ENGLISH POETRY AND
OLD NORSE MYTH

English Poetry and
Old Norse Myth

A History

HEATHER O'DONOGHUE

OXFORD
UNIVERSITY PRESS

OXFORD

UNIVERSITY PRESS

Great Clarendon Street, Oxford, OX2 6DP,
United Kingdom

Oxford University Press is a department of the University of Oxford.
It furthers the University's objective of excellence in research, scholarship,
and education by publishing worldwide. Oxford is a registered trade mark of
Oxford University Press in the UK and in certain other countries

© Heather O'Donoghue 2014

The moral rights of the author have been asserted

First Edition published in 2014

Impression: 1

Published in the United States of America by Oxford University Press
198 Madison Avenue, New York, NY 10016, United States of America

British Library Cataloguing in Publication Data
Data available

Library of Congress Control Number: 2013957856

ISBN 978-0-19-956218-3

Printed and bound by
CPI Group (UK) Ltd, Croydon, CR0 4YY

For Bernard

Acknowledgements

This book is greatly indebted to previous scholars who have documented the impact of Old Norse literature and culture in various periods. As will be evident from what follows, without the work of Ethel Seaton, Frank Farley, Margaret Clunies Ross, Margaret Omberg, and Andrew Wawn, I could hardly have even begun my own. In addition, three young scholars—Tom Birkett, Eleanor Parker, and Josie O'Donoghue—gave so generously of their expertise and time that without their help with this book I could hardly have finished it. I am deeply grateful to them all.

Contents

Introduction

The primary subject of this book is the engagement of poets writing in English with Old Norse mythology. The influence of Norse myth is evident in English poetry from the Anglo-Saxon period right up until the present day. The reasons why a poet might be drawn to Old Norse myth of course vary over time, and this book takes a chronological approach, tracing both the developments in what was received as Old Norse myth—the various texts poets had to hand—and the different ways in which poets have responded to it. During the Anglo-Saxon period, Viking Scandinavians were at once a terrifying enemy and at the same time recognized as an ethnically similar people. As we shall see, this chequered relationship is mirrored throughout English literary history in attitudes towards Old Norse myth, a subject by turns thrillingly alien and yet part of the ancestral inheritance of English-speaking peoples.

In the context of Old Norse in general, and this book in particular, a working definition of "myth" might be *representations of pre-Christian beliefs about the beginnings and end of creation, and stories about the gods, and the giants and monsters associated with them.* The overwhelming majority of such representations are, as one would expect, literary ones: poems and prose narratives. But it is important to bear in mind from the outset that mythological texts make up only a proportion (though a significant one) of Old Norse literature as a whole, which ranges far more widely over historical, fictional, and legendary subject matters. My concern here will be almost exclusively with mythological texts in Old Norse.

Although Old Norse language and culture persisted to some degree—and perhaps for some centuries—in the parts of the British Isles where Scandinavians had settled during Anglo-Saxon times, knowledge of Old Norse literature eventually died away, and there ensued a long period during which Old Norse literature was effectively lost to the wider European world. But in the seventeenth century, the fact that the origins of the English nation were traced back to the Goths, as the progenitors of both the English and Scandinavians, meant that references to Old Norse were loaded with positive connotations—for Parliamentarians at least—of political liberty and the rule of law, which were believed to have been inherited from the nation's Gothic ancestors.

In Britain in the eighteenth century, a craze for Scandinavian and Celtic "ancient" poetry, and a taste for sublimity in literature, fuelled keen interest in Old Norse mythological poetry, though contemporary critics were slow to warm to what they regarded as its wildness. In subsequent decades, Victorian mythographers sought what they believed to be the real, hidden meanings of Old Norse myth, and saw in the Norse gods, especially Odin and Baldr, figures comparable with or analogous to Christian divinities. And finally, the advent of Old Norse as an academic subject, especially in the literature degrees studied by so many twentieth- and twenty-first-century poets, together with a new interest in the Scandinavian settlement (as opposed to Viking ravaging) of the British Isles and Ireland, have provoked a fresh response to Old Norse myth as a poetic subject.

Individual poets have also had their own particular motivations for turning to Old Norse myth: the antiquarian and scholarly leanings of Thomas Gray, or Walter Scott; William Morris's politicized medievalism; the deep concern for the religious element in all myths shown by David Jones; Hugh MacDiarmid's double fascination with both the disputed ethnicity of the Scots and the modernist mythic symbol; Paul Muldoon's and Don Paterson's post-modernist playfulness with Old Norse mythic motifs, and the latter's reaching-out for cosmic symbols in his more sombre elegiac poetry.

Many of the poets discussed in this book are canonical names in the history of poetry in English, but by no means all of them. The quality of poetry influenced by Old Norse myth is extremely variable. Nevertheless, I think it can be demonstrated that so-called "minor poetry" is just as fascinating as the work of more major writers in the way its authors use Old Norse myth. This book cannot, of course, hope to be exhaustive in its coverage of the influence of Old Norse mythological material on poetry in English. The four chapters, together with the prologue and epilogue, might easily have been expanded to fill six whole volumes. I have limited myself to myth on the one hand, and poetry on the other, not only for reasons of scale, but also because it seems to me that the imaginative potential of poetry responds particularly well to the metaphysicality of myth—which is perhaps why so much Old Norse myth was originally transmitted in poetic form. It is my hope that for both major and minor poets, Old Norse myth will be shown to have been a surprisingly widespread, sustained, and fundamental influence in English literary history.

Finally, how evident the debt to Old Norse myth is also varies considerably. Sometimes a reference, or source, is explicitly acknowledged, and relatively easy to identify. More often, the Norse material is transformed or disguised: perhaps naturalized to conform to the poetic conventions of the time, or presented in a playfully oblique manner, or reduced to an arcane allusion. Indeed, the more creative the poet has been with the material, or the more fruitful the engagement with it, the more difficult it is to identify the source. Such references have often been overlooked or misunderstood by scholars and critics, and the full significance of even explicitly identified Norse allusion is not always appreciated. Some allusions must remain speculative, a matter of critical opinion.

Myth itself is always a representation, usually in literary or sometimes in visual or ritual form, of an unreachable antecedent. An original, unitary body of material, coherent and systematic—what we might assume "Old Norse myth" to designate—simply does not exist, and never did. What we are dealing with is a diverse collection of literary texts, in different forms and genres, and from different times and places. There have been any number of attempts—from the earliest medieval scholars in Iceland to contemporary mythographers—to reconstruct some hypothetical original mythology. But this is very far from being my concern here, not least because the focus of this book is on the actual textual materials—however inauthentic, or derivative, or mistaken—with which poets engaged, and most of all, with what was made of them. Nevertheless, it will be useful to offer a brief account of the origins of the literature which is the vehicle for Old Norse myth.

In the year 870 AD, the year before Alfred the Great came to the throne in Anglo-Saxon England, and a year after the death of King Edmund of East Anglia at the hands of Viking invaders (a particularly horrible death, as later tradition had it), the first Norwegians set sail for Iceland, then uninhabited apart from a few Irish monks on retreat for the summer months. The Norwegians' aim was to make a new life there as settlers. Many more Norwegians followed them, and they were joined by other migrants, largely Scandinavians who had settled first in the Western Isles of Scotland, and in Ireland, and intermarried there. Just over half a century later—by the year 930 AD, according to early Icelandic sources— Iceland was fully settled: *albyggt*.

There are many theories as to the causes of this swift and substantial migration. Lack of farmable land at home, an autocratic king of Norway (King Haraldr Finehair, nicknamed thus after the successful completion of a vow not to cut or comb his hair until he had brought the whole of Norway under his rule), the threat of a northward expansion of the Emperor Charlemagne's Frankish empire, and sheer pioneering spirit have all seemed good reasons to historians both medieval and modern. But whatever the causes of their move, once in Iceland the settlers set about creating a unified, cohesive new nation. This was not a scattered colony of subsistence farmers, but a tightly knit community with a strong sense of independent identity, its own laws, and a precocious parliament; it was a remarkable, almost democratic, republic. When Iceland was converted to Christianity around the year 1000 AD, the change of faith was debated in the national parliament, the Althing (literally, the meeting for everyone, or General Assembly), and the clinching argument was not theological, but political: that Iceland as a nation would not survive division, and that all Icelanders must therefore share the same laws and, thus, the same religion.

No doubt there is an element of simplification and understand-able national pride in this version of events. Iceland's conversion is rep-resented as the outcome of rational debate and collective compromise, utterly unlike the "top-down" conversions imposed by kings elsewhere in Europe, especially in Anglo-Saxon England. But it is how Icelanders themselves remembered and recorded the fundamental shift from pagan-ism to Christianity, a shift which most importantly ushered in the transi-tion from orality to literacy, for Christianity is a religion of the book. At first, Icelanders put their new literacy to Christian purposes, and from the very beginning, their concern was with the vernacular: they translated the Bible, the lives of saints, the exegetical works of the church fathers and sermons, and with the help of foreign scholars, especially Anglo-Saxons, adapted the Roman alphabet to accommodate the sounds of the Icelandic language—the language now commonly referred to as Old Norse. Around the middle of the twelfth century, an Icelandic linguistician set out a com-plete spelling system "for us Icelanders" and detailed all the texts which were being translated, composed, or written down in the vernacular at that time: history, laws, genealogies, and Christian exegesis.

A Latinate faith never came to dominate the native literary culture. The range of learned texts recorded on vellum broadened dramatically to include imaginative literature: poems—eddic and skaldic—and fictional prose narratives of all kinds, including one completely new and unique lit-erary form, the Icelandic family saga. What unites this wide-ranging body of material is that in their different ways the texts present us with images of the past—and, crucially, the mostly pre-Christian past. Either because the texts themselves originated in this pre-Christian period, and were written down later, or because their authors were recreating a pre-Christian past they knew about, or could invent or elaborate on the basis of oral tradi-tions, this substantial body of material, in all its variety, provides us with the primary literary sources of Old Norse myth.

This raises an immediate difficulty. With a few dramatic exceptions—for instance, Viking age picture stones in Sweden and Viking age sculp-ture in Britain which may illustrate mythic scenes, or the stanza of skaldic poetry inscribed on a stone in Sweden—the primary surviving represen-tations of Norse myth derive from literary texts written down in Iceland by Christians. The difficulty of distinguishing originally oral material from the rewriting, elaboration, and transformation which inevitably accompanies the "recording" of oral texts is widely recognized. But one might expect this to be especially difficult in the case of Christian writers transmitting texts dealing with pagans, and their beliefs and traditions. Would not the pagan material have been diminished, treated cursorily, been recounted with an ironic, scornful, or dismissive gloss, or intrusively moralized? Might we not be left with a threadbare and distorted record, something for patient scholars to restore, patch, and reconstruct?

In fact, the ingrained and dominant nativism of Icelandic authors seems to have resulted in a correspondingly less dominant clerical culture, and a much more tolerant attitude to pre-Christian material, and the depiction of pre-Christian forebears, than was the case elsewhere in Christian Europe. Of course we cannot assume that what has survived is a completely authentic version or representation of what existed before conversion. But the special circumstances of Icelandic literary culture have resulted in two very striking features of Old Norse mythic literature. The first is the large quantity of such literature: there is simply a very great deal of surviving mythological material by or about pagans in Old Norse. The second is the high literary artistry of that surviving Old Norse mythological literature. We are not dealing with scraps and shadows, with tired re-tellings or pale derivatives. We are dealing with authors at the height of their imaginative and technical abilities, with the dramatic narrative poems of the *Edda*; the dense and intricate verbal imagery of skaldic verse; and prose fictions and chronicles—sagas—of great power and authority. This is crucial because the influence of Norse myth on later poets proved to be so strong not only because of the inherent attraction of the subject matter—the drama of the myths themselves—or because of the mythology's profound cultural and political significances for those writing in English (though these two factors were of course very potent), but also because the literature which encodes the mythic material is so compelling.

The major literary sources of Old Norse myth are four kinds of text: eddic poems, skaldic stanzas, sagas, and Snorri Sturluson's *Prose Edda*. These texts are very different in literary form, and vary widely in how authentically they may transmit pagan material, or reliable accounts of pagan beliefs and attitudes. But it is not their authenticity or relia- bility, but rather the subsequent reception history of the mythological elements in these texts, which will concern us in the main body of this book. Sometimes the most inauthentic material was the most influen- tial. And very few English-language poets encountered the primary texts in their original Icelandic: the earliest post-Reformation poets in English knew their Norse literature in Latin translation—or paraphrase—at best.

Nevertheless, for the sake of completeness at least I will sketch out a brief account of the earliest forms of this literature.

Almost all skaldic verse—so-called after the Icelandic word for poet, *skald*—survives as quotation in prose narrative. The earliest skalds (the first whose poetry survives, Bragi, seems to have lived in the ninth century) were Norwegian court poets, pagans employed by pagan Scandinavian kings and earls to produce praise poetry for living and, where politically appropriate, dead rulers. Icelandic poets soon established a reputation at Norwegian courts, and came to dominate the poetry associated with them. The form of skaldic verse has led most scholars to believe that it changed little in the period between its composition and its quotation in later written prose narratives. Its distinctive metre—*dróttkvætt*, or "court(ly) metre"—is extraordinarily intricate, involving not only patterns of stress and alliteration, in common with other forms of Germanic poetry, but also syllable counting and internal full and half rhyme in the eight short lines of each stanza. This renders it unusually (if not completely) resistant to corruption or purposeful tinkering, and so the earliest skaldic verse is usually held to transmit the pagan beliefs of its practitioners and recipients with very little alteration, even if it was not written down until much later than its original composition.

The poetic diction of skaldic verse, drawing on a lexis exceptionally rich in synonyms, is characterized by the use of kennings; that is, cryptic poetic circumlocutions consisting of a sequence of two or more nouns in which the first—a so-called "base word"—is then successively re-defined by the next—the "determinant"—in a string which may extend to four or five elements. Thus, in a simple warrior kenning, "tree of battle", the base word, "tree", seems to have only the slightest connexion with its ultimate referent, "warrior". The listener must first extend the possible referent of "tree" to any organic, upright object, and then re-define it according to the determinant term "battle". The mental process frames the question "What organic, upright object is associated with battle?", and the answer is "warrior". If the poet extends his kenning further, so that "battle" is itself designated by a kenning—let's say, "storm of Odin"—the poetic image created by the three-element kenning "tree of the storm of Odin" is a strikingly rich and vivid one, as we imagine trees battered and bent in a storm, and spears falling on the enemy showering down like piercing rain.

I have spent some time analyzing the workings of the skaldic kenning for two reasons. Firstly, in building a kenning, poets often drew on mythological stories or alluded to mythological figures—calling battle "the storm of Odin" is one very simple example of this. Some kennings require a detailed knowledge of Norse myth, since they contain allusions to specific stories, and some remain a puzzle. There are some sequences of skaldic stanzas which might be described as mythological poems in themselves, and the praise of a pagan aristocrat may involve associating or even identifying him with a pagan deity. However, it is the mass of mythological allusions in skaldic kennings—continuing as a literary technique, though somewhat abated, in the work of later, Christian skalds—which contributes so very much to our knowledge of Norse myth. Secondly, although the intricate metre and cryptic kennings may have helped stanzas to survive a period of oral transmission, and thus helped to preserve authentic mythological material, the very difficultness of the stanzas has been an important factor in the way they have been received by post-medieval readers: sometimes the translation has been little more than loose paraphrase; sometimes the kennings have been misconstrued. What modern readers may take as fundamental aspects of Norse myth are sometimes actually the result of early mistranslations or misconceptions.

Eddic verse is almost always defined in contradistinction to skaldic poetry: it is much looser in metre and contains comparatively few kennings; it is anonymous and hard to date; and it is mostly preserved as discrete poems in a thirteenth-century anthology, now known as the *Poetic Edda,* in a manuscript known as the Codex Regius, or in Icelandic, *Konungsbók.* The compiler of this collection of poems carefully arranged them into two sections, mythological poems and heroic ones, and it is in these poems—and a small number of others found in other manuscripts but similar in form and type of content—that much of the sustained mythical material in Old Norse is preserved. The Codex Regius opens, for example, with the magnificent poem *Völuspá,* in which a powerful prophetess, summoned by Odin, relates the creation of the cosmos, and looks ahead to the final apocalypse, Ragnarök, which will mean the end of the gods and the world as we know it, though as in the poem's biblical counterpart, the account of apocalypse in the book of Revelation, a new world is predicted which will replace the old one. Following *Völuspá* in the Codex Regius is a poem entitled *Hávamál*—the words of the High One—which consists of various pieces of Odinic wisdom, some purporting to be spoken in the voice of the god Odin himself. There follow poems in which Odin and a giant engage in a wisdom contest, each trying to ask a question the other cannot answer, and narrative poems—some comic, some serious—concerning the Norse gods and their continual struggles against the old enemy, the giants.

The heroic poems in the *Poetic Edda* concern the exploits of the heroes of the Völsung dynasty—notably Sigurðr the Dragon-Slayer (Wagner's Siegfried), and his wife Guðrún, who, after Sigurðr is murdered by her brothers, goes on to marry first Attila the Hun, and then (having killed him) a king called Jónakr, whose sons by him she sends off to the Gothic king Jörmunrekkr and certain death to avenge the killing of her daughter by Sigurðr. These poems have an oblique but undeniable relation to what historians can piece together about the Germanic heroic age, long before Iceland was settled, and even before the Anglo-Saxons left continental Europe for Britain, a time when Goths, in fragile alliances with Burgundians, fought Huns, and their leaders died violent or mysterious deaths. The savage perpetrators and tragic victims of these extraordinary events are presented in the poetry not only as encountering supernatural creatures such as valkyries or shape-shifting giants, but also as sometimes rubbing shoulders with the gods themselves: the activities of the Völsungs, for instance, are closely monitored by the god Odin, who on occasion intervenes, in disguise, in the human world. Both the mythological and the heroic poems of the *Edda* sustain a substantial body of traditional pagan material in highly dramatic and accomplished literary form, and were to prove enormously influential in the hands of later poets in English, especially in the eighteenth century.

The word *saga* is related to the Norse word *segja*, "to say", and is used of very many kinds of prose narratives in Old Icelandic: saints' lives, royal biographies, geographical treatises and translated continental romances, as well as for what is perhaps the most celebrated kind of saga—the Icelandic family saga, or, in Icelandic, the *Íslendingasaga*, or saga of Icelanders. The family sagas are not mythological texts. Rather, they are naturalistic prose narratives which detail the lives of the first settlers in Iceland and the generations succeeding them. Since the earliest generations of settlers were pagan, the family sagas do to some extent represent customs and beliefs relating to Norse myth, although in fact saga authors tend not to dwell on the religious aspects of early Icelandic life. However, the Icelandic *fornaldarsögur*, or legendary heroic sagas (the term means "sagas of olden times"), are quite different from the family sagas, for they are freely fictional, even fantastic, in their narratives, which are packed with magic, sensational event, and the supernatural, and most take place in Scandinavia, at some unspecified historical period before the settlement of Iceland. The most celebrated of the *fornaldarsögur* is *Völsunga saga*—the story of the Völsung dynasty, based on the heroic poems of the *Poetic Edda*, and many *fornaldarsögur* contain eddic poetry. Ironically, the earliest Scandinavian historians took *fornaldarsögur* as valuable sources for the ancient history of their own nations. For this reason, such sagas, in scholarly Latin editions, were amongst the first Icelandic texts to reach a wider European public, and their quoted verses especially were very influential in forming a taste for extravagant supernatural incident and heroic action thought to be characteristic of Icelandic tradition.

In Iceland, by the middle of the thirteenth century, a major project to collect, preserve, order, and interpret Old Norse myth had been completed. The Icelandic historian and antiquarian Snorri Sturluson composed a great cycle of biographies of Norwegian kings, *Heimskringla*, beginning with the earliest pagan rulers, and quoting in his prose very many skaldic stanzas attributed to the court poets of both these early pagan rulers, and later Christian kings, and thus a substantial amount of mythological material, including some extended sequences of skaldic stanzas. Snorri may also have composed the saga about Egill Skalla-Grímsson, an Icelandic Viking poet whose pagan beliefs, expressed vividly in his poetry, quoted copiously in the saga prose, mark him out as a distinctively Odinic hero. But Snorri's key role in the dissemination of Old Norse myth was his authorship of what is now known as the *Prose Edda*, or *Snorra Edda* ("Snorri's *Edda*"), a bipartite treatise on myth and on skaldic diction, followed by the *Háttatal* or "List of metres", a demonstration of 101 varieties of *dróttkvætt* in the form of a sequence of skaldic stanzas each exemplifying a different metrical variation.

The first section of the treatise, *Gylfaginning*, is set in a narrative framework whereby a Swedish king called Gylfi determines to find out more about a mysterious and powerful race of people called the Æsir—the name of the Norse gods. Arriving at their court in Asgard—in mythic texts, the name of the gods' stronghold—he begins his questioning of a strange trinity of throned figures: High, Just-as-High, and Third. This sets the stage for a lengthy interrogation which Snorri uses as the basis of a carefully ordered exposition of Norse myth. Gylfi's questions move logically and cogently through Norse mythological lore. He asks about creation and cosmology, and the answers he is given are based largely on *Völuspá*, the first poem in the *Poetic Edda*, supplemented by information taken from other eddic poems. He asks about the Norse gods, their relationships, attributes, and exploits, and finally about Ragnarök, the end of the world and the gods themselves. The answers to his questions often include relevant quotations from eddic poems, and Snorri's considerable story-telling skills are well demonstrated in the fluent, detailed, and lengthy speeches he puts into the mouth of his Æsir trinity. *Gylfaginning* is a brilliantly realized account of Norse mythology, based largely, but not completely, on eddic verse. The potential embarrassment for a Christian author in re-telling pagan myth is elegantly avoided by the device of having not Snorri himself, but ostensibly, in the fictional frame, the Æsir, recounting the material.

Skáldskaparmál—"the art of poetic language"—is the second part of Snorri's *Edda*, and it too takes the form of a dialogue initiated by a visitor to Asgard; this time a figure called Ægir questions Bragi, the god of poetry. These questions prompt replies which together set out a comprehensive account of the Norse myth of the origin of poetry, and move on to explain skaldic kennings, thickly illustrated from skaldic sources. Sometimes the narrative is no more than a list of poetic quotations: for instance, in response to the question "How can Thor be designated?" there are sixteen examples of kennings referring to Thor, with quotations from almost as many different skalds. But at other times, the sheer force of the narrative takes over, and there are long stretches of continuous narrative telling the mythological stories which lie behind kennings. So Snorri's *Skáldskaparmál* is a rich source of skaldic quotation and related mythological stories, just as *Gylfaginning* re-tells and quotes (though to a lesser extent) mythological and heroic material from the *Poetic Edda*. Together with the skaldic praise poetry quoted in *Heimskringla*, and the possibility that Snorri was the author of the saga about the Viking poet Egill, with its many verses, our total knowledge of Norse mythology is overwhelmingly due to his antiquarian scholarship. Snorri's *Edda*, in one of its many translations, together with the eddic poetry Snorri quotes, was the vivid and compelling form in which most poets in English have known Norse myth.

I will conclude this introduction with a brief account of the individual chapters in this book.

Although Anglo-Saxon authors, working in the centuries before Old Norse myth was written down, could not have had access to Old Norse myths in written form, there are, as we shall see, traces of what looks like Old Norse myth in certain early medieval English texts. There are two ways in which such mythic elements might have been available to Anglo-Saxon authors, and both are problematic in their way. Firstly, it may be that some of the ancient pre-Christian beliefs of the first Anglo-Saxons were similar to those carried to Iceland by its first settlers. In fact, the common assumption that the earliest Anglo-Saxon and Icelandic settlers shared the same ancestral—that is, continental Germanic—pagan beliefs must be at the least a major simplification, and the passage of time would in any case have dimmed similarities. However, just as Anglo-Saxon and Old Norse are plainly cognate languages, there are good reasons for believing that the mythological beliefs of the two communities might have been cognate too. Secondly, it may, additionally or alternatively, be the case that the Scandinavian settlement in Anglo-Saxon England during the ninth century, or perhaps more fleeting cultural contacts between the Norse and the Anglo-Saxons in earlier centuries, led to Norse myth becoming known in some form to the Anglo-Saxons, and thus finding its way into literary texts. It has long been argued that hostile relations and linguistic differences between the two communities are likely to have limited cultural interaction, but scenes from Old Norse myth—often alongside Christian iconography—carved on traditionally English stone crosses in parts of Anglo-Scandinavian England provide strong counter-evidence. But whether we tend towards the shared cultural inheritance model, or the theory of fresh Viking age contacts—and they are not mutually exclusive—we cannot expect to see Old Norse mythic elements in precisely the form they take in the later written sources, and dealing with the oral transmission of material of course involves many variations and uncertainties.

Added to all this, there is one even stronger reason why any allusions to pre-Christian traditions in Anglo-Saxon literature may be difficult to discern and interpret. The conversion of Anglo-Saxon England to Christianity, though a piecemeal affair, protracted and regionally uneven, was more or less complete by the time of the Scandinavian settlements, and by the time of the conversion of Iceland, around 1000 AD, almost all of Anglo-Saxon England had been Christian for several centuries. Anglo-Saxon authors were Christians, perhaps mostly clerics, and clerical culture dominated literary production. There is nothing in Old English literature even approaching the apparently free-reined transmission of pagan traditions in Old Norse, but only the terse dismissals or shadowy allusions one might expect from a literary culture largely controlled by a clergy naturally hostile to paganism, and possibly responding to the threat of recidivism in the early period, and then to the influx and influence of large numbers of Scandinavian settlers in later times.

Nevertheless, the Anglo-Saxon poem *Beowulf*, which is set in a semi-historical Scandinavian pagan past, shows many traces of what look like versions of Old Norse myth. Identifying possible Norse influence in the poem is a delicate matter, precisely because the poem's Christian, and probably clerical, author would surely have had to temper any mythic material in an attempt to balance his own, or perhaps his patron's, ideological and religious convictions against an artistic engagement with his pre-Christian subject matter. Claims about veiled references to Old Norse myth or pagan beliefs in *Beowulf*—and more widely in Anglo-Saxon poetry—are still justifiably contested by sceptical scholars. Whether Anglo-Saxon poetry—like *Beowulf*, or *Widsith*, or *Deor*—takes the characters of the Germanic heroic age as its subject matter, or whether, as in the reflective poems in the Old English elegiac tradition, poets concerned themselves with the resigned but wistful recreation of a distant and faded past, and meditations on ends and beginnings, we might look to find Norse-related material, but can only expect carefully mediated allusions at best. And in the post-Conquest period, while it is possible to argue for instances of Old Norse material still leaving traces in literary texts, such material has by this time become part of the collective body of English story matter, and there is rarely any sense that poets are working with non-native traditions.

The scope of my prologue, which considers the influence of Old Norse myth on pre-Conquest literature, and focuses on the Anglo-Saxon poem *Beowulf,* is thus somewhat separate from that of the main chapters of the book, since the circumstances of influence are so different, and identification of the traces of it so speculative.

At the close of the Middle Ages, Iceland entered into a period of cultural and economic decline. It had lost its independence to Norway in 1262, although it is not clear to what extent this impacted on either everyday life in Iceland, or literary production. However, by the end of the next century, control of Iceland's affairs had passed to Denmark, and Iceland was both isolated and neglected. After the Reformation, though Icelanders continued to copy by hand and disseminate saga manuscripts, new literary production was in church hands, and such secular literature as was produced tended to be highly derivative of either earlier forms or European models. But Icelanders maintained their own language, and isolation and neglect only helped to preserve the language from the degree of change experienced by other European language communities in the British Isles and Scandinavia. So when in the sixteenth and seventeenth centuries Denmark and Sweden began to construct the earliest histories of their own nation, it became evident that in Iceland there were texts which not only seemed to provide copious evidence for Scandinavian history, but also could be readily expounded by Icelanders. With the help of Icelandic scholars, Danes and Swedes began producing Latin editions of Old Icelandic texts, thus opening up access to them for scholars throughout Europe. Foremost among these texts, ironically enough, were examples of *fornaldarsögur,* legendary adventure narratives set in a distant Scandinavian past, nowadays (and to some extent even in the Middle Ages) regarded as highly fictional, and eddic verse, closely followed by Snorri's own *Edda.*

This urge to investigate early history, fuelled to a great extent by nationalism, was felt all over Europe, and seventeenth-century English antiquarians such as Sir Henry Spelman or Robert Sheringham were at the forefront of such scholarship, and in close touch with their Scandinavian colleagues. The Goths, seen as the ancestors of northern European peoples, were celebrated by English historians as bearers of political liberty and democracy, and in this period the image of Norse culture is dominated by references to a Gothic Odin—a chieftain, who had been deified by his gullible followers—as a great lawgiver, a champion of liberty, and a military hero. But Odin was also seen as the inventor, or at least disseminator, of runes, and of poetry, and allusions to Old Norse myth began to appear in the work of better-read English poets such as Dryden or Pope. Seventeenth- and early eighteenth-century responses to Old Norse myth form the subject of the first chapter.

The Norse-influenced poets of the eighteenth and early nineteenth centuries are the subjects of the second chapter. Thomas Gray and William Blake were the most prominent poets in this period to draw on Old Norse myth in their work, but there were dozens of others. The increasing availability of the central texts of Old Norse myth (Snorri's *Edda*, and the major mythological poems of the *Poetic Edda*), together with a Europe-wide interest in poetry of earlier ages, led to an explosion of Norse-derived poetry, imitations, translations, and free adaptations. This is without doubt the richest period for poetry in English which was produced under the influence of Old Norse—rich in volume, that is, if not in quality, with the notable exceptions of Gray and Blake. But ironically, just as the English literary world was gradually gaining in knowledge and appreciation of Norse mythological literature in its original language, the taste for the wild and supposedly "sublime" poetry of the ancient North began to wane.

Although the major poets of the English Romantic movement did not take up Norse themes in any significant way, very many poets whose reputation has not endured—for example, the Poet Laureate Robert Southey—or writers who have become more celebrated for non-Norse works, such as Thomas Love Peacock, did. The figure of Odin—as a chieftain rather than a god—was particularly popular, and many Viking clichés continued to flourish, as in Walter Scott's self-mocking and extremely readable Norse narrative poem, *Harold the Dauntless*, and a number of long narrative poems on Viking themes which also deployed familiar and popular motifs from Old Norse myth. In North America, the influence of Old Norse on poets such as Longfellow constituted a distinctive and alternative Romantic movement, in which Viking valour was softened by a celebration of romantic and even peace-loving Vikings inspired originally by the Swedish poet Tegnér. All this poetry is the subject of the third chapter.

Chapter 4 shows how, during the nineteenth century, Old Norse myth was treated to scholarly analysis by British and Continental scholars, and read as evidence of an ancient religion which might offer comparisons with Christianity itself. Its attraction for poets was not so much the thrilling subjects of Old Norse poetry, but myth as a reflection of an earlier theology. This is true, for instance, of Matthew Arnold's representation of Norse material in his poem 'Balder Dead', and in the work of other Victorian poets who followed the lead of Thomas Carlyle (himself influenced by German scholarship) in seeing Baldr as a figure analogous to Christ. Towards the end of the century, medievalism was clearly an important element in William Morris's employment of Norse themes.

Into the twentieth century, the project of modernist poets to break with the accepted beliefs of the previous century and to turn to alternative structures occasioned the use of Norse myth in a different way. Hugh MacDiarmid, for example, adopted the central symbols of Old Norse myth in ways analogous to the methods of Russian symbolist poets, and he was also inspired by his political understanding of Scottish ethnicity, then (as now) fiercely disputed between Celticists and Nordicists. Poets such as David Jones, or C. S. Lewis, used Old Norse mythic themes in their exploration of Christian theology. In *The Anathemata*, for instance, David Jones expressed a vision of "the genuine tradition of the Island of Britain" in which what he called "signs"—transcendental vehicles of fundamental cultural beliefs—encompassed Norse myth as well as Christian symbolism. The poetry of contemporary poets such as Pauline Stainer has continued this mystical tradition.

My epilogue considers the work of contemporary poets and its relation to Old Norse myth. In the second half of the twentieth century, the history of the Vikings themselves was beginning to be re-written: from lawless invaders or intrepid explorers to settled and productive migrants, integral elements in the ethnic make-up of Britain and Ireland. These shifts in the imaging of a people still popularly—and inaccurately—termed "Vikings" led to new relationships between English poetry and Old Norse literature. Poets such as Ted Hughes and Seamus Heaney worked from the knowledge that the bearers of Norse myth were, in simple or complicated ways, their and our ancestors. Heaney notoriously drew a comparison between Viking violence and the troubles in Ulster. But neither he nor Hughes can be said to have engaged with actual mythological material from Old Norse. W. H. Auden also felt a strong connexion with Scandinavian and specifically Icelandic literature and culture. But from around the beginning of the twentieth century, Old Norse literature had been introduced as a subject in university curricula, and Auden's re-workings of Old Norse mythological poems were primarily prompted by the academic study of Old English and Norse literature. Poets such as Paul Muldoon and Don Paterson—who might be labelled post-modernist—have taken further still the somewhat arcane academic and intellectual status of Old Norse myth, and used references to it to destabilize, or at least make very difficult, the derivation of any transparent unitary meaning from their work. The contemporary poets whose work is the focus of the epilogue have inherited the conception of Old Norse culture as an essential constituent of the history of the British Isles, and some have engaged with even the more arcane elements of Old Norse myth, often based on academic knowledge or their reading of Old Norse literature as part of their literary inheritance.

A NOTE ON THE NAMES

In the process of anglicization, different poets used various forms of Old Norse names. I have tried in what follows to echo the usage of each individual poet when referring specifically to his or her work, even if the differences between that and the original Old Norse are very slight. I myself use the usual Old Norse forms of most names, apart from standard anglicizations such as the names of the two most familiar Norse gods, Odin and Thor, and their home, Asgard. Where reference is made to some idea of the "Old North", I have capitalized "Northern" and "Northernness", and also when designating an actual geographical location: "the North". And throughout, the term "English poetry" refers to poetry written in English and (perhaps less justifiably, in order to accommodate the work of Hugh MacDiarmid and Kathleen Jamie) Scots.

Prologue
Earliest Contacts: Medieval Poetry
and Old Norse Myth

Beowulf is an Anglo-Saxon poem detailing the adventures of its eponymous Scandinavian hero, Beowulf, and set in pre-Christian Scandinavia,
though the poet of *Beowulf* was evidently a Christian—recent scholarship has identified more and more biblical, apocryphal, and patristic
learning in the poem.[1] But the date of the poem remains uncertain, and
whether we date the poem to the beginning, the middle, or the end of the
Anglo-Saxon period bears on how the poet might have received, related
to, and understood the beliefs and stories he attributes to his sixth-century
pagan Scandinavian characters, and the allusions to Old Norse myth with
which he creates a Scandinavian backdrop to his poem.

Whatever our favoured date for the poem's composition—if, indeed,
we may view its composition as a single, dateable creative act—it would
be ill-advised to expect allusions in the poem to match elements of Old
Norse myth as it has come down to us with any degree of neatness. For
example, an early poet might well have drawn on mythological traditions inherited from pre-Christian times and shared by Anglo-Saxons
and Scandinavians, though transmitted to us otherwise only in Old
Norse texts. But Old Norse myth in its late, written, form might have
been quite unlike such hypothetical early beliefs and traditions. And further, it is by no means certain that the pre-Christian cultures of the many
and various early Germanic tribes were ever the same as each other, or
even similar.

A middle period dating for *Beowulf* would have to take into account
the obvious obstacles to cultural exchange presented by hostile relations
between Anglo-Saxons and Scandinavians during the Viking age, though
the hostilities were not continuous, and attacks on Northumbria, for
example, would not necessarily preclude peaceful and culturally productive relations elsewhere. Roberta Frank has argued that the *Beowulf*-poet's
knowledge of Old Norse myth was newly learned from his Danelaw

---

[1] See Andy Orchard, *A Critical Companion to Beowulf* (Cambridge: D. S. Brewer, 2003),
pp. 130–68. References to the poem are to George Jack (ed.), *Beowulf: A Student Edition*
(Oxford: Clarendon Press, 1994), by line number.

neighbours, and that his aim was to undermine and counter it.[2] If Frank is right, then what we can discern in *Beowulf* will be Old Norse myth arguably different from its later, written form, having been purposefully modified rather than uncritically imported.

The latest possible date for the poem—the proposed date of the one surviving manuscript—would place it in the time of the new Scandinavian rulers of England, Sveinn Forkbeard and his son Knútr (King Canute).[3] This would account well for the poem's range and perspective, its mighty frame of reference, and the poise and wisdom of the narrator's voice as he seems to look back at an era long past, commenting on its strengths and weaknesses, its lessons for the present, and its irrecoverable pastness. But a late *Beowulf*-poet's knowledge, or memory, of Old Norse myth might well have been blurred or faded by the passage of time. And in any case, the literary culture of conquering dynasties has more usually taken over native traditions and re-presented them in new colonial forms, while the author of *Beowulf*, an Anglo-Saxon poem about Scandinavians, has done exactly the opposite.

Given the history of Anglo-Saxon relations with raiding, invading, and settling Scandinavians, it is in fact hard to fit the poem and its audience into a time and place in which allusions to Scandinavian myth would be both known by the poet and enjoyed by his audience. But as long as we do not expect mythic material which precisely reproduces what has come down to us in Old Norse written sources, we may recognize echoes of Old Norse myth in several different forms in *Beowulf*. Further, whatever date we assign to the poem, the Anglo-Saxon poet's apparent, and understandable, concern to "sanitise", "euhemerise", and "disguise" (to use Andy Orchard's terms[4]) his material does mean that identification of mythic allusions can be very uncertain, and not all identifications are as convincing as others. However, as Orchard has noted, "if we must dig deep to find traces of pagan myth in the text, it is surely striking that the *Beowulf*-poet should so reveal his antiquarian interest as to include them at all".[5]

Beowulf's three great fights which structure the poem are set in the context of semi-legendary Scandinavian history, and this background to the poem is packed with names and details, some familiar, some mentioned nowhere else. It is striking how many of these allusions—included

---

[2] Roberta Frank, 'Skaldic Verse and the Dating of *Beowulf*' in Colin Chase (ed.), *The Dating of Beowulf* (Toronto: University of Toronto Press, 1981), pp. 123–39.

[3] See Kevin S. Kiernan, *Beowulf and the Beowulf Manuscript* (Ann Arbor: University of Michigan Press, 1996), pp. 13–63.

[4] Orchard, *Companion to Beowulf*, p. 113.

[5] Orchard, *Companion to Beowulf*, pp. 113–14.

apparently at will by the poet, and not integral to his story—bear some relation to Old Norse mythic material, as if imported by him to provide Scandinavian colour. And as we shall see, it is invariably the darker shades which these allusions introduce. For example, the poet compares his Scandinavian hero Beowulf with the great dragon-slayer of Old Norse legend, Sigurðr the Völsung, but names this hero as Sigemund, in Old Norse Sigurðr's father, and a much more ambivalent character, associated in Old Norse tradition with incest and shape-shifting.[6]

After his success against Grendel, Beowulf is rewarded with praise and with treasure, including the most magnificent neck ring the poet has ever heard of—apart, that is, from the necklace of the Brosings (1197–1201). In Old Norse, the *Brísingamen*—"the necklace of the Brísings"—is a necklace stolen from the goddess Freyja, who paid for it by sleeping with four dwarves.[7] Such a highly charged treasure with powerful sexual associations would seem to have no place in the morally upright world of *Beowulf*— upright at least with regard to sexual morality—but it is hard to believe that there is no connexion. Might the poet again be evoking the darker side of Norse tradition without alluding to it directly?

When Beowulf is facing his final great challenge against the dragon, he recalls a family tragedy: his lord's brother, Hæðcyn, accidentally killed another brother, Herebeald (2425–71). Many scholars have remarked on an apparent parallel between Hæðcyn's killing of his brother Herebeald— mentioned nowhere else in Old English tradition—and the Old Norse myth of Baldr's death, caused by an inadvertent shot from his brother Höðr.[8] The brothers' father, the Geatish king Hrethel, is paralyzed by grief. But in Old Norse poetic traditions, Odin contravenes the law of

---

[6] *Beowulf*, 874–915; for Sigemund see R. G. Finch (ed.), *Völsunga saga: the Saga of the Volsungs* (London: Nelson, 1965). The story of Sigemund and the dragon leads the *Beowulf*-poet to mention the Danish king Heremod, who does not feature anywhere else in Old English literature, although he is mentioned in a semi-historical genealogy of West Saxon kings (Kenneth Sisam, 'Anglo-Saxon Royal Genealogies', *Proceedings of the British Academy* 39 (1953), 287–346). However, the Norse god or hero, Hermóðr, appears in three very early (perhaps tenth-century) Old Norse poems, and in all three instances Hermóðr is associated with Sigmundr; see Orchard, *Companion to Beowulf*, p. 107, and Mark Griffith, 'Some difficulties in *Beowulf*, lines 874–902: Sigemund reconsidered', *Anglo-Saxon England* 24 (1995), 11–41.

[7] *Sörla þáttr eða Heðins saga ok Högna*, in Guðni Jónsson (ed.), *Fornaldar sögur Norðurlanda* (Reykjavík: Íslendingasagnaútgáfan, 1950), vol. I, pp. 365–82; see Helen Damico, '*Sörlaþáttr* and the Hama episode in *Beowulf*', *Scandinavian Studies* 55 (1983), 222–35.

[8] For contrasting interpretations of the evident parallel, see for instance Richard North, *Heathen Gods in Old English Literature* (Cambridge: Cambridge University Press, 1997), pp. 198–202, Roberta Frank, 'Skaldic verse', p. 132, and Heather O'Donoghue, 'What has Baldr to do with Lamech? The Lethal Shot of a Blind Man in Old Norse Myth and Jewish Exegetical Traditions', *Medium Ævum* LXXII (2003), 82–107.

nature, seducing a giantess by magic to beget a son, Vali, who magically reaches maturity in the space of one day, solely to wreak revenge on his half-brother's killer.[9] Can we infer that the *Beowulf*-poet deliberately created the Geatish tragedy in order to engineer an implied contrast between a grieving father and a mythological sorcerer? And finally, at the very beginning of the poem, the mythical progenitor of the Danish dynasty is introduced as Scyld Scefing—"Shield Sheafson", as Seamus Heaney has it.[10] But while the Danish royal family are known in Norse tradition as the Skjöldungar—"descendants of Skjöldr", Scyld in Old English—there is evidence that a figure with a name like Sceaf was a mythic fertility figure in Old English tradition.[11] Has the *Beowulf*-poet combined the two, producing not only a doubly potent mythic founder, associated with both military success and fertility, but also a progenitor with an Anglo-Scandinavian heritage?

I now turn to the two central aspects of the poem which have claims to have been influenced by Old Norse myth: the hero, Beowulf himself, and the overall structure and ethos of the poem. Beowulf's career has been compared with the exploits of the Norse god Thor, especially in their final, mutually fatal, encounters with a monstrous serpent. In Norse myth, this final fight is an element in the Norse apocalypse, Ragnarök, whose doom-laden finality has been held to permeate the *Beowulf*-poet's representation of his characters'—and perhaps his own—heroic past.

Thor is the hero of the Æsir, fighting their battles, defending Asgard and taking on giants (and giantesses), the old enemies of the gods. His giant-killings feature widely in Old Norse poetry and prose; a number of eddic poems are given over to such episodes, and Snorri Sturluson adds to their number in his *Prose Edda*.[12] Of course, protection from monsters, or enemies, is what heroes offer, and as Lord Raglan pointed out long ago, the biography of the hero is remarkably similar in narratives across many times and places; in fact, its climax is very often a fight against a monster or other powerful figure.[13] It would be surprising if Beowulf the champion of the Geats did *not* share certain features with the god whose physical courage

---

[9] *Völuspá*, st. 32–3, in Ursula Dronke (ed.), *The Poetic Edda* (Oxford: Clarendon Press, 1969–2011), vol. II, pp. 15–16.

[10] Seamus Heaney, *Beowulf* (London: Faber and Faber, 1999), l. 4.

[11] See Orchard, *Companion to Beowulf*, pp. 100–5, and Clive Tolley, 'Beowulf's Scyld Scefing Episode: Some Norse and Finnish Analogues', *Arv* 52 (1996), 7–48.

[12] For a translation of the *Poetic Edda* see Carolyne Larrington, *The Poetic Edda* (Oxford: Oxford University Press, 1996), and of the *Prose Edda*, Anthony Faulkes, *Edda* (London: Dent, 2003). References to the *Prose Edda* are to this translation.

[13] Lord Raglan, *The Hero: A Study in Tradition, Myth, and Drama* (London: Methuen, 1936).

and might were his primary attributes. But three of Thor's exploits—his first attempt at hooking the World Serpent, and two of his adventures at the court of the giant Útgarða-Loki—are arguably similar to episodes in *Beowulf's* career. Both Thor and Beowulf, when young, contend with a sea monster or monsters, out in the ocean, and best their companion; their safe return is carefully noted.[14] Both Thor and Beowulf wrestle with an old woman—perhaps the greatest of Thor's humiliations at the court of Útgarða-Loki is his wrestling match with Elli, an old woman whom the giant, ostensibly despairing of Thor's ability to meet the feeblest of challenges, brings on as a suitable opponent. Thor struggles hard against Elli, and when he stumbles to one knee, the giant steps in and stops the fight. But Thor was deceived. The name Elli means "old age" in Norse, and no-one can be expected to prevail against her.[15] Beowulf also fights a woman—Grendel's mother, savage with revenge and a powerful opponent for Beowulf, who is, like Thor, brought to his knees by her. But there is no big friendly giant to stop the fight; instead, Beowulf's mail coat—and God—protect him against her potentially fatal knife thrust (1537–56).

Finally, both Thor and Beowulf have a close encounter with a giant's glove. On his way to giantland, searching for a place to spend the night, Thor comes across a large building whose doorway is as wide as the structure itself, and entering, they find a smaller room off to the side, about halfway down, and huddle there, with Thor guarding them. His night shelter turns out to be the giant's glove.[16] The comedy is broad, and Thor is a figure of fun, looking all the sillier for the giant's grave politeness towards him in their exchanges. But there is no comedy to be had from Beowulf's encounter with the giant's glove. The poet does not include this episode in his main narrative, but introduces it as Beowulf gives an account of how he fought and killed the monster Grendel. Though it was not mentioned in the earlier narrative of Beowulf's fight with Grendel, Beowulf now reports that Grendel was carrying a great glove made out of dragon skins—perhaps a sinister allusion to Beowulf's eventual fate at the hands of a dragon. Grendel's intention was to have put Beowulf in the glove (2085–92). Why did the poet not include the detail about the glove in his own narrative of Beowulf's fight with Grendel? Perhaps he was trying to avoid a difficulty only too obvious in Snorri's narrative: it is simply not possible to envisage any real interaction between Thor and the giant if the disparity in size were

---

[14]   *Beowulf,* 499–589, and *Hymiskviða,* in Dronke, *The Poetic Edda,* vol. III, pp. 67–75. This parallel has been under-emphasized because Beowulf's swimming contest with Breca is overshadowed in the poem by his dragon and monster fights.

[15]   Faulkes, *Edda,* pp. 44–6.

[16]   Faulkes, *Edda,* pp. 38–40.

so great as to allow Thor and his companions to spend the night in the giant's glove. By the same token, Beowulf's fight with Grendel would have been an altogether different encounter if the poet had represented Beowulf as tiny enough to fit inside Grendel's glove.

It may be, then, that Snorri and the *Beowulf*-poet[17] drew on similar mythic sources, but that Snorri has inherited, or transformed his sources into, tales in which the hero—identified as Thor—is successively ridiculed, while in *Beowulf,* the register is completely different: the hero's opponents and their attributes are terrifying and the narrative epic, and serious.

That scholars have seen echoes of Christ in the figures of both Thor and Beowulf is the most fundamental link between the two heroes. Significant parallels between Thor's hooking of the World Serpent and Christ catching the Devil on a fish hook have been set out by Ursula Dronke; she also points out that Thor is presented in Old Norse sources as the son of Odin—the father of men.[18] Art historians have proposed that the depiction of mythological scenes on Viking age Christian monuments—for example, the Gosforth Cross, and the "Fishing Stone" which may have formed part of a frieze decorating the church in Gosforth—may indicate that a strong typological connexion was perceived between Christian and pagan motifs; as Richard Bailey puts it, "[w]hat we see on the Gosforth cross is an exploitation of the links and the contrasts between a Scandinavian and a Christian theology".[19] This raises the possibility of a new kind of attitude from the poet of *Beowulf* towards Old Norse myth: a poet who was not disapproving, or rivalrous, as Frank has claimed in connexion with the apparent undermining of Odinic myth, but one ready and willing to draw on both traditions in his depiction of a celebrated hero. It may even be worth making a distinction between the acceptability of Thor, the god of farmers and settlers, like the Danish Scandinavians in eastern England, and the much more risky figure of Odin, the necromancer, the god of aristocratic Norwegians, whose country, as Frank astutely points out, the *Beowulf*-poet "studiously ignores".[20]

If we can see traces of a Christ-Thor figure in Beowulf, it may be that the poet did not himself invent this composite, and even that it was

---

[17] And the author of the most celebrated analogue to *Beowulf,* the Old Norse *Grettis saga;* see Jesse Byock (trans.), *Grettir's Saga* (Oxford: Oxford University Press, 2009), and Magnús Fjalldal, *The Long Arm of Coincidence: The Frustrated Connection between Beowulf and Grettis saga* (Toronto: University of Toronto Press, 1998).

[18] Dronke, *The Poetic Edda,* vol. III, pp. 89–101.

[19] Richard N. Bailey, *Viking Age Sculpture in Northern England* (London: Collins, 1980), p. 129; see also Lilla Kopár, *Gods and Settlers: The Iconography of Norse Mythology in Anglo-Scandinavian Sculpture* (Turnhout: Brepols, 2012), pp. 57–104.

[20] Frank, 'Skaldic verse', p. 129.

familiar to his audience as a site where Old Norse myth might be held to meet the Christian beliefs of the Anglo-Saxons. But it is clear that Thor's final encounter with the World Serpent, in its context of the final battle between the gods and their adversaries—Ragnarök—was not something easily paralleled with Christian eschatology. Echoes of Ragnarök are evident not only in Beowulf's fight against the dragon, but also in the ethos and outline of the whole poem, and they mark out the epic, heroic, and in many ways glorious pagan past depicted by the poet as something wholly foreign to Christian traditions.

Ursula Dronke has examined the fundamental parallels between the myth of Ragnarök and the *Beowulf*-poet's depiction of the world of Hrothgar and Beowulf himself.[21] Challenging Tolkien's claim that "both Norsemen and Anglo-Saxons believed that the Gods waged a continual struggle against the monsters" and that "within Time the monsters would win"—a profoundly pessimistic credo—Dronke points out that "Chaos and Unreason—the monsters—do not win; they destroy what is ripe for destruction, a decaying and tainted world, but a world whose defenders have sufficient strength to destroy their destroyers".[22] This is the key element of Ragnarök: in a series of cataclysmic encounters, the gods engage in single combat with their enemies, and neither side survives. Odin fights Fenrir, the great wolf, and the poet of *Völuspá* gives us to understand that this is the death of him, for it is his wife Frigg's second sorrow, her first being the death of Baldr.[23] Fenrir perishes too, when Odin's son Viðarr avenges his father by stabbing the monster. Týr fights the savage hound Garmr, and both are killed. Freyr advances on the fire-giant Surtr, and falls; Surtr later sets fire to the whole world, so that the flames lick the heavens themselves. But before this all-consuming conflagration, Thor meets the World Serpent, and although he attacks the creature with characteristic vigour, his strength fails in the face of its deadly poison, and both fall.[24] Here, then, is the clearest parallel between Thor and the hero Beowulf: both die fighting a mighty dragon, and with them ends a whole epoch—in Beowulf's case, the end (as Frank points out, an unhistorical closing[25]) of the whole race of the Geats. Beowulf has no heirs; there is no successor to the throne, and though his helper Wiglaf survives the dragon

[21] Ursula Dronke, '*Beowulf* and Ragnarök', *Saga-Book of the Viking Society* 17 (1966–9), 302–25.

[22] Dronke, '*Beowulf* and Ragnarök', 302–3; see J. R. R. Tolkien, '*Beowulf*: The Monsters and the Critics', *Proceedings of the British Academy* 22 (1936), 245–95.

[23] *Völuspá*, st. 51, in Dronke, *The Poetic Edda*, vol. II, p. 21. For Snorri's account of Ragnarök see Faulkes, *Edda*, pp. 52–55.

[24] *Völuspá*, st. 53, in Dronke, *The Poetic Edda*, vol. II, p. 22.

[25] Frank, 'Skaldic verse', p. 125.

fight, there is no indication that the Geats have any future, especially in the face of attacks from their old enemies the Swedes. Beowulf is burnt on his funeral pyre, and heaven swallows up the smoke (3137–55). The Danes, as we know from analogous Norse sources, and might infer anyway from the poet's own dark hints, have been engulfed in another conflagration: the burning of Heorot—once a beacon of civilized heroic life built with such pride and hope—and the notorious familial violence amongst the generation after Hrothgar (2009–69).[26]

The pessimism of this conception of the end of the world (though to some extent tempered by rebirth in *Völuspá*, perhaps under the influence of Christian theology) runs quite counter to Christian belief. Craig Davis describes how "the hero's career recapitulates on a secular level the movement of pagan myth from the violent creation of order out of primeval chaos to an apocalyptic collapse of that order back into chaos", and argues that "virtually every narrative in the poem ... follows the pattern of temporary success but ultimate disaster".[27] His conclusion is that "the larger world-view inherent in heroic legend, formulated under the influence of a late pagan fatalism, is fundamentally antipathetic to the consolations of Christian sacred history".[28] John Halverson believes that "the Christian consolation of salvation has no significant part in *Beowulf*",[29] and Charles Moorman makes a persuasive distinction between the triumphant closing passages of Old English biblical poems such as *Judith* and *Andreas*, and the "negative" colours of the end of *Beowulf*.[30] Although there have been some dissenting voices,[31] parallels between *Beowulf* and accounts of Ragnarök are hard to resist. The poet insists—in spite of Wiglaf's loyalty and bravery, and in spite of historical evidence that the Geatish line did not in fact end here—on a mood of hopeless resignation for the end of his poem, and it seems that for this he turned to Old Norse myth.

We will probably never know in just what form the *Beowulf*-poet knew Norse mythology, but it is perhaps significant that the arguable allusions in the poem range widely across the whole body of this material—and thus contrast with most of the allusions in post-medieval poetry in English, in

[26] For the Norse sources see G. N. Garmonsway and Jacqueline Simpson (eds.), *Beowulf and its Analogues* (London: Dent, 1968), pp. 238–47.

[27] Craig Davis, *Beowulf and the Demise of Germanic Legend in England* (New York and London: Garland, 1996), pp. 140 and xii.

[28] Davis, *Beowulf and the Demise of Germanic Legend*, p. 160.

[29] John Halverson, 'The World of *Beowulf*', *English Literary History* 36:4 (1969), 593–608 (603).

[30] Charles Moorman, 'The Essential Paganism of *Beowulf*', *Modern Language Quarterly* 28 (1967), 3–18 (4).

[31] See 'Christian and Pagan in *Beowulf*', in Arthur G. Brodeur, *The Art of Beowulf* (Berkeley: University of California Press, 1959), pp. 182–219.

which it is evident that the poet was responding to one or two specific Old Norse texts, rather than to a great mass of material.

Identifying Norse mythic allusions in *Beowulf*, with its pre-Christian Scandinavian setting, characters, and backstory, is necessarily a speculative endeavour—partly because the poet may have transformed his sources, and partly too because these sources might well not have been the same as those which have come down to us as Old Norse myth. It is not surprising, then, that traces of Norse myth elsewhere in Old English poetry are even fainter and less certain. The bleak winter which the speaker in the Exeter Book poem *The Wanderer* suffers may owe something to the Old Norse *fimbulvetr*, the monstrous winter presaging Ragnarök.[32] When the poet of the eighth-century Old English poem *The Dream of the Rood* writes that "all Creation wept" at the death of Christ on the cross, is he alluding to the myth of the Christ-like Baldr, for whom almost all creation wept, like the thaw which presages the coming of spring?[33] Or is it perhaps that the Old Norse myth itself borrowed the topos from Christian tradition? Might the mysterious female speaker in *The Wife's Lament* share some characteristics with the valkyrie figure of Brynhildr in eddic poetry?[34]

Traces of Old Norse myth in post-Conquest traditions are still fainter, and more uncertain. Gradually, knowledge of Old English, and appreciation of its literature, disappeared until early modern antiquarians resurrected it.[35] But of course a literary culture—whether oral or written—never simply comes to a stop, however clean the break may seem to be. No-one can be certain how long the Scandinavian language lingered in England after the Norman Conquest, nor whether Scandinavian stories continued to be told, and therefore were available to influence later generations of poets.[36] There are some intriguing hints. In 1076, for

[32]   *The Wanderer*, in Bernard J. Muir (ed.), *The Exeter Anthology of Old English Poetry: An Edition of Exeter Dean and Chapter MS. 3501* (Exeter: University of Exeter Press, 1994), vol. I, pp. 218–22, and Faulkes, *Edda*, pp. 52–3.

[33]   Michael Swanton (ed.), *The Dream of the Rood* (Manchester: Manchester University Press, 1970), l.55, and Faulkes, *Edda*, p. 51.

[34]   *The Wife's Lament*, in Muir, *The Exeter Anthology of Old English Poetry*, vol. I, pp. 331–3, and Heather O'Donoghue, '*The Wife's Lament* and *Helreið Brynhildar*' in Natalja Gvozdetskaja et al. (eds.), *Stanzas of Friendship: Studies in Honour of Tatjana N Jackson* (Moscow: Dmitry Pozharskiy University, 2011), pp. 310–20.

[35]   How long the understanding of written Old English lasted in England after the Norman Conquest has been a matter of debate, and the persistence of the spoken language is even more difficult to chart; see Mary Swan and Elaine Treharne (eds.), *Rewriting Old English in the Twelfth Century* (Cambridge: Cambridge University Press, 2000), and Mark Faulkner, 'Archaism, Belatedness and Modernisation: "Old" English in the Twelfth Century', *Review of English Studies* 63 (2011), 179–203.

[36]   See R. I. Page, 'How long did the Scandinavian language survive in England? The epigraphical evidence', in Peter Clemoes and Kathleen Hughes (eds.), *England Before the Conquest: Studies in Primary Sources Presented to Dorothy Whitelock* (Cambridge: Cambridge

instance, William the Conqueror ordered the execution of Earl Waltheof of Northampton, who was of Danish descent. Waltheof had sworn allegiance to him in 1066, but twice rebelled against him in the decade after the Conquest. Waltheof's body was taken to Crowland Abbey, in Lincolnshire, of which he had been a benefactor. He eventually came to be regarded as a saint by the monks there, and a cult developed around him.[37] Two quite separate and very different bodies of tradition about Waltheof have survived. Thirteenth-century Norse accounts of his death present him as a martyr and claim that though he was born and lived in England, in the time-honoured tradition of Scandinavian earls he had employed an Icelandic skald to sing his praises.[38] After Waltheof's death, according to the Norse sources, this skald duly composed a memorial eulogy to Waltheof, the *Valþjófsflokkr* ("poem about Waltheof"). This would seem to testify to an audience in England not only understanding Old Norse, but also versed in the complicated prosody and metaphorical lexis of skaldic poetry. The verses preserved in these Old Norse histories, if genuine, are just as cryptic and intricate as verses composed in Scandinavia, and even contain mythological kennings.[39]

The second body of tradition about the earl is completely different, comprising a thirteenth-century Latin compilation concerning Crowland saints, including Waltheof. One of these texts, the *Gesta antecessorum comitis Waldevi*, contains some remarkable details about the life of Waltheof's father, Earl Siward, who is said to have killed a dragon, and had an encounter with an Odinic old man who gives him advice, and a war banner with a raven on it (we shall come across the raven banner again in the next chapter). Siward's father—St Waltheof's grandfather—was the result of a union between the daughter of an earl and a white bear; according to the *Gesta*, he had furry ears as a mark of his strange ancestry.

Both of these traditions would seem to be evidence of lively narratives of Old Norse myth and legend current in England in the century after the Conquest.[40] And it is in the nature of such stories to be perpetuated—though

University Press, 1971), pp. 165–81, and D. N. Parsons, 'How long did the Scandinavian language survive in England? Again', in James Graham-Campbell et al. (eds.), *Vikings and the Danelaw* (Oxford: Oxbow, 2001), pp. 299–312.

[37] See Forrest S. Scott, 'Earl Waltheof of Northumbria', *Archaeologia Aeliana* 30 (1952), 149–215, and Carl Watkins, 'The Cult of Earl Waltheof at Crowland', *Hagiographica* 3 (1996), 95–111.

[38] See Forrest S. Scott, 'Valþjófr jarl: an English earl in Icelandic sources', *Saga-Book of the Viking Society* 14 (1953–7), 78–94.

[39] For the verses see Kari Ellen Gade (ed.), *Poetry from the kings' sagas 2: from c.1035 to c.1300* (Turnhout: Brepols, 2009), Part 1, pp. 382–4, and Judith Jesch, 'Skaldic Verse in Scandinavian England', in Graham-Campbell et al., *Vikings and the Danelaw*, pp. 313–25.

[40] See E. C. Parker, *Anglo-Scandinavian Literature and the Post-Conquest Period*, D.Phil thesis (University of Oxford, 2013).

not without alteration or development—through further centuries. Sometimes it is even possible to trace the line of descent. For instance, in the twelfth century, Henry of Huntingdon included material about Siward in his chronicle of English history, and from there Siward found his way into Holinshed's Chronicle, and thus probably into Shakespeare's *Macbeth*.[41] Elsewhere, the appearance of a Norse-derived story element may be more difficult to source. Given its subject matter (and its setting, Lincolnshire again) it would seem likely that the thirteenth-century English medieval romance *Havelok the Dane* might include material derived from local and ultimately Scandinavian sources, but specific evidence is hard to come by. By the same token, one might expect to find Norse-derived material in Shakespeare's *Hamlet*, and there does indeed seem to be a faint, attenuated but plausible link between the eponymous hero of the play and the mysterious figure of Amloði in an Icelandic poem quoted by Snorri.[42] Moreover, the underlying structure of the play—a disaffected nephew in the royal house of Denmark, and the suspicious death of the ruling king's brother—clearly echoes Norse legends about the early Danish monarchy, legends which as we have seen are also reflected in the Old English poem *Beowulf*.[43] And Siward may not be the only Norse connexion in *Macbeth*. Saxo Grammaticus tells the story of Høther who "happened to be hunting when he wandered from his path in a mist and came upon a retreat of forest maidens. As they saluted him by his own name he asked who they were, to which they replied that their special function was to control the fortune of wars by their guidance and blessings."[44] Saxo claims that he used medieval Icelandic sources for his history, and these women, who "were able to award success or defeat at pleasure", are clearly based on valkyries. But they are just as readily identified with the three weird sisters of *Macbeth*, and there are a number of other (slighter) echoes reminiscent of Old Norse tradition elsewhere in the play.[45]

Returning to the Middle Ages, one might also make a claim for elements of Old Norse myth in Chaucer's *Canterbury Tales*. In the 'Pardoner's Tale', for instance, Chaucer's three young dissolutes meet, like Earl Siward, an old

[41] See Heather O'Donoghue, *Old Norse-Icelandic Literature: A Short Introduction* (Oxford: Blackwell, 2004), pp. 144–7.

[42] O'Donoghue, *Old Norse-Icelandic Literature*, pp. 147–8, and Faulkes, *Edda*, pp. 92–3.

[43] Is it merely coincidence that in Act V, ii 220–1, following a discussion on culpability and responsibility, Hamlet begs forgiveness from Laertes on the grounds that any injury has been accidental—"That I have shot my arrow o'er the house/and hurt my brother"—a striking echo of the accidental fratricide in *Beowulf*?

[44] Saxo Grammaticus, *History of the Danes*, trans. Peter Fisher and ed. Hilda Ellis Davidson (Woodbridge: D. S. Brewer, 1979), vol. I, p. 69.

[45] See Nora Chadwick, 'The Story of Macbeth: A Study in Gaelic and Norse Tradition', *Scottish Gaelic Studies* 6:2 (September 1949), 189–211.

man who tells them the way to Death; "al forwrapped" apart from his face, he is reminiscent of Odin, usually represented in Old Norse sources as an old man with a hat pulled down low over his face in disguise.[46] Paul Taylor has compared the Wife of Bath's admiration for her young fifth husband's legs and feet—"so clene and faire"—with the story Snorri tells in *Skáldskaparmál* about the giantess Skaði, who was allowed to choose a husband from amongst the gods, but was only granted a view of their legs and feet.[47]

However, it would be surprising if a story compendium as wide-ranging in its sources and materials as the *Canterbury Tales* did *not* include stories ultimately from Norse tradition. Though these correspondences are endlessly fascinating, and could easily be multiplied, they are necessarily highly speculative, and do not represent the direct and knowing engagement with evidently non-native traditions which I am primarily concerned with in this book. This sort of engagement was simply absent for several centuries, and it was not until the seventeenth century that knowledge of Norse literary traditions began, slowly, to spread amongst antiquarians and poets in England.

Outside the British Isles, European knowledge of Old Norse literature had experienced a more major rupture. Iceland suffered an extraordinary degree of cultural and economic decline after the Reformation, as the power base in Scandinavia shifted eastwards, from Iceland and Norway to Denmark and Sweden. But in parallel with developments in England, for similar reasons, and in similar ways, Scandinavian antiquarians in the sixteenth and seventeenth centuries began to investigate the early literary records of their cultures, and what they rediscovered were the medieval Icelandic manuscripts in which the rich literature—and mythology—of Old Norse was not only preserved, but was still fully accessible to hitherto neglected Icelandic scholars and *littérateurs*, whose native language had barely altered from the medieval idioms of the manuscripts. And since Latin remained the scholarly lingua franca of western Europe, the exchange of ideas, texts, and philological speculation brought the mythology of medieval Iceland to a wider audience. Some English poets were inspired by this body of knowledge, imperfect as it was, and the subject of the first chapter will be precisely those first brief, scattered allusions to Old Norse mythic themes and figures in early modern English poetry.

---

[46] See R. A. Barakat, 'Odin: Old Man of the Pardoner's Tale', *Southern Folklore Quarterly* 28 (1964), 210–15.

[47] Paul Beekman Taylor, *Sharing Story: Medieval Norse-English Literary Relationships* (New York: AMS Press, 1998), pp. 237–44; see Faulkes, *Edda*, pp. 60–1. Taylor's link between the giantess's name—Skaði—and the use of the word "scathe" in relation to the Wife in the *General Prologue* is perhaps less convincing.

1

Antiquarians and Poets: The Discovery of Old Norse Myth in the Seventeenth and Eighteenth Centuries

Direct literary relations between England and Scandinavia were few and far between in the Elizabethan period. As Ethel Seaton notes at the beginning of her invaluable survey of such interaction between England and Scandinavia in the seventeenth century, "the connexion that had existed in the Middle Ages between England and Iceland, and England and Norway, becoming attenuated, had been forgotten"[1] and as she concludes, tersely, "Elizabethans knew very little about the Scandinavian countries, and most of that little was wrong".[2] Old Norse myth in its literary form was not known. Classical sources concerning Scandinavian (or more generally, Germanic) peoples formed the basis of some idea of the North, but they provided little mythological information. What we shall see in this chapter is that it was growing antiquarian interest in works which were thought to bear on the early history of the ancestors of the English—and particularly, the constitutional and political ideals these ancestors were believed to have passed on—which began to awaken an interest in Northern religion, literature, and mythology.

Early insular sources such as Gildas, Bede, Asser, and Æthelweard had made it quite clear that the English had Germanic origins, and Tacitus's highly favourable portrait of the Germanic tribes in the *Germania*, once it had been rediscovered in the early modern period, was to become extremely influential—though more for its idealized depiction of the political or constitutional traditions of the Germanic tribes than for its account of their religious practices. According to Tacitus, in the land he called "Germania" the powers of a king were limited: major issues were debated in a democratic way by whole tribes, and kings ruled by consent

---

[1] Ethel Seaton, *Literary Relations of England and Scandinavia in the Seventeenth Century* (Oxford: Clarendon Press, 1935), p. 7.
[2] Seaton, *Literary Relations*, p. 329.

and persuasion, not as autocratic tyrants.[3] Of course this politically auspicious origin myth came to be frequently cited by English parliamentarians in the seventeenth century. Tacitus also stressed the virtue, bravery, and powerful sense of honour amongst these people. As Samuel Kliger puts it, "Tacitus wrote an epitaph to Roman *virtus*, not a prophecy of German greatness, yet his treatise was fated to immortalize for English history the Germanic love of liberty and democratic procedures".[4]

Tacitus does make oblique reference to the gods worshipped by Germanic tribes. He refers to "traditional songs" in which Germanic peoples recorded their history, and tells us that in these songs "the Germans celebrate an earth-born god called Tuisto".[5] His son, Mannus, according to Tacitus, was held to be the progenitor of three groups of Germanic tribes: the Ingaevones, the Herminones, and the Istaevones. However, when detailing the religious practices of the Germans, Tacitus writes of a trinity of gods: "Above all other gods they worship Mercury, and count it no sin, on certain feast-days, to include human victims in the sacrifices offered to him. Hercules and Mars they appease by offerings of animals, in accordance with ordinary civilized custom".[6] With these Roman names, Tacitus is usually understood to be denoting Germanic equivalents of Odin, Thor, and Týr, though he does not use these names.

The pre-Christian gods of the Anglo-Saxons might have had their counterparts in Norse mythology and literature, but there are very few references to the pagan gods in Anglo-Saxon sources. The Saxon god Woden figured as an ancestral name in familiar Anglo-Saxon royal genealogies, but the link between Anglo-Saxon deities and the Scandinavian gods was not readily made in the post-medieval period, even though some learned Anglo-Saxon scholars had recognized it.[7] For instance, William Camden,

[3] Tacitus, *The Agricola and The Germania*, trans. H. Mattingly and S. A. Handford (Harmondsworth: Penguin, 1970), *Germania* ch. 7, p. 107. Subsequent references are to this edition.
[4] Samuel Kliger, *The Goths in England: A Study in Seventeenth and Eighteenth Century Thought* (Cambridge, Mass.: Harvard University Press, 1952), p. 112. For a brief account of the later, pernicious, influence of the *Germania*, see Anthony Birley, 'Introduction', in Tacitus, *Agricola and Germany* (Oxford: Oxford University Press, 1999), pp. xxxvii–xxxviii.
[5] Tacitus, *Germania*, ch. 2, p. 102.
[6] Tacitus, *Germania*, ch. 9, p. 108.
[7] The homilist Ælfric, in his references to Danish paganism in *De falsis diis*, does not mention a link between the Saxon and Norse gods, and neither does Wulfstan in his version of the homily, but at least one reader of Wulfstan recognized the connexion: a note in the margin of the sole manuscript reads "Oþon unde Wodones deg", identifying Odin with Woden (Dorothy Bethurum (ed.), *The Homilies of Wulfstan* (Oxford: Clarendon Press, 1957), p. 223, and see John C. Pope (ed.), *Homilies of Ælfric: A Supplementary Collection* (Oxford: Oxford University Press, 1967–8), vol. II, p. 684). For the link between Woden, Odin, and Mercury in learned writing about paganism in the Anglo-Saxon period, see

in his *Britannia* (1586, translated into English in 1610), writes about a Saxon god Wooden—"that false imagined God, and Father of the English Saxons"[8]—and notes that he was also worshipped by the Danes. But although Camden had read one of the first Scandinavian histories to gain currency amongst English scholars—Saxo Grammaticus's *Gesta Danorum,* which had been published in Paris in 1514—he saw "no connexion whatever between the war-god Woden of the Saxons...and the hero-god sorcerer Odin of Saxo's history".[9]

Saxo Grammaticus's history of the Danes, the *Gesta Danorum,* had been written around AD 1200, though the manuscript was not published until the beginning of the sixteenth century. The *Gesta Danorum* is an extraordinary compendium of pseudo-historical and legendary material. Saxo says in his preface that he used Old Icelandic sources,[10] and it is indeed possible to discern the outlines of familiar Old Norse mythic figures and even the bare bones of the central Old Norse myth of the death of Baldr: Odin, and his wife Frigg; Odin's son Balder, who was killed; and Odin's celebrated revenge, begetting a son, Wale, by seducing Rindr, a son who avenges his dead brother. But crucially, Saxo presents this material not as myth, derived from Old Norse poetry, but as history: he fundamentally euhemerizes these figures, explaining of Odin, for example, that "there was a man called Odin who was believed throughout Europe, though falsely, to be a god".[11] The whole Norse pantheon could be accounted for in this way, their divinity attributed to the ignorant misconceptions of early Scandinavians: "At one time certain individuals, initiated into the magic arts, namely Thor, Odin and a number of others who were skilled at conjuring up marvellous illusions, clouded the minds of simple men and began to appropriate the exalted rank of godhead. Norway, Sweden and Denmark were ensnared in a groundless conviction, urged to a devoted worship of these frauds and infected by their gross imposture. The results of their deception spread, so that all other realms came to revere some kind of divine power in them, believing they were gods or the confederates of gods. They rendered solemn prayers to these wizards and paid the respect

---

Richard North, *Heathen Gods in Old English Literature* (Cambridge: Cambridge University Press, 1997), pp. 78–132.

[8]   *Britannia,* translated by Philemon Holland as *Britain, or A Chorographicall Description of the most flourishing Kingdomes, England, Scotland and Ireland, and the Ilands adioyning, out of the depth of Antiquitie* (London, 1610), p. 241.

[9]   Seaton, *Literary Relations,* p. 245.

[10]   Saxo Grammaticus, *History of the Danes,* vol. I, p. 5.

[11]   Saxo Grammaticus, *History of the Danes,* vol. I, Book I, p. 25.

to an impious heresy which should have gone to true religion."[12] Thus the Norse gods became a part of the ancient history of Scandinavia.

But if he did not link the Anglo-Saxon gods with their Scandinavian counterparts, William Camden does seem to have been the first to make a parallel link. He took the very significant step of identifying the Jutes— one of the Germanic tribes who, in Bede's celebrated account, settled in England in the fifth century—as Goths, whom the early Scandinavian historians celebrated as their progenitors. This claim of Gothic origins was ultimately based on the work of the sixth-century historian Jordanes, who argued that Scandinavia was the *vagina gentium* or "womb of nations" from which the Goths, the indigenous peoples of Europe, had "burst forth like a swarm of bees".[13] The metaphor of the swarm of bees became enormously popular, and recurs again and again in the poetry and essays of the seventeenth and eighteenth centuries in England. There is no mention of Gothic gods or religion in the *Gothic History*, but Jordanes's use of the term "Gothic" to include everything that we might call Germanic meant that English writers adopted the term as a common label for both Anglo-Saxon and Old Norse—and for medieval traditions more generally.[14]

Camden's identification of Jutes and Goths meant that a direct connexion could be made between the ancestors of the English—the primary concern of the English antiquarians—and the new historical scholarship beginning to come out of Scandinavia. And when these Scandinavian scholars included in their work not only legendary history but also accounts of religious beliefs and ancient literature, even more information about Norse myth could be disseminated amongst English writers. For instance, in 1555, the Swedish scholar Olaus Magnus had published his *Historia de Gentibus Septentrionalibus*, translated into English as *A Compendious History of the Goths, Swedes and Vandals, and other Northern Nations*, though not until 1658. His brother Johannes's slightly earlier *Historia . . . de omnibus Gothorum Sveonumque Regibus* was especially influential in Sweden, since, in David Wilson's words, "it glorified the Gothic heritage of the Swedish state and refuted Saxo".[15] However, Camden

---

[12] Saxo Grammaticus, *History of the Danes*, vol. I, Book VI, pp. 170–1. See D. F. Johnson, 'Euhemerisation versus Demonisation: The Pagan Gods and Ælfric's *De Falsis Diis*' in T. Hofstra, L. A. J. R. Houwen, and A. A. MacDonald (eds.), *Pagans and Christians* (Groningen: E. Forsten, 1995), pp. 35–69, for a useful account of the euhemerization of pagan gods.
[13] Charles Christopher Mierow (trans.), *The Gothic History of Jordanes* (Princeton: Princeton University Press, 1915), pp. 57, 53.
[14] For an account of the various meanings of "Gothic" in this period see Kliger, *The Goths in England*, pp. 10–26.
[15] David Wilson, *Vikings and Gods in European Art* (Højbjerg: Moesgård Museum, 1997), p. 15.

himself does not seem to have used either of these works. Olaus adopted Saxo's euhemeristic explanation of the Old Norse pantheon, and also drew heavily on his brother's work. At the beginning of his third book he acknowledges the debt to his "most dear brother and predecessor, Johannes Magnus" for a description of the three chief gods of the "ancient Goths": "the mighty Thor, who was worshipped sitting in the middle of a cushioned couch, flanked on each side by two other deities, Odin and Frigga".[16] The woodcut at the head of the chapter—also taken from Johannes Magnus's book—vividly depicts this triumvirate of idols. Frigg has a bow and a sword, and Olaus notes that "her image... shamelessly vaunted its sex", although this is far from apparent in the illustration. Odin, heavily armoured, also has a sword, and is described by Olaus as "holding sway over wars, affording men help against their foes". Thor, in pride of place, has "a crown and sceptre and... twelve stars, since people thought there was nothing of equal worth that could be compared to his grandeur".[17] Saxo Grammaticus is also acknowledged as a source for this information about the Gothic gods, and the ultimate source is probably Adam of Bremen's account of the temple at Uppsala.[18] Olaus's work was to become extremely influential, and especially this illustration.

One final aspect of Elizabethan engagement with the ancient history of northern peoples was distinctly literary: the belief that rhyme in English poetry was a legacy from the Gothic tribes. Judy Quinn and Margaret Clunies Ross have traced the history of the debate about the desirability— or otherwise—of rhyme amongst the English poets.[19] It was contended that rhyme was not simply adopted from the Goths, but was a direct result of their overthrow of the Roman Empire and, with it, classical learning and literature which had valued quantitative as opposed to rhyming verse. Whether disparaging or defending the use of rhyme, everyone agreed that it had come into English poetry because of the Goths. In 1602 Thomas Campion published his pamphlet 'Observations in the Art of English Poesie', attacking the wholesale use of rhyme as "a vulgar and easie kind of Poesie".[20] Campion was swiftly challenged by Samuel Daniel, whose 'A

---

[16]   Olaus Magnus, *Historia de Gentibus Septentrionalibus: Description of the Northern Peoples*, ed. Peter Foote (London: Hakluyt Society, 1996), III.3, vol. I, p. 151.
[17]   Olaus Magnus, *Historia de Gentibus Septentrionalibus*, p. 152.
[18]   Adam of Bremen, *History of the Archbishops of Hamburg-Bremen*, trans. F. J. Tschan (New York: Columbia, 1959), Book IV, ch. 26, p. 207. Adam mistakenly calls the third god Fricco, an error for Freyr, and this gave rise to the identification of the idol as Frigg.
[19]   Judy Quinn and Margaret Clunies Ross, 'The Image of Norse Poetry and Myth in Seventeenth-Century England', in Andrew Wawn (ed.), *Northern Antiquity: The Post-Medieval Reception of Edda and Saga* (Enfield Lock: Hisarlik Press, 1994), pp. 189–210 (195–203).
[20]   G. Gregory Smith (ed.), *Elizabethan Critical Essays* (Oxford: Clarendon Press, 1904), vol. II, pp. 327–55 (329).

Defence of Ryme was published the following year, but like Campion, he saw the fall of the Roman Empire as being due to the "Gothes, Vandales, and Longobards, whose comming downe like an inundation ouerwhelmed, as they say, al the glory of learning in Europe".[21]

In summary, Elizabethan scholars could have described the Germanic tribes as noble and blessed with constitutional liberty, and defended the belief that the English were descended from them. These Germanic peoples were identified as Goths, but the link between the Scandinavian Odin and the Saxon Woden was still little more than a note in the margin. Olaus Magnus had described and illustrated runes, which he called "Gothic characters", but they were not yet known by that name, and apparently could not be deciphered in Britain.[22] And rhyme, whether approved of or not, was seen as having come into English poetry as a result of the barbarian invasions. There was still no direct experience of Old Norse mythological literature.

Throughout the seventeenth century we see the same concerns and themes repeatedly alluded to—the legacy of liberty, and the "inundation" of the Goths and their effect on English prosody. Olaus Magnus's triumvirate of gods headed by Thor remained influential, but Odin, though more often represented as a mighty and inspirational Gothic leader than as a diabolical magician, let alone a deity, became by far the most often alluded to of the Norse gods.

At the beginning of the seventeenth century, the scholar and antiquarian Richard Verstegan produced his *Restitution of Decayed Intelligence in Antiquities, concerning the most noble and renowned English Nation*, published in Antwerp in 1605, in London in 1628, and in five editions altogether. Verstegan repeats and elaborates the arguments for the Gothic origins of the English; as Kliger puts it, though this was not new, he was "the first to devote an entire book to a discussion of the historical, cultural and linguistic proofs of his theory".[23] His glowing account of the nobility and political freedoms of England's Gothic ancestors—including the purity of their race—was ultimately based on Tacitus's *Germania*. But Verstegan, unlike Camden, also used the work of Olaus Magnus on Northern culture, and offers a good deal of "information" about the Norse

[21] Smith, *Elizabethan Critical Essays*, vol. II, pp. 356–84 (367). See Amina Alyal, "'In what Scythian sorte soeuer': Tudor Debate on Rhyme', in Z. Almási and M. Pincombe (eds.), *Writing the Other: Humanism versus Barbarism in Tudor England* (Newcastle: Cambridge Scholars, 2008), pp. 159–76.
[22] Olaus Magnus, *Historia de Gentibus Septentrionalibus*, I.34, vol. I, pp. 73–4, and see Seaton, *Literary Relations*, pp. 222–4.
[23] Kliger, *The Goths in England*, p. 115.

gods.[24] Following earlier native English traditions,[25] he links the Norse pantheon to the names of the days of the week. Seven gods are represented as idols in a temple, and there is a series of illustrations—some of uncertain origin, though Woden, Thor, and Friga are recognizable from Olaus Magnus's triumvirate woodcut.[26] Even Verstegan himself seems puzzled by some of them. The idol of Monday's moon, for example, he describes as "very strange and ridiculous"—a woman with a man's coat, and two long rabbit-like ears.[27] Tuesday's idol is not of the god of war, Old Norse Týr, but of the god Tuisto, from Tacitus. In keeping with his status as the most ancient of the Germanic deities, he is illustrated in a "garment of a skin, according to the most ancient manner of the Germans' clothing".[28] Woden (armed and armoured, as in Olaus Magnus) is equated with the Roman god of war Mars, and in a brilliantly insightful etymology, Verstegan connects his name with the English word "wood", meaning mad, or furious (the cognate Old Norse word *óð* has been proposed by modern scholars as the origin of his Norse name *Óðinn*). Thor, enthroned and crowned with stars, as in Olaus, is still presented as the most powerful and popular of the pantheon. Friga too is depicted as in Olaus, but Verstegan's comments about her reveal the confusion surrounding this figure. She carries a bow and a sword, which he interprets as a meaning that "women as wel as men should in tyme of need be ready to fight". But Friga is "an Hermaphrodite" with "both the members of a man, and the members of a woman". Verstegan continues: "Some do call her Frea and not Friga, and say shee was the wyf of Woden, but shee was called Friga".[29] Here, perhaps, may lie the origins of the hermaphrodite information: Freyr and Freyja were brother and sister in the Old Norse pantheon, members of the incestuous Vanir. The confusion between Frigg and Freyja, which went back as far as Adam of Bremen, was to persist (on neo-pagan internet sites especially) to this day.

[24] An enlarged edition of Camden's *Britannia* adds material on the gods from Verstegan; see Rolf H. Bremmer, 'The Anglo-Saxon Pantheon according to Richard Verstegen (1605)', in Timothy Graham (ed.), *The Recovery of Old English: Anglo-Saxon Studies in the Sixteenth and Seventeenth Centuries* (Kalamazoo, Mich.: Medieval Institute Publications, 2000), pp. 141–72 (159–60).
[25] For instance Ælfric in *De falsis diis* (Pope, *Homilies of Ælfric*, vol. II, pp. 683–6), and William of Malmesbury in *Gesta Regum Anglorum*, ed. R. A. B. Mynors, R. M. Thomson, and M. Winterbottom (Oxford: Clarendon Press, 1998), I.5, vol. I, pp. 22–3.
[26] Richard Verstegan, *A Restitution of Decayed Intelligence in Antiquities, concerning the most noble and renowned English Nation* (Antwerp, 1605), pp. 68–81. The illustrations are reproduced in Bremmer, 'The Anglo-Saxon Pantheon', pp. 149–59.
[27] Verstegan, *Restitution of Decayed Intelligence*, p. 70.
[28] Verstegan, *Restitution of Decayed Intelligence*, p. 71.
[29] Verstegan, *Restitution of Decayed Intelligence*, pp. 76–7.

Information about the Norse gods was also circulating in England around this time from a very different source. Elizabethan tall tales about Iceland—for instance that Icelanders were bestial creatures who ate candle wax and raw meat and fish, and that "they haue no houses, but yet doth lye in caues, al together, lyke swyne"[30]—had so incensed the Icelander Arngrímr Jónsson that in 1593 he wrote a brief factual account of Iceland, the *Brevis Commentarius*, which was translated into English.[31] In 1609 Arngrímr wrote a fuller history of Iceland, the *Crymogaea*, which was also translated into English.[32] It includes paraphrases from a number of Old Norse texts, and there are accurate references to *Njáls saga,* and a number of other family sagas, but disappointingly, the references to the Norse gods do not come from Arngrímr's direct knowledge of Old Norse literature, and add little to what was known from Saxo and Olaus Magnus.

However, in a chapter called in English "Of their Politie, and Religion in old times", we learn of temples that were built in Iceland for the worship of the heathen gods, some apparently still standing. The idols themselves, duly related to the names of the days of the week, and to their supposed Roman equivalents, are familiar from Olaus, with Thor "the chiefe and middlemost". The names are accurate representations of the original Old Norse, as one might expect. Arngrímr names Freyr and Njörðr, and then identifies "As"—the Old Norse name for a divinity—as "that famous Odinus". He continues with the medieval etymology of the plural form Æsir: that it derives from Asia, their original home. Arngrímr calls Odin "the chiefe of the people of Asia, who came hither in to the North".[33] Like Saxo, Arngrímr writes of Odin as an historical leader who "affected a Divinitie after his death". And like Verstegan, he sees that although the naming pattern of the days of the week would equate Odin with the Roman Mercury, in Old Icelandic tradition he is more obviously the equivalent of Mars, the god of war. Arngrímr adds that "the ancients honoured Odin in the place of Mars: and such as were slaine in the warres, they say were sacrificed to Odin". This looks tantalizingly like knowledge taken from a literary text. There follows a detailed description of a heathen temple, and a rather sensational account of human sacrifices—"a lamentable matter", Arngrímr remarks piously, but not widespread in Iceland, and short-lived.

[30] Andrew Boorde, *The Fyrst Boke of the Introduction of Knowledge,* ed. F. J. Furnivall (London: N. Trübner, 1870), pp. 141–2; see Seaton, *Literary Relations,* pp. 12–14.

[31] *The True State of Island,* included in Richard Hakluyt, *The Principal Navigations, Voyages, Traffiques and Discoveries of the English Nation* (London, 1599), vol. I, pp. 515–91 (repr. Glasgow: J. Maclehose and Sons, 1904, vol. IV, pp. 1–195).

[32] In Samuel Purchas, *Hakluytus Posthumus, or Purchas His Pilgrimes* (London, 1625, repr. Glasgow: J. Maclehose and Sons, 1906), vol. XIII, pp. 519–59.

[33] Purchas, *Hakluytus Posthumus,* vol. XIII, p. 547.

And for his English audience, Purchas notes in the margin to the passage about Odin "Odinus the same that Woden in our Saxon storie". Bit by bit, fragments of knowledge were beginning to come together and take shape. However, Arngrímr's partial and pious references to heathen practice are the nearest thing yet to any direct quotation of Old Norse mythological literature. It is all the more surprising, then, that as Ethel Seaton points out, two early seventeenth-century poets seem to echo passages from Snorri's *Prose Edda*.[34]

William Browne's poem *Britannia's Pastorals* (1613–16) is stuffed with classical allusions, and there are many references to the early history of "Britannia", with footnotes to antiquarians such as Camden and John Selden. Its lyrical nationalism contains nothing Germanic; there is no reference to Goths. In Book I, the allegorical figure of Riot is pictured roaming the world, and compared, in an extended heroic simile, to an adventurer in strange and far-off climes, travelling "Unto the shores of monster-breeding Nyle/Or through the North to the unpeopled Thyle". As sites of exotic terror, Ultima Thule and the River Nile form a convenient if dubious rhyming pair. In keeping with the sparse and patchy knowledge of the time about northern matters, Browne claims that the sun—"Titan's golden Ring"—never sets between the spring and autumn equinoxes, and that by the same token, all is "gloomy darknesse" for the other half of the year.[35]

In Book II, however, Browne elaborately depicts the onset of night with another allegorical figure, "All-drowsie Night", who sets out "in a Carre of Iet,/By steeds of Iron-gray (which mainely swet/Moist drops on all the world) drawne through the skye".[36] This is remarkably close to Snorri Sturluson's account of the alternation of day and night in his *Gylfaginning*. Snorri writes, "All-Father took Night and her son Day and gave them two horses and two chariots and set them up in the sky so that they have to ride around the earth every twenty-four hours. Night rides in front on the horse called Hrimfaxi, and every morning he bedews the earth with the drips from his bit".[37] Snorri is here following a source such as the eddic poem *Vafþrúðnismál*, which names Hrímfaxi (Soot, or Frost, Mane) as the horse which drags the night, and from whom flecks of foam from the bit fall each morning as dew over the valleys.[38] In the heroic eddic poem

---

[34] Seaton, *Literary Relations*, pp. 326–7.

[35] William Browne, *Britannia's Pastorals* (London, 1613–16), Book I, Song 5, pp. 66–7.

[36] Browne, *Britannia's Pastorals*, Book II, Song 1, p. 21.

[37] Faulkes, *Edda*, p. 14.

[38] *Vafþrúðnismál*, st. 14, in Gustav Neckel and Hans Kuhn (eds.), *Edda: Die Lieder des Codex Regius nebst verwandten Denkmälern* (Heidelberg: C. Winter, 1962), vol. I, pp. 45–55; see Larrington, *The Poetic Edda*, p. 42.

Helgakviða Hjörvarðssonar the same idea is expressed; here, the valkyries ride horses that drip dew from their manes into the valleys.[39] And as Seaton notes, "this is not a classical idea".[40]

James Shirley's masque, *The Triumph of Peace* (1633), also contains what looks like an odd echo of Snorri's mythic material. There is a parade of "projectors"—inventors—the first of which is a jockey, "he seeming much to observe and affect a bridle which he had in his hand".[41] His invention is "a rare and cunning bridle,/Made hollow in the iron part, wherein/A vapour subtly conveyed, shall so/Cool and refresh a horse, he shall ne'er tire".[42] This invention is reminiscent of the mysterious bellows attached to the horses Árvakr and Alsviðr which Snorri tells us drag the chariot of the sun across the sky. According to Snorri, under the horses' shoulders, the gods had fixed two "windbags" to keep the animals cool; Snorri adds the cryptic comment that "in some poetic sources, this is called *ísarnkól* (iron cold)".[43] In the eddic poem *Grímnismál*, the same information is related: the horses have the same names, and "under their withers/the blithe powers/implanted/eternal currents of iron-cold air".[44]

It is odd that this bizarre contraption should figure in both Old Norse sources and in an early seventeenth-century English masque. A contrivance to prolong indefinitely the power of the horse belongs in the widespread folk tale motif of the endless supply of some commodity: the ever-full bottle, or the spinning wheel which turns straw into gold. But the correspondence is very close, and it is striking that the mysterious "ísarnkól" in the poetry is closer to Shirley's inventor's device than the bellows imagined, or rationalized, in Snorri's narrative. Striking too is the fact that Snorri's detail of the cooling tackle follows on directly from the description of dew dripping from Hrimfaxi's mane. One relatively brief passage from Snorri could provide poets with both motifs.

Shirley's other inventions, proudly paraded by his projectors, are a threshing machine, a pressure cooker, an aqualung, a chicken fattener, and a "kind of sea-gull" designed to "compose a ship to sail against the winds". Later in Snorri's *Gylfaginning*, we hear of the ship Skiðblaðnir, which is so large that all the gods—together with their weaponry—can fit on board, and which raises a fair wind whenever its sails are hoisted. And yet, when it is not needed, it can be folded up like a handkerchief and put into a

---

[39] *Helgakviða Hjörvarðssonar*, st. 28, in Larrington, *The Poetic Edda*, p. 128.
[40] Seaton, *Literary Relations*, p. 326.
[41] James Shirley, *The Triumph of Peace* (London, 1633); see Shirley, *James Shirley* (London: Vizetelly, 1888), pp. 437–66 (442).
[42] Shirley, *James Shirley*, p. 452.
[43] See Faulkes, *Edda*, p. 14.
[44] *Grímnismál* st. 37, in Dronke, *The Poetic Edda*, vol. III, pp. 113–24 (121).

pocket. Again we have the concept of the self-sustaining device, if not the striking correspondence of detail.[45]

If these allusions do indeed relate to Old Norse sources, how Browne and Shirley came across them is unexplained. According to Seaton, the Danish scholar Ole Worm visited London in 1611–13, but there are no details of who he met or what manuscripts he might have brought with him, if any.[46] A Norse reference in Thomas Heywood's *Gunaikeion* ('The Generall History of Women', first published in 1624) is more typical of the confused and confusing knowledge of Norse matters in the period. In a section entitled "Of the Goddesses" Heywood lists "*Tro* and *Thor*", adding "These are the names of a goddesse and a god, spoken of in the history of Saxo Grammaticus".[47] Since the entry comes between "Flora" and "Fuvina" we can assume that "Tro" is a misprint for "Fro". In Saxo, the god Frø (Saxo's name for Freyr) presided over a sacrifice of "dark-coloured victims"—the Frøblot.[48] As Davidson notes, these were practices "which shocked Christian writers".[49] But Heywood, with his misspelt, sex-changed divinity, makes no mention of this. Later in the *Gunaikeion*, in the section "Of Adulteresses", Heywood's information from Saxo is more reliably transmitted: "*Friga* was the wife of *Othinus* King of the Danes; and as Saxo Grammaticus affirms, prostituted her body to one of her servants".[50] These two items, along with a brief reference to Olaus Magnus, are the sum total of Heywood's Norse allusions.

As well as spending some time in London, Ole Worm was in correspondence with English antiquarians, among them Sir Henry Spelman. Spelman was himself immersed in the investigation of English law and the constitution, writing anti-Norman tracts in support of the antiquity of pre-Norman—that is, Saxon—laws, and supporting his claims with references to Tacitus and Jordanes about Germanic—that is, Gothic—polity.[51] Spelman's *Glossarium Archaiologicum* (1664) was a study of obsolete

---

[45] See Faulkes, *Edda*, pp. 36–7. Seaton (*Literary Relations*, p. 328) also cites a possible analogue to the story of Thor's fishing expedition in Davenant's *Britannia Triumphans*, in which a "giant vile" fishes with an enormous rod and line. But his bait is a dragon's tail, and hooking the whale entails not a terrifying stand-off, as it does in the story of the god Thor and the World Serpent, but only a satisfyingly large quantity of food for the giant.

[46] Seaton, *Literary Relations*, pp. 154–8.

[47] Thomas Heywood, *Gunaikeion, or Nine Books of Various History concerning Women*, repub. as *The Generall History of Women* (London: W. H., 1657), Book I, p. 38.

[48] Saxo Grammaticus, *History of the Danes*, vol. I, Book I, p. 30.

[49] Saxo Grammaticus, *History of the Danes*, vol. II, p. 151.

[50] Heywood, *The Generall History of Women*, Book IV, p. 275.

[51] On Spelman's study of English constitutional history see J. G. A. Pocock, *The Ancient Constitution and the Feudal Law: A Study of English Historical Thought in the Seventeenth Century* (Cambridge: Cambridge University Press, 1987), pp. 91–123.

words in current ecclesiastical and legal terminology—another example of how constitutional interests also served to increase knowledge of Old Norse material. But his most celebrated—and perhaps most significant—contribution to philology was his suggestion, to Ole Worm himself, in a letter dated 1630, that the word "rune" was derived not, as Worm had proposed, from a word for "furrow", denoting the incised nature of the letters, but was rather related to the Old English word *run* meaning secret.[52] This was a coup for Spelman, not least because Worm's great work, which marked a new phase in Northern knowledge outside Scandinavia, was his *Runer, seu Danica Literatura Antiquissima* (1636), a treatise on runes themselves, a script Worm claimed was derived from Hebrew, and thus of great antiquity.

Literatura Runica ("Runic letters"), as the work is usually known, is an exhaustive study of runes, with disquisitions on their origins, their names, the order of the characters, and much else. But for our purposes, it was extremely significant in that Worm quotes Old Norse poetry—which he believed was all originally written in runes—and not only snippets to illustrate poetic lexis and metre, but also three whole poems. These poems were to become the backbone of the Old Norse poetic canon as it was known to English poets, and in addition they supplied, in E. V. Gordon's words, "a conception of the viking which appealed to romantic taste in England, an incredibly heroic viking, completely indifferent to death, eager to enter Valhalla and drink beer from the skulls of his enemies".[53]

The first whole poem quoted is, naturally enough, the Icelandic rune poem, in which the proper name of each rune in turn forms the basis of a half line of poetry, which is then completed by an apparently unconnected, but rhyming, second half line. Thus the first letter of the runic alphabet, F, is called "fé" which means "wealth" or "property". The first half line proclaims "Fé veldr frænda rógi" (wealth causes dissension amongst kinsmen) followed up with "Fæðisk ulfr í skógi" (the wolf is nurtured in the wood).[54] There are occasional mythological references in the poem. For instance, the name of the "T" rune is that of the god Týr, who is identified as the one-handed god, alluding to the myth about his hand being bitten off by the wolf Fenrir when he laid it in the wolf's jaws as a pledge of good faith to trick Fenrir into being fettered. However, the poem as a

---

[52] For an engaging account of their exchanges on the matter, see Seaton, *Literary Relations*, pp. 226–7.
[53] E. V. Gordon, *An Introduction to Old Norse* (Oxford: Clarendon Press, 1927), p. lxix.
[54] For a meticulous analysis of possible relations between the half lines in the poem, see T. E. Birkett, *Ráð Rétt Rúnar: Reading the Runes in Old English and Old Norse Poetry*, D.Phil thesis (University of Oxford, 2011), pp. 170–87.

whole is so enigmatic that it would hardly be likely to spark off any literary fashion for Old Norse myth or legend.

It was a different matter with the poems in Worm's appendix, apparently supplied by the Icelander Þorlákr Skúlason. The first is the so-called Death Song of Ragnar Lothbrok—the legendary hero Ragnar Loðbrók.[55] Ragnar rejoices in fighting, killing, and even dying; the final line of the poem (printed by Worm in runes transliterated from an Icelandic original, with interlinear Latin translations) was particularly influential for later poets in English: in Worm's Latin, *ridens moriar*; in the original Icelandic, *hlæjandi skal ek deyja*; in English, therefore, "laughing, shall I die". There are also a number of mythological references in the poem, such as synonyms for Odin, or mythological kennings, which Worm explains in his notes.

Worm's contention that Icelandic poetry was originally written in runes was not the only misconception he passed on to English antiquarians and poets, however. He was responsible for two striking mistranslations which, because English scholars and readers could read his Latin, but not the Icelandic original, became staples in the English image of the Viking. The celebrated image of Vikings drinking from cups made from the skulls of their enemies arose from a misunderstanding of a kenning in the Death Song. Worm seems to have mistaken a kenning for drinking horns, "the curved trees of skulls", as denoting skulls themselves, explaining in a Latin note that the verse depicts warriors drinking "ex craniis eorum quos occiderant".[56] The second error was grammatical: the poem's speaker, boasting about the rigours of warfare, twice mockingly claims that fighting was not like lovemaking, whether sleeping next to a virgin, or kissing a merry widow at a feast. Icelandic has a suffixed negative, so that *varat* means "was not". Perhaps misled by the formal echo of the Latin past tense *erat* ("was"), Worm omits the negative and mistakenly gives us a hero for whom killing is as much fun as sex.

The second whole poem quoted by Worm is Egill Skalla-Grímsson's *Höfuðlausn*, the Head-Ransom Poem. This too became one of the handful of Old Norse poems which were early rendered or imitated in English. It is not strictly a mythological poem (though there are mythological references, especially in the kennings); it is a praise poem, composed, according to the author of *Egils saga*, to flatter Eric Bloodaxe who, incited by his

---

[55] The "Death Song", now known as *Krákumál*, is a twelfth-century poem, supposedly spoken by Ragnar as he lay dying in a snake-pit; for the text see Finnur Jónsson (ed.), *Den norsk-islandske skjaldedigtning* (Copenhagen: Gyldendal, 1912), B I pp. 649–56, and for discussion of the poem see Rory McTurk, *Studies in Ragnars Saga loðbrókar and its Major Scandinavian Analogues* (Oxford: The Society for the Study of Mediæval Languages and Literature, 1991), pp. 125–33.

[56] Worm, *Runer, seu Danica Literatura Antiquissima* (Amsterdam, 1636) pp. 222–3.

malevolent wife Gunnhildr, was planning to have Egill executed.[57] Unlike every other surviving praise poem in Old Norse, its lines are end-rhymed; it has even been suggested that Icelandic poets would have regarded end-rhyme as cheap and trashy, and that the poem was actually a disguised insult to Eric. The Rune Poem too is a rhymed composition, though since it is presented in parallel with the Icelandic original, the rhyme is more evident than with *Höfuðlausn,* which is presented with a parallel Latin version; one would need to transliterate the runes to see the Icelandic rhyme. It is certainly striking that two of the three whole poems quoted by the influential Worm were rhymed, and the unrepresentative nature of these first translated Old Norse poems may well have confirmed the general belief that ancient Gothic poetry was rhymed.[58] Certainly, in English writing the commonest term for Old Norse verse was the catchily alliterative phrase "runic rhyme".

Later in the seventeenth century, after Worm's pioneering work, came the great scholarly edition of the key mythological texts in Old Norse: in 1665, Peder Hansen Resen's *Edda Islandorum,* comprising Snorri's *Prose Edda* and editions, with Latin renderings, of the major mythological poems *Völuspá* and *Hávamál.*[59] In 1644, S. J. Stephanius had published a new edition of Saxo's *Gesta Danorum;* the following year he published a set of notes and a preface to it, together with material from *Ynglinga saga,* the opening part of Snorri's *Heimskringla,* a history of the Norwegian kings— beginning, crucially for our purposes, with Odin, and the mythological pre-history of the dynasty.[60]

In *Ynglinga saga* Snorri presents Odin as a great leader of his people, whose fame and prestige led to him being worshipped as a god. At first, his gifts are plausibly human ones: Odin is handsome in appearance, a fearsome warrior, and a compelling orator. But Snorri goes on to cite stranger qualities. Odin "could change his appearance and shape at will", and exercised magic powers over his enemies in battle, causing them to suffer blindness, deafness, or incapacitating fear. And next, Snorri details even more sinister powers: Odin is presented as an arch-magician who can use words

[57] Sigurður Nordal (ed.), *Egils saga Skalla-Grímssonar,* Íslenzk fornrit II (Reykjavík: Hið Íslenzka Fornritafélag, 1933), ch. 60, pp. 183–92, and Christine Fell (trans.), *Egils saga* (London: Dent, 1975), pp. 107–12.

[58] Quinn and Clunies Ross try to account for the misconception that "runic"—that is, Old Norse—poetry was rhymed, noting the slippage in such terms as *rhythmus,* which meant both simply "verse" and also accentual verse which, unlike quantitative, might rhyme (Quinn and Clunies Ross, 'Norse Poetry and Myth', pp. 198–9).

[59] For facsimile and discussion see Anthony Faulkes (ed.), *Two Versions of Snorra Edda from the 17th Century* (Reykjavík: Stofnun Árna Magnússonar, 1977), vol. II.

[60] Bjarni Aðalbjarnarson (ed.), *Heimskringla,* Íslenzk fornrit XXVI (Reykjavík: Hið Íslenzka Fornritafélag, 1941), pp. 9–29.

to supernatural effect, putting out fire, calming storms, raising winds. He can resurrect corpses from their burial places, or sit under hanged men, presumably to hear what they might have to say from the other world; Snorri explains that this is where his title "Lord of Hanged Men" comes from. He also has two ravens, who can speak to him, and bring him news from far and wide as they fly over the earth. This is not Odin the euhemerized battle leader, but the God of the Dead from Old Norse myth. Snorri completes the picture with a reference to *seiðr*, a form of Norse sorcery which he purports to shy away from describing in any detail: "this sorcery is attended by such wickedness that manly men considered it shameful to practice it, and so it was taught to priestesses".[61]

Snorri also tells us that Odin spoke only in verse, and not in prose. Significantly, he links this superior eloquence to Odin's knowledge of runic charms, the means by which he accomplished all the sinister and supernatural feats which have been cited. He even, Snorri adds, "knew all about hidden treasures, and knew such magic spells as would open for him the earth and mountains and rocks and burial mounds; and with mere words he bound those who dwelled in them, and went in and took what he wanted". Given all these powers, it is no wonder that, as Snorri concludes, "people worshipped Odin, calling him a god". This picture of Odin, together with the section on runic magic, and Odin's sacrifice on the tree in the eddic poem *Hávamál* (newly available in Resen's edition), which seems to depict Odin fetching up runes from the world of the dead he had briefly visited, established the image which English antiquarians, and later, poets, inherited: a leader, a warrior, a magician, and, in one further stretch, the inventor of runes, and of poetry itself.

The most impressive of the English antiquarians to inherit and transmit all this new knowledge about Norse myth in general, and Odin in particular, was Robert Sheringham. As its title indicates, his *De Anglorum Gentis Origine Disceptatio* ("A treatise on the origin of the English people"), published in 1670, was first of all designed, like the majority of historical work of the time, as an exploration of national origins (he is clear about England's Germanic origins, for instance, and links Jordanes's Goths with Bede's Jutes). But he makes ample room for the literary texts only very recently made available. Sheringham had been sent a copy of Resen's *Edda*, with its Latin translations of *Völuspá* and *Hávamál*, from which he quotes.[62] He calls Odin the father of poetry and the inventor of runes, presiding over Valhalla, the Hall of the Slain. Following Worm, he quotes

---

[61] Lee M. Hollander (trans.), *Heimskringla: History of the Kings of Norway* (Austin: University of Texas Press, 1964), p. 11.

[62] See Quinn and Clunies Ross, 'Norse Poetry and Myth', p. 193.

a Latin translation of the Death Song of Ragnar Lothbrok, and adds a list of minor gods who had not previously been cited.[63] Seaton describes Sheringham's work as "sound and scholarly",[64] although he apparently did not have any knowledge of the Old Norse language.

An even more influential treatment of Odin and Norse myth, though a much less reliable guide to it than Sheringham's *Disceptatio,* was Aylett Sammes's *Britannia Antiqua Illustrata,* written in English, and published in 1676. Sammes's extraordinary theories about the Phoenician contribution to the English nation, and other flights of fancy, have completely discredited the work's claim to be a scholarly history of England. For Sammes, the Phoenician element is everywhere evident: in a host of English place names (Thule itself is said to be derived from Phoenician), and throughout the English language itself; the god Thor is described as "the true Phoenician Hercules"; and the building of Stonehenge is attributed to Phoenicians. But Sammes offers a considerable amount of Northern knowledge, including a reprinting of the runic alphabet, and translates into English (though from Sheringham's Latin, and not any original) long quotations from *Völuspá* and *Hávamál.* Sammes's range of reference is impressive: he cites all the authorities mentioned so far, from Tacitus and Jordanes to Worm and Sheringham. He even discusses the derivation of the word "rune", and Spelman's brilliant intervention in the debate. He calls for an informed and tolerant allegorical reading of mythology, cautioning those who "cry out all is false and ridiculous, when indeed, we only want the key to unlock those Mysteries, which they purposely wrapt up in obscurity".[65] This is particularly good advice, warns Sammes, when we come to read what the ancients have written about Odin.

Odin is explicitly identified with the "Saxon" god Woden, and the story—as told by Snorri—of his migration from Asia is clearly set out. Odin is credited with the use of runes in magic spells, though not with their invention, and with the introduction of rhymed poetry. To him as law-giver is attributed the institution of the twelve-man jury. There is a good deal of information about Valhalla, though there are some confusions, and familiar misconceptions persist: the Saxons "believed that after death they were to go into *Woden's* Hall ('Valhalden'), and there drink Ale with him, and his Companions, in the Skulls of their Enemies. To this end they imagined a certain Goddess called *DYSER,* employed by *Woden,* to

---

[63] Robert Sheringham, *De Anglorum Gentis Origine Disceptatio* (Cambridge: Joann. Hayes, 1670), pp. 252–4 and 322.

[64] Seaton, *Literary Relations,* p. 208.

[65] Aylett Sammes, *Britannia Antiqua Illustrata: or The Antiquities of Ancient Britain* (London: Tho. Roycroft, 1676), vol. I, pp. 395–467 (431).

convey the Souls of the Valiant into his drunken Paradice". At this point, Sammes's imagination takes flight: "And methinks I see the *Danish King, LOTHBROCK,* in his Fur-Leather Breeches (for so his name importeth) in as good Verses as Ale could inspire, hugging himself with the hopes of Full-pots in the World to come".[66] There follows a quotation, attributed to Worm, concerning the infamous skull drinking cups, and then the final stanza from Ragnar's Death Song, in which Ragnar's celebrated courage in the face of death ("laughing, I die") is implicitly motivated by sheer greed for drink. The details are accurate, but the tone is all wrong.

References to so many sources, not always harmonized (for instance, Valhalla is mentioned again, from a different source, a few paragraphs further on, but appears as Walholl), mean that the writing, though teeming with information, is sometimes confused and repetitive, and as we have seen, Sammes's judgement—historical, philological, and literary—is often suspect. His chapter about Odin is rightly summed up by F. E. Farley as "most amusing".[67]

In 1689, the Danish scholar Thomas Bartholin published his *Antiquitatum Danicarum de Causis Contemptae a Danis adhuc Gentilibus Mortis* ("Danish Antiquities concerning the reason for the pagan Danes' disdain for death"). As is obvious from the title, the Death Song was a key text for Bartholin, but in the course of his whole treatise, he quotes from very many Old Norse poetic sources, and for those who could read Latin, a whole new selection of Old Norse literature—both poetry and prose—was put on show. And yet, in spite of the availability of all these literary texts, their influence on English literature was minimal. As F. E. Farley puts it, until at least the middle of the eighteenth century, although "opportunities were at hand, and fairly accessible, for the scholar who wanted to make a special study of these 'Gothic' matters, ... the great mass of English people knew little and cared little about them".[68]

Interest in the history of the nation had inspired works like those of Sheringham and Sammes which contained so much information about Old Norse myth and literature. But this was still literature to be mined for information, and not primarily of interest in itself. Perhaps the first English writer to express an explicitly *literary* judgement on an Old Norse text was Sir William Temple.

Temple's short treatise *An Introduction to the History of England* (1695) is a straightforward summary of the by now well-known orthodoxy

[66] Sammes, *Britannia Antiqua Illustrata*, p. 436.
[67] Frank Edgar Farley, *Scandinavian Influences in the English Romantic Movement* (Boston: Ginn, 1903), p. 13.
[68] Farley, *Scandinavian Influences,* p. 27.

regarding English history. The Saxons are a Gothic tribe, in the conventional metaphor "swarming from the Northern hive". They were "a sort of idolatrous Pagans" who worshipped the familiar triad of gods: Woden, Thor, and Frea; these names are duly related to the days of the week. The Danish and Norman invasions constitute another "mighty Swarm of the old Northern Hive".[69] Trial by jury, and common law, practised by the Saxons, and inherited from the Goths, survived these invasions. But two of Temple's earlier essays, 'Of Heroic Virtue' and 'Of Poetry', are much more directly engaged with the literature.[70]

In 'Of Poetry', Temple appears less than impressed with "Gothic", or "runic" verse. Repeating several misconceptions about such poetry (that it was all rhymed, for instance, and that the term "rune" came to refer to the poetry itself, and its practitioners as "runers") and even contributing a new unreliable etymology (that the word "rhyme" was actually derived from "rune", and not Greek at all), Temple sides with the old Elizabethan anti-rhyme party, complaining that rhyme drove out classical prosody like "a Cloud of Ignorance... coming from the *North*".[71] Even when he seems to be analyzing the complex metre of skaldic *dróttkvætt*, he dismisses the effect as "a sort of Gingle, that pleased the ruder Ears of that People".[72] His concluding remarks are harsh: "The common Vein of the *Gothick Runes*...was of a raving or rambling sort of Wit or Invention, loose and flowing, with little Art or Confinement to any certain Measures or Rules." According to Temple, its only achievement was "to Charm the Ignorant and Barbarous Vulgar", and the association of runes (and therefore, poetry itself) with the black arts is the last straw: "the Charms of their *Runick* Conceptions, were generally esteemed Divine or Magical at least".[73]

But in a second essay, 'Of Heroic Virtue', Temple's engagement with the texts produces an entirely different result. Much of the opening of the essay is familiar enough: Goths issue from the north like bees swarming out of a hive, and fall upon the Roman Empire. But Temple has a new answer to a difficult contradiction: was Odin a "devillish magician", as the old authorities such as Saxo or the Icelander Arngrímr had it, or was he the great leader of the Goths, an invincible warrior and wise lawgiver who

---

[69] William Temple, *An Introduction to the History of England* (London: Richard Simpson and Ralph Simpson, 1695), pp. 44–80 (44, 66, 70).
[70] These essays were first published in William Temple, *Miscellanea: The Second Part* (London: J. R. for Richard and Ralph Simpson, 1690), and are edited by Samuel H. Monk in William Temple, *Five Miscellaneous Essays* (Ann Arbor: University of Michigan Press, 1963), pp. 98–203.
[71] 'Of Poetry', in Temple, *Miscellanea*, p. 314.
[72] Temple, *Miscellanea*, p. 316.
[73] Temple, *Miscellanea*, p. 318.

"instituted many excellent Orders and Laws" and even "made the distinction of Seasons, the division of time"? Temple neatly squares the circle. Odin started well, but became "infamous" because of his association with charms and magic, and was worshipped as a god after his death.[74]

Temple attributes to the Goths "three Principles of a strain very extraordinary": bravery in the face of death, reverence for learning and knowledge, and political liberty. As we have seen, Gothic claims to political liberty had a long history going back to Tacitus and Jordanes. Respect for learning was demonstrated by the esteem in which their poets, who recorded the deeds of their patrons in praise poetry, were held. But it was bravery in the face of death which so very much impressed Temple. And in elaborating the "great principle" of contempt for death, and following (roughly) Snorri, Temple tells us that it was believed that those who died natural deaths were consigned to "vast Caves under ground, all dark and miry, full of noysom Creatures". But those who died heroic deaths might die laughing, for they were believed to go to "the vast Hall or Palace of *Odin*" (the term "Valhalla" is not used) where they can drink from bowls made out of the skulls of their enemies.[75] Temple goes on to quote the two relevant stanzas from Ragnar's Death Song, and refers his readers to "Olaus Wormius", where they may find the whole sonnet, which is "very well worth reading". Temple notes admiringly that "such an alacrity or pleasure in dying, was never expressed in any other Writing, nor imagined among any other People". Temple quotes the two stanzas from Worm's Latin rendering, and adds enthusiastically; "I am deceived, if in this Sonnet, and a following Ode of *Scallogrim* ... there be not a vein truly Poetical".[76]

Ethel Seaton credits Temple with introducing English readers to the apprehension of an ancient Scandinavian "national principle or philosophy of life, and in the runic verses an application of this principle", an idea which was "new and original in English".[77] S. H. Monk, in the introduction to his edition of Temple's essays, writes that even if 'Of Heroic Virtue' "did not immediately set off a Gothic revival, it did help to popularize the virtues of the Goths, from whom the English believed themselves to be descended".[78] And finally, Temple's great advance was that he passed a literary judgement on Old Norse poetry, and it was with a distinct "ring of enthusiasm" that he pronounced it "truly poetical".[79] It is precisely this

---

[74] 'Of Heroick Virtue', in Temple, *Miscellanea*, pp. 229–32.
[75] Temple, *Miscellanea*, pp. 233–4.
[76] Temple, *Miscellanea*, pp. 234–6.
[77] Seaton, *Literary Relations*, p. 134.
[78] Monk, *Five Miscellaneous Essays*, p. xxxvi.
[79] Monk, *Five Miscellaneous Essays*, p. xxxvi.

enthusiasm for the "vein truly poetical" in Old Norse literature which drove the passion for it amongst English poets and readers, as we shall see in the next chapter.

Some of the literature which was to inspire such enthusiasm appeared in the seventeenth century, notably, perhaps, a Swedish edition of *Hervarar saga* by Olaus Verelius, who provided notes, but not a translation, in Latin. *Hervarar saga* is now classed as a *fornaldarsaga*; that is, an adventure saga about legendary times, so it is ironical that Verelius published his edition as part of the larger Scandinavian project to explore the historical origins of the Scandinavian nations. *Hervarar saga* contains a poem which came to be known as 'The Waking of Angantyr', in which a valkyrie figure calls up her father from the dead, to reclaim his magic sword Týrfing.[80] George Hickes, who used Verelius's work with help from a Swedish scholar, included the whole poem in his *Thesaurus*, published in 1703–5, and the striking aspect of Hickes's presentation of the poem is that (unlike Verelius) he set it out as poetry, and in half lines clearly comparable with Old English verses.[81] 'The Waking of Angantyr' thus became the very first whole Icelandic poem to be translated into English, and joined the handful of Old Norse poems which established the taste for ancient poetry in England in the eighteenth century; Bishop Percy based his 'Incantation of Hervor' on Hickes's English translation. But that was later. In spite of Temple's enthusiasm, the Gothic craze had not yet caught on, and Hickes's hugely scholarly *Thesaurus*, which had been preceded by his *Institutiones Grammaticæ Anglo-Saxonicæ et Meso-Gothicæ* (1689), and would have enabled interested scholars to tackle the poetry in its original language and see parallels with native Old English, served not as a beginning, but as an end: as Andrew Deacon puts it, it "proved to be something of a funeral monument to English Septentrional scholarship".[82]

In fact, for many English seventeenth-century poets the Goths were simply synonymous with destruction and barbarity, and casually alluded to in such contexts. In 'The Dampe', John Donne in an elaborately playful metaphor urges his mistress to kill her disdain and even her honour,

---

[80] For a parallel-text translation of the saga, see Christopher Tolkien (ed.), *The Saga of King Heiðrek the Wise* (London: Nelson, 1960); 'The Waking of Angantyr' is in ch. 3, pp. 14–19.

[81] See Christine Fell, 'The first publication of Old Norse literature in England and its relation to its sources', in Else Roesdahl and Preben Meulengracht Sørenson (eds.), *The Waking of Angantýr: The Scandinavian Past in European Culture* (Aarhus: Aarhus University Press, 1996), pp. 27–57 (34–52).

[82] A. N. Deacon, *The Use of Norse Mythology and Literature by some 18th and 19th Century Writers, with special reference to the work of Bishop Thomas Percy, Thomas Gray, Matthew Arnold and William Morris*, B.Litt thesis (University of Oxford, 1964), p. 40.

"And like a Goth and Vandall rize,/Deface Records, and Histories/Of your owne arts and triumphs over men".[83] The barbarian tribes are responsible not only for murder and mayhem, but also for the obliteration of literate culture. More straightforwardly, in 'Cooper's Hill', Sir John Denham likens the ruins of an English abbey to the devastation caused by marauding barbarians: "Who sees these dismall heaps, but would demand,/What barbarous invader sackt the land?/But when he heares, no Goth, no Turk did bring/This destruction, but a Christian King...".[84] The Goths (and the Turks, here) are seen as the antithesis of civilized Christendom.

And as we have seen, for some writers this destruction ushered in the curse of rhyme. Roscommon's *Essay on Translated Verse* (1684) roundly deplores in familiar terms the coming of rhyme, which "in Greece or Rome, was never known/Till by Barbarian Deluges o'erflown". However, if rhyme came in with the Goths, then Roscommon is forced to concede that it must have had a long history in English literature: "I grant that from some Mossy, Idol Oak/In Double Rhymes our Thor and Woden spoke".[85] But Roscommon's urbane concession was bluff, as Dr Johnson pointed out acerbically a century later in his *Lives of the Poets*: "He has confounded the British and Saxon mythology... The oak... belonged to the British druids, and Thor and Woden were Saxon deities". Johnson also scorns Roscommon's reference to "Double Rhymes" (presumably, rhymes involving two syllables) of which, Johnson mocks, "he certainly had no knowledge".[86] Roscommon's vagueness about the Germanic gods and poetry was of course not at all unusual, and the confusion of Celts and Norsemen was to persist for years. Perhaps most significant in this passage is Roscommon's nonchalant assumption that Thor and Woden are "our" deities. As we shall see, in characterizing the Saxons—especially in contradistinction to the Britons, or Welsh—the Norse gods are appropriated alongside Woden as Saxon—that is, hereditary—accessories.

In 1685, John Dryden wrote a preface to the second edition of Roscommon's essay in verse, endorsing the view that rhyme was the fault of "barb'rous Nations", and that early rhymed poetry was poor stuff: "a

---

[83] John Donne, *The Elegies and The Song and Sonnets*, ed. Helen Gardner (Oxford: Clarendon Press, 1965), p. 49, ll. 13–14.
[84] John Denham, *Coopers Hill* (London: Humphrey Moseley, 1655), p. 8. The poem was first published in 1642, but this reference did not appear until later editions.
[85] Roscommon, *An Essay on Translated Verse* (London: Jacob Tonson, 1684), p. 23.
[86] Samuel Johnson, *The Lives of the Poets*, ed. John H. Middendorf (New Haven and London: Yale University Press, 2010), The Yale Edition of the Works of Samuel Johnson vol. 21, p. 249.

kind of hobbling Prose:/That limp'd along, and tinckl'd in the close",[87] though he conceded that poets such as Dante and Petrarch had made the best they could of a bad form, and ultimately contributed to its improvement. Dryden himself had just completed a play, or semi-opera, mostly in blank verse, about the power struggle between the British, led by Arthur, and the invading Saxons, led by their pagan leader Oswald.[88] Oswald is ruling the kingdom of Kent, which was particularly associated with the Jutes, and therefore, the Goths. In this work, *King Arthur,* we see both the exploitation of Norse knowledge in the portrayal of the pagan Saxon "Goths", and the calculated use of rhyme in a "Gothic" context.

Although *King Arthur* is only extremely loosely based on history, it is clear that Dryden was not simply relying on commonplaces about the Saxon past: in his dedication to the play, he describes his researches into Saxon and Gothic cultural history, citing "Beda, Bochartus, and other sources".[89] Dryden's depiction of Oswald's Germanic ancestors follows the familiar Tacitean line: they are described as "revengeful, rugged, violently brave" (I.i, l. 39) and as Kliger notes, Dryden could easily have derived such an image from Camden, who praises the Germans as "the most glorious of all now extant in *Europe* for their morall and martiall virtues".[90] But in his description of the Saxons' religious rites in advance of battle, Dryden includes a remarkable amount of detail, and it is evident that his researches must have gone much farther than the modest acknowledgement in the dedication.

Act I, Scene ii opens at "a place of Heathen worship". Around an altar are idols of "three Saxon gods, Woden, Thor and Freya". This scene clearly recalls the description and woodcut of the pagan temple in Olaus Magnus, with its three idols. Oswald bows before the idols, and in the tradition of his ancestors prays to them that he may avenge his father's death (Dryden makes Oswald the son of Hengist, the first Saxon invader, thus contradicting Bede, and indeed Milton). But Woden is addressed as "Father of Gods and Men"—a clear advance on Olaus Magnus, for whom Thor was still pre-eminent, and probably the result of the knowledge spread by the Scandinavian editions of actual Old Norse poems, and the use made of

---

[87] John Dryden, 'To the Earl of Roscomon, on his Excellent Essay on Translated Verse', in *The Works of John Dryden: Poems 1681–1684*, ed. H. T. Swedenburg, The Works of John Dryden vol. II (Berkeley: University of California Press, 1972), p. 172.

[88] *The Works of John Dryden: Plays*, ed. V. A. Dearing, The Works of John Dryden vol. XVI (Berkeley: University of California Press, 1996), vol. XVI, pp. 1–68. *King Arthur* was written c. 1684 (vol. XVI, p. 285).

[89] *John Dryden: Plays*, p. 6, and see pp. 294–5 for the form in which Dryden encountered these sources.

[90] See Kliger, *The Goths in England*, p. 75.

them by Sheringham and Sammes. The gods are begged to use "Sacred Runick Rhimes" to give them victory in battle, and spare their lives, to "Edge their bright Swords, and blunt the *Britons* darts" (12–13). This is plainly influenced by Old Norse poems—quoted in Sheringham and Sammes—such as *Hávamál*, in which Odinic magic ensures success in battle.

Dryden's pagans embark upon human sacrifice to Woden (and, in another Tacitean touch, "Mother Earth"). Oswald has already arranged the sacrifice of three white horses; Saxo Grammaticus has Othinus ride a white horse,[91] and in the *Germania*, Tacitus recounts how the Germanic tribes would use pure white horses as instruments of divination, their priests and king "taking note of their neighs and snorts".[92] With one final Tacitean reference, to Tanfan (according to Aylett Sammes, an ancient Germanic God of Lots), the die is cast, and Dryden's Saxon chorus celebrates imminent victory in two resoundingly rhyming stanzas.

The first stanza pithily expresses the traditional Germanic attitude towards death, as described by Sammes, Sheringham, and Bartholin, and exemplified in the Death Song of Ragnar Lothbrok: "Honour prizing/Death despising/Fame acquiring/By Expiring" (68–71). The second stanza is very clearly based on the two verses of the Death Song which had been quoted, in English translation, by Aylett Sammes. Sammes's rather risible quotation of the first of these two verses, ostensibly translated from Ole Worm's Latin, reads:

> We have stood true to *Snick* and *Snee*,
> And now I laugh to think,
> In *Woden's* Hall there Benches be,
> Where we may sit and drink.
> There we shall tope our bellies-full
> Of Nappy-Ale in full-brim'd skull.

The second verse is similar:

> Methinks I long to end,
> I hear the *Dyser* call;
> Which *Woden* here doth send,
> To bring me to his Hall.
> With Asians there in highest Seat,
> I merrily will quaff,
> Past-hours I care not to repeat,
> But when I die I'le laugh.[93]

91 Saxo Grammaticus, *History of the Danes*, Book I, pp. 24–5.
92 Tacitus, *Germania*, ch. 10, pp. 109–10.
93 Sammes, *Britannia Antiqua Illustrata*, vol. I, p. 436.

Dryden's slightly classicized version of the two is not much of an improvement on them:

> I call ye all,
> To *Woden's* Hall;
> Your Temples round
> With Ivy bound,
> In Goblets Crown'd,
> And plenteous Bowls of burnish'd Gold;
> Where you shall Laugh,
> And dance and quaff,
> The Juice, that makes the *Britons* bold. (74–82)

Of course facile and flippant doggerel such as this could never kindle any enthusiasm for Old Norse poetry amongst English writers, in spite of the acknowledged novelty of the sentiments expressed. In fact, as Ethel Seaton notes, "the sing-song verses of Aylett Sammes, and of Dryden, meant to represent the rhythms of the Death Song of Ragnar Lothbrok, were responsible for the poor opinion of 'Runic rhymes' that Samuel Garth [in *The Dispensary*, 1699, iv, 127ff] expressed when he classed them as 'Gothic lumber'".[94] However, Dryden's *King Arthur* does contain here a clear engagement with an actual piece of Old Norse poetry, the Death Song, albeit in a loose, risible translation (and it scarcely bears repeating that the original Death Song—in common with the overwhelming majority of Old Norse verse—does not contain end-rhyme). But if Dryden's "runic rhymes" did not prove an inspiration to later poets in English, they did nevertheless have an interesting afterlife. Dryden himself, in his *Miscellany* of 1716, reprinted Hickes's translation of the Old Norse poem 'The Waking of Angantyr', which brought it to much greater public literary attention, and led to its becoming one of the most popular—and influential—of the Norse poems in English. And Thomas Gray, the poet most responsible for the craze in ancient—that is, Norse—poetry in the later eighteenth century, wrote of his admiration for *King Arthur*, which may thus perhaps be counted amongst Gray's own formative influences.[95]

The struggle between Saxon and Briton naturally had political connotations in seventeenth-century England. It is clear, as Dearing notes, that Merlin's concluding prophecy of "a harmonious merger of Briton and Saxon" not only represents (though somewhat rosily) the actual course of history, but also reflects a contemporary ideal: a harmonious merger of

[94] Seaton, *Literary Relations*, p. 256.
[95] Paget Jackson Toynbee and Leonard Whibley (eds.), *Correspondence of Thomas Gray* (Oxford: Clarendon Press, 1935), vol. I, pp. 36–7.

"royal prerogative and parliamentary democracy".[96] A rather less politically engaged—and certainly less learnedly researched—Arthurian work was Sir Richard Blackmore's *Prince Arthur* (1695). Blackmore's "absurd epic", as Seaton calls it,[97] is plainly in the British, rather than the Saxon, camp, as his opening lines make clear: "I sing the *Briton*.../To re-enthrone fair Liberty, and break/The Saxon Yoke, that gall'd *Britannia*'s Neck".[98] The subject of *Prince Arthur* is again the power struggle between Britons and Saxons, but its setting is not England, but a semi-imaginary historical world, in which Thor, living in Lappland, is called upon by Lucifer to raise up storms to shipwreck Arthur off the coast of Brittany. The Saxons, with their "senseless gods, of barb'rous Northern names", are blatantly the villains of this piece, and historical Scandinavians are no better: the ninth-century Vikings are "Northern locusts" and King Canute is dismissed as a "cruel, slothful Dane".[99]

Much of the antiquarian paraphernalia is familiar: the Goths and Huns are "a barbarous Flood" who Rome's "Banks broke down"; and the Saxons swarm like bees, their heroes descended from "the farthest snows of Scythia". Blackmore's anti-hero, Octa the Saxon, is the son of Hengist, and descended from Odin (though not Woden); the warlike Saxons worship idols in groves. But Octa's gods are a strange collection of old-lore scraps: Irmansul, and Tuisto, from Tacitus, stand alongside Odin and "mighty Jove", and in addition a litter of minor deities: "rural Gods, who rule the Hills and Woods" and "wat'ry Powers, who dive beneath the Floods,/By gloomy Styx".[100]

The battle scenes are unexpectedly reminiscent of Old English poetry, especially *The Battle of Maldon*, with its set piece encounters between Anglo-Saxon and Norse warriors, its focus on weaponry, and rousingly defiant speeches.[101] Amidst this bombast, there is one unusually oblique allusion which may reference the raven banner which appears first in the Anglo-Saxon Chronicle and was picked up in the story of Earl Waltheof.[102] According to the early English chroniclers, this banner was used as an

[96]   *John Dryden: Plays*, p. 288.
[97]   Seaton, *Literary Relations*, p. 257.
[98]   Richard Blackmore, *Prince Arthur: An Heroick Poem in Ten Books* (London: Printed for Awnsham and John Churchil, 1695), Book I, p. 1.
[99]   Blackmore, *Prince Arthur*, Book V, pp. 147–9.
[100] Blackmore, *Prince Arthur*, Book X, pp. 291–2.
[101] For instance, Cerdic's encounter with a Briton in Book VIII, pp. 237–8, or the battle in Book X, pp. 278–83.
[102] See *The Anglo-Saxon Chronicle*, trans. G. N. Garmonsway (London: Dent, 1972), p. 77 and note (entry for 878), and Niels Lukman, 'The Raven Banner and the Changing Ravens: A Viking Miracle from Carolingian Court Poetry to Saga and Arthurian Romance', *Classica et Medievalia* 19 (1958), 133–51.

augury: the raven depicted on it seemed to flap its wings if victory was in prospect, but to droop if defeat lay ahead. The raven banner certainly caught the imagination of later poets of northern themes; Farley rather scornfully calls it "one of the theatrical properties regularly employed by 'runic' poets".[103] There may just be an early poetical reference to this banner in *Prince Arthur:* Blackmore writes of the martial success of the Saxon hero Octa who "Had tir'd the flaggy Wings of weary Fame"—that is, perhaps, won victory so often that the raven wings on the banner were tired out.[104]

Many early eighteenth-century references to the Germanic gods continued to promulgate old confusions. For instance, John Phillips's long poem 'Cyder' (1706) describes a fruitful apple orchard in the south of England sited on what was once apparently a Roman city, Ariconium. This city, according to Phillips, was subject to a volcanic earthquake, which swallowed it up completely, together with its "Heroes, and Senators":

> nor is there found a Mark,
> Whereby the curious Passenger may learn
> Her ample Site, save Coins, and mould'ring Urns,
> And huge unweildy Bones, lasting Remains
> Of that Gigantic Race; which, as he breaks
> The clotted Glebe, the Plowman haply finds,
> Appall'd.[105]

But describing the terror and despair of the original inhabitants, Phillips unexpectedly writes that

> some to Fanes repair'd, and humble Rites
> Perform'd to *Thor*, and *Woden*, fabled Gods,
> Who with their Vot'ries in one Ruin shar'd,
> Crush'd, and o'erwhelm'd. (I.214–17)

But sometimes there may be more deliberate manipulation. Thomas Tickell's *A Poem, to his Excellency the Lord Privy-Seal, On The Prospect of Peace* (1713) celebrates a peace ostensibly brokered by Queen Anne. Tickell describes how "the Painted Kings of India" have made docile obeisance to glorious Queen Anne, calling them "Chiefs who full Bowls of hostile Blood had quaff'd".[106] This line is an unmistakable echo—slightly

[103] Farley, *Scandinavian Influences*, p. 103, n. 1.
[104] Blackmore, *Prince Arthur*, Book IV, p. 106.
[105] John Philips, 'Cyder', in *The Poems of John Philips*, ed. M. G. Lloyd Thomas (Oxford: Blackwell, 1927), pp. 44–87 (51), I.236–42.
[106] Thomas Tickell, *A Poem, to his Excellency the Lord Privy-Seal, On The Prospect of Peace* (London: J. Tonson, 1713), p. 9.

sensationalized—of a familiar image, repeated as we have seen by Aylett Sammes and John Dryden, of Vikings in "Woden's hall" quaffing ale in bowls made from the skulls of enemies. Tickell has applied motifs from Old Norse myth to characterize emphatically non-northern nations.

That Alexander Pope based *The Temple of Fame* (1715) on Chaucer's *House of Fame* demonstrates at the very least an interest in and commitment to what would, in the eighteenth century, have counted as "Gothic"; that is, generally medieval.[107] Pope's imagined temple has four faces, "Of various structure, but of equal grace" (66), looking east, west, north, and south, and each is decorated with images of "fabled Chiefs", or "Worthies old, whom arms or arts adorn", or "Heroes . . . and Legislators". The northern side is decorated with runic letters, perhaps prompted by the preceding account of the southern, Egyptian side, which is embellished not only with statues of Egyptian priests, immensely learned scholars "Who measur'd earth, describ'd the starry spheres,/And trac'd the long records of lunar years" (111–12), but also with hieroglyphics. Pope's description of the runic inscriptions on the temple's northern face may be the first example of runic letters being used to characterize an object—in this case, a part of a building—as distinctively Norse.

Only two statues on the northern face are named: Zamolxis and Odin. Zamolxis is identified in Pope's own note as "the disciple of Pythagoras, who taught the immortality of the soul to the Scythians". The information in Lucan's *Pharsalia* that the Gauls—a Celtic people—had been taught about the transmigration of souls by druids had been misapplied to Scandinavian, or Germanic, nations by a number of influential writers, including Sammes, Bartholin, and Temple.[108] On Pope's edifice unnamed Scythian heroes, "on rude iron columns, smeared with blood", mingle indiscriminately with "Druids and Bards" whose characteristic harps are now unstrung; as Kliger says, there is "hopeless confusion" of the two ethnic groups.[109] What connects them both, of course, is their longing for glory, and their contempt for death given their faith in a life after death: as Pope puts it, they are "youths that dy'd to be by Poets sung" (128).

Pope's depiction of Odin, and the note appended to it, is extremely interesting. In the note, Odin is identified as "the great legislator and hero of the Goths"; Pope is clearly following Temple here, and Odin takes his place alongside Alcides, or Orpheus, or Zoroaster, or Confucius. Pope

---

[107]   'The Temple of Fame', in Alexander Pope, *Poetical Works*, ed. Herbert Davis (Oxford: Oxford University Press, 1978), pp. 132–46. References are to this edition, by line number.

[108]   For instance, see Temple, 'Of Heroick Virtue', *Miscellanea*, pp. 225–39.

[109]   On this prevalent confusion see Kliger, *The Goths in England*, pp. 84–9.

adds that Odin "is said to have been the inventor of runic characters" and claims that "being subject to fits, he persuaded his followers, that during those trances he received inspirations, from whence he dictated his laws".[110] So what Odin's self-sacrifice effects is neither the magic of runes nor the mystery of poetic inspiration, but his law-giving, an interesting twist on the usual distinction between Odin the devilish magician and Odin the venerable Moses figure, instituting laws and leading his people to their final homeland. Pope depicts the statue of Odin on the northern face of the temple of Fame at one of these moments of self-sacrifice: "And Odin here in mimic trances dies" (124). This would be a statue worth seeing.

In January 1721, in a letter to Pope, Jonathan Swift expressed his admiration for supposedly Gothic parliaments and governance, which he understood, in the conventional way, to have been introduced into England by the Saxons.[111] This suggests that Pope's interest in Northern matters—at least insofar as constitutional matters were concerned—was a continuing one. But elsewhere, knowledge of Norse myth and religion was still very vague; in a work of reference called *A Dictionary of All Religions* (1724), attributed to Daniel Defoe, proper names are so thoroughly mangled as to be almost unrecognizable: Odid; Ascardie; and Vall-kell.[112] And as Quinn and Clunies Ross point out, "Alexander Pope names one Worm in his caricature of antiquarian dullness in *The Dunciad* III 185–190".[113]

Pope's temple, with its Gothic face, is, like its Chaucerian original, an imaginary structure. But in 1732, the poet Gilbert West wrote an admiring account of an actual structure on a Gothic theme. In *Stowe*—dedicated to Pope—he takes the reader on a tour of "Stowe, the Gardens of the Right Honourable Richard Lord Viscount Cobham". In addition to the delightful monuments in classical style—"*Dorick* edifices"—and a series of statues—"a sacred Band/of Princes, Patriots, Bards and Sages"—of great Britons (such as Shakespeare, Queen Elizabeth I, Locke, and Newton), one may "pass... to where a sylvan Temple spreads/Around the *Saxon Gods*, its hallow'd Shades".[114]

West grandly salutes these statues—"Hail! Gods of our renown'd Fore-Fathers, hail!" He praises them for protecting old England, "a Nation valiant, wise, and free,/Who conquered to establish Liberty!", and to whom

[110] Pope, *Poetical Works*, ed. Davis, p. 136, n. 119.
[111] Harold Williams (ed.), *The Correspondence of Jonathan Swift* (Oxford: Clarendon Press, 1963–5), vol. II, pp. 366–75.
[112] See Farley, *Scandinavian Influences*, p. 22.
[113] Quinn and Clunies Ross, 'Norse Poetry and Myth', p. 207.
[114] Gilbert West, *Stowe, the Gardens of the Right Honourable Richard Lord Viscount Cobham* (London: L. Gilliver, 1732), pp. 4, 6, 17.

Britannia owes thanks for the care of her laws and "equal Government".
There follows a detailed description of these idols, which are quite plainly
the seven days of the week gods illustrated in the woodcuts accompanying
Verstegan's text more than a century before:

> First radiant *Sunna* shews his beamy Head,
> *Mona* to Him, and scepter'd *Tiw* succeed,
> *Tiw*, ancient Monarch of remotest Fame,
> Who led from *Babel's* Tow'rs the *German* name.
> And warlike *Woden*, fam'd for martial Deeds,
> From whom great *Brunswick's* noble Line proceeds.
> Dread *Thuner* see! on his Imperial Seat,
> With awful Majesty, and kingly State
> Reclin'd! at his Command black Thunders roll,
> And Storms and fiery Tempests shake the Pole.
> With various Emblem next fair *Friga* charms,
> In female Coats array'd and manly Arms...
> Last of the Circle hoary *Seatern* stands;
> Instructive Emblems fill his mystick Hands.[115]

The descriptions of the statues of Saxon deities follow precisely what is
depicted in Verstegan. In the woodcuts, Sunna is little more than a "beamy
head", and West himself passes tactfully over the illustration of Mona,
which Verstegan had called "very strange and ridiculous". In West's poem,
Verstegan's Tuisto has been updated to Tiw, and credited with the exodus
after Babel, but Woden is clearly armed and armoured, as in Verstegan's
own source, Olaus Magnus, and suitably identified by West as "warlike"
and "fam'd for martial Deeds". Thunor is given a Saxon form of the name
Thor, but is, like Verstegan's Thor, the chief of the gods, "on his Imperial
Seat/With awful Majesty". Friga is especially interesting. As we have seen,
Verstegan calls her frankly "an hermaphrodite", but West is more dis-
creet: for him, the statue is "In female coats array'd and manly arms".

Another poem celebrating the felicitous garden architecture at Stowe is
Samuel Boyse's 'The Triumphs of Nature' (1742).[116] Boyse too describes
the "awful *grove*/Sacred to *Woden* and the Saxon *Jove*". But Boyse had earlier
produced a very remarkable take on the well-worn idea of the Germanic
scorn for death. 'The Vision of Patience' (c.1740), a work included in an
anthology of "Poems imitative of Spenser", and thus a priori "Gothic", is
an elegy for a young man, Mr Alexander Cuming, the son of a friend of

---

[115] West, *Stowe*, pp. 18–19.
[116] Published in instalments in *The Gentleman's Magazine* XII (June–August 1742),
pp. 324, 380–2, 435–6. On Boyse's life and work see Edward Hart, 'Portrait of a
Grub: Samuel Boyse', *Studies in English Literature 1500–1900*, 7 (1967), 415–25.

Boyse's. According to the poem's subtitle, Cuming was "unfortunately lost in the Northern Ocean on his Return from China, 1740". Why his route back from China should take in the northern ocean is only clear from the poem itself, in which Cuming confronts his own death in a manner clearly appropriate to the northern, Germanic heroes who despised the fear of it.

Boyse presents himself as seeing a vision of Patience in a dream; she takes him to "Thulé's sky-girt coast:/Where *Silence* sits", listening only to the "hollow winds,/Or the shrill mew".[117] Here, Boyse is shown a vision of a shipwreck, in which a young man, undaunted by the proximity of his death, bravely prepares himself for it. Patience glosses the vision: the young man, by his attitude, is "unvanquish'd" by death, and as Patience opines, "The truly valiant dares to meet the foe,/Nor shrinks from danger, but with honour dies".[118] Poor Cuming in his bravery and innocence is given a Germanic hero's death—and, indeed, funeral. For in spite of some introductory classical-sounding references—"blushing virgins weep around his urn" and "virgins drop the artless tear"—the funeral is positively Beowulfian: these female mourners, like the Geatish woman in *Beowulf,* "sing the funeral dirge in Runic rhyme". Germanic pagan and classical meet in the anomalous reference to Cuming's "ashes", although it is elsewhere made plain that he has been buried. In fact, the only Christian reference anywhere in the poem is to eventual resurrection, when "the last trump emit the dead-awakening sound!". Cuming has been given the Germanic hero's end, though whether this would have been of any comfort to his grieving family cannot be known.

With James Thomson's long poem 'Liberty' (1735–6) we return, as its title suggests, to the conventional association of the Gothic origins of England, its political freedoms, and yet the damage the barbarian Goths wreaked on classical culture.[119] Gothic taste has "only loaded Earth/with labour'd heavy Monuments of Shame" (II.378–9), and Gothic architecture is tersely condemned as "the Chissel's Shame" (III.510). And yet these barbarous nations have the potential for greatness, for "Long in the barbarous Heart the bury'd Seeds/Of *Freedom* lay, for many a wintry Age" (III.540–1). Liberty is working on them, if only by "slow Degrees", and when "*Roman Virtue* slacken'd into Sloth" (III.383), the barbarian tribes descend, impelled by the goddess herself. Thomson employs all the

[117] Samuel Boyse, 'The Vision of Patience', in *Bell's Classical Arrangement of Fugitive Poetry, vol. XI: Poems imitative of Spenser and in the Manner of Milton* (London: John Bell, 1790), pp. 49–60 (51).
[118] Boyse, 'The Vision of Patience', p. 55.
[119] 'Liberty, A Poem', in James Thomson, *Liberty, The Castle of Indolence, and Other Poems,* ed. James Sambrook (Oxford: Clarendon Press, 1986), pp. 31–147.

conventional tropes to describe this inundation: "a Race of Men prolific swarms", and "from almost perpetual Night they broke/As if in Search of Day; and o'er the Banks/of yielding Empire.../Resistless rage'd" (III.535–8). Rome falls, and "Gothic darkness" falls on Europe. In Britain too, as elsewhere, Liberty's Dark Ages are characterized by "barbarous force", "scholastic discord", "holy slander", and "idiot superstition". Liberty moves on, northward, "O'er vast *Germania*, the ferocious Nurse/Of hardy Men and Hearts affronting Death" (IV.364–5)—a familiar Tacitean characterization of the Germanic tribes which Thomson has already formulated in his poem 'Winter'.

Once in "wintry *Scandinavia's* utmost Bound"—the "Parent-Hive" of the Germanic tribes—Liberty transforms the natural, indigenous political freedom there into a State which exemplifies what came to be known in England as the "Gothic balance"—in which kings, lords, and commoners took an equal share in government. Thomson's goddess puts forward at this point an idea which was to become very important in later ideas about the supposed racial supremacy of northern peoples: she claims that "keener Air/Their Genius purg'd, and temper'd hard by Frost" (IV.374–5). But they are still easily recognizable as the death-defying tribes "Whose only terror was a bloodless Death" (IV.377).

Having set up this impressive realm of brave, hardy, and politically emancipated northerners, Liberty moves on to Britain, still languishing in a confusing blend of Gothic darkness and Celtic night. To Celtic Britain "deep-blooming, strong/And yellow-hair'd, the blue-eyed *Saxon* came" (IV.669–670), and brought not only to British blood "a fresh, invigorating Stream", but also to British culture a religion and mythology which was actually Scandinavian, but ascribed by Thomson to the Saxons. Norse myth has been taken over as Anglo-Saxon history. Liberty describes these Saxon invaders in very familiar terms:

> Unpeaceful Death their Choice: deriving thence
> A Right to feast, and drain immortal Bowls,
> In *Odin's* Hall; whose blazing Roof resounds
> The genial Uproar of those Shades, who fall
> In desperate Fight, or by some brave Attempt. (IV.678–82)

Thomson appends a long note taken from Temple's description of the "dark and miry" otherworld, and repeats the misunderstanding about drinking out of bowls made from enemy skulls.

Thomson's Saxons were impressively advanced politically, and thus made eminently suitable predecessors in this respect: as Liberty boasts,

> Wisdom was likewise theirs, indulgent Laws
> The calm Gradations of Art-nursing Peace,

And matchless Orders, the deep Basis still
On which ascends my British Reign. (IV.686–9)

Britain now exemplified the celebrated "Gothic balance": "*Monarchical*
their State,/But prudently *confin'd*" (IV.695–6). However, this "happy
Government" was to face a serious threat:

No sooner dawn'd the fair disclosing Calm
Of brighter Days, when Lo! the *North* anew,
With stormy Nations black, on England pour'd
Woes the severest e'er a People felt. (IV.705–8)

The actual sons of Odin had arrived.

Having characterized the Saxons in terms we now recognize as stereotypical Viking motifs, fighting all day and drinking all night in Valhalla with
Odin, Thomson introduces a different motif to characterize the invading
Danes: the raven banner. McKillop suggests that Thomson may have been
the first poet to pick up the raven banner "and to give it poetic currency",[120]
though as already noted, Richard Blackmore does seem to allude to it—
so obliquely that it was perhaps already a known motif—in *Prince Arthur*.
Thomson's raven banner is not, of course, associated with Odin, who has
already been cited as the god of Saxon warriors who have fallen in battle. But
it gives a good indication of the nature of the Viking raids on Anglo-Saxon
England: "lur'd by annual Prey", it "Hung o'er the Land incessant" (IV.709–
10). Again, the reference is allusive, ostensibly referring to the bird itself, a
vulture-like beast of battle circling over the prospect of carrion.

McKillop traces the reference to the Huguenot historian Rapin, since
Thomson's note on the passage—"The Danes imagined that, before a
Battle, the Raven wrought upon this Standard clap'd its Wings or hung
down its Head, in token of Victory or Defeat"—is clearly taken from
Rapin's work.[121] Rapin includes an additional piece of information: that
the standard had been woven by the sisters of the great Viking invader Ívarr
the Boneless, a legendary scourge of the English.[122] Though he makes no
mention of this in 'Liberty', in the patriotic masque *Alfred* (which contains
the song 'Rule Britannia') Thomson elaborated the theme of the weaving
of the standard by the sisters, who by their "enchanted song" conjure up
the "baleful power" of the "Demons of destruction".[123]

---

[120] A. D. McKillop, *The Background of Thomson's Liberty* (Houston: Rice Institute,
1951), p. 83.

[121] McKillop, *Background*, pp. 82–3.

[122] For theories about the origin of this nickname, see McTurk, *Studies in Ragnars saga
loðbrókar*, pp. 40–41.

[123] *Alfred*, Act II, Scene IV, in *The Plays of James Thomson*, ed. Percy G. Adams (New York
and London: Garland, 1979), pp. 187–229 (223).

In spite of this intriguing nugget of northern lore, McKillop can still rightly maintain that Thomson "had but little interest in Norse mythology". And disparagement of the Gothic was still common. Even as late as 1753, Sir John Armstrong's *Taste: An Epistle to a Young Critic*, which preaches the undeniable virtues of literary discrimination, denigrates the Gothic. Classical literature, Armstrong argues, requires the "hardy Skill" of a critic such as Horace, who "dar'd to tell us Homer nods", and without whom "*Homer* might slumber unsuspected still". And a terrible fate awaits the young student, lately "enfranchis'd from his Tutor's care" who does not exercise carefully enough his own critical taste. For him, the consequences will be dire: he will "die a Goth: and nod at *Woden's* Feast". Armstrong's footnote exudes distaste—"Alluding to the *Gothick* heaven, *Woden's* Hall; where the Happy are for ever employed in drinking Beer, Mum, and other comfortable Liquors out of the Skulls of those whom they had slain in Battle"[124]—and reveals that Armstrong still felt it necessary to explain the allusion to his fashionable readers.

As we have seen, Sir William Temple can be credited with making the first specifically literary judgement on Old Norse poetry—quoting two stanzas in Latin from the Death Song of Ragnar Lothbrok, and discerning in them "a vein truly poetical". We can trace the influence of Temple on the work of Thomas Warton the Elder, whose poems were published posthumously (he died in 1745) by his son Joseph Warton in 1748, and included two 'Runic Odes', versions of Temple's Latin stanzas. But even earlier, in 1741, Sir John Campbell published *The Polite Correspondence*, in which the virtues of "Danish" poetry are carefully, and surprisingly knowledgeably, discussed, followed by two versions of heroic poetry in English, one attributed to Saxo Grammaticus, and the other to Worm. Oddly, expanded versions of both of these two poems, 'An Ancient Danish Ode' and 'Another, on Victory', were printed in 1770, in an anthology of the works of Michael Bruce,[125] obscuring the fact that both poems, and Warton's 'Runic Odes', were written well before the craze for Gothic literature had begun.

The Polite Correspondence: Or, Rational Amusement; Being a Series of Letters, Philosophical, Poetical, Historical, Critical, Amorous, Moral and Satyrical appeared in 1741. It was published anonymously, but a later edition revealed one of the authors to be Sir John Campbell.[126] Introducing

---

[124] John Armstrong, *Taste: An Epistle to a Young Critic* (London: R. Griffiths, 1753), p. 4.
[125] Michael Bruce, *Poems on Several Occasions* (Edinburgh: J. Robertson, 1770), pp. 48–52.
[126] See A. D. McKillop, 'A Critic of 1741 on Early Poetry', *Studies in Philology* 30:3 (1933), 504–21, for a full account of *The Polite Correspondence*.

the poetic version of what are claimed to be original verses, Campbell (writing as "Leander") discusses the Viking raids on the British Isles, and the character of the Danes he held to be responsible for them.[127] Campbell's account of the poetry of Viking-age Danes is sensible and informed. The favourite activities of these Danes, he explains, were "War and Feasting"; thus it is that these are the main topics of their verse, especially since their warlike ways allowed them so much opportunity for victory, plunder, and, hence, feasting and "the Pleasures of a jolly Life".[128] With their record of conquest, it is no wonder, Campbell concludes, that so much of their poetry consists of "Panegyricks on their Princes". But further, this poetry was highly prized and much respected, so that it was "warily transmitted to Posterity" in oral form—which led Campbell to speculate (again, quite rightly) that there was probably a lot more of it to be discovered. He pays graceful tribute to the Scandinavian scholars who have been making this material known. He even realizes that it is from Iceland that much of the poetry derives, since what he calls "the Zeal of the Popish Clergy" was not so influential to the detriment of the preservation and understanding of the verse. And finally, he declares himself at a loss to understand why Anglo-Saxon monks did not exercise the same care for their native literary traditions as Icelanders did.

Moving on to Old Norse myth, Campbell touches on the fundamental contention of this book: that "these People, being Pagans, had a Religion wonderfully calculated for Poetry".[129] He gives a fairly standard account of the Odin myth, and though the proper names he includes are not very accurately represented—"Asgardia", "Val Holt"—his final remarks on Old Norse myth, with its giants, dwarves, and gods, are both tolerant of pagan belief and appreciative of the Norse mythic system: "'Tis easy to conceive, that Men of strong Fancies might raise a Diversity of beautiful Structures, capable of amazing, and at the same Time pleasing, such as contemplated them".[130]

Campbell's account of the affective power of ancient Danish verse is particularly interesting. Following his source, Worm, he refers to Egill Skalla-Grímsson's poem *Höfuðlausn* (Head-Ransom) and its ability to placate Eric Bloodaxe when Egill recited it to him, though the proper names are askew again ("Eric Blodock", for example). But Old Norse verse, Campbell claims, could also "excite all the Human Passions, and

[127] John Campbell, *The Polite Correspondence* (London: John Atkinson, 1750), Letter VI, pp. 283–93.
[128] Campbell, *The Polite Correspondence*, p. 285.
[129] Campbell, *The Polite Correspondence*, p. 286.
[130] Campbell, *The Polite Correspondence*, p. 287.

carry them to the utmost Height" (which, Campbell understands, is true
of contemporary Icelandic poetry). What is remarkable, writes Campbell,
is that these poets ascribe poetic skill to "Science, not to Study"; it is "a
Gift from Heaven" and the product of "Genius". Campbell was ahead of
his time in diagnosing the sublime.

His account of the technicalities of skaldic verse is also remarkable
(though perhaps the characteristic half-rhyme of *dróttkvætt* is not ideally
demonstrated by the pairing of "Guardian and Pardon").[131] And Campbell
is also persuasive on the amount of Danish blood in British veins, such
that the genius of this ancient poetry must have been inherited (as well as
such vices as excessive drinking). At length, Campbell modestly ventures
to "enliven a little so dry a Subject" (as this account of ancient Danish
poetry) by offering two translations, one from "Saxo Gramaticus", and
the other from Worm. Be merciful in judgement, he pleads, for this is his
first attempt. There follow 'An Ancient Danish Ode', and 'Another, on
Victory'.

It is hard to match the first with anything in Saxo, not least because
the implied context of the verse is the Danish invasion of Anglo-Saxon
England. The speaking voice of the poem acknowledges the glory of Danish
ancestors who "feared not thro' the Stormy Sea/To urge their Course".
They might serve as a lesson to contemporary imperialist Britons: "Why
should not we as well as they/Teach vanquish'd Nations to obey?" The
mythic element is minimal—an invocation to Odin to send a favourable
wind, and eventually, victory, to these neo-Viking adventurers, and an
interesting reference to the "lazy Rites" which do not please Odin (perhaps
echoing William Temple's remark that those who lived "lazy and inactive
lives" would never be welcomed into Odin's hall after death; Campbell
never acknowledges Temple as a source though there are a number of echoes of his work). The poem ends with what McKillop calls a weak echo
of the celebrated final line of the Death Song: in Worm's Latin, "ridens
moriar"; in Campbell, the upbeat metre of "He chearful lives who does
not fear to die".[132]

The second of these two pieces, 'on Victory', is a loose rendering of the
familiar final stanza of Ragnar's Death Song, as printed by Worm, and
quoted by Sammes and Dryden. But it effects a very major change in
the dynamic of the work, and indeed the whole idea of warriors who die
in battle being conducted to Valhalla by Odin's valkyries. A fundamental
problem with this concept is that the warriors welcomed by Odin are by

---

[131] Campbell, *The Polite Correspondence*, pp. 289–90.
[132] Campbell, *The Polite Correspondence*, p. 294; McKillop, 'A Critic of 1741', p. 519.

definition those who have been killed in battle, and who can therefore scarcely celebrate their victory. This is a curious contradiction at the heart of Old Norse myth. Campbell's version of stanza 29 of the Death Song neatly sidesteps the difficulty. His warriors are celebrating the end of the battle—but it has been a victorious one: "The Foe is fled, the Field is Won". This means that there can be no valkyries acting as psychopomps, and in his second three-line rhyming stanza, Campbell substitutes a reference to the supernatural raven banner, which signals victory as the raven "claps her sable Wings".[133] The drinking and feasting is dedicated to fighting another day; a "homecoming" to Odin's hall is yet to take place. At this feast, Odin is being praised for granting victory.

In one of the "Danish odes" attributed to Bruce nearly thirty years later, and plainly based on Campbell's original, Bruce expands a little on the goings-on in the hall where the warriors feast: "When mimic shrieks the heroes hear/And whirl the visionary spear" are evidently references to Odin's magical practices as reported by the antiquarians.[134] There is also an intriguing Ossianic reference, as Bruce's raiders vow to worship Odin "At Loda's Stone". But in spite of Temple's clear references to it, neither Campbell nor Bruce alludes to the bizarre notion, based on Worm's misconceived note, that the goblets brimming with ale were crafted from the skulls of fallen enemies, although this misconception became even more widespread during the next hundred years or so.[135] Bruce ends his poem by attributing a strangely proleptic sentiment to his conquering Vikings: "With Odin's spirit in our soul/We'll gain the globe from pole to pole". This powerfully positive sense of invincible and unstoppable conquering forces—so different from earlier anxieties about destructive Gothic barbarians—was to be characteristic of the later Victorian concept of Vikings as bold, intrepid, and technologically advanced adventurers. But further, the notion that the spirit of Odin might inspire the founding of great empires inspired much more sinister and dangerous expansionism in the twentieth century.

Thomas Warton the Elder's posthumously published 'Runic Odes' are explicitly sourced to Temple—"Taken from the *Second Volume of Sir William Temple's* MISCELLANIES"[136]—and they too are plainly based on the stanzas quoted in Latin by Temple, numbered 25 and 29 in Worm.

---

[133] Campbell, *The Polite Correspondence*, p. 294.

[134] Bruce, *Poems*, p. 49, and compare Pope's reference to Odin's "mimic trances" in *The Temple of Fame*.

[135] I. A. Blackwell's revised edition of *Northern Antiquities* (London: Henry G. Bohn, 1847), p. 105, corrects the error at last.

[136] Thomas Warton Sr, *Poems on Several Occasions* (London: R. Manby and H. S. Cox, 1748), pp. 157–9 (157).

In both, following the originals, the speaking voice is that of Ragnar himself, dying from snakebites. In the first, Warton's hectic images make the Latin translation of the Old Norse look restrained. "Pugnavimus ensibus" ("We have fought with swords") becomes "my Sword no more/Shall smoke and blush with hostile Gore", and the festive ale is turned into "luscious Wines", drunk, as (wrongly) explained by Worm and echoed by Temple, "from the hollow Sculls.../Of Kings in furious Combat slain". Ragnar is not, of course, facing death in battle, but Warton has him welcoming the chance to end up in "awful *Odin's* Court" where he will take his place amongst the bravest of brave fighters, and exchange stories with other old warriors about wounds and victories. In the second, Warton dwells on Ragnar's death throes—"Tremble my Limbs, my Eye-balls start,/The Venom's busy at my Heart" which serves to point up how his "glad Soul" rejoices in imminent death. Ragnar claims to hear the valkyries coming for him (Warton appends a note alluding to the Dysæ, the term used in Worm and Temple's Latin), and Ragnar dies looking forward to the impending banquet, proudly scorning life—"this idle Breath"—and repeating almost verbatim the last line of the stanza and the Death Song itself: "I smile in the Embrace of Death!"

The verses of Campbell, Warton, and Bruce are typical of the response to Old Norse myth we have seen as characterizing seventeenth- and early eighteenth-century writers: the focus on Odin, and Ragnar's Death Song, as disseminated by Worm and Bartholin, with its attendant expressions of scorn for impending death, and rejoicing in anticipation of Valhalla. Proper names are still rather hit and miss, unsurprisingly given the prominence of Latin translations in the scholarly texts, and there is no attempt to echo, let alone reproduce, the distinctive metres or poetic diction of the Old Norse. The context of the poetry is still firmly associated with British history, politics, patriotism, and military action. But the significant innovation we can see in these poets, and even more so, in the next chapter, with the poetry of Thomas Gray, is that Norse mythic poetry is beginning to be engaged with for its own poetic qualities, not simply because it illustrates a facet of the lives of those of British, or English, ancestry, or the inheritance of British liberty, or provides exotic local colour for an historical setting. Ancient poetry, appreciated for its own aesthetic value and affective power, is being made available as poetry, for contemporary readers of poetry, even though the end product may be of variable quality.

2

Preromantic Responses: Gray, Blake, and the Northern Sublime

The poet Thomas Gray—the most learned man in Europe, according to an obituary written by a friend shortly after Gray's death in 1771[1]—combined antiquarian and poetic talents; with his celebrated versions of two Old Norse poems, the 'Norse Odes', he was the first major poet in English to engage with Old Norse myth, and heralded the great surge in the popularity of Old Norse poetry, and the consequent flood of poetic imitations of Old Norse verse in the later eighteenth century. Of course, one could not overestimate the influence of two other roughly contemporary writers on the recognition and dissemination of Old Norse myth. The Swiss scholar Paul-Henri Mallet, whose two learned works on ancient Danish history and culture—including Old Norse myth—were published together in 1763, was a very important figure whose work became a crucial resource for enthusiasts about Northern matters—septentrionalists, as they came to be known—throughout Europe.[2] The volume was translated into English as *Northern Antiquities* in 1770 by Thomas Percy, Bishop of Dromore, and its range of scholarly material is indicated by Percy's subtitle: "A description of the Manners, Customs, Religions and Laws of the Ancient Danes, and other Northern Nations, including those of our own Saxon Ancestors". But it also included an almost complete translation of Snorri's *Gylfaginning*, with much scholarly comment; an "idea" of *Skáldskaparmál*; a translation of most of *Hávamál*; and an account of *Völuspá*.[3] This was mythological riches. Percy's other great contribution to Old Norse studies was his own *Five Pieces of Runic Poetry Translated from*

[1]   Quoted by Samuel Johnson in *The Life of Gray* (Johnson, *The Lives of the Poets*, ed. Middendorf, vol. 23, pp. 1452–71 (1460)).
[2]   On Mallet's work and its extensive influence, see Margaret Clunies Ross, *The Norse Muse in Britain 1750–1820* (Trieste: Edizioni Parnaso, 1998), pp. 41–50.
[3]   Percy notes that he "need not here quote any passages from [*Völuspá*]; the text of the EDDA is...quite full of them" (*Northern Antiquities* (London: T. Carnan and Co., 1770), vol. II, p. 204; quotations from *Northern Antiquities* are taken from this edition).

the Islandic Language, published in 1763.[4] This volume added translations
of *Hákonarmál* ('The Funeral Song of Hacon') and a sequence Percy called
'The Complaint of Harold', verses attributed to King Haraldr harðráði
("hard-ruler"), to the three poems already available and influential: the
Death Song of Ragnar Lothbrok (which Percy called 'The Dying Ode
of Regner Lodbrog'), Egill's *Höfuðlausn,* and the Angantýr poem, which
Percy called 'The Incantation of Hervor'. But Percy was not a poet, and
his prose translations from Latin translations of Old Norse poems were
not enthusiastically received.[5] Nevertheless, through Percy's translations,
knowledge of Old Norse literature, and hence, of its myths, took a major
new turn from the middle of the eighteenth century, and the poetry of
Thomas Gray, and that of his somewhat less impressive successors, will be
the focus of this chapter.

As is clear from his correspondence and entries in his Commonplace
Book, during the 1750s Thomas Gray was working on a projected "History
of English Poetry", which would be illustrated by specimens of Gaelic,
Welsh, and Norse poetry.[6] This ambitious project was never completed,
but Gray's notes towards it show that as well as the usual Old Norse poems
illustrating supposedly Viking virtues such as love of warfare and contempt
for death, as quoted in Worm and Bartholin, and translated by Percy in
his *Five Pieces of Runic Poetry,* Gray would have made available the two
great central poems of Old Norse mythology, *Völuspá* and *Hávamál,* as
well as the two poems he was to publish as his 'Norse Odes': *Darraðarljóð*
and *Baldrs draumar.*[7] Gray's work on Old Norse marks a major departure
from those writers who were interested in promulgating the stereotype of
the valiant Viking laughing in the face of death, since in selecting *Baldrs
draumar* and *Darraðarljóð* he reveals an interest in mythic themes outside
that now familiar area; indeed, the protagonists of both poems are not
Viking heroes, but commanding and powerful women. In 'The Descent
of Odin', Gray's version of *Baldrs draumar,* Odin is not an historical Asian
war-leader, a celebrated legislator who was deified by a grateful (or deluded)
people after his death, and associated with runes and magic, but a figure of

    [4]   See Margaret Clunies Ross, *The Norse Muse* and *The Old Norse Poetic Translations of
Thomas Percy: A New Edition and Commentary* (Turnhout: Brepols, 2001), for exhaustive
accounts and analyses of Percy's important work with Old Norse poetry, as well as a useful
survey of the popularity of "ancient poetry" in this period.
    [5]   See Frank Farley's harsh assessment of Percy's work: "the translations...were all in
prose, inaccurate, and jejune to the verge of grotesqueness" (*Scandinavian Influences,* p. 33).
    [6]   See Paget Jackson Toynbee and Leonard Whibley (eds.), *Correspondence of Thomas
Gray* (Oxford: Clarendon Press, 1935), vol. II, p. 517 and note.
    [7]   For text and translation of *Darraðarljóð,* see R. G. Poole, *Viking Poems on War and
Peace: A Study in Skaldic Narrative* (Toronto: University of Toronto Press, 1991), pp. 116–
19, and for *Baldrs draumar,* Dronke, *The Poetic Edda,* vol. II, pp. 154–8.

vivid immediacy, an animated Norse god so troubled by intimations of his son Baldr's death that he braves a terrifying passage to the underworld in an attempt to trick a hostile sibyl into letting slip the secrets of the future of the mythic cosmos. But he fails, outwitted by the sibyl he has conjured up.[8] And in 'The Fatal Sisters', Gray's version of *Darraðarljóð*, the valkyries are not shadowy extras serving Odin's superannuated warriors in Valhalla, but wild and warlike women, revelling in death and bloodshed, and their power over human lives. These frantic subjects prefigure the characteristic mood and setting of the sublime, an aesthetic which itself revels in the grotesque, in charged emotions, and in extremes.[9] With the 'Norse Odes', Gray moved from the reflective "graveyard poetry" of his enormously successful 'Elegy Written in a Country Churchyard' to the wholly different register of the sublime, with its terrifying images, its supernatural action, and its mythic settings.

The first complete poem of Gray's to have survived was a translation of Psalm 84 into Latin, and translations—and imitations—continued to figure prominently in his published works.[10] Given his own scholarly inclinations, the new material about Old Norse literature beginning to circulate—Gray had read Mallet's work very shortly after it appeared in French, and well before Percy translated it[11]—and the growing popularity of "ancient" poetry, it is perhaps only to be expected that he would turn to Old Norse, especially given his project on the early history of English poetry. Gray was thrilled by a visit to Cambridge by the blind Welsh harper John Parry in 1757, with his "ravishing blind Harmony" and "names enough to choak you",[12] and he was excited by Macpherson's Ossian, translations "from the Erse-tongue", published in 1760: he writes with typical flamboyance "I am gone mad about them ... *extasié* with their infinite beauty",[13] though he did have doubts about their authenticity. But it is clear that a number of other forces impelled him towards the Old

---

[8] 'The Descent of Odin', in H. W. Starr and J. R. Hendrickson (eds.), *The Complete Poems of Thomas Gray* (Oxford: Clarendon Press, 1966), pp. 32–4. Quotations from the poems are from this edition.

[9] 'The Fatal Sisters', in Starr and Hendrickson, *Complete Poems*, pp. 27–31. For contemporary ideas of the sublime, see Andrew Ashfield and Peter de Bolla (eds.), *The Sublime: A Reader in British Eighteenth-Century Aesthetic Theory* (Cambridge: Cambridge University Press, 1996).

[10] For an account of contemporary debates about imitative poetry and Gray's place in this, see Roger Lonsdale, 'Gray and "Allusion": The Poet as Debtor', in R. F. Brissenden and J. C. Eade (eds.), *Studies in the Eighteenth Century IV* (Canberra: Australian National University Press, 1979), pp. 31–55.

[11] See Toynbee and Whibley, *Correspondence*, vol. II, pp. 550–2, Letter 262.

[12] Toynbee and Whibley, *Correspondence*, vol. II, p. 502, Letter 238.

[13] Toynbee and Whibley, *Correspondence*, vol. II, pp. 679–80, Letter 313.

Norse. A portrait of Gray as a young boy shows him seated next to a table with two books on it. One is by John Locke, and one of Gray's biographers makes much of the significance of this.[14] But the other is even more significant for our purposes: a volume by Sir William Temple, who, as we have seen, did so much to advance the literary appreciation of Old Norse verse. Further, Gray met Thomas Percy in Cambridge in 1761, when Percy was evidently deep in his own Old Norse work, though we do not know from his account of the meeting whether or not the two men discussed Old Norse poetry, and Percy's "minutes" of the encounter have not survived. But there are several telling references in Gray's own correspondence to the appeal Old Norse poetry held for him. In a letter to James Beattie, he describes how his publisher Dodsley has suggested a volume of his complete poems, and how he plans to send Dodsley "imitations of two pieces of old Norwegian poetry, in wch there was a wild spirit";[15] these were the two 'Norse Odes', 'The Fatal Sisters' and 'The Descent of Odin', which had been written several years before. Such "wild spirit"—though very evident in the original poems—was not the only attraction of these pieces. In a letter to his friend William Mason, dated 28 September 1757, in which he politely praises Mason's risible historical drama *Caractacus,* Gray puts forward "one great advantage" of re-working ancient literature: such works "leave an unbounded liberty to pure imagination, & fiction (our favourite provinces) where no Critick can molest, or Antiquary gainsay us".[16]

It is in the light of all these comments and trends that we should read Gray's 'Norse Odes', the work of a learned poet nevertheless taking advantage of freedom from scholarly constraints, and thrilled by the mood and atmosphere of the originals—at least, the original poems as Gray read them, in a Latin translation. Before turning to an analysis of the Odes themselves, I want briefly to sketch out the most striking features of the original poems, each in turn, in their original literary contexts, and to consider too the form in which Gray encountered them; that is, in Latin, quoted in the works of Scandinavian scholars. But the focus will be firmly fixed on Gray's poetic achievement—the target—rather than how he and his predecessors differ from the original poems—the source.

Both *Darraðarljóð* ("The Song of Dörruðr") and *Baldrs draumar* ("Baldr's Dreams") are found in anomalous contexts in Old Norse. *Darraðarljóð* is unusual in being a long poem quoted in an Old Icelandic

---

[14]   Robert L. Mack, *Thomas Gray: A Life* (New Haven and London: Yale University Press, 2000), p. 101.

[15]   Toynbee and Whibley, *Correspondence*, vol. III, p. 983, Letter 457.

[16]   Toynbee and Whibley, *Correspondence*, vol. II, p. 529, Letter 250, and see Lonsdale, 'Gray and "Allusion"', p. 45.

family saga—*Njáls saga,* often regarded as the greatest of its kind. Many family sagas quote verse in their narratives, but more usually skaldic stanzas, often incorporated individually as the dialogue of the characters in the narrative, or as an authority with which the saga author purports to corroborate what he is relating.[17] *Darraðarljóð* is a poem of eleven stanzas, of varying lengths,[18] in the eddic metre *fornyrðislag,* in which pairs of short lines, each with two stresses, contain a varying (though very limited) number of syllables, and are linked by alliteration. It may be worth stressing at this point that there is no syllable counting, and that rhyme is not part of the scheme, so that the metre of the original poem is not at all reflected in Gray's regular rapid couplets:

> Now the storm begins to lower,
> (Haste, the loom of hell prepare)
> Iron-sleet of arrowy shower
> Hurtles in the darken'd air. (1–4)

On the other hand, Gray's use of alliteration, though inconsistent, does suggest the rich alliterative patterns of the original, without imitating it very precisely. Gray copied out part of the original poem in Old Norse in his Commonplace Book; it would have been perfectly possible for him to have recognized the alliteration without needing to fully understand the language. In fact, he quotes the first two short lines of the poem—"Vitt er orpit/fyrir valfalli"[19]—which, if one elides the two syllables of the word "fyrir" into one, actually form one octosyllabic line, and might possibly have suggested to Gray the overall metre of 'The Fatal Sisters'.

The narrative context of *Darraðarljóð* prepares the reader to identify the verses as the overheard speech of women weaving. The poem itself begins by describing a grim but indistinct scene: the creation on a loom of a bloody fabric apparently made from human remains, the warp being formed by men's intestines, weighted with severed heads, and the moving parts of the loom—the shuttle, and the beater—being weapons. As the third stanza makes plain, these women are valkyries: they have the power of life or death over the warriors, the mysterious product of their loom standing as an imaginative symbol of men's destinies. By exercising their power over individual warriors, they can also control the fate of whole nations: in something between prophecy and speech act, the women foretell or actually cause the coming to dominance of a once marginalized

---

[17] On verse in the sagas, see Heather O'Donoghue, *Skaldic Verse and the Poetics of Saga Narrative* (Oxford: Oxford University Press, 2005).

[18] Though this may be due to incomplete preservation; see Poole, *Viking Poems on War and Peace,* pp. 154–5.

[19] Starr and Hendrickson, *Complete Poems,* p. 29.

people, the death of a great king, and defeat for the Irish. According to the original poem, the outcome of the battle will be victory for a young king.

The author of *Njáls saga* associates the poem with the eleventh-century battle of Clontarf, in which the Irish high king, Brian Boru, supported by Norse mercenaries fought against the King of Leinster allied with two Norse leaders, Sigtryggr silkiskeggi (silk beard) and Sigurðr, earl of Orkney. Both Irish leaders died in the battle. The connexion with Clontarf, as set out in the saga, and echoed in Gray's preface, is tenuous: according to the saga author, on the morning of the battle, a man in Caithness, in Scotland, named in the saga as Dörruðr, a name which occurs nowhere else, saw a vision of the weaving women, and heard them speak the verses which constitute the poem. This is presented as only one of the strange events in Scandinavian Europe which marked the momentous battle in Ireland; others included a similar vision in the Faroe Islands, the appearance of blood on a priest's vestments in Iceland, and dreams about the battle or its participants in the Hebrides, and Orkney.[20]

The reason why Clontarf features in *Njáls saga* at all is that some of the characters in the saga fought in the battle. But it is far from certain that the author of the saga was right to identify the battle of *Darraðarljóð* with Clontarf, and even the saga's own account of the events of the battle is inconsistent with what the poem implies.[21] It is tempting to propose that the saga author, like Gray himself, centuries later, knew and was very taken with the poem, enthralled by its sensational metaphors and forceful female voices. The poem stands out as a lurid departure from the sober and complex social pseudo-realities of the *Njáls saga* prose. Oddly enough, the poem stands out just as much from its prose context in Gray's source, the work of the Icelander Þormóðr Torfason, perhaps more usually known by the Latin form of his name, Torfaeus.[22] In Þormóðr's *Orcades* (1697), a scholarly collection of texts relating to Orkney, *Darraðarljóð* is the only poem which is quoted as a complete whole, though in Latin translation. But its relation to Þormóðr's central focus, Orkney, is quite clear, since one of the protagonists at Clontarf was Earl Sigurðr of Orkney, though he is not mentioned in the poem itself. Þormóðr discusses *Njáls saga* elsewhere in the *Orcades*, but he does not mention the saga in his introduction to the poem.

---

[20]   Einar Ól. Sveinsson (ed.), *Brennu-Njáls saga*, Íslenzk fornrit XII (Reykjavík: Hið Íslenzka Fornritafélag, 1954), ch. 157, pp. 448–60, and Robert Cook (trans.), *Njals saga* (London: Penguin, 2001), pp. 301–8.

[21]   On this question see Poole, *Viking Poems of War and Peace*, pp. 120–5.

[22]   Gray acknowledges a debt to Torfaeus and Bartholin on his title page (see Starr and Hendrickson, *Complete Poems*, p. 29).

Darraðarljóð is a difficult poem, even by Old Norse standards. Kennings, the characteristic kind of periphrastic metaphors used by Old Norse poets, can be very cryptic, and the first kenning in *Darraðarljóð* has caused difficulty for most translators of the poem. The phrase *rifs reiðisky̆* probably denotes the bloody fabric the women are weaving, and may be translated literally as "the swinging cloud of the warp beam", a cloud signifying a moving, indefinite, and almost two-dimensional object which, in association with part of a loom, is redefined as a piece of fabric. But the Latin translation quoted in Bartholin and Þormóðr substitutes "sagittarum nubes" (cloud of arrows) which Gray, following this translation, renders as "arrowy shower", a phrase he got from Milton's *Paradise Regained*, as his own note tells us.[23] Other difficult kennings are simply side-stepped by Gray, who openly advocated shying away from the more difficult and obscure details of Old Norse myth, as in his letter to William Mason in 1758: "I would venture to borrow from the Edda without entering too minutely on particulars: but if I did so, I would make each image so clear, that it might be fully understood by itself, for in this obscure mythology we must not hint at things".[24]

The original title of the poem Gray wrote out in his Commonplace Book was 'The Song of the Valkyries'.[25] He also used the title 'The Song of the Weird Sisters', which may well owe something to Shakespeare's *Macbeth*; the women in *Darraðarljóð* are not identified as sisters. In fact, Gray's own note on the term "valkyrie"—which incidentally demonstrates that the contemporary reader of his poetry would have needed the help the note provides—does not suggest that valkyries are sisters either.[26] The final title as printed by Dodsley, 'The Fatal Sisters', with its punning allusion to the classical Fates, or Parcae, thus stresses the role of the valkyries as, in Gray's words, "Chusers of the slain"; that is, supernatural women with power over men's lives, rather than Odin's waitresses in Valhalla. This move not only increases the force of the poem itself, but also brings its sensational subject-matter into alignment with a classical milieu his audience would have felt more comfortable with. Of course, the term "ode" in itself contributes to this, as do the references to hell, or fate itself, and indeed the Latinized versions of proper names, especially those of the valkyries themselves. And finally, as Lonsdale has painstakingly noted, 'The Fatal Sisters'

[23] See Roger Lonsdale (ed.), *The Poems of Thomas Gray, William Collins, and Oliver Goldsmith* (London: Longmans, 1969), p. 217.
[24] Toynbee and Whibley, *Correspondence*, vol. II, p. 568, Letter 269. See Clunies Ross, *The Norse Muse*, p. 116, and Lonsdale, *Poems of Gray*, p. 217, for discussion of another particularly obscure kenning, *vinur Randvés bana*.
[25] See Lonsdale, *Poems of Gray*, p. 213.
[26] Lonsdale, *Poems of Gray*, p. 216.

is packed with allusions to and echoes of earlier English poets, including Shakespeare, Dryden, and Milton.[27] But equally, as Arthur Johnston has shown, Gray was searching for "'Poetry endued with new manners, and new images', for what Shenstone called 'the more striking efforts of wild, original, enthusiastic genius'"—a quest Johnston argues is typical of the later eighteenth century.[28] And Samuel Johnson remarked of the 'Norse Odes' that "the language is unlike the language of other poets".[29]

Although 'The Fatal Sisters' is not by any means a close translation of *Darraðarljóð*, it conveys and even intensifies the energy and pace of the original. This is partly to do with the alliteration, which ties the unrhymed lines tightly together, and the rhyme, which rushes the reader on to each succeeding couplet. But it is also a function of Gray's vigorous style and lexis. The poem is full of monosyllabic imperatives—"Haste!", "See!", "Join!", "Cease!"—which are not represented in *Darraðarljóð*. The description of the bloody weaving at the beginning is suitably dramatic—the fabric is "griesly" (9), the warriors' heads, acting as loomweights, are "gasping" (12), the shuttles are "dipt in gore" (13)—and the fighting itself is loud: javelins "sing", bucklers clatter, hauberks "crash", and helmets "ring" (22–4). All this drama is intensified by Gray's skilful handling of the narrative voice of the poem. For example, the opening line, full of foreboding—"Now the storm begins to lower"—suggests an anonymous narrative voice describing the scene, with the added immediacy of the first word "Now". But we learn from Gray's prose introduction to the poem that "the following dreadful song" is sung by "twelve gigantic figures resembling Women" and "employ'd about a loom",[30] and the second line, with its imperative opening—"Haste, the loom of hell prepare"—is clearly not addressed to the reader, but is the direct speech of these terrifying women, addressed to each other. The first line of the third stanza—"See the griesly texture grow" (9)—and the final line of the following stanza—"Keep the tissue close and strong!" (16) are also the direct speech of the weavers themselves, but the first also invites the reader to envisage the scene. Gray thus pulls the reader into this fantastic prospect, and the end result of their work, the carnage of a great battle.

In the original poem, the first person plural is repeated in what might be called the refrain of the poem, "vindum, vindum/vef darraðar" (we shall wind, *or* we are winding, the web of *either* Dörruðr, *or* of a battle

[27]   See Lonsdale's extensive notes to the text in *Poems of Gray*, pp. 215–20.
[28]   Arthur Johnston, 'Poetry and Criticism after 1740', in Roger Lonsdale (ed.), *Dryden to Johnson*, History of Literature in the English Language IV (London: Sphere, 1971), pp. 357–95 (371–2).
[29]   Johnson, *Lives of the Poets,* p. 1470.
[30]   Starr and Hendrickson, *Complete Poems*, pp. 27–8.

flag³¹). Similarly, in 'The Fatal Sisters', Gray introduces a comparable refrain—"Weave the crimson web of war" (25) and the collective voice of the valkyries is clearly heard: "Let us go, & let us fly" (26); "As the paths of fate we tread" (29); "Ours to kill, & ours to spare" (34). Gray closely follows the emotional rhythm of the original as their hectic urging to action subsides into a more measured account of the various outcomes of the battle, so that a comparative calm settles over the poem: "Low the dauntless Earl is laid" (41); "Long his loss shall Eirin weep" (45). But, just as in *Darraðarljóð*, the pace suddenly picks up after this, and the bloody, almost apocalyptic imagery returns: "Horror covers all the heath,/Clouds of carnage blot the sun" (49–50). The weaving is brought to an end—"Sisters cease. The work is done" (52)—and a brief note of triumph is sounded, since where there is defeat there must also be victory, both equally brought about by the valkyrie women. The ending of 'The Fatal Sisters' also echoes the conclusion of the original. In the prose context of the original poem we are told that the women's song is overheard, and Gray follows this up in his poem, as they explicitly address their eavesdropper: "Mortal, thou that hear'st the tale" (57). As with *Darraðarljóð*, this apostrophe to *hinn.../er heyrir á* (he who is listening) includes us as readers too. But Gray concludes his poem with a surprising change. In *Darraðarljóð*, the valkyries, whose song, as Russell Poole has pointed out, represents a commentary on presently, or progressively, unfolding action,³² declare that they will now ride away, and this is clear in the Latin translation. Gray, by contrast, has them determining to ride *towards* the battle, which is thus still impending, and the poem ends with repeated urgency: "Hurry, hurry to the field" (64).

Gray's second Norse ode, 'The Descent of Odin', is similar in many ways—especially in its relation to the Old Norse poem on which it is based—to 'The Fatal Sisters'. *Baldrs draumar* ("Baldr's dreams") is also something of an anomaly in Old Norse literary tradition, since although it is generally categorized as an eddic poem, it does not appear in the Codex Regius, the great thirteenth-century anthology of eddic poetry, but only survives in a fragmentary manuscript which also contains full or partial texts of five other poems which do.³³ In a Latin translation, it is quoted by Bartholin, whom Gray acknowledges as a source, although Bartholin did not base his translation on this manuscript, but on one of the seventeenth-century paper copies, which was in fact interpolated at

³¹ On the difficulty of interpreting *darraðr* see Poole, *Viking Poems of War and Peace*, pp. 125–31.
³² Poole, *Viking Poems of War and Peace*, pp. 142–54.
³³ The manuscript is AM 748 I 4°.

several points.³⁴ Thus, what Gray based his poem on was not only a Latin translation of *Baldrs draumar*, but also a slightly different version of the poem; 'The Descent of Odin' is thus at two removes from the poem as it is now generally edited or translated.

Several of Gray's translation practices are familiar from 'The Fatal Sisters'. The metre of *Baldrs draumar* is the same as that of *Darraðarljóð*, and Gray again uses rhyming couplets, with alliteration, in his work. The alliteration is rather less regular than in 'The Fatal Sisters', picking out and emphasizing key phrases—"the Dog of darkness" (5); "runic rhyme" (22); "Flaming on the fun'ral pile" (70). The proper names are similarly treated, too, being sometimes discreetly Latinized—Hela, for Hel, Rinda for Rindr, and Vala for the Old Norse word for sibyl, *völva*. But strikingly, unfamiliar names are sometimes translated or omitted: the name of Odin's horse Sleipnir, represented unchanged in Bartholin's Latin, is replaced by the Spenserian "coal-black steed" (2), and the two key names for Odin himself, Vegtamr ("one accustomed to travel") and Valtamr ("one accustomed to slaughter") are translated as "Traveller" (37) and "Warriour's Son" (38). And the poem is even more packed than 'The Fatal Sisters' with phrases taken from the work of other English poets: Dryden, Spenser, Pope, Shakespeare. Gray evidently measured very carefully the degree to which he conveyed the alterity of his source, wedded as he was to the idea of a whole new poetic form and subject.

In the Old Norse, Odin, in his role as a god who can call up the dead and speak to them, makes a daring journey down into the underworld in order to summon a prophetess who can tell him the future—and specifically, what lies in store for his beloved son Baldr, who, according to an opening stanza which Bartholin, and hence Gray, omits, has been troubled by ominous dreams.³⁵ According to Old Norse sources, Baldr's forebodings are justified, for his death, and, following that, Ragnarök, the end of the world of gods and men, is imminent. Odin withholds his identity from the sibyl, and in answer to his urgent questions she reveals that Baldr will die, that his brother will be the death of him, but that Odin will beget "A wond'rous Boy" (65) who will avenge his brother's death. In all this, Gray follows very closely the emotional rhythm of his source. But at this point, the original poem takes a strange turn. Having asked his factual questions about Baldr's fate, Odin poses a riddle question: in the Old Norse, "who are those maidens/who weep for their pleasure,/and fling to the sky/the scarves on their necks?"³⁶ The answer to the riddle seems to be "waves",

³⁴ Bartholin calls his poem *Vegtamskviþa*, the name given to the poem in the paper manuscripts (Bartholin, *Antiquitatum Danicarum* (Hafniæ: Joh. Phil. Bockenhoffer, 1689), p. 632).
³⁵ Dronke, *The Poetic Edda*, vol. II, p. 154.
³⁶ Dronke, *The Poetic Edda*, vol. II, p. 156.

daughters begotten of their father, the ocean, whose windswept crests are reminiscent of the linen headdresses of women. A similar riddle occurs in the Old Norse *Hervarar saga*, a legendary saga which, as we have seen, was amongst the first works edited by Scandinavian scholars in the seventeenth century. In this saga, it is again Odin, incognito, who poses the riddle.

Odin engages in wisdom contests in several Old Norse poems. Sometimes, it seems that the question and answer format is simply a lively vehicle for the expression of information about Old Norse myth; the contest is based on knowledge, and the correct answer is a matter of mythological "fact". This is true, for instance, of the eddic poem *Vafþrúðnismál* ("the words of Vafþrúðnir") in which Odin, again incognito, visits the eponymous giant in order to ask fundamental questions about the origin of the cosmos. In this poem, Odin has one unanswerable question up his sleeve: "What did Odin say to Baldr when Baldr lay dead on his funeral pyre?" The giant concedes defeat, but Odin has revealed his identity.[37] In *Baldrs draumar*, Odin's riddle about the waves also apparently reveals the identity of the questioner to an angry sibyl, and the poem ends with recrimination, as Odin insults her, calling her the mother of three ogres,[38] and she sarcastically congratulates him on his success in the contest, whilst alluding triumphantly to the horror which is about to engulf the gods.

It is hard to see why the question about the waves reveals Odin's identity to the sibyl, thus bringing the contest to such an abrupt and angry end. But Gray seems not to be troubled by this. Although in his version, Odin's question is slightly differently posed: not, "Who are they?" as in the Old Norse, but "whence their sorrows rose?" (79), Gray's sibyl responds just as immediately and peremptorily as the Old Norse *völva*—"Ha! No Traveller art thou!" (81)—and Odin is just as abusive in return. In her final retort, the sibyl makes a dramatic allusion to Ragnarök, the Norse apocalypse. She tells Odin that her "iron-sleep" will not be broken again until "*Lok* has burst his tenfold chain" (90). According to Snorri, Loki was bound by the gods as a punishment for the killing of Baldr, and a poisonous snake drips venom on to his face. His loyal wife Sigyn tries to catch the drops in a bowl, but when she turns to empty each full bowl, Loki writhes so desperately that the whole world shakes, and this, says Snorri, is the origin of earthquakes. But at Ragnarök, when many things bound or contained will become loose, Loki will be freed to take part in the fight against the gods.[39] *Baldrs draumar* alludes explicitly to Ragnarök, describing it as

[37] *Vafþrúðnismál*, st. 54–5, in Larrington, *The Poetic Edda*, pp. 48–9.
[38] Perhaps a reference to the giantess Angrboða: see Dronke, *The Poetic Edda*, vol. II, p. 158.
[39] *Gylfaginning*, ch. 50, in Faulkes, *Edda*, pp. 51–2.

"riúfendr"—destroying. Gray does not use the term Ragnarök, though his description of what will happen is powerful—"wrap'd in flames, in ruin hurl'd,/Sinks the fabrick of the world" (93–4). In a note to these lines, he gives us a brief account of Loki's fate, and explains that he "continues in chains till the *Twilight of the Gods* approaches", referring his reader to Mallet for more information.[40] It is possible that his phrase "Twilight of the Gods" is taken from Bartholin's Latin, "crepusculum Deorum", and tempting to suppose that his reference to "ruin" was inspired by Bartholin's Old Icelandic text "Ragnarök riufendr".[41]

A close examination of Gray's 'Norse Odes' shows very clearly that his combined talents of scholarship and inventiveness produced versions of Old Norse poems—via Latin translations—which were remarkable in a number of ways. Gray was evidently closely and continuously aware of the need to balance the old and the new, the familiar and the novel, the traditional and the pioneering. And sensational as the subject matter of the 'Norse Odes' must have seemed to contemporary audiences, as Gray's biographer William Mack points out, the underlying subjects were undeniably serious, and perhaps closely connected with Gray's own life: the Fatal Sisters are "the forces of fate... now vigorously and threateningly animated", and 'The Descent of Odin' is "a poem which positions its subject as inquiring into the greater 'divine' causes which motivate and lie beneath the subsidiary tragedies of human experience... engaged in the activity of seeking some explanation for the fact of death".[42]

Gray's earlier odes—'The Bard' and 'The Progress of Poetry'—had had a mixed critical reception. W. L. Phelps sums up readers' reservations: "The public did not take to them kindly... Their obscurity was ridiculed, and they were freely parodied."[43] Obscurity was indeed the key word; in a letter of 1757, to Wharton, Gray writes ruefully: "I hear, we are not at all popular. The great objection is obscurity, no body knows what we would be at".[44] In 'The Bard', Gray had tried out an image taken from his knowledge of Old Norse, and specifically, *Darraðarljóð*: the bard envisages himself and the ghosts of his fellow poets as they "weave with bloody hands the tissue of [Edward's] line", and urges them "Weave the warp, and weave the woof/ The winding sheet of Edward's race".[45] The similarities to the imagery of

[40] Lonsdale, *Poems of Gray*, p. 228.
[41] Bartholin, *Antiquitatum Danicarum*, p. 640.
[42] Mack, *Thomas Gray: A Life*, p. 520.
[43] W. L. Phelps (ed.), *Selections from the Poetry and Prose of Thomas Gray* (Boston: Ginn and Company, 1894), p. xxvi.
[44] Toynbee and Whibley, *Correspondence*, vol. II, p. 518, Letter 246.
[45] 'The Bard: A Pindaric Ode', in Starr and Hendrickson, *Complete Poems*, pp. 18–24, ll. 48–50.

'The Fatal Sisters' are very clear; a few lines earlier, Gray describes the bards as a "griesly band" (44), echoing the "griesly texture" of the valkyries' web. Samuel Johnson was unsparing in his mocking criticism of these lines:

> The "weaving" of the "winding sheet" he borrowed, as he owns, from the northern bards; but their texture, however, was very properly the work of female powers, as the art of spinning the thread of life in another mythology. Theft is always dangerous; Gray has made weavers of his slaughtered bards, by a fiction outrageous and incongruous. They are then called upon to "Weave the warp, and weave the woof," perhaps with no great propriety; for it is by crossing the "woof" with the "warp" that men "weave" the "web" or piece; and the first line was dearly bought by the admission of its wretched correspondent, "Give ample room and verge enough." He has, however, no other line as bad.[46]

And yet it was clear that these lines, whether admired or not, caught the public imagination. W. Powell Jones quotes a letter written very shortly after Gray's response to the charge of obscurity, in September 1757, by Mrs Elizabeth Montagu, which contains a casual aside about weaving the web for Edward's line.[47] And in Boswell's *Life of Johnson*, Johnson quotes "Weave the warp, and weave the woof" which Boswell at once completes: "The winding sheet of Edward's race".[48] But the reviewers, though struck by the weaving imagery, were not impressed: in the *Literary Magazine* of autumn 1757, Gray's verse was dismissed as "Spittle-fields poetry".

The 'Norse Odes' were better received. Even Johnson said that they "deserve praise".[49] Margaret Clunies Ross asserts that there was "a general feeling, even among other poets and translators of Old Norse, that Gray's poem's could not be bettered", basing this on the decision of William Herbert, a later translator of Old Norse poetry, not to include *Baldrs draumar* in full in his 1804 anthology *Select Icelandic Poetry*, simply advising the reader to read Gray.[50] However, Margaret Omberg, citing a piece in the *Monthly Review* of 1768, notes that the "immediate response of the literary public to the northern odes was largely unfavourable". Omberg goes on to show that nevertheless, nearer the end of the eighteenth century, "Gray's Scandinavian paraphrases had become established as two extraordinarily fine examples of the poetic sublime and models of the way in which

---

[46] Johnson, *Lives of the Poets*, p. 1469.
[47] W. Powell Jones, 'The Contemporary Reception of Gray's *Odes*', *Modern Philology* 28:1 (1930), 61–82 (68).
[48] James Boswell, *Life of Johnson*, ed. R. W. Chapman (Oxford: Oxford University Press, 2008), p. 600.
[49] Johnson, *Lives of the Poets*, p. 1470.
[50] Clunies Ross, *The Norse Muse*, pp. 105–11 (105), and see also Amanda Collins's Appendix, pp. 207–31.

northern myth could be applied to English poetry".[51] Horace Walpole's careless sneer—"Gray has translated two noble incantations from the Lord knows who, a Danish Gray, who lived the Lord knows when"[52]—is matched by his contempt for Norse themes: "Who can care through what horrors a Runic savage arrived at all the joys and glories they could conceive, the supreme felicity of boozing ale out of the skull of an enemy in Odin's hall?"[53] And as Susie Tucker has shown, some reviewers shared this low opinion of Old Norse material in general: "Scandinavian mythology is little adapted to the purposes of modern poetry. The images that it exhibits are for the most part incomprehensibly wild and uncouth"; this mythology is dismissed as a "tissue of the most absurd and preposterous fictions" and represents "intractable materials" for poetry.[54] But a decade or so later, the *Critical Review* shows that opinion was coming round to this strange new stuff: Norse myth "is a wild and magnificent system, calculated powerfully to impress an unenlightened people, and which may take place, in poetry, of the tame fictions of Greece and Rome... The historian will find in it the creed of his ancestors; and the poet will acquire a variety of images peculiarly adapted for poetry by their novelty, their strangeness, and their sublimity".[55] That many took this to heart is evident from the wealth of poets who followed in Gray's footsteps, producing free versions or imitations of Old Norse poetry, even if few of them approached the quality of their model.

In the second half of the eighteenth century, as we have seen, three very different—but almost equally influential—works were available to English poets who were minded to write on Old Norse themes: Paul-Henri Mallet's two scholarly volumes (first published in French, in 1755 and 1756, and then in English translation by Thomas Percy as *Northern Antiquities* in 1770); Percy's own translations of Old Norse poetry, *Five Pieces*; and Gray's 'Norse Odes'. Mallet provided the learning, and Percy set the poetic agenda for a century by making available a selection of thrilling, death-defying texts. But Gray offered not simply free translations of Old Norse poetry, but versions of the originals which were themselves

---

[51] Margaret Omberg, *Scandinavian Themes in English Poetry, 1760–1800* (Uppsala, 1976), pp. 45–6, and see Farley, *Scandinavian Influences*, p. 36.

[52] W. S. Lewis and Ralph S. Brown (eds.), *Horace Walpole's Correspondence with George Montagu*, The Yale Edition of Horace Walpole's Correspondence vols. 9–10 (New Haven: Yale University Press, 1941), vol. 9, p. 364.

[53] Lewis and Brown, *Horace Walpole's Correspondence with George Montagu*, vol. 10, p. 255.

[54] These were the opinions of *The Monthly Review* in 1781 and 1784, quoted in Susie Tucker, 'Scandinavica for the Eighteenth-Century Common Reader', *Saga-Book of the Viking Society* 26 (1962–5), 233–47 (241–2).

[55] *Critical Review* 22 (1798), quoted in Tucker, 'Scandinavica', p. 247.

taken seriously as poetry, and importantly, engaged with Old Norse texts, *Darraðarljóð* and *Baldrs draumar*, which lay outside the legendary or heroic corpus made prominent by Percy.

However, the impact of these three works was neither immediate nor revolutionary. The name of Odin, or Woden, continued to be invoked by poets in connexion with the supposed political virtues of the Germanic tribes. A good example is Joseph Spence's paean of praise to Britain's Germanic roots in his poem 'On the Royal Nuptials', celebrating the marriage of George III to Princess Charlotte of Mecklenburg-Strelitz in 1761. George is described as "great heir of Anglo-Saxon kings" but the teenage princess's own heritage is paid "grateful homage" by an England indebted to Germania for "her name, her tribes, her generous race". Germania, from where "our sires" issued, is the home of "old Woden's high-born sons;/Great Woden deem'd a god, with uncouth rites/By his rude offspring worshipp'd".[56] The old Gothic balance is commended—"civil freedom tempering royal power"—and the poem itself, with its "kindred accents", will show Charlotte that she may feel perfectly at home on English soil, even though she had yet to meet her bridegroom.

Similarly, in his long poem *Almada Hill* (1781), William Mickle disparages Rome in familiar terms as "a luxurious prey", "debased in false refinement", and has "northern hords" bringing liberty to Europe, and Freedom dwelling in "Saxony's wild forests".[57] And in 1775, William Stevens was still including in a collection of "Miscellaneous pieces" a version of the two familiar verses of Ragnar Lothbrok's Death Song which Temple had praised almost a century before. Though Stevens attributes them to "Rednor Ladbrog" he does not otherwise depart from a familiar and instantly recognizable idiom: his speakers have "quaff'd/from hollow Skulls", and he claims that the poem had been composed "in the Runic language".[58]

In Tobias Smollett's strange allegory *Ode to Independence* (1773), Independence is born in "the frozen regions of the north", of "a goddess violated"—Liberty herself. Taking cover on "the bleak Norwegian shore" after Charlemagne's massacre of "the sons of Woden" she catches the eye of Disdain, who is dressed in a "shaggy vest" made of bearskin, snow clinging to his "yellow beard". He is smitten, and in an unexpected echo of Thomas

[56] Joseph Spence, 'On the Royal Nuptials', in *The Annual Register, or A View of the History, Politicks, and Literature of the Year 1761* (London: R. and J. Dodsley, 1762), pp. 225–6.

[57] William Julius Mickle, *Almada Hill: An Epistle from Lisbon* (Oxford: W. Jackson, 1781), pp. 11–12.

[58] William Bagshaw Stevens, *Poems, Consisting of Indian Odes and Miscellaneous Pieces* (Oxford: J. and J. Fletcher and S. Parker, 1775), pp. 81–5.

Gray's allusion to Odin's seduction of Rindr in 'The Descent of Odin', he "seiz'd th'advantage Fate allow'd/And straight compress'd her in his vig'rous arms". Independence is "th'auspicious fruit of stol'n embrace", and will go on to prevail against a host of barely personified social evils: Vice, Vanity, Insolence, Falsehood ("pert and vain"), pale Disease, and Gluttony and Sloth.[59]

The "General Observations" in a piece of prose which Smollett appends to this Ode may reveal, however, that a new kind of poetry was coming into vogue. Smollett writes: "Lyric poetry imitates violent and ardent passions. It is therefore bold, various, and impetuous. It abounds with animated sentiments, glowing images, and forms of speech often unusual, but commonly nervous and expressive. The composition and arrangement of parts may often appear disordered, and the transitions sudden and obscure; but they are always natural".[60] The hectic and impassioned character of Old Norse verse would come at last to catch the public imagination. In 1774, Thomas Warton's *History of English Poetry* was published, prefaced with a dissertation 'Of the Origin of Romantic Fiction in Europe'. This piece put Old Norse literature into the heart of English poetic tradition in a novel and powerful way: Warton contends that the origin of "our old romances of chivalry" was Gothic (meaning, by this, Old Norse) poetry, citing Mallet as evidence of the "love and admiration for the profession of arms which prevailed among our ancestors even to fanaticism", and classical sources on female chastity amongst the Goths as evidence underlying the principles of chivalry.[61] Warton also described the diction of Old Norse poetry as having "a certain sublime and figurative cast" which was the result of "warmth of fancy".

What all this amounts to is the growing sense that what were perceived as the characteristic qualities of Old Norse mythological poetry—sublimity, passion, extravagant diction, supernatural incident—were features attractive to contemporary poets and their readers. I want now to turn to poets who engaged with Old Norse myth on these terms, producing poems in what was supposed to be the Old Norse mode. Further, perhaps influenced by Gray, poets were moving beyond the heroic or legendary material covered in Percy's anthology to confront the great cosmic myths of Old Norse tradition: the beginnings and end of the world.

Margaret Omberg describes Thomas Penrose's 'The Carousal of Odin' (1775) as "the first and only instance of an original poem [on Old Norse

[59] Tobias Smollett, *Ode to Independence* (Glasgow: Robert and Andrew Foulis, 1773), pp. 1–7.

[60] Smollett, *Ode to Independence*, p. 9.

[61] Thomas Warton Jr, *The History of English Poetry* (London: J. Dodsley, 1774), vol. I, Dissertation I.

themes] to appear in the [seventeen] seventies".[62] At first, the poem seems
to be situated squarely in the well-established tradition based on the two
most widely disseminated verses of Ragnar's Death Song, numbered 25
and 29 by Worm, and quoted by William Temple in Latin a century
before. The scene is one of warriors feasting in Odin's hall, drinking mead
from skulls. Gray's influence is apparent: the poem begins with emphatic
octosyllabic couplets reminiscent of the 'Norse Odes', and there are echoes of Gray's diction, with Odin described as the "griesly lord" of warriors.[63] These warriors are distinctly Spenserian figures, couching quivering
lances, and equipped with maces, gauntlets, and morions (according to
the Oxford English Dictionary, a sixteenth-century helmet, with a brim,
like a hat). Like Sir John Campbell's *einherjar*, these celebrating warriors
are not the defeated dead in the afterlife, but are triumphing in victory.
Nevertheless, all that eating and drinking takes its toll, and "the gust of
War subsides". A valkyrie, Hilda, calls up minstrels to rouse the warriors from their indulgence. The poetry of the skalds does the trick: "the
charm prevailed, up rush'd the madden'd throng/Panting for carnage",
and disorder is restored. "Fierce Odin's self led forth the frantick band,/
To scatter havock wide o'er many a guilty land". Here we see poetry itself
as the hero of the hour. However, in 1781, Hugh Downman returned to
familiar ground and published yet another version of the Death Song,
complete with drinking goblets fashioned from "skulls of recreant foes",
and a thick sprinkling of echoes from Gray's 'Norse Odes'. Downman
praises his source for exhibiting "a species of savage greatness, a fierce and
wild kind of sublimity, and a noble contempt of danger and death";[64] the
familiar figure of the death-defying warrior, inspired by Odinic principles,
could meet the demand for sublimity, too.

There had been very little reference to the overall system of Old Norse
mythology, its myths of creation and destruction, its cosmology, and stories of the other gods in the Norse pantheon. In Old Norse literature,
the primary poetic source for such material was the poem *Völuspá*, but
although it had been summarized by Mallet, translated by Percy, and had
appeared a century earlier in Resen's seventeenth-century Latin edition of
the *Edda*,[65] little attention had been paid to it by English poets. Margaret
Clunies Ross suggests that "it was simply too hard, and its allusive

[62] Omberg, *Scandinavian Themes*, p. 60.
[63] Thomas Penrose, *Flights of Fancy* (London: J. Walter, 1775), pp. 11–14, reprinted in
Omberg, *Scandinavian Themes*, pp. 160–1.
[64] Hugh Downman, *The Death-Song of Ragnar Lodbrach, or Lodbrog, King of Denmark,
translated from the Latin of Olaus Wormius* (London: Fielding and Walker, 1781), p. vi.
[65] See Faulkes, *Two Versions of Snorra Edda*, vol. II, pp. 77–88.

mythological references too obscure".[66] As she points out, *Völuspá* was not translated into English as a whole until the nineteenth century. But in the second half of the eighteenth century, a number of English and Irish poets attempted to use material from *Völuspá*, with mixed results and reception, as we shall see.

The first poet to use the material of *Völuspá* in any substantial way was Thomas James Mathias, whose *Runic Odes* was published in 1781. The title does not signal any departure from the usual ways of receiving Old Norse literature, and indeed a number of the old misconceptions persist: Valhalla is a place where warriors "drain the skull", for instance. Or rather, cease their feasting and drinking, for Mathias's first runic ode is "The Twilight of the Gods, or, The Destruction of the World" and the gods and their champions are preparing for their final battle against the giants and their monstrous kin. Mathias refers his readers to Percy's translation of Mallet "for a farther Account of this wild and curious System of Mythology"[67] and has himself clearly based his details on *Northern Antiquities*: the great World Tree is referred to as "Ydrasil", for instance, Percy's mistaken form of Yggdrasill there. Other less explicable differences include the substitution of the giant Ymir, from whose murdered corpse the earth was made, for the ancient frost-giant Hrymr, who in *Völuspá* surges forward in the vanguard against the gods.[68] And the names are carefully latinized: Hlín becomes Lina, Hlöðyn, Lodina, and so on. But essentially, Mathias's poem is a rendering of the Ragnarök narrative as set out in Mallet/Percy, and taken originally from Snorri Sturluson's composite prose account, largely based on *Völuspá* and quoting many stanzas from the poem.[69]

Mathias presents the whole volume to Thomas Gray, prefaced by a notably feeble dedicatory sonnet which begins "Pardon me, Mighty Poet, that I turn/My daring steps to thy supreme abode". In spite of the extreme violence and extravagant action of the original, Mathias's ode lacks drama or urgency, unlike Gray's own 'Norse Odes', and his octosyllabic couplets are statelier than Gray's breathless quatrains, though the horror of the scene is emphasized rather than played down. Mathias tries to temper the allusiveness of the original, but fleshes out what would perhaps be better left to the imagination. Thus, for instance, when the World Serpent heaves itself up from the depths to make its assault on the gods, even Snorri scarcely elaborates on the relevant stanza from *Völuspá*, which reads "Mighty Wraith coils/in giant wrath./The snake flails the

[66] Clunies Ross, *The Norse Muse*, p. 41.
[67] Thomas James Mathias, *Runic Odes imitated from the Norse Tongue, in the manner of Mr. Gray* (London: T. Payne, T. Becket, J. Sewell, and T. and J. Merrill, 1781), pp. 1–2.
[68] *Völuspá*, st. 47, in Dronke, *The Poetic Edda*, vol. II, pp. 7–24 (20).
[69] *Gylfaginning*, chs. 51–4, in Faulkes, *Edda*, pp. 52–8.

waves,/and the eagle exults—/pale-beaked, rips corpses".[70] Mathias
expands this to eight lines:

> The serpent dread, of dateless birth,
> Girds the devoted globe of earth;
> And, as charm'd by pow'rful spell,
> Ocean heaves with furious swell.
> The plumed Monarch whets his beak,
> Seeking where his wrath to wreak;
> Till on the plain, with corses strew'd,
> He sates his maw with bleeding food.[71]

The final line of the original stanza alludes to the great boat Naglfar, cap-
tained by the advancing frost giant Hrymr, and according to Snorri, constructed from the parings of the nails of corpses who have failed in their
duty to trim them whilst alive. Snorri notes tersely that everyone should
take care to keep their nails short, since gods and men will want this ship
to take a long time to be built, so that Ragnarök may be deferred as long
as possible.[72] The poet of *Völuspá*, almost certainly assuming the reader's
knowledge of this grotesque vessel, confines himself to two words: "Naglfar
losnar" ("Naglfar will be loosed"). But, as if the original poem were not
difficult enough, Mathias complicates the allusion to produce both obscurity and error: he writes that the eagle is searching out its carrion "While
the vessel's floating pride/Stems duration's rounding tide".[73]

Gray's policy was to simplify whatever the reader might find difficult in
Old Norse myth, but Mathias tries to keep the reader informed with footnotes, and he does well to convey something of the voice of the sibyl herself: her bad-tempered refrain in the original poem—"Do you know yet?
Or what?"—is rendered, perhaps a little limply, by Mathias as "Know'st
thou what is done above?"[74] But perhaps his major contribution to making
the material of *Völuspá* accessible for English readers is to have abstracted
from the whole poem, with its complex time schemes and sudden shifts of
scene and emphasis, the Ragnarök narrative itself, the final confrontation
between the gods and their old foes, stripping away the sibyl's mysterious
memories of creation, and the uncertain place of her visions of torments
for wrongdoers. By the same token, Mathias's second ode in the collection,
entitled 'The Renovation of the World and Future Retribution', takes as
its subject the concluding stanzas of *Völuspá* which allude to the coming
of a new world after the ruin of Ragnarök. In stately four-line stanzas, this

[70] *Völuspá*, st. 47, in Dronke, *The Poetic Edda*, vol. II, p. 20.
[71] Mathias, *Runic Odes*, p. 2.
[72] Faulkes, *Edda*, p. 53.
[73] Mathias, *Runic Odes*, p. 3.
[74] Mathias, *Runic Odes*, p. 4.

hymn-like ode opens with the surviving gods singing a "prophetic Song of Triumph", celebrating the creation of a "renovated earth;/Pine-clad mountain, shaded plain", with "murm'ring fountain, rapid flood".[75] In a welcome break from the hectic sublimity of the monstrous last battle, there is a distinct harking back to the old style of eighteenth-century pastoral verse: eagles are "tyrants of the finny brood", and the new earth is depicted in terms of an English countryside magically idealized—socially as well as visually:

> From the kindly teeming soil,
> Ripen'd harvests wave unsown;
> Wherefore need the peasant's toil?
> Nature works, and works alone.[76]

The third ode in Mathias's collection returns to an old favourite, the 'Incantation of Hervor' as translated by Percy, and by Hickes as 'The Waking of Angantyr' at the very beginning of the century. There follow an ode entitled 'Battle', with "Images selected from the Works attributed to Ossian" (full of craggy rocks and sanguinary torrents) and a fourth, 'Tudor'; the reader is recommended to look at "Mr Evans's specimens of the Welsh Bards". All this gives a very clear idea of the company which Old Norse-derived verse was likely to keep in the period. But the final piece is an interesting departure—an original composition "founded on the Northern Mythology", not a version of existing material, or a scrap of Norse myth projecting local colour onto a northern medieval setting, but a poet creating a completely new piece.

This poem, Ode VI, 'An Incantation', seems to be spoken by an enchantress, Thorbiorga, a witch, or sibyl, who figures in the Old Norse *Eiríks saga rauða* (The saga of Erik the Red) and who is mentioned by Bartholin.[77] Perhaps inspired by *Völuspá*, in which the sibyl begins with a call for attention from all the gods, Thorbiorga in Mathias's poem demands, "Hear, ye Rulers of the North,/Spirits of exalted worth".[78] Calling for aid in casting her magic spells, she invokes a number of mysterious occult but non-Norse names "Peolphan, murky king/Master of th'enchanted ring", "Glauron's Lord" and "Coronzon" with his "awful power", and so on.[79] But whilst

[75] Mathias, *Runic Odes*, pp. 9–10.
[76] Mathias, *Runic Odes*, p. 11.
[77] *Eiríks saga rauða*, in Einar Ól. Sveinsson and Matthías Þórðarson (eds.), *Eyrbyggja saga*, Íslenzk fornrit VI (Reykjavík: Hið Íslenzka Fornritafélag, 1935), pp. 206–9; for a translation see Gwyn Jones (trans.), *Eirik the Red and Other Icelandic Sagas* (Oxford: Oxford University Press, 1988), pp. 133–7.
[78] Mathias, *Runic Odes*, p. 27.
[79] These are names taken from occultism: Coronzon is another name for Lucifer in the writings of John Dee and Edward Kelly (see Meric Casaubon (ed.), *A True and Faithful Relation of what passed for many Yeers Between Dr. John Dee... and Some Spirits* (London: D.

being heavy on atmosphere—the setting is midnight, "some moss-grown ruin silv'ring o'er" by torchlight, on some "unfrequented shore"—the poem is light on substance: we are not told what form the spells take (though they are "inly-thrilling") or what their purpose is.

Mathias helpfully concludes his slim volume with a Latin translation of the relevant stanzas from *Völuspá,* and an English version of 'Angantýr', since "the books whence they are taken are rather scarce". All in all, Mathias's *Runic Odes* offers a full spectrum of how poets might deal with Old Norse mythological poetry: English versions, radically adapted for English readers, a conventional translation, an original composition, and sight of his sources (though not the original Old Norse).

As Farley notes, reviews of Mathias's volume reveal that "English readers were beginning to have some definite idea as to the sort of subject that might be consistently dealt with in a poem purporting to imitate the Norse manner".[80] In other words, reviewers were quick to pick fault with Mathias's work. For example, it was objected that "Pale Cynthia's beam" (said by Mathias to be outshone by the midnight torches lighting Thorbiorga's spells) is a classical reference, and thus inappropriate in a Norse milieu—though one might claim in Mathias's defence that there is an implicit allegory of Norse myth outshining classical sources. Similarly, Mathias was taken to task in that he "improperly gives the Norns the attributes of the Parcae". But more generally, Mathias was attacked for lack of poetic skill: the lines from 'The Twilight of the Gods' about the monsters' advance—"Mark the murd'rous monster stalk/In printless majesty of walk"—were much mocked, and so too the description of the earth as "this pensile mundane ball", or a reference to "the curtain close and murk" which "veils Creation's ruin'd work".[81] And finally, and even more generally, some reviewers felt that the project itself—basing English poems on Old Norse themes—was doomed. Despite its occasional "sublime or magnificent image", Norse poetry was believed by some to be simply unsuitable as an inspiration for modern works. For some critics, Mathias's *Runic Odes* seemed to confirm this. But poets were not deterred.

In 1784, Edward Jerningham published *The Rise and Progress of the Scandinavian Poetry,* a bold and ingenious meta-myth based on Norse mythological material, in which he was well read. Jerningham's big idea was to begin with the shadowy first creator of life in the Norse—indeed,

---

Maxwell, 1659), pp. 92–3), and Peolphan is king of the Hunters of the North in Reginald Scot's *Discovery of Witchcraft* (London: Andrew Clark, 1665), pp. 219–26, in which all three names appear.

[80]   Farley, *Scandinavian Influences,* p. 101.
[81]   For a variety of scathing reviews, see Farley, *Scandinavian Influences,* pp. 98–101.

the universal—cosmos. According to Snorri Sturluson's account of creation, the first living creature was the primeval giant Ymir, whose corpse was
to provide material for the physical features of the landscape: mountains,
rivers, oceans, and so on. But who created him? The original Icelandic
describes the genesis of Ymir from drops of thawed frost in a sentence
crucially lacking a specific grammatical subject. Two modern translations
reflect this impersonality: Anthony Faulkes suggests "there was a quicken-
ing from these flowing drops due to the power of the source of the heat,
and it became the form of a man";[82] Jesse Byock has "life sprang up, taking its force from the power that sent the heat".[83] In *Northern Antiquities*,
quoted in Edward Jerningham's "Advertisement" to the Rise and Progress,
Mallet/Percy gives this grammatically effaced subject a distinct identity: "a
powerful being had with his breath animated the drops out of which the
first giant was formed", and distinguishes this figure—"whom the Edda
affects not to name"—from both gods and giants. But for Jerningham, he
is a key figure; he is the creator not of this world—our world—but of "a
new Poetic World", the world of Old Norse myth.

    Jerningham begins with the creation of the giant Ymir, and then the
Power "bad the splendid city Asgard rise". Jerningham's Asgard is rather
like the New Jerusalem, a glittering edifice with a crystal wall, mansions
of sapphire, and towers of opal. The creative Power peoples it with the
gods, and conjures up Yggdrasill, the mighty ash. "Three virgin forms"
are the next to appear: the Norns, Urda, Vernandi [sic], and Skulda. The
production of Valhalla—"great Odin's festive hall!"—is the occasion for
a mention of warriors "who welcom'd pain, and with a smile expir'd"—a
familiar echo of the ubiquitous Death Song.[84] But Jerningham does not
delay here, but moves on to the creation of valkyries, and the "drear abode"
of the goddess Hel. Diverging from the standard sources, he describes the
raven banner, which, as we have seen, Farley described as one of the familiar "theatrical properties" of Old Norse-themed verse.[85] The banner seems
to be made out of the ravens themselves: their wings "into one vast texture grew" and their "gory heads conjoin'd in one dread fold". Jerningham
notes carefully that though this banner is not mentioned in the *Edda*, it is
a motif "of great antiquity".[86]

[82] Faulkes, *Edda*, p. 10.
[83] Jesse Byock (trans.), *The Prose Edda* (London: Penguin, 2005), p. 14.
[84] Edward Jerningham, *The Rise and Progress of the Scandinavian Poetry: A Poem, in Two Parts* (London: James Robson, 1784), pp. 5–8.
[85] Farley, *Scandinavian Influences*, p. 103, n.1.
[86] Jerningham, *Rise and Progress of the Scandinavian Poetry*, pp. 9–10.

Having set out in this ingenious frame the basics of Old Norse myth, Jerningham now describes the creation of "the living fathers of the Runic rhyme"—the poets themselves. Their creator commands them to produce poetry which will "engrave the sacred form of truth" on the "bosom of the list'ning youth"; it must "rouze the tyrant from his flatt'ring dream", "a glowing, unabating fire proclaim" and "strike the solemn deep, mysterious chords". In other words, all the qualities for which Jerningham and his contemporaries valued Old Norse verse are shown being inculcated by the creator of its poets and poetic world. Finally, Jerningham's Great Power dictates the subject matter of this poetry: Fenrir, bursting his chains; Naglfar, the gigantic ship; the World Serpent ("mighty whale")—in sum, Ragnarök. But composition is not in itself enough; transmission must be ensured. In a remarkable passage, Jerningham depicts the Power describing how Old Norse poetry should be set down in runic inscriptions:

> The lofty pine that meets the mountain gale,
> Th'expanding oak that crowns the lowly vale,
> Shall as your fingers touch the furrow'd rind,
> Display the treasures of the musing mind:
> There by the voice of whisp'ring nature call'd,
> In future times shall stand the youthful Scald,
> There shall he meditate the Runic store,
> There woo the science of the tuneful lore;
> There view the tree with speechless wonder fraught,
> Whose womb mysterious bears the poet's thought.[87]

Even aside from the ingenious presentation of the creation of Old Norse myth—as a creation myth in itself—Jerningham's poetry has a certain grandeur, and even sublimity, by the standards of the period. And his Creator's final instruction to the Poets—"Disturb, exalt, enchant the human soul"—might almost serve as a definition of the contemporary fashion for sublimity.

Jerningham's debt to Gray is evident everywhere in his diction. Mention of the raven banner, for example, evidently called to mind Gray's description of the weaving in 'The Fatal Sisters' and prompted a slew of Gray-isms: its own "vast texture"; the description of the ravens' heads as "gory"; the "grisly" aspect of the banner's frame. And for Jerningham, the goddess Hel is Death's "terrific maid"—though this phrase was perhaps better suited to its original subject, Mista, one of Gray's "Fatal Sisters".

The second part of *The Rise and Progress* concerns the demise of the skalds in the face of Christianity, and is a much less engaging piece.

---

[87] Jerningham, *Rise and Progress of the Scandinavian Poetry*, p. 17.

Christianity is presented as enriching the poets' store of images and subjects, and a somewhat uninspiring "various allegoric band" includes Hope,
Conscience, and Grace—but also Celibacy ("Dead to the bliss that from
affection flows") and Disappointment with its "meagre form" and "incessant tears". More conducive to the poetic imagination are new images
of horror: Lapland hags (who similarly "spread the texture of the fatal
loom"), wolf-dogs howling savagely, owls, bats, and "they whose talons
reek with infants' gore". These are the new "forms that peopled the poetic
land" in the post-pagan world.[88]

Reviews of Jerningham's work were mixed; Farley notes that Jerningham
was "well-known and not over-appreciated".[89] But the *Literary Review* was
impressed: "We have often admired Mr J's compositions, but we freely
confess, that he has never, in our opinion, assumed the character of a poet
with more success, in any of his performances than in the Rise and Progress
of Scandinavian Poetry".[90] The 1786 edition of *The Rise and Progress* was
dedicated to Horace Walpole, who, in a letter to William Mason, offered
a frank and not over-generous assessment of the piece (as indeed he had
done for his friend Gray's 'Norse Odes'): "It is far superior to his previous
works. The versification is good; very many expressions and lines beautiful…It might have been thrown into a better plan; and it ends rather
abruptly and tamely. He seems to have kept the 'Descent of Odin' in his
eye, though he had not the art of conjuring up the most forceful feelings,
as Gray has done…Though one has scarce any idea of what the whole is
about, yet one is enwrapt by it".[91]

A reviewer's antipathy to Norse themes was not of course the only reason
why a poet might attract a harsh review. Joseph Sterling's 'Odes from the
Icelandic' from his collection *Poems*, published in 1782, were criticized on
two further counts: that he had confused Norse and Celtic mythologies,
and that his poetic technique was poor.[92] Sterling prefaces his odes with
a sonnet dedicated to a friend praised as one for whom "immortal Odin
waits" and "Valhalla shall unfold its golden gates"—but "the Noble Isle",
Flath Innis, the paradise of Celtic mythology, is also keen to receive him.[93]
However, as Sterling himself makes perfectly clear in the dissertation

[88] Jerningham, *Rise and Progress of the Scandinavian Poetry*, pp. 21–31.
[89] Farley, *Scandinavian Influences*, p. 102.
[90] Anon., Review of Jerningham, *The Rise and Progress of the Scandinavian Poetry, Literary Review* (1784), Article LII, pp. 237–9 (237).
[91] Quoted in Farley, *Scandinavian Influences*, p. 105, n.1.
[92] Joseph Sterling, *Poems* (Dublin: Joseph Hill, 1782); quotations are taken from the second, revised edition (London: G. G. J. and J. Robinson, 1789).
[93] Sterling, *Poems*, p. 142.

which precedes the Icelandic odes, he was not confusing the two mythological systems, but rather conflating them, or drawing on both.

Sterling's dissertation is a very helpful document (though it is of course
significant that it was still felt necessary to help readers with some background information). He praises "the ancient inhabitants of the North";
on the evidence of their poetry "their sentiments, though tinctured with
ferocity, were liberal and generous... their language... nervous and expressive... their songs breathe all the enthusiasm of poetry".[94] A number of
old ideas about Norse culture are re-hashed: to these Goths—who "broke
the splendid shackles with which domineering Rome had fettered mankind for so many ages"—should be attributed the institution of Liberty.
The Death Song is represented as the testimony of Ragnar himself. But
Sterling is impressively sceptical about the myth of Odin as 'Asiatic' settler
(it "seems to be nothing more than a splendid fiction"[95]).

Interestingly, Sterling is not uncritical of Old Norse verse: it is "at times
turgid and obscure", he warns, and "we must not expect that justness of
sentiment, or that purity of diction, which is to be met with in the poets
of Greece and Rome".[96] And perhaps Sterling gave his reviewers too much
ammunition, for he concedes that Old Norse myth may still be "obscure and
uninteresting to many", and adds footnotes to his verses for those still ignorant of the subject. Nevertheless, he maintains that the style of Norse poets
is "extravagantly noble", and that "nothing less than the dissolution of the
world is the object of their contest; and when Odin falls, creation expires".
Sterling's conclusion is that "the sublime Gray has been his guide; and happy
should he think himself, if... he could pursue the steps of so great a master".[97]

Sterling's first Icelandic ode 'The Scalder' describes a host of magnificent
Norse warriors pouring out of Valhalla—"the mansion of the brave"—on
their way into battle. The battlefield is grim: "Death and carnage load the
plain./Pale fear, grim horror, stalk around". Many are killed, but at the
call of a brazen trumpet (echoing the biblical trumpet in I Corinthians
15:52: "the trumpet shall sound, and the dead shall be raised incorrupt-
ible") they spring back to life, and make their way back to Valhalla, and
to Odin. There they feast on the boar Serimner, attended by valkyries
who "present the goblet foaming o'er:/Of heroes skulls the goblet made".[98]
The scene then shifts abruptly to an isle "far in the west"—the far gentler
paradise of Celtic myth, where departed warriors play the harp, or hunt

[94] Sterling, *Poems,* pp. 143–4.
[95] Sterling, *Poems,* p. 146.
[96] Sterling, *Poems,* p. 145.
[97] Sterling, *Poems,* pp. 146–7.
[98] Sterling, *Poems,* p. 150.

deer with hounds. Whichever tradition the archetypal warrior belongs to, Sterling concludes, his praises will be sung, whether by bards with harps, or in runic rhymes. Plainly influenced by Gray, the final stanza depicts an Icelandic poet, who is clearly inspired to sublime poetry by the wildness of the landscape:

> A shaggy rock o'erhung the raging flood,
> Here sat the tow'ring bard in dreadful state;
> Loud roar'd the tempest through the crashing wood;
> Rude was the scene, majestically great...[99]

Romantic notions of an untamed landscape meshed well with Norse themes.

In 'The Scalder' Sterling does not depart far from familiar ideas of Odin, Valhalla, savage warriors and the power of practitioners of runic rhyme. But his second ode, 'The Twilight of the Gods', as its title suggests, engages with Ragnarök. Sterling apparently based his verse on Snorri's prose account in *Gylfaginning*, though with some significant changes and omissions. There is plenty of blood and horror from the beginning, even before the last battle: the poem opens with the line "The dusky moon is streak'd with blood", for instance, and goes on to describe how "The clouds descend in streams of gore". As in *Gylfaginning*, Ragnarök is heralded by a great winter, but Sterling omits all mention of the celebrated moral chaos of pre-Ragnarök society, when brothers will fight brothers, and sexual depravity will be rife, and moves straight on to the World Serpent's terrifying incursion on to land, and the advance of the giant Surtr. The ship Naglfar, which gave Mathias such trouble, is also passed over. As in *Gylfaginning*, Heimdallr, the watchman of the gods, blows his great horn, and the single-combat encounters between the gods and the giants are as represented in *Gylfaginning*, though the drama is exaggerated: Fenrir the wolf "bleeds in agonizing pangs", for instance, and Surtr "launces a deluge of devouring flame".[100] But suddenly, four lines from the end of the poem, Sterling announces the coming of "a second earth, serenely bright" and ends with a rushed and bathetic mention of the Norse equivalent of the final judgement—"In Gimle's halls reside the just and brave,/While the base Caitiff's chain'd in Nastrond's dreary cave"[101]—which requires a lengthy footnote to be comprehensible to a reader not familiar with the details of Old Norse eschatology.

Sterling's poetic shortcomings will have been evident from the short quotations above. His language rarely matches the grandeur of the subject

---

[99] Sterling, *Poems*, pp. 152–3.
[100] Sterling, *Poems*, p. 156.
[101] Sterling, *Poems*, p. 157.

matter. The World Serpent, for instance, "shoots the seas along", like a surfer; Surtr "pricks his steed"; Loki "puts his lance in rest"; Sleipnir (Odin's eight-legged horse) "gives a dreadful bound"; Odin "darts from file to file" and "the sounding bowstring twangs". Contemporary reviewers did not spare Sterling either, complaining particularly about what they imply are Hibernicisms in his verse: Irish rhymes such as "toil" and "isle", for example, or "care, appear, share, severe, cease, face, sway, sea", and failures of logic, or tautologies, are sneeringly condemned as having "a dash of the Shannon".[102] Sterling responded indignantly, accusing his reviewers of simple prejudice, but he did amend some of the rhymes in later editions of his work. And their criticisms of other aspects of his style—especially the repeated use of formulations such as "the board is spread" and "the goat is fed"—are clearly justified.

Sterling wrote a number of poems on Spenserian themes and in Spenserian metre as well as a long continuation of Chaucer's 'The Squire's Tale', and agrees with Warton in attributing the origin of romance to Norse poetry. But direct influence from Old Norse has not been great, according to Sterling; in an unexpectedly poetic flight of fancy, he writes: "The abilities of the Scalder may be compared to the rays of passing light, when launched out into the regions of infinite space, from whence they are never to return, and where their heat and splendor will be diffused in vain".[103] In direct contrast to the bulk of Sterling's Old Norse-derived poetry, this judgement misrepresents his sources, but is elegantly expressed.

In spite of the appearance, in 1787, of the Copenhagen *Edda,* an edition in Norse and Latin of full texts of a wider selection of the mythological poems of the *Edda,* the influence of Percy's translations continued to be very potent, and extremely long-lasting: for example, Anna Seward published a version of 'The Incantation of Hervor' in 1796 (this was reprinted by Scott in 1810),[104] and Gray's friend William Mason reworked a version of 'The Complaint of Harold', which had appeared in 1766, as 'The Song of Harold the Valiant', published in 1797.[105] And in 1792, a collection

---

[102] Anon., Review of Sterling, *Poems,* in *The English Review,* October 1787, vol. 10 (Article 13, pp. 281–4), and again in March 1790, vol. 15, (Article 22, p. 229), in response to Sterling's protests.

[103] Sterling, *Poems,* p. 146.

[104] 'Herva at the Tomb of Argantyr: A Runic Dialogue', in Anna Seward, *Llangollen Vale, with Other Poems* (London: G. Sael, 1796), pp. 22–36, and *The Poetical Works of Anna Seward,* ed. Walter Scott (Edinburgh: James Ballantyne and Co., 1810), vol. III, pp. 90–103.

[105] William Mason, *The Works of William Mason* (London: T. Cadell and W. Davies, 1811), vol. I, pp. 196–8.

entitled *Poems, Chiefly by Gentlemen of Devonshire and Cornwall*, edited by
Richard Polwhele, included a number of similar works.[106]

I want to mention briefly an interesting short poem which, even more
than Penrose's 'Carousal of Odin' or Mathias's 'An Incantation', may be
regarded as neither imitation nor adaptation, but actually an original
poem "in the Norse manner". This is 'The Haunting of Havardur' by
C. Lestley, published in 1793.[107]

'The Haunting of Havardur' tells the story of the eponymous anti-hero
who has seduced "Coronzon's lovely maid"—it will be remembered that
Mathias used the name Coronzon in one of his *Runic Odes*, though it
belongs in the context of early modern occultists, not Old Norse. The
woman has drowned herself, and is now "a frantic, pale, and shrouded,
ghost". The voice of a messenger from Odin—perhaps a valkyrie—con-
demns Havardur to Hel, with Lok the evil demi-god, instead of an afterlife
in Valhalla until Ragnarök, when the world will be destroyed by Surtr's
fire. Odin's curse has made a mockery of all Havardur's warlike exploits,
since there will be no glorious afterlife for him. His fate will be truly hor-
rific: "famish'd eagles" will tear at his corpse, and "sea-mews" will drink his
blood. But as dawn comes, this spirit fades, with a valedictory warning:

> At night, when weary'd Nature's still,
> And Horror stalks along the plain,
> Remember—we must meet again.

This is pure Gothic horror. The usual trappings of Old Norse motifs are
evident: Havardur is condemned never to "pass the scull" in Valhalla, and
as we have seen, the beasts of battle are invoked. But Lestley's twist on the
customary celebration of a Norse warrior's defiance of death is to imagine
its opposite: Havardur's terror of a death which will bring him not to
Valhalla, but to the torments of Hel, and which will make him a coward in
battle. 'The Haunting of Havardur' has no basis in Norse myth but simply
uses Norse motifs and the familiar hectic battle imagery to produce an
atmospheric ghost story.

By the end of the eighteenth century Norse sources had become far
more widely known, even though common misconceptions persisted. In
1801, the Reverend William Lisle Bowles published a collection of poems
including 'Hymn to Woden', in which the speaking voice beseeches the

---

[106]   Richard Polwhele (ed.), *Poems, Chiefly by Gentlemen of Devonshire and Cornwall*
(Bath: R. Cruttwell, 1792). See Farley, *Scandinavian Influences*, pp. 44–90, for a useful and
full list of Percy-inspired material.
[107]   First published anonymously in *The Gentleman's Magazine*, May 1793; see Farley,
Scandinavian Influences, p. 129. The poem is reprinted in Omberg, *Scandinavian Themes*,
pp. 168–9.

"god of the battle" to grant victory—or at least, a hero's death and an afterlife in Valhalla. The poem is prefaced by a telling little note: "I need not
perhaps mention, that WODEN was the god of the Gothick or Northern
nations—his hall was called 'VALHALLA;' where those who were slain
in battle drank ale with him out of the skulls of their enemies." It is of
course significant that Bowles felt the note necessary, and perhaps not
unexpected that the old misconception about the skulls is repeated. The
poem itself uses the old cliché "Runick rhyme", and notes of the phrase
"weird Sisters" (printed in inverted commas) that these were "Valkyriae,
or Choosers of the Slain", referring the reader back to Gray's poem. The
poem itself repeats the enemy skull-cup topos, and its speaker begs to be
saved from "slow disease".[108] It is perhaps even more significant that the
god of battle is Woden, not Odin, Bowles employing a name familiar
from much older learning, and associated not with Scandinavians, but
with the Saxons. There are extensive end notes to the poem, mostly taken
from Mallet, and interestingly, the confusion of Celtic and Scandinavian
seems to have been uncritically imported from Mallet's original, since the
warriors set off to the battle "o'er Cumri's hills of snow". In fact, another
poem in Bowles's volume, 'St Michael's Mount', betrays a similar confusion, since there the Britons "rear their axes huge", and call on Thor. The
notes also include extensive citation from "The Gothick 'Ode on Hacon'"
(*Hákonarmál*) from Mallet, which Bowles calls "wild and poetical". Such
was the mix of learning, misconception, and muddle which still characterized Norse-inspired poetry in English.

I want to conclude this chapter by looking at the poetry of William
Blake, who also combined Celtic and Norse mythology in his mythic
prehistory of Britain, but who completely transformed his sources and
influences.[109] In spite of this creative transformation, the influence of
Old Norse mythology on William Blake's poetry has not been overlooked. If anything, it has been rather grandly overstated—as in Harold
Bloom's sweeping declaration that Blake's "own true Sublime comes
in...a Northern [mode]...in the tradition of the Icelandic Eddas".[110]

[108] 'Hymn to Woden', in W. L. Bowles, *Sonnets, and Other Poems* (London: T. Cadell,
1801), vol. II, pp. 67–72.
[109] I am very grateful to Sebastian Kalhat Pocicovic, University College, Oxford, for
his expert advice on Blake. For a fuller account of Blake and Old Norse literature, focusing
on female voices, see Heather O'Donoghue, 'Valkyries and Sibyls: Old Norse Voices of
Authority in Blake's Prophetic Books', in Helen P. Bruder (ed.), *Women Reading William
Blake* (Basingstoke: Palgrave Macmillan, 2007), pp. 179–88.
[110] Harold Bloom, 'William Blake', in Frank Kermode and John Hollander (eds.), *The
Oxford Anthology of English Literature* (New York and London: Oxford University Press,
1973), vol. II, pp. 10–14 (12).

Northrop Frye has similarly pronounced that "eddic myths" are "integral to Blake's symbolism", claiming that "we cannot understand Blake" without understanding how to read the *Prose Edda*, "at least as he read [it]".[111] More recently, Vincent De Luca compared what he understands to be the characteristic form of individual (mythological) eddic poems— "dramatic exchanges between characters in conflict... [which are] usually mere pretexts for long expository accounts chronicling divine history and eschatology, cataloguing mythic names, and mapping out supernatural geography"—with Blake's own work: "One might be describing the typical features of *Jerusalem* itself".[112] But these critics are tellingly unspecific about what it was, precisely, that Blake read, and in what forms it is found in his poetry.[113]

It is certain that Blake knew Old Norse myth, for in an annotation to a tract about the theological shortcomings of "primitive peoples", Blake angrily demanded "Read the Eddas!". So it is not surprising that in his prophetic books, we may glimpse the outlines of some of the most basic elements of Old Norse myth. Thus, in *The Book of Urizen*, which has been described as "an ironic version of the biblical Book of Genesis",[114] it might be argued that there are also echoes of the Old Norse creation myth, especially as represented in *Völuspá*. But for Blake, the great primordial void, the *ginnunga gap*, is itself a creation of the figure he calls Urizen: "what Demon hath form'd this abominable void/This soul-shudd'ring vacuum?—Some said/'It is Urizen'" (I.3–6; E70).[115] Throughout Blake's work, the great creative spirit Los, like the Norse gods of Asgard, is always creating, building, constructing. But faced with the great void, he begins, just like the primeval forces in *Völuspá*, to divide chaos into times and places: "Times on times he divided, & measur'd/Space by space in his ninefold darkness". Like Thor, Los is defined by his wielding of a hammer, and the blows of his hammer denote not only the physical act of manufacture, like a blacksmith hammering in a forge, but also by imaginative extension, the hammer beats of poetic metre, as Los/Blake creates poetry as well as material objects.

---

[111]   Northrop Frye, *Fearful Symmetry* (Princeton: Princeton University Press, 1947; 4th printing 1974), p. 418.
[112]   Vincent Arthur De Luca, *Words of Eternity* (Princeton: Princeton University Press, 1991), p. 131.
[113]   De Luca's footnote to this remark makes the vague assertion that Blake "presumably" would not have had access to the poems themselves.
[114]   *William Blake, The Complete Poems*, ed. Alicia Ostriker (London: Penguin, 2004), p. 913.
[115]   References to Blake's work are taken from *The Complete Poetry and Prose of William Blake*, ed. David V. Erdman, revised edition (Berkeley: University of California Press, 2008).

In *The Book of Ahania*, Blake links the great void with the tree of mystery: "The Tree still grows over the Void/Enrooting itself all around". Elsewhere in Blake's work, this tree recalls Yggdrasill even more insistently, for there are secrets deep beneath its roots: in *The Four Zoas*, a lake "irrigates" its roots, like the well of wisdom beneath Yggdrasill, and there is a dark realm below its roots, "in the deeps beneath the roots of Mystery in darkest night" (FZ VIIb: 1; E360). There is no emphasis on the below-ground existence of the two great trees of Judeao-Christian mythology, the tree of Knowledge, and the cross on which Christ was crucified. Above ground, however, the parallels are striking, and even disturbing. For Blake, the Tree of Mystery is accursed, since Urizen "naild Fuzon's corse", "the corse of his first begotten" on its topmost stem. Urizen clearly acts like the Christian god here, and Blake makes this identification more explicit in *The Four Zoas*, in which the Lamb of God is "naild upon the tree of Mystery". But in Norse myth, Odin too may have sacrificed his own son, Baldr, and Odinic sacrifice—insofar as we may rely on Old Norse allusion to it—involved death on a gallows, or tree. A similar conflation of Old Norse and Christian ideas is attempted in the twentieth-century poetry of David Jones, whose work will feature in a subsequent chapter.

I want now to single out two specific forms in which Blake would have encountered Norse mythology: Thomas Gray's 'Norse Odes', and the work of Paul-Henri Mallet, translated and re-worked by Thomas Percy as *Northern Antiquities*. If we assume, with Omberg, that Blake could not read Latin, then "his acquaintance with northern mythology...was almost certainly made through *Northern Antiquities*".[116] But while this might be termed a primary source for Old Norse learning, it seems inconceivable that Blake would not have come across some of the poetic imitations and adaptations of Old Norse poetry which have formed the essential subject matter of this chapter. However, his engagement with Gray's work was of a wholly different order, for he was commissioned, in 1797, to illustrate Gray's *Poems*, and used pages from a disbound copy of the 1790 edition as the basis for his plates.[117] Blake must have absorbed in a concentrated way these poems based on Norse mythology; he must have internalized the texts in an unprecedentedly intense way. We can trace his understanding and interpretation of Gray's work first in the illustrations, and then in his own poetry. And throughout his poems, there are verbal echoes of Gray's

---

[116] Omberg, *Scandinavian Themes*, p. 126. See also Whittaker's note on the verbal correspondences between *Jerusalem* and *Northern Antiquities* (Jason Whittaker, *William Blake and the Myths of Britain* (Basingstoke: Macmillan, 1999), p. 28).
[117] See David Bindman, *Blake as an Artist* (Oxford: Phaidon, 1977), p. 113.

'Norse Odes': red clouds, wheels of blood, cloudy terrors—and a fondness for Miltonic echoes which are also a feature of Gray's poetry.

Given the violent power and drama invested in Blake's illustrations to 'The Fatal Sisters', Blake's image of valkyries was evidently more of controlling destinies than of Mallet's heroic waitresses. Further, as Irene Tayler points out, Blake "almost always pictures the sisters as three, perhaps conflating them in his mind with the three Norns, or Fates".[118] It is, I think, striking that in the face of Gray's clear reference in the preface to the poem (Blake's plate 4) to twelve women, and the poem's mention of five valkyrie names, Blake nevertheless repeatedly pictures three women. It may be that the poem's new title, 'The Fatal Sisters', suggested the three classical Fates to Blake, but elsewhere in Old Norse, three Norns are figured as creating or determining the fates of human beings and, indeed, of the gods themselves. According to the Old Norse poem *Völuspá*, for instance, three maidens, "deep in knowledge...laid down laws,/they chose out lives/for mankind's children,/men's destinies".[119] These three Norns are sometimes confused with the valkyries, so Blake may well have known other sources which fed his imaginings of these supernatural women.

Blake's debt to 'The Fatal Sisters' has been carefully documented by Paul Miner[120] and Morton Paley.[121] As Paley notes, in Blake's work after 1797, "the imagery of weaving suddenly assumed a major importance".[122] Weaving is identified in Blake's work with the production or controlling of destiny, and Enitharmon's primary creative process—in tandem with the hammering of Los—is her weaving. She weaves spectres in *The Four Zoas* (including the spectre of Tharmas).[123] In *Milton*, she is "weaving the Web of Life" (M6.28; E100). And this weaving/creation is invariably accompanied by song, "lulling cadences" (M6.6; E99). We may remember that Gray's Fatal Sisters are also singing, though their song is very far from a lullaby. The dark side of weaving (in its own way, textual/textural

---

[118] Irene Tayler, *Blake's Illustrations to the Poems of Gray* (Princeton: Princeton University Press, 1971), p. 111. Tayler suggests that the plate illustrating the beginning of the poem (plate 5) may show more than three figures, but I am inclined to disagree.

[119] *Völuspá*, st. 20, in Dronke, *The Poetic Edda*, vol. II, p. 12.

[120] Paul Miner, "Two Notes on Sources", *The Bulletin of the New York Public Library* LXII (1958), pp. 203–7.

[121] Morton Paley, 'The Figure of the Garment in *The Four Zoas, Milton*, and *Jerusalem*', in Stuart Curran and Joseph Wittreich (eds.), *Blake's Sublime Allegory* (Madison, WI, and London: University of Wisconsin Press, 1973), pp. 119–39.

[122] Paley, 'The Figure of the Garment', p. 121. Paley also notes that Blake does not use the word "loom" before *The Four Zoas*.

[123] For instance, FZ VIII: 51–3 (E372) and FZ VIII: 182–5 (E376); see Paley, 'The Figure of the Garment', p. 127. Enitharmon and Los are, repeatedly, twin creators: "Enitharmons looms and Los's forges" (FZ VIII: 200 (E376).

production, like Los's hammer beats) is represented too in Blake's poetry. In the same poem, Religion is imagined as a detrimental veil over the truth, with its "direful Web". However, the dominant association of weaving in Blake's work is with war, and often recalls Gray's Fatal Sisters. In *Milton*, for instance, the sisters of Tirzah recall the bloody valkyries. As they "weave the black Woof of Death" (M29[31].56; E128),

> The stamping feet of Zelophehads Daughters are covered with Human gore
> Upon the treddles of the Loom, they sing to the winged shuttle.
>   (M29[31].58–9; E128)

In *Jerusalem*, Cambel and Gwendolen "wove webs of war" (J7.44; E150), a precise echo of the refrain in 'The Fatal Sisters', "Weave the crimson web of war", and similarly, the "flaming treddles" of Ragan's loom "drop with crimson gore", as too do Vala's shuttles. The blood is apparently inexhaustible:

> Red run the streams of Albion: Thames is drunk with blood:
> As Gwendolen cast the shuttle of war; as Cambel returnd the beam.
> The Humber & the Severn: are drunk with the blood of the slain.
>   (J66.61–3; E219)

Perhaps the clearest allusions to Old Norse occur when Blake imagines the weaving, or its product, the web, with its many negative connotations in his work, being spun from the bowels of the weavers, a disturbing variation on the "texture" which is "of human entrails made" in Gray:

> The Daughters of Enitharmon weave the ovarium & the integument
> In soft silk drawn from their own bowels in lascivious delight
> With songs of sweetest cadence. (FZ VIII: 209–11; E376)

Tirzah and her sisters sit within a monstrous 'Polypus', "Spinning it from their bowels with songs of amorous delight" (M34 [38].28; E134). In the work known as 'The Circle of Life' or 'The Arlington Court Picture',[124] S. Foster Damon identifies the figure at the foot of the picture, holding "a phallic hank of rope, the line of material life, which the Three Fates... grasp", as Tharmas.[125] One of these fates is about to cut the rope; it's not clear whether Tharmas is the spinner or the spun. But there is one final, strange connexion to be made with Old Norse before we move on. The threads on the fatal sisters' hideous loom are made, as we have seen, out of men's intestines. It seems unlikely that Gray knew much Old Norse, and still less likely that Blake had access to the original, as quoted in

---

[124] S. Foster Damon, *A Blake Dictionary* (London: Thames and Hudson, 1973), plate IV. See also Martin Butlin, *William Blake* (London: Tate Gallery, 1978), p. 142 (plate 307).
[125] Damon, *A Blake Dictionary*, pp. 400–1 (entry under "Tharmas").

Bartholin and Torfaeus. But it is a curious coincidence that the Old Norse word used for intestines in its plural form is *parmar*, almost the same word as Blake's Tharmas.[126]

What could *Northern Antiquities* tell Blake about the sibyl, the great female voice of authority in Old Norse? Describing the Germanic culture of ancient Denmark, Mallet quotes Tacitus as his authority for the respect with which this voice was treated: "The Germans suppose some divine and prophetic quality resident in their women, and are careful neither to disregard their admonitions, nor to neglect their answers".[127] This follows Mallet's (somewhat comic) contention that "Nothing was formerly more common in the North than to meet with women who delivered oracular informations".[128] Mallet's brief summary of the Old Norse poem *Völuspá* is striking:

> The Prophetess having imposed silence on all intellectual beings, declares, that she is going to reveal the decrees of the Father of Nature, the actions and operations of the Gods, which no person ever knew before herself. She then begins with a description of the chaos; and proceeds to the formation of the world, and of that of its various species of inhabitants, Giants, Men and Dwarfs. She then explains the employment of the Fairies or Destinies; the functions of the Gods, their most remarkable adventures, their quarrels with Loke, and the vengeance that ensued. At last, she concludes with a long description of the final state of the universe, its dissolation and conflagration: the battle of the inferior Deities and the Evil Beings: the restoration of the world; the happy lot of the good, and the punishment of the wicked.[129]

This is massive intellectual authority: wisdom unparalleled in its range and profundity. This female voice has absolute command of the sum of human—and, even more significantly, divine—knowledge. As we have seen, Gray's poem 'The Descent of Odin' also features an Old Norse prophetess, or *völva*, whom the pre-eminent god Odin has to consult about the fate of his own son Baldr, pleading with her to yield up her transcendent knowledge of the future.[130] Gray shows Odin conjuring up a "prophetic maid", but when she angrily realizes his hitherto concealed identity, he slanders her in turn, denying her virginal status:

---

[126] Bartholin, *Antiquitatum Danicarum*, p. 617.
[127] Percy, *Northern Antiquities*, vol. I, p. 317.
[128] Percy, *Northern Antiquities*, vol. I, pp. 316–7.
[129] Percy, *Northern Antiquities*, vol. II, p. 204.
[130] Margaret Clunies Ross notes that both 'The Descent of Odin' and 'The Fatal Sisters' feature what she calls "vatic" speech by female figures, and claims it was Mallet's remarks about Germanic prophetesses which led to "eighteenth-century translators' fondness for vatic poetry either delivered by female speakers or verses in which they are shown playing a prominent part" (Clunies Ross, *The Norse Muse*, p. 46).

No boding Maid of skill divine
Art thou, nor Prophetess of good;
But Mother of the giant-brood! (84–6)

Blake's illustration of the first appearance of the sibyl shows a stern and sorrowful mature woman, face heavily lined, and lips parted, about to speak—a stark contrast to the blank, unlined faces of his Fatal Sisters. They are completely distinct from the post-sexual prophetesses figured in *The Book of Los* and, most importantly, *Vala, or the Four Zoas*, which are, as we shall see, plainly derived from the Old Norse *völva*.

The Book of Los opens with "Eno, the aged mother, a monumental figure who has been

> Since the day of thunders in old time.. .
> Sitting beneath the eternal Oak. (BL3.3–4; E90)

Unlike the sibyl, who is associated with the great ash tree Yggdrasill, the Old Norse World Tree, Eno is "sitting beneath the eternal oak", apparently a druidic association.[131] But everything else about Eno—the chariot she guides, the tree which is associated with the shaking of the earth, and even the mention of thunder—is unmistakably Norse. In *Völuspá*, as quoted in Mallet, the shaking of the great ash tree presages the coming violent apocalypse, and throughout *Northern Antiquities* Thor is identified as the god of thunder, who rides a chariot. And like the sibyl in *Völuspá*, who can look back to a time before the world was created, Eno too commands an immeasurable span of time; she looks back eons,[132] to a golden age in "Times remote" (BL3.7; E90), before moving on, like her Old Norse counterpart, to a creation myth.

In *Northern Antiquities,* following Snorri's work, this creation myth is recounted, in prose, by a trinity of mysterious interlocutors whose Old Norse names are Hárr, Jafnhárr, and Þriði—their names translate as High, Just-as-High, and Third.[133] And their account is closely based on the poem *Völuspá*, the prophecy of the sibyl. To begin with, Percy's Har explains, "All was one vast abyss". Thridi takes over to describe a burning world,

---

[131] W. H. Stevenson (*Blake: The Complete Poems* (Harlow: Pearson, Longman, 2007) p. 285, n. 4) suggests that the oak may be understood as being distinct from the "pernicious trees of the druids", but then goes on to claim that "Eno speaks as a prophetic female bard". I cannot find any contemporary source which allows the possibility of female druids (see A. L. Owen, *The Famous Druids* (Oxford: Clarendon Press, 1962)).

[132] See Damon, *A Blake Dictionary*, p. 125, under *Eno.*

[133] It is worth noting that Blake introduces the figures Har and Heva in the book of Tiriel, and they figure throughout his work. Har is the regular anglicized version of Snorri's Hárr, "the High One"; Heva sounds like a version of the genitive form of this name, "Háva", as in the name of the poem *Hávamál*, "The Words of the High One".

"luminous, glowing", and Har and Jafnhar speak of a corresponding world of ice in which "many strata of congealed vapours were formed, one above another, in the vast abyss". Thridi concludes: "And as to that part of the abyss which lay between these two extremes; it was light and serene like the air in a calm. A breath of heat then spreading itself over the gelid vapours, they melted into drops; and of these drops were formed a man...This man was named YMIR...From him are descended all the families of the Giants".[134] There are suggestive echoes of this creation myth—so very unlike Genesis—in Chapter I of *The Book of Los*: the begetting of the giant race and the void between two great realms (E91) in which Los takes shape. Just as Eno resembles the Old Norse sibyl, so the creation myth which follows her exordium closely resembles the sibyl's vision.

A cancelled opening line to *The Four Zoas* once read "This is the dirge of Eno" (E819). But this was replaced by "The Song of the Aged Mother which shook the heavens with wrath" (FZ I: 1; E300)—clearly our female prophetess, and the third line, with its reference to "the day of Intellectual Battle" (FZ I: 3; E300), vividly recalls Mallet's sibyl who "imposed silence on all intellectual beings". A little further on, we are told that Urthona "his Emanations propagated" (FZ I: 18; E301); in *Northern Antiquities* too we are told that "from [the] supreme God were sprung (as it were emanations of his divinity) an infinite number of subaltern deities and genii".[135] Blake's conception of the universal man is also strongly suggestive of the fate of Ymir: in the Norse, the gods "dragged the body of Ymir into the middle of the abyss, and of it formed the earth. The water and the sea were composed of his blood; the mountains of his bones; the rocks of his teeth; and of his hollow bones, mingled with the blood that ran from his wounds, they made the vast ocean".[136]

But throughout the whole poem, whatever Blake's original intentions might have been, the female figure called Vala is portrayed not as a speaking authority, but as a character—an evil one—in the drama. It has still seemed axiomatic to some critics that, in name at least, Vala is derived from the Old Norse sibyl, or *völva*. But others have scorned this identification—for instance, Margoliouth, who notes tersely: "This is a mistake. The name Blake could have found in Mallet's *Northern Antiquities* (1770 ii 202) is not Vala but Vola".[137] However, it was standard practice amongst British writers to anglicize this form as "Vala". William Herbert, for instance, one of the first to translate Old Norse poetry into English

---

[134]   Percy, *Northern Antiquities* vol. II, pp. 8–15.
[135]   Percy, *Northern Antiquities,* vol I, p. 79.
[136]   See, for instance, E328, or FZVII: 283–6 (E 359), where veins are figured as rivers.
[137]   H. M. Margoliouth, *William Blake's* Vala (Oxford: Clarendon Press, 1956), p. xviii.

directly from the original (and not via Latin), calls his version of *Völuspá* 'The Song of Vala'.[138]

It is clear that, like *Völuspá*—the sibyl's prophecy itself—Blake's poem is an account of Creation and Apocalypse. And nowhere are Blake's debts to Old Norse myth more evident than in its final section, 'Night the Ninth, Being the Last Judgement' (E386).

Blake's 'Night the Ninth' opens with Los and his wife Enitharmon weeping over the body of Christ crucified, just as the Old Norse gods weep at the death of Baldr, the radiant young son of Odin, a son who, like Christ, was perhaps sacrificed by his own father in the hope of resurrection. In Old Norse, the death of Baldr is the final act before Ragnarök, the doom of the gods. The first cosmic loss in the ensuing cataclysm is the disappearance of sun and moon, just as in *The Four Zoas* Los's first action wrenches the sun and moon from the sky. And while in *The Four Zoas*

> With thunderous noise & dreadful shakings rocking to & fro
> The heavens are shaken & the Earth removed from its place
> The foundations of the Eternal hills discoverd (FZ IX: 15–17; E387),

so at Ragnarök, in Percy's translation, "the earth and the mountain shall be seen violently agitated; the trees torn up from the earth by the roots, the tottering hills to tumble headlong from their foundations";[139] similarly, Los is described as "cracking the heavens across"(FZ IX: 9; E386), just as in the Norse "the heaven shall cleave asunder".[140]

Of course, much of this imagery is echoed in Biblical sources, especially the Book of Revelation (in fact Percy's note in *Northern Antiquities* draws attention to the similarities, quoting at length from Revelation).[141] But the verbal correspondences with the text of *Northern Antiquities* are very close. There, the gods and the giant monsters engage in battle: the World Serpent bears down on Thor and all the time "the great ash Tree of Ydrasil is shaken"[142]—recalling "the serpent Orc" and "The tree of Mystery" (FZ IX: 69–70; E388). Further, we can see elsewhere in *The Four Zoas* a number of incidental Old Norse motifs. In 'Night the seventh', a battle is attended by the characteristic Old Norse beasts of battle: "swords rage where the Eagles/cry... the drunken Raven shall wander/All night among the wounded". This raven is even associated with a banner "clothd in blood" on the battlefield, and Blake continues: "I hear the northern

---

[138] See Chapter 3 of this work.
[139] Percy, *Northern Antiquities*, vol. II, p. 160.
[140] Percy, *Northern Antiquities*, vol. II, p. 161.
[141] Percy, *Northern Antiquities*, vol. II, pp. 176–7.
[142] Percy, *Northern Antiquities*, vol. II, p. 162.

drum/Awake, I hear the flappings of the folding banners/The dragons of the north put on their armour".

In both *The Four Zoas* and *Northern Antiquities* a new world is born from a great conflagration. Again, we must take account of parallels in Revelation (especially "And I saw a new heaven and a new earth", Rev.21:1). But the pastoral images of regeneration in Blake are clearly influenced by Mallet/Percy: compare

> The sun arises from his dewy bed & the fresh airs
> Play in his smiling beams, giving the seeds of life to grow (FZ
>   IX: 846–7; E407)

with

> There will arise out of the sea, another earth most lovely and delightful; covered it will be with verdure and pleasant fields; there grain shall spring forth and grow of itself, without cultivation,[143]

or

> And Man walks forth from the midst of the fires, and evil is all
>   consumd (FZ IX: 828; E406)

with

> While the fire devoured all things, two persons of the human
>   race...lay concealed...They feed on the dew.[144]

At the end of the poem, Blake's "spectre of prophecy", his "delusive phantom" (FZ IX: 851; E407), disappears. So too, at the end of the *Prose Edda*, as in Percy/Mallet: "Gangler heard a terrible noise all around him; he looked every way, but could discern nothing, except a vast, extended plain".[145] All, in the end, is immaterial discourse.

Blake's *Jerusalem* has been called "his monumental equivalent of Milton's *History of England*".[146] It is a mythic pre-history of England—Albion— with England as a new Holy Land, with the druids as Old Testament patriarchs, and the figure of Albion like a great giant, who falls like mankind, or an empire, becoming alienated from Jesus, and in need of reconciliation. Blake's Los –"a projection of [Blake's] character, desires and struggles as an artist"[147]—is trying to save Albion.

---

[143] Percy, *Northern Antiquities*, vol. II, p. 165.
[144] Percy, *Northern Antiquities*, vol. II, p. 166.
[145] Percy, *Northern Antiquities*, vol. II, p. 167.
[146] Blake, *Complete Poems*, ed. Ostriker, p. 993.
[147] Blake, *Complete Poems*, ed. Ostriker, p. 996.

In this mythical Albion, Blake's supernatural universe, populated by "Fairies & Genii & Nymphs & Gnomes", is not at all Scandinavian. Oddly, there is one explicitly Scandinavian reference—to the Wicker Man, a site of human sacrifice graphically illustrated in Aylett Sammes's extraordinary history of Britain. Blake seems here to conflate the Celtic, or druidic, and the Norse. But King Arthur is a druid, and there are no Vikings. Vala has been completely transformed from Norse sibyl to a malevolent emanation of Luvah, one of the four Zoas. She is still, however, associated with Germanic heathenism—according to Alicia Ostriker, she "takes vengeance on Albion by producing a Walpurgisnacht of superstition"[148] in which, according to Blake, "the Human Victims howl to the Moon and Thor and Friga", and "The Giants and the Witches and the Ghosts of Albion dance with Thor and Friga". Warriors still tend to turn to the pagan gods: "the Hearts of their Warriors glow hot before Thor and Friga". And the cosmography is still Nordic: "In the south remains a burning fire…in the North, a solid darkness". We may remember that at Ragnarök, Surtr comes from the south with his all-consuming fire.

In *Jerusalem*, Blake's concluding vision of a reconciled and united Albion, articulated by Los, is rapturous: "What do I see? The Briton Saxon Roman Norman amalgamating/In my Furnaces in One Nation the English". Vikings are not included. And the loom is transformed too, while retaining its essential qualities:

> Swift turn the silver spindles, & the golden weights play soft
> And lulling harmonies beneath the Looms, from Caithness in the north
> To Lizard-point and Dover in the south. (J83:69–71; E242)

But it cannot be coincidence that the original female weavers, according to Gray's introduction to 'The Fatal Sisters' and the original Old Norse context of their weaving song, made their mysterious appearance in Caithness. Although Blake air-brushes the Vikings from the history of Albion and gives them no place in his harmonious national melting pot, transformed traces of Old Norse myth nevertheless linger in his imagination, and show themselves in his work.

---

[148] Blake, *Complete Poems*, ed. Ostriker, p. 1021.

3

Parallel Romantics: The Alternative Norse-Influenced Tradition

The major influence on the knowledge and popularity of Old Norse myth in the second half of the eighteenth century was, as we have seen, the work of Mallet, Percy, and Gray, in three quite distinct kinds of text: Mallet's scholarly treatises, Percy's translations, and Gray's 'Norse Odes'. All three writers continued to inspire poets throughout the nineteenth century, and were often explicitly acknowledged or cited in footnotes and prefaces. But there were other milestones, perhaps most importantly the publication of the 1787 Copenhagen edition of the *Edda*, which made available Old Norse eddic poetry in the original, with facing Latin translations, and prompted fresh interest in Old Norse myth.[1] Following this, Amos Cottle published his notorious translation of the *Edda* in 1797,[2] followed in 1804 by William Herbert's *Select Icelandic Poetry*, which marked the high point of accurate and readable translations, by an English-language poet who worked for the first time with the original Icelandic.[3]

However, the canonical poets of the Romantic movement did not take up the baton. Old Norse myth remained on the very fringes of English literary culture. Robert Southey, appointed Poet Laureate in 1813 (on the recommendation of Walter Scott, who had refused the post), was much involved with Norse literature, as we shall see, but he never wrote the great Norse poem he had projected.[4] Coleridge planned to write an epic about the god Thor, but never did.[5] William Wordsworth was given a copy of

---

[1] Arnamagnæan Commission, *Edda Sæmundar hinns Fróda. Edda Rhythmica seu Antiquior, vulgo Sæmundina dicta* (Hafniæ: Sumtibus Legati Magnæani et Gyldendalii, 1787). Further volumes were published in 1818 and 1828.

[2] A. S. Cottle, *Icelandic Poetry, or The Edda of Saemund Translated into English Verse* (Bristol: N. Biggs, 1797).

[3] William Herbert, *Select Icelandic Poetry, Translated from the Originals, with Notes* (London: T. Reynolds, 1804).

[4] See Herbert G. Wright, 'Southey's Relations with Finland and Scandinavia', *Modern Language Review* 27:2 (1932), 149–67, and Farley, *Scandinavian Influences*, pp. 131–3.

[5] See Kathleen Coburn (ed.), *The Notebooks of Samuel Taylor Coleridge* (New York: Pantheon Books, 1957), vol. I, 1794–804, entry 170.

Cottle's *Icelandic Poetry,* but although polite about it, was not inspired.[6] Shelley famously called poets "the unacknowledged legislators of the world" but was not interested in Odin or the role of skalds and skaldic verse. And though, intriguingly, Byron composed a Spenserian romance with Child Harold as its (anti-)hero, at a time when there were several Norse-themed poems with titles such as 'Harold the Valiant' (William Mason), or 'Harold the Dauntless' (Walter Scott) which were inspired by the Old Norse poem translated by Percy as 'The Complaint of Harold', there is little trace of the North in Byron's poem, or in John Keats's poems or letters.

I want therefore now to go back to the work of poets who *were* inspired by the new eddic translations, and then move on to the dramatic poetry of those who continued older traditions of Norse-themed long romances, sometimes using classically derived conventions—not odes, but a strange hybrid of Greek models and Norse subject matter. All of these poets, though in very different ways, pressed their Norse learning into the service of narratives about the history of Britain, whether fantastic, legendary, or actual, though none approached the mythic visionary history of Blake's prophetic books.

The first volume of the Copenhagen *Edda* included a wider and fuller selection of the mythological poems of the *Edda,* although it did not at first include *Hávamál,* or more especially, *Völuspá*—"the most important poem of all the old Edda", according to one disappointed reviewer.[7] English translations were made by Amos Cottle and William Herbert, though their efforts have been very differently valued. Cottle's reputation as a bungling translator may well have been sealed by Herbert's own withering judgement on his work: that had Cottle claimed the poems as his own compositions, he "could scarce have been accused of plagiarism".[8] In fact, as we shall see, Cottle's translations were not as bad as all that, though Herbert's, together with his immensely learned and lengthy notes, certainly marked the highest point so far of scholarly translations, not least because for the first time, the translator, Herbert, with help, actually engaged with the Icelandic originals, not simply with Latin paraphrases of them.

We learn from Amos Cottle's brother Joseph that Amos originally translated the *Poetic Edda* into prose, and completed it in one long vacation

---

[6] For his response to Cottle's work, see Ernest de Selincourt and Chester L. Shaver (eds.), *The Letters of William and Dorothy Wordsworth* (Oxford: Clarendon Press, 1967), vol. I, 1787–805, p. 196, Letter 79.

[7] See Farley, *Scandinavian Influences,* pp. 106–8.

[8] Herbert, *Select Icelandic Poetry,* p. 46.

when Amos was studying at Cambridge, for "a young friend". It was on the advice of Robert Southey that this was redone as a verse translation— "in the free manner of Gray's 'Descent of Odin'".[9] Cottle's preface, largely derived from Percy's 'Translator's Preface' to *Northern Antiquities,* provides a good introduction to Old Norse myth, in spite of William Taylor's deprecation of it as superficial.[10] Cottle explains how, "when Rome had sunk into depraved slavery, the enthusiasm of a fierce superstition prevailed... The tenets of this superstition must be sought for in the Edda".[11] He draws a careful and clear distinction between Celtic and Germanic mythology and culture, contending that while the druids refused to commit their secrets to writing, "Odin and the Gothic Scalds or Poets were quite the reverse. No barbarous people were ever so addicted to writing", adducing runic inscriptions, the reverence for poetry, and the ascription of supernatural virtues to letters.[12] He offers salutary warnings about supposing all Germanic tribes to have had the same mythology and religion. However, he describes the death of Odin in sensational terms which do not come from Old Norse sources: "with the sharp point of a lance, he made in his body nine different wounds in the form of a circle, and when expiring he declared that he was going to Scythia, where he should become an immortal god".[13] In contrast to the shadowy origins of James Macpherson's Ossianic verse, Cottle provides a sober account of Saemund, the twelfth-century Icelandic scholar who was until relatively recent times supposed responsible for anthologizing the *Poetic Edda,* and traces the history of the manuscript since its discovery in 1639—material he found in the Copenhagen Edda. Finally, he adduces detailed parallels between Norse and Classical myth, equating Loki with Apollo, Odin with Adonis, Frigg with Venus, Thor with Jupiter, and Tyr with Mars, and confidently contradicts Verstegan, an authority on this subject for so long.

Cottle omits three poems from his *Edda.* Following the Copenhagen edition, he does not include *Völuspá* or *Hávamál.* And on his own account he dismisses *Sólarljóð,* a strange and difficult Old Norse vision of an apparently Christian afterlife, as being "filled with little else but

---

[9] Joseph Cottle, *Early Recollections, chiefly relating to the late Samuel Taylor Coleridge* (London: Longman, Rees and Co., 1837), vol. I, p. 110.

[10] In the Monthly Review for December 1798; see Farley, *Scandinavian Influences,* pp. 133–4.

[11] Cottle, *Icelandic Poetry,* p. iii.

[12] Cottle, *Icelandic Poetry,* pp. x–xi.

[13] Cottle, *Icelandic Poetry,* p. xvi. The nine wounds are taken from Sammes' chapter on Odin, an elaboration on the account of Odin's death in *Ynglinga saga,* ch. 9 (Sammes, *Britannia Antiqua Illustrata,* vol. I, p. 435).

the absurd superstitions of the Church of Rome".[14] But those poems he does include are perfectly serviceably translated, with relatively few inaccuracies.[15] Proper names are not very accurately reproduced, but the footnotes, taken mostly from Snorri's *Edda*, are informative and scholarly, and include many insightful and appreciative comments about the poems. From time to time, Cottle perceptively and plausibly interprets what the original poems leave unsaid, often anticipating the speculations of modern scholars.

However, Herbert was not the only one to pour scorn on Cottle's *Edda*. In the *Monthly Magazine* for 1798, William Taylor seems to pay tribute to Cottle, writing that his "Icelandic Poetry is by this time"—a bare year later—"in the hands of every lover of wild imagery and harmonious verse".[16] But for Taylor, such wide circulation is regrettable because Cottle's translation—which he disparages as merely "a rimed paraphrase"—"departs widely from the text". For this reason, he now offers "a less free translation of the first and most curious of these sagas [sic], which unfolds the Gothic cosmogony": a translation of *Vafþrúðnismál* (literally, the words—*mál*—of Vafþrúðnir, a learned giant whom Odin visits in his pursuit of wisdom). That Taylor calls his poem 'The Meal of Vafthruthni' anticipates the shortcomings of his translation.

Cottle calls his version 'The Song of Vafthrudnis';[17] he mistakes the genitive form of the giant's name—Vafþrúðnis—for the nominative—Vafþrúðnir—but at least translates the element *mál* properly. His rhymed octosyllabic couplets echo the swift rhythms of Gray's 'Norse Odes', and although the original poem is not rhymed, its insistent alliteration and repetitions are quite well conveyed by Cottle's fluent couplets. We can see the tripartite structure of the eddic metre *fornyrðislag* in a modern translation of the poem's repeated refrain:

> Much have I travelled, much have I tried,
> Much have I tested the powers.[18]

[14] Cottle, *Icelandic Poetry*, pp. xxix–xxx; *Sólarljóð*, ed. Carolyne Larrington and Peter Robinson in Margaret Clunies Ross (ed.), *Poetry on Christian Subjects, Part 1: The Twelfth and Thirteenth Centuries* (Turnhout: Brepols, 2007), pp. 287–357, and see C. Carlsen, 'Old Norse Visions of the Afterlife', D.Phil thesis (University of Oxford, 2012).
[15] But Herbert picked up on them; see Herbert, *Select Icelandic Poetry*, pp. 9–11, and Farley, *Scandinavian Influences*, p. 134.
[16] William Taylor, 'Original Poetry', Review of Cottle, *Icelandic Poetry*, in *The Monthly Magazine* (July–December 1798), vol. VI, pp. 451–5.
[17] Cottle, *Icelandic Poetry*, pp. 3–39.
[18] Andy Orchard (trans.), *The Elder Edda: A Book of Viking Lore* (London: Penguin, 2011), p. 40.

Cottle's translation echoes the characteristic repetition of the first two statements:

> Much have I seen, and much have known,
> And wise in ancient mist'ry grown.

But Taylor, with his statelier, unrhymed lines, produces a very different effect:

> Far I've wander'd, much sojourn'd,
> In the kingdoms of the earth.

The snappy urgency of the Old Norse—a quality which Gray has been praised for importing into English poetry after the excesses of Augustan politeness[19]—is lost in the soggy formal grandeur of Taylor's diction. The original Old Norse poem opens with a disarmingly casual conversation between Odin and Frigg: in a modern translation,

> Advise me now, Frigg, since I feel keen to go
> to visit Vafthrúdnir.[20]

Cottle begins with a similarly peremptory dialogue between Odin and Frigg:

> Valhalla's Queen! I pray thee say
> Which to Vafthrudnis' hall the way.[21]

But again Taylor is both wordier and slower paced:

> Friga, counsel thou thy lord,
> Whose unquiet bosom broods
> A journey to Vafthruni's [sic] hall.[22]

Taylor's failure to divide the poem into stanzas also decreases its velocity, especially since he dispenses with the steadily increasing enumeration of the questions which increases the tension of the original—and of Cottle's translation.

While Cottle's footnotes, derived largely from Snorri's *Edda*, are mostly learned and perceptive, by turns informative and interpretative, Taylor continually contradicts his sources, and brings his often eccentric opinions to both footnotes and text. Thus he always translates the Old Norse word for giant, *jötun*, as Jute, so that the giant Vafþrúðnir becomes "the crafty Jute". He is no respecter of the Danish editors: "The Danish interpreters

---

[19] C. H. Herford, *Norse Myth in English Poetry* (Manchester, 1919), pp. 10–14.
[20] Orchard, *The Elder Edda*, p. 39.
[21] Cottle, *Icelandic Poetry*, p. 3.
[22] Taylor, *Monthly Magazine*, p. 452.

should not always be followed in the use of the words *god* and *giant*", he asserts.[23] Instead of being represented as a giant, Vafþrúðnir becomes a king, addressed by Odin as "monarch", or "king of men". Taylor has done his own euhemerizing of a mythological frame, since his preface also identifies Odin as a legendary chieftain rather than a god.

Taylor's 'The Meal of Vafthruthni' is heavily influenced by Gray's 'Norse Odes' (the fatal sisters put in an inauthentic appearance, for instance, and Odin setting out for the giant's hall "rose with speed"). The word "Runic" is used three times in the first thirty lines or so, and difficult expressions in the original are carefully omitted, following Gray's practice. But most interesting is an extraordinary attempt to represent a disputed line in the original, when Odin answers Vafþrúðnir's question about Hrímfaxi, the horse which draws the night behind it. The Old Norse phrase "dregr/ nótt of nýt regin" is usually translated literally as "draws/night over the gifted [or useful] gods", and Cottle, himself departing somewhat from the Latin, has "o'er the sight/Of Gods, drags on the veil of night".[24] But Taylor is not happy; he complains that the line has been "misrendered by the Danish interpreter" and that a literal translation should be "(drags) night eke bliss showers"—apparently reading the Norse word for gods, *regin*, as its English cognate "rain". Taylor therefore translated "bears the night/ Fraught with showering joys of love". The *regin*/rain confusions occurs a number of times, most notably when the wise gods become, bafflingly, "showers of fruitage".[25]

Taylor's footnotes also creatively etymologize the mythological names in the poem. He explains the name of the gods' final battle field, Vígríðr, as "drunkenness" (in fact, it means "battle field"), and the name of the destructive fire giant Surtr is "funeral flame". This produces an allegory which "intimates that a loss of the faculties is the harbinger of death". Similarly, Taylor notes, the name of the giant Ymir signifies "chaos" (nowadays most scholars would relate it to the verb *ýma*, to groan; many giants have names which seem to allude to wordless utterances). The father of the moon is named Mundilfoeri in the poem; Taylor construes this as "gift-bestowing" and adduces an allegory which "describes beneficence as producing the sun and moon".[26] Later on in the poem, when Vafþrúðnir tells Odin about what will happen after the end of the world, Taylor allegorizes the surviving deities Vali and Víðarr as "apparently the gods of death

[23] Taylor, *Monthly Magazine*, p. 452.
[24] *Vafþrúðnismál*, st. 13–14, in Neckel and Kuhn, eds., *Edda*; Cottle, *Icelandic Poetry*, p. 8.
[25] Taylor, *Monthly Magazine*, p. 453.
[26] Taylor, *Monthly Magazine*, p. 453.

and sleep", and Móði and Magni are explained as "mould" and "nobody". Thus, concludes Taylor, the new reigns of these gods after Ragnarök "obviously describe the state of the departed".[27] In his preface, Taylor compares the *Poetic Edda* unfavourably with Snorri's *Prose Edda*—the poetry has "no adventures equally prodigious, no descriptions equally romantic [to] startle and reward the curiosity". But "in their stead occur definite allegories, which throw much light on the manner in which rude nations endeavour to account to themselves for the origin of things, and in which moral facts assume in their minds a mythic form".[28] Based on dubious etymologies, such allegorizing of myth seems risible, but the impulse anticipates the work of later Victorian, and indeed present-day, mythographers. Taylor's "Meal", in spite of its linguistic failings, represents a real engagement with the myth: in the original poem, the god Odin and a giant, Vafþrúðnir, engage in a wisdom contest, each trying to outdo the other in a question and answer contest to the death. It may be that Odin's repeated seeking after knowledge is an integral part of Old Norse myth: his need to hear a different version of the future from the one he already knows, that his son Baldr will die young, and the gods be destroyed at Ragnarök. On the other hand, this question and answer frame may be a vehicle invented by a poet to convey in time-honoured dialogue form a store of mythological lore. But Taylor has transformed the poem into something subtly different again: a dramatized encounter between two legendary figures who exchange mythic information which can be interpreted by modern—that is, late eighteenth-century—scholarship as a primitive but intelligent way of understanding the world and man's place in it. For Taylor, Old Norse poetry is not simply sensational, but is evidence of what would come to be known as "Old Thought".

Prefixed to Cottle's *Icelandic Poetry* was a remarkable poem by Robert Southey. Southey planned, but never wrote, a major poem on Norse themes.[29] However, amongst his earliest poems are 'The Race of Odin' and 'The Death of Odin', both published in 1795.[30] The former begins with a spirited account of the old Odin myth, with Pompey scattering the forces of Mithridates, and Odin leaving Asgard and swearing "never to quaff the sportive bowl" until he returns to wreak his vengeance on Rome.[31] Odin and his race are followed north by "genuine poesy, in freedom bright" and

---

[27] Taylor, *Monthly Magazine*, p. 455.
[28] Taylor, *Monthly Magazine*, p. 452.
[29] See Wright, 'Southey's Relations with Finland and Scandinavia', 149–67.
[30] Robert Southey and Robert Lovell, *Poems: Containing The Retrospect, Odes, Elegies, Sonnets, etc.* (Bath: R. Cruttwell, 1795), pp. 97–109.
[31] Southey, *Poems*, p. 98.

they all gain strength "nurtur'd by Scandinavia's hardy soil".[32] The son of Odin looks forward to a hero's afterlife, when he too shall quaff foaming ale from a foeman's skull, and welcomes his end: "Death is bliss—I rush to bleed". Southey continues with more examples of Old Norse heroism and poetic achievement, for example an account of the recitation of Egill Skalla-Grímsson's *Höfuðlausn* or 'Head-Ransom' (translated by Percy), and Ragnar Lothbrok's ever popular Death Song, represented tersely by Southey in two lines:

> "We fought with swords," the warrior cry'd,
> "We fought with swords," he said—he dy'd.[33]

The climax of the poem is the fall of Rome—"and lo, the world again is free!"

'The Death of Odin' is a similar conglomeration of familiar Norse motifs, as Odin, anxious to avoid "pale disease's slow-consuming power", informs the shade of Freyja (Southey's mistake for Frigg) that he will soon be joining her, killed by his own hand.[34] He tells all the other gods not to lament, and lifting up his "death-denouncing eyes" demands that Valhalla be opened for him, where he will live on to welcome warriors who die bravely, their corpses left behind to feast the eagle and the wolf, conveyed to him by valkyries, to feast themselves forever on the never-ending boar Serimner, and drink from Roman skulls. Warning against "Luxury's enerving snare"—the downfall of Rome—Odin "pierc'd his breast" and "rush'd to seize the seat of endless rest".[35]

These two poems are significant not as literary achievements—far from it—but as full-blown examples of the old-fashioned representation of what we might call "the Odin myth" at the end of the eighteenth century. But Southey's poem for Cottle, written not much later, when Southey was still only in his early twenties, is very different.

The poem begins with a pleasant description of a time spent by Southey at Cottle's home.[36] The scene is fetchingly pastoral: "mazy streams and tufted villages" in the distance, and in the foreground, a river edged with ferns which "seem'd to form/A little forest to the insect tribes". How thrilling, then, Southey reflects, that Amos's imagination should dwell on such very different scenes—"strange sublimity"; "Niflhil's nine worlds, and Surtur's fiery plain". Alluding to the "strange and savage faith" of the

[32] Southey, *Poems*, p. 99.
[33] Southey, *Poems*, p. 101.
[34] Southey, *Poems*, p. 103.
[35] Southey, *Poems*, p. 109.
[36] 'To A. S. Cottle, from Robert Southey', in Cottle, *Icelandic Poetry*, pp. xxxi–xlii.

Norse, who "laugh'd in death",[37] Southey is clearly basing his idea of Norse themes not on Cottle's actual translations, but on the widely accepted notion of what they constituted: essentially, still Ragnar Lothbrok and his snake-pit, and warriors quaffing mead from skulls.

Southey goes on to describe Norse poets—the Scalds—and attributes the wildness of their work to Scandinavian landscape: "pine-cover'd rocks,/ And mountain forests of eternal shade". William Phelps has suggested that one can trace the beginnings of the English Romantic movement in the travel writing of Gray, with his rapturous descriptions of untamed scenery;[38] here we see Southey linking Old Norse verse with similar settings, and making reference to picturesque views of Norwegian scenes "taken by Mr Charles Fox", and the work of Mary Wollstonecraft. Southey's landscape poetry is accomplished and readable, and he is particularly good at special effects in moonlight:

> Sweet to walk abroad at night
> When as the summer moon was high in heaven
> And shed a calm clear lustre, such as gave
> The encircling mountains to the eye, distinct,
> Disrobed of all their bright day-borrow'd hues,
> The rocks' huge shadows darker, the glen stream
> Sparkling along its course, and the cool air
> Fill'd with the firs' faint odour.[39]

This distinctly Wordsworthian subject and tone gives way suddenly to an appealing, down-to-earth voice: in fact, Southey says, attractive as these landscapes may be, he would rather imagine them from the comfort of his armchair, with a book of ancient poetry, than actually go off travelling. But he laments what he learns from these old poets: about the impulse to "humanize their God"—to be unsatisfied with the sheer beauty and richness of nature and to want to worship it as a deity. But this is not the strangest thing—which is, that religion should support bloody wars in the name of God. Southey maintains that Christian priests may "pour/Prayers of bloodier hate than ever rose/At Odin's altar". The poem ends with a denunciation of "these evil and tumultuous times" and invokes "the easy precepts of the Nazarene … The law of peace and love".[40]

Clearly there are many ideas jostling around in this remarkable and unconstrained poem. Of especial significance are the ideas which speak

[37] Southey, 'To A. S. Cottle', p. xxxiv.
[38] William Lyon Phelps, *The Beginnings of the English Romantic Movement* (Boston: Ginn and Company, 1893), pp. 166–70.
[39] Southey, 'To A. S. Cottle', p. xxxvii.
[40] Southey, 'To A. S. Cottle', p. xli.

of distinctly Romantic preoccupations: landscape, the imagination, the superiority of the beliefs of "our" ancestors, or of a simple faith, or just the appreciation of Nature herself, and reference to the turmoil of the wider world. There had been stirrings of all of these themes in the poetry in English considered in Chapter 2, perhaps chiefly because of Thomas Gray's remarkable precocity and even more remarkably dominant influence. The use of Norse myth involved the evocation of the wild and desolate northern landscapes believed to be its home, or the terrifying scenes of the imaginary spaces populated by its giants and witches. But the complacent inheritance of Liberty (from the Goths) is now gradually replaced by the realization that times are "tumultuous"—old certainties are no longer stable, and the place of poetry and poets in political action becomes increasingly important.

In spite of the new translations of mythological poems in the wake of the Copenhagen *Edda*, and Southey's distinctively Romantic reflections on ancient poetry, some poets continued in the old ways, and it is not clear that Old Norse myth was becoming any more familiar to the general reading public. For example, when, in 1790, Frank Sayers's *Dramatic Sketches of the Ancient Northern Mythology* was published, the reviews were grudging, and praised Sayers for taking on such a difficult subject rather than admiring his achievement.[41] Sayers himself, in the Preface to his work, complains that "Mr Gray is the only one among our more celebrated poets, who has chosen to notice the mythology of the Goths", and that "it is much to be lamented that scarcely any traces are to be discovered of the splendid and sublime religion of our Northern ancestors".[42] Leaving aside for the moment Sayers's automatic equation of mythology and religion, I want to concentrate on his assertion that Old Norse myth has been neglected (though as Farley notes, in the fourth edition of his work, published in 1807, Sayers revised this opinion).[43] Sayers concludes his preface by suggesting that it might have been advantageous to his readers had he prefixed a dissertation (as Sterling had done, rather impressively) but claiming that it would have needed "more time and labour to effect than I could conveniently bestow". Instead, Sayers appends a great number of footnotes to his work, many of which are inaccurate.

Dramatic Sketches comprises a masque, in two acts, 'The Descent of Frea', and two "tragedies", 'Moina' and 'Starno'; a fourth work, 'Oswald', was added to a later edition. The first of these clearly references Gray's 'Norse

---

[41] See Farley, *Scandinavian Influences*, pp. 122–5.

[42] F. Sayers, *Dramatic Sketches of the Ancient Northern Mythology* (London: J. Johnson, 1790), p. iii.

[43] Farley, *Scandinavian Influences*, p. 122.

Odes', and owes much to Gray, but the title itself announces a major departure from its source in Old Norse myth. Its subject is an episode in Old Norse myth different from but parallel to Gray's subject of Odin's descent to solicit a prophecy about Baldr's fate from a sibyl. Sayers's 'Descent' derives ultimately from the story of the descent of the god Heremod into the realms of the goddess Hel, to bargain with her about releasing Baldr, now dead, back to the gods in Asgard. But evidently for Sayers Heremod's attempted deliverance of the god Baldr from the realms of Hel was not sufficiently dramatic or sentimental. He had a better idea: according to his introduction, "Frea, the goddess of beauty, was peculiarly afflicted by the loss of her lover, and resolved to undertake a journey to the regions of death". In Old Norse sources, Baldr has a wife, Nanna; there are no references to Freyja (often spelled Frea in English sources) as his lover. Perhaps Sayers felt that he could adapt his sources with greater freedom than would have been the case had Old Norse myth been better known.

The masque opens with Baldr lamenting his fate in Hel's underworld, which is depicted as a Northern wasteland "where eternal Frost/Has built his icy throne". Baldr is imagined as sharing this space with the frost giants—"the giant-brood"—and a series of horrors. He is destined to "shudder at the death-owl's song,/And shrink aghast from speckled snakes that rear/Their venom'd jaws". The Valhalla from which he has been exiled has been transformed by Sayers into a luxurious paradise where "ambrosial eve with fragrant hand/Scatters her sweets", and where Baldr once trod "flowery paths,/Holding celestial converse" and where "Frea blooming as the orient day/Would blushing meet her Balder's steps retir'd" and gaze contentedly on his "godlike limbs".[44]

After a longish soliloquy lamenting his fate, Baldr is surprised by the arrival of Frea, whose perilous journey down to Hel—a descent which is the focus of the drama in Gray's Ode—is lightly passed over in her own account: "On Odin's winged steed I sped my course", she explains.[45] After a joyful embrace, Frea calls on Hela (the goddess Hel), who refuses to give up Baldr until "all the gods of nature lave/With briny tears [her] Balder's grave".[46] In the Norse, it will be remembered, Hel demands tears from all things in the world, alive or dead, which Snorri relates to the natural phenomenon of condensation, or the melting of frost, as all things seem to weep when they are brought from extreme cold into warmth.[47]

[44] Sayers, *Dramatic Sketches*, pp. 1–4.
[45] Sayers, *Dramatic Sketches*, p. 6.
[46] Sayers, *Dramatic Sketches*, p. 12.
[47] *Gylfaginning*, ch. 49, in Faulkes, *Edda*, p. 51.

Sayers's version allows a roll call of gods: Odin "drops the tear", and also his consort Hertha (Old Norse Jörðr, confusingly footnoted by Sayers as the goddess Herthus—actually Nerthus—described by Tacitus in his *Germania*[48]). Thor and Niord (Frea's father) follow suit, and so too does the fire-giant Surtr, an unexpected visitor to Valhalla, since he is the chief opponent of the gods at Ragnarök and the cause of the conflagration which is to be their doom. But Lok—Loki—refuses to weep, in spite of Frea's horror-packed imprecation:

> By the ghosts' eternal moan,
> By the murderer's dying groan,
> By the screech-owl's song of death,
> By the night-mare's baneful breath,
> By the famish'd eagle's scream,
> By the meteor's awful gleam,
> By the slaughter'd infant's blood,

and so on.[49] Lok is not deterred by this catalogue of ghastly items, nor even by Thor's "iron mace" (an interesting variant on the usual hammer) or Odin's golden spear. The masque ends with his triumphant, defiant refusal to weep Baldr out of Hel.

Sayers's 'Moina, a Tragedy in five acts' is quite different: it is set in the Viking age, "on the coast of Ireland, which the Northern nations were accustomed to plunder".[50] The heroine Moina has been abducted by Harold, and is living with him. Harold and his Viking warriors and poets are unfavourably contrasted with Moina's own Celtic people. Harold's pleasures are savage and martial: to slay, to conquer, to stab, to shed blood. But Moina's companion, a Nordic bard, explains that the Norse gods are just the same. A chorus of Norse bards prays to Odin that Harold shall be victorious in battle, and their prayer is stuffed with mythic references: Odin "from the spring of Mimer/Quaff[s] liquid lore divine" rides, like Gray's Odin, a "coal-black steed", and is even attended by "the Fatal Sisters".[51] Oddly, Moina, a Celtic princess, is described by the Norse bards as one specially favoured by Frea. Carril, her lover, having gained access to Moina in the disguise of an ancient holy man, fails to persuade her to escape with him—"tho' force compell'd me/To share the bed of Harold, whilst he breathes/I'm his alone"—but agrees on her suggestion to visit

[48] Sayers, *Dramatic Sketches*, p. 16.
[49] Sayers, *Dramatic Sketches*, pp. 23–4.
[50] Sayers, *Dramatic Sketches*, 'Moina', Introduction.
[51] Sayers, *Dramatic Sketches*, pp. 37–40.

"A prophetess deep skill'd in Runic lore".[52] And then comes the news that Harold has been killed in battle, and is en route to Valhalla.

The sibyl whom Carril visits is a fine creation, living in a "deep dark gulph" in a gloomy wood; she seizes him with "a dead cold hand" and addresses him "in a hoarse voice".[53] Evidently echoing the response of the sibyl in Gray's 'Descent of Odin' (and also, in its Norse sources), she angrily recognizes Carril, but he wins her over with his bravery, and she agrees to bring back to life with her spells a newly dead (indeed, still bleeding) corpse from Harold's last battle to give Carril the news which readers already know: that Harold is dead too. But this does not free Moina, for the Nordic bard informs her that in Norse culture, wives are buried alive with their husbands (Sayers's footnote here refers the reader to Mallet for the various citations of "this barbarous law" in Old Norse sources[54]).

Harold's funeral paves the way for a description of the delights of Valhalla, and the gloomier prospect of Ragnarök, the "most striking parts" of which Sayers attributes to Mallet.[55] By and large, Sayers presents an accurate account, and concludes by picturing Harold amongst the Odin's warriors, the *einherjar,* in the final battle. The whole masque is concluded when Moina (for whom Frea now drops a tear) lies dead and cold, and Carril, despairing, throws himself off a rock. Sayers's footnote explains that "the practice of suicide was neither unfrequent, nor dishonourable among the Northern nations".[56]

As the appearance of a chorus of bards suggests, Sayers wrote both 'Moina', and the third tragedy, 'Starno', "on the ancient Greek model", thus perpetuating the use of classical forms so evident in Gray's odes. But 'Starno' is given a British, and not Viking setting, so that Sayers was, as he explains, "obliged to desert the mythology of the Saxons for the institutions and ceremonies of the Druids", and even though he pronounces that "the variety and magnificence of the Gothic religion is by no means rivalled by the Celtic",[57] the complete absence of Old Norse allusions in 'Starno' makes it clear that Sayers could confidently distinguish the elements of the two mythologies. Later editions of *Dramatic Sketches* included 'Oswald' (a "monodrama"), in which Sayers depicts a "gothic chieftain" facing his demise: Oswald is dying of old age and sickness, so he stabs himself with his "friendly steel" in order to secure a place in Valhalla, and like Ragnar Lothbrok, dies joyfully, just like Southey's suicidal Odin.[58]

[52] Sayers, *Dramatic Sketches*, p. 54.
[53] Sayers, *Dramatic Sketches*, p. 60.
[54] Sayers, *Dramatic Sketches*, p. 64.
[55] Sayers, *Dramatic Sketches*, p. 69.
[56] Sayers, *Dramatic Sketches*, p. 79.
[57] Sayers, *Dramatic Sketches*, 'Starno', Introduction.
[58] 'Oswald', in F. Sayers, *Poems* (London: J. Johnson, 1792), pp. 105–10.

Very shortly before Sayers's *Dramatic Sketches*, Richard Hole published his Arthurian epic, *Arthur, or, the Northern Enchantment*, a long poem in seven books which evidences all the now familiar attractions of a blend of history, patriotism, magic, chivalry, and Gothic horrors. *Arthur* is a story based loosely on Arthurian legend, like Dryden's *King Arthur*, or Blackmore's "absurd epic" *Prince Arthur*, written a century earlier. References to Norse myth again appear as the sensational beliefs of a savage enemy. Hole's representations of what he calls "the characteristic features of the Northern nations at the time when the action of the poem is supposed to have taken place" are carefully justified in the preface and footnotes.[59] He draws on the current theory that chivalry and romance originated in the North, and discusses at some length his depiction of "the Weird Sisters", tracing a development from the Old Norse Norns to the witches in Shakespeare's *Macbeth,* and arguing for cultural exchange and the influence of Christianity to explain it.[60] Hole regularly cites Mallet, and sometimes even goes back to Olaus Magnus. It is in itself significant that Hole felt that his Norse references still required footnoting; indeed, it seems that there was no limit to the amount of help a reader might need, and Hole very often footnotes his footnotes.

Arthur opens on the west coast of Scotland, with an encounter between Ivar,[61] son of the chieftain of the Western Isles, and Arthur himself, who has been shipwrecked there. Merlin appears, and fills in the romantic backstory: wicked Hengist has designs on Merlin's daughter Imogen, whom Arthur loves. The kingdom of Britain, moreover, faces a double threat: in a surprising verbal echo of much earlier texts, we hear that both Norwegians and Danes (Hole has smoothly conflated the Saxons who opposed Arthur's Britons with the Vikings who raided—ironically—Anglo-Saxon England centuries later) are on the attack, and that the North "had pour'd her iron swarms/On Britain's coast",[62] just as Goths swarmed out of the Northern hive in so many earlier texts. The Weird Sisters appear throughout the story of *Arthur* as forces responsible for the fates of all the characters, and a terrifying witch, Urda, also makes several appearances, often in a shape-shifted disguise, and once even as Odin himself.

Arthur sets off to regain his kingdom, helped by a series of magic aids, such as a white-plumed helmet with a dragon crest which appears beside

---

[59] Richard Hole, *Arthur, or The Northern Enchantment: A Poetical Romance, in Seven Books* (Dublin: Zachariah Jackson, 1790), p. xiii.

[60] Hole, *Arthur*, pp. xii-xvi.

[61] This is an unexpected name for a Scottish ally of Arthur's, since it is the name of the notorious Viking who according to legend murdered and mutilated St Edmund of East Anglia.

[62] Hole, *Arthur*, Book II, p. 35.

him when he wakes one morning: this is reminiscent of Horace Walpole's much-mocked magical helmet with its gently waving plume in *The Castle of Otranto*. He needs all the help he can get: a shepherd tries to dissuade him from his path (ostensibly warning him of dangers ahead, rather as Gawain is warned by his malevolent guide in *Sir Gawain and the Green Knight*[63]); when Arthur scorns flight, the shepherd disappears and Urda takes his place, with "terrific cries/(Like famish'd wolves contending o'er the slain,/Or wintry blasts that howl along the main)".[64] She is Hengist's protector, and vows that Arthur will never overcome him. But Arthur is not deterred, and makes his way into Hengist's formidable castle.

Hengist is magnificently attired, and wears a helmet with a raven on it, its beak "distain'd with blood"; it is "Omen of death and havock". This prompts Hole to a long and extremely learned and wide-ranging footnote about the significance of ravens in very many cultures, not only Norse.[65] Arthur overcomes his extraordinary opponent, but Urda spirits Hengist away before he can be killed, and indeed the whole castle suddenly dissolves from sight, much as Utgarða-Loki's castle vanishes in Snorri's *Gylfaginning*—but unlike Stonehenge, Hole suddenly remarks, which still stands, and still bears Hengist's name.[66]

In Book Four, the scene shifts to a castle in Carlisle, where the Danish chief Valdemar, now also in contention with Hacon of Norway, whose realm includes "distant Thule", is feasting with his warriors. Odin makes a dramatic appearance, castigating the idleness and luxury of the castle, and urging war, reminding them that otherwise they will never gain a place in Valhalla (and thus prompting another long footnote from Hole).[67] Hacon will not join forces with Valdemar, and declares that he feels no obligation to do what Odin tells him. Hole here cites Bartholin about the religious independence of the Goths.[68] Their actual religion, as depicted by Hole, is vague but sinister. They perform "barbarous rites" before altars, and, inevitably, chant "Runic rhyme"—directed, as they suppose, to Odin, "Dread god of battle!", but in fact, Odin is no more than a "vain shadow", and Urda is instead the controlling spirit.

Book Five continues with more fierce battles, warriors urged on by poets promising Valhalla and "Hydromel divine", whilst warning of the torments of Hel for those who do not die bravely. Fearing that their hero

---

[63]   *Sir Gawain and the Green Knight*, ed. J. R. R. Tolkien and E. V. Gordon, rev. Norman Davis (Oxford: Clarendon Press, 1967), ll. 2087–159.

[64]   Hole, *Arthur*, Book III, p. 60.

[65]   Hole, *Arthur*, Book III, p. 62.

[66]   Hole, *Arthur*, Book III, p. 69.

[67]   Hole, *Arthur*, Book IV, pp. 93–5.

[68]   Hole, *Arthur*, Book IV, pp. 96–7.

Valdemar will be struck down by Arthur, the "sisters dire" cause his horse to bolt and carry him to safety—though one may perhaps wonder why they did not leave him to certain death and thus glory in Valhalla. He himself is mortified by this removal, and begs his comrades to explain to his lover Thora that he did not flee willingly. Here we find ourselves once more in the realm of the death-defying warriors of Percy's translations: Thora is the name of Ragnar's lover in the Death Song. And as one might expect, Hacon later "grimly smiles and dies". Hole's original contribution to this well-worn theme is a surprising one: he notes a similarity between Bartholin's accounts of Norse bravery in the face of death with "the ferocious contempt with which the North-American Indians display at its approach" and points out that Ragnar's Death Song "greatly resembles the death-song of the Canadian savage". He even proposes that this may have come about after the Norse voyagers to Vinland came into contact with North American native culture, but draws back from what he concedes may be "too hazardous a conjecture".[69]

Hole's epic draws on material which had been often used in English poetry over the course of the whole century, but his evident command of his sources—not to mention his willingness to speculate, and formulate theories—does mark him out from his predecessors. Perhaps most notable is his Shakespearian transformation of the Norns—Hole's "dire sisters", whose names are still a little mangled (Urda, Valdandi, and Skulda)—into the Weird Sisters, who "dimly fate's mysterious volumes scan"[70] but in their rituals perform a Shakespearian "deed without a name".[71] The influence of Gray's 'Fatal Sisters' is very clear: the weaving metaphor carried over into English from *Darraðarljóð* dominates their presentation. From the beginning of the epic, the Weird Sisters have "weav'd, with artful malice to impede/What heaven's eternal wisdom has decreed/Round Imogen and Arthur",[72] and control the fate of Hengist too: Urda "weav'd in fate's mysterious loom/The web of Hengist's life".[73] Perhaps this blend of Norse and Shakespearian allusion is Hole's most significant debt to Gray.

Arthur ends happily; Arthur and Imogen are reunited, ironically through the agency of the Weird Sisters. Curiously, Arthur, triumphant, is compared to the god Thor, as he appears at the humble dwelling of a peasant and his wife and children—another echo of the story of Thor in Snorri's *Gylfaginning*: "Not mighty Thor, in Runic rhymes renown'd",

---

[69] Hole, *Arthur*, Book VI, pp. 163–5.
[70] Hole, *Arthur*, Book II, p. 40.
[71] Hole, *Arthur*, Book VI, p. 141.
[72] Hole, *Arthur*, Book II, p. 40.
[73] Hole, *Arthur*, Book VI, p. 142.

freshly returned to Odin's Valhalla from giant-killing in the "realms of frost", cut a more majestic figure than Arthur.[74] Hole's use of Norse motifs thus goes beyond the characterization of the "Gothic" characters. In fact, the whole epic is a tissue of Norse references, whether Hole's subject is Arthur and his Britons, or the Norse warriors he is depicting. Although Hole's focus is still the death-defying warrior theme made popular by Percy's *Five Pieces*, effectively intermingled with the magic and chivalry of Gothic romance, he still incorporates a good deal of mythological mate-rial—even if mostly in the form of learned footnotes.

Thomas Love Peacock's dramatic poem 'Fiolfar, King of Norway', pub-lished in 1806, is a similar but even more fantastic tale set in Scotland, in which the heroine Nitalpha is abducted by "Lochlin's proud monarch, the bold Yrrodore", but is rescued by the Norse hero Fiolfar.[75] Again, refer-ences to Norse myth are plentiful and they are not limited to the cultural colouring of the Norse characters, but permeate the narrative voice too: the poem opens at night, when "The steeds of DELLINGER had hasten'd to rest"—a reference to *Vafþrúðnismál*[76]—and Hrimfax "shook the thick dews from his grey-flowing mane".[77] The hero Fiolfar calls on his Norse gods, lamenting the mysterious disappearance of his beloved Nitalpha, and a Voice breaks in to his solitary reflections, with "accents portentous and dread,/Like the mystical tones of the ghosts of the dead.../As the thunder resounds in the vaults of the tomb": this "sable-clad form" tells Fiolfar about Nitalpha's fate, and urges him to reclaim her from Yrrodore. Fiolfar swears a vengeance which will "burst, in a death-rolling flood,/And deluge thy altars, Valfander, with blood!".[78] Valfander seems to be a ver-sion of one of Odin's names—Valföðr, "father of the slain"—but otherwise the Norse references are swamped by a more general Gothic horror.

Fiolfar's poets are not Norse skalds, but "harp-bearing bards", and they process to the Ossianic stone of Loda—the Odin stone. But their singing ascends to Valhalla, as they invoke Odin and Thor for success in battle, and the raven and eagle put in an appearance as beasts of battle—the former, "on dark-flapping wing", evoking the raven banner described by earlier poets. The bards' chorus calls down from Valhalla the ghosts of dead warriors, and the coming battle is dramatically prefigured in a show of the aurora borealis, the Northern Lights: "Fantastical arrows and jav'lins were

---

[74] Hole, *Arthur,* Book VII, p. 170.
[75] 'Fiolfar, King of Norway', in Thomas Love Peacock, *Palmyra, and other poems* (London: T. Bensley, 1806), pp. 69–92.
[76] *Vafþrúðnismál,* st. 25, in Larrington, *The Poetic Edda,* p. 44, and see Faulkes, *Edda,* p. 14.
[77] Peacock, *Palmyra, and other poems,* p. 69.
[78] Peacock, *Palmyra, and other poems,* pp. 71–3.

hurl'd", "flashing and falling in mimic array" until the illuminated sky fades with another reference to the "blood-dropping banner" which seems to "expand its red folds to the death-breathing gale". Fiolfar eagerly antici-pates the battle; after all, he will either be victorious, or will die a hero, and "Hilda and Mista" will bear him to Valhalla.[79]

In the battle itself, valkyries "guided the death-blow, and singled the slain". Fiolfar, "Majestic as Balder, tremendous as Thor", overcomes Yrrodore, who is condemned to the regions of Hel, because although he too dies in battle, he is "base and guilty" in his abduction of Nitalpha, and must be forever "toss'd/Through Niflhil's nine worlds of unchangeable frost".[80] But Yrrodore's defeat does not automatically release Nitalpha, because Yrrodore has imprisoned her in a cavern surrounded by "Duergi"—presumably, an anglicization of the Old Norse plural noun *dvergir*—dwarves. Worse still, Nitalpha will remain their captive until Fiolfar himself is dead, at which time Nitalpha will awake from her magic sleep and grieve for him for the rest of her life. Yrrodore dies, destined, according to Peacock, to wander around Hel's realms until Ragnarök, when

> the last final twilight on earth shall descend,
> When Fenris and Lok, by all beings accurst,
> Their long-galling chains shall indignantly burst,
> When the trump of Heimdaller the signal shall peal
> Of the evils Creation is destin'd to feel,
> And Surtur shall scatter his ruin-fraught fire,
> And earth, air and ocean, burn, sink, and expire![81]

But there is a happy ending. The sable-clad form appears again to Fiolfar, now naming itself as "Nerimnher"—a curious variant on the name of the everlasting roast boar in Valhalla, anglicized as Serimner—and identifying itself as a messenger from Odin. Nerimnher has a spell which will over-come Nitalpha's dwarfish guards, and moreover, her virtue has remained intact, since Yrrodore dared not "By force to obtain what affection denied". The spell itself is packed with mythological allusion. Nerimnher drives away the dwarves "By the hall of Valhalla, where heroes repose,/ And drink beer and mead from the skulls of their foes".[82] He invokes Thor, Freyer and the valkyries—"twelve giant-sisters, the rulers of war"—their number following Gray. And with his reference to "the unreveal'd accents, in secret express'd/Of old by Valfander to Balder address'd"[83] he alludes

[79] Peacock, *Palmyra, and other poems*, pp. 74–7.
[80] Peacock, *Palmyra, and other poems*, p. 79.
[81] Peacock, *Palmyra, and other poems*, p. 81.
[82] Peacock, *Palmyra, and other poems*, p. 85.
[83] Peacock, *Palmyra, and other poems*, p. 85.

to the deal-breaking question Odin poses to the giant Vafþrúðnir in their wisdom contest: what did Odin whisper to his son Baldr on his funeral pyre? With concluding references to Hela and Surtr, the dwarves flee and Fiolfar and Nitalpha are reunited.

Peacock appends some notes to his poem, explaining that although the basics of Old Norse myth will be familiar enough "to the readers of English poetry", what he calls "the minutiae of the Gothic mythology" may not be—a revealing observation about the progress of Old Norse knowledge.[84] Peacock's notes are not wholly reliable. Baldr is said to drive the chariot of the sun, and that when he was killed by his brother Höðr, "his office was transferred to Dellinger"—a bold attempt to make sense of the plethora of names in Snorri and the mythological poems. But there is a good deal of Norse learning in the whole piece, and 'Fiolfar' is a spirited, if hectic, engagement with Norse myth on Peacock's part.

George Richards's play *Odin*, in his 1804 collection *Poems*—significantly subtitled "Dramatic Poems on the Model of the Greek Theatre"—takes place in an ostensibly historical setting: Odin's homeland in Asia, on the eve of his battle with the victorious Pompey, which leads to his migration north. In the dedicatory verse—to the Earl and Countess of Harcourt, in Oxfordshire—Richards describes his muse as local: Cherwell's lonely banks" at first inspire him.[85] But shortly, "She bade before my wondering eyes/The bleak Caucasian mountains rise/And Odin's pile funereal tower". Richards explains that his drama "is intended as an imitation of the manner of Æschylus", and hopes that this will account for the "severe simplicity" of the narrative, and the "supernatural cast of the actions, the characters, the sentiments and the imagery".[86] But Richards has taken what pains he could with authenticity: he has based the dialogue of his Greek chorus on what classical sources have to say about the women of ancient Germania, and in his depiction of Odin, "has been desirous of drawing, not the composed and dignified hero of ancient Rome, but the savage Chieftain, who lived in a state of society even less civilized than that in which Achilles was produced, and to whom fabulous historians have imputed a romantic wildness of character, and on many occasions even a phrensy of passion".[87] For Richards, Odin is a fully historical figure.

So if Odin is not a god, but a chieftain, to whom might he pray? Richards has a surprising answer: Odin's god is Woden. This allows for a complete separation of historical chieftain and mythological figure,

[84] Peacock, *Palmyra, and other poems*, p. 89.
[85] George Richards, *Poems* (Oxford: Oxford University Press, 1804), vol. I, pp. 5–7.
[86] Richards, *Poems*, vol. I, p. 12.
[87] Richards, *Poems*, vol. I, p. 13.

and also for plenty of Norse mythic reference, since what pertains in the work of most poets to Odin is simply transferred by Richards to Odin's god Woden. Thus *Odin* opens with a distinctly classical chorus invoking "Valhalla's mighty lord" to solicit help for the Asæ—Odin's people, the Æsir, or Norse gods in the original sources—in their forthcoming battle against the Romans. The Romans are sacrificing to their gods too, so the conflict not only pits pseudo-historical Asæ against the Romans, but also implicitly sets Norse myth against classical—a long-running rivalry in the history of Norse myth and English poetry. The plea of the chorus— "Let not the Roman gods/Bear down the whole submitting world before them"[88]—can almost be read as a coded statement of the literary struggle between the two.

A figure called Balder plays a major part in *Odin*, as Baldr does in Old Norse myth, but here he is simply another chieftain of the Asæ, who first appears to report that Odin has gone to consult a "prophetic priestess"— an oracle, in classical terms, but here clearly the Norse sibyl of Gray's 'Descent of Odin'. There are a number of echoes of Gray's poem: Odin rides a "coal-black steed", for instance. Höðr appears too, but again as just another general, marshalling the troops. The horrors of Ragnarök are represented as grim portents of defeat: along with a more conventional appearance of a comet, the "Deadliest of Loke's terrific brood" appear, sent "in wrath divine", followed by cliffs toppling down "in ruin" (another echo of Gray's Ragnarök diction) and then full Gothic horror: "dancing hand in hand with Death,/Moves many a rude and ghastly form!", attended by Blakean abstractions, Flight, Uproar, Agony, and finally, Despair.[89]

In place of Baldr and Höðr as a son for Odin, Richards unexpectedly introduces Morcar, the name of an actual Anglo-Saxon earl. Poor Morcar takes Baldr's place in a very particular way, since he is sacrificed (though to Thor, not Woden) in an attempt to secure victory. The sacrificial ritual is described in sensational detail culminating in Morcar's death, at which "Far burst in ample stream/The blood propitious"; this blood is sprinkled over the whole scene, and Morcar's body is hung on an ash tree (Richards borrowing here from Adam of Bremen's account of the sacrifices at Uppsala) to remain there "Till Loke shall burst his chain, and fire the world"—that is, until Ragnarök.[90]

Odin's account of his visit to the sibyl—here named as Rinda, in the Norse sources the giantess whom Odin seduced by magic in order to beget an avenger for the death of Baldr—is also packed with echoes of Gray's

[88] Richards, *Poems*, vol. I, p. 20.
[89] Richards, *Poems*, vol. I, pp. 28–30.
[90] Richards, *Poems*, vol. I, pp. 30–3.

Ode, but there is an effective twist to the plot: Rinda has prophesied that it will be a long time before "Valhalla's golden doors" will be opened to Odin, which he naturally takes as a prediction of victory—not, as we readers know, an allusion to the long exile in Scandinavia which is to come. Odin and his fellow-warrior Balder face the battle in "proud expectation" and there is a great deal of confident boasting and battle fervour. Interestingly, Odin calls for his poets to place themselves in a protected vantage point to be able to observe the course of the conflict—just, indeed, as Snorri's biography of St Óláfr depicts him placing his own skalds behind a defensive wall, like war correspondents observing and reporting on the action.[91] This detail, together with the unexpected appearance of the figure identified as Morcar, and, a little later, an Asæ chieftain called Triggueson, strongly suggests that Richards used a translation of Snorri's historical compilation *Heimskringla*—itself in fact the chief source for the origins of Odin as a deified leader—though he does not acknowledge this debt.[92]

Balder is killed in the ensuing battle. With his sword, "inscrib'd/With mystic characters of mighty power", and his shield, on which his "noblest feats are pictur'd", he expires in conventional ecstasy: "My days are past: I come,/ Woden, I come; rejoicing I shall meet thee;/Rejoicing die".[93] After this, Woden—"the high, the terrible, in clouds/Involv'd, and darkness"—deserts the Asæ. Having disdainfully refused to parley with the Romans, Odin prepares a "funereal pile" for himself and his horse Sleipnir, and steadies himself to fall on his sword. But a voice suddenly interrupts his funeral orations: Gondula, a valkyrie ("The god of battles is my lord"), directs him to head north, to "the land of winter, nurse of frost and snows", where he and the remaining Asæ, made strong by the harsh climate, will nurture liberty, so that in due course, revenge will return to Rome. With his sons Segdeg, Sigge, and Baldeg (taken from Snorri's genealogy of Odin[94]) Odin will establish a dynasty in Scandinavia, like "the sacred ash, that spreads/O'er the bright city of the gods her boughs".[95] It is now time for Gondula to get back to Valhalla, and she makes a memorably pithy farewell speech:

> My steeds, o'er yonder pines, await me,
> Veiled in a cloud. Remember me. Revere
> The gods. Love war. And glow with hate of Rome.[96]

[91] *Óláfs saga helga*, ch. 206, in Hollander, *Heimskringla*, pp. 496–7.
[92] The sacrifice of Morcar before the battle may have been suggested by Earl Hákon's sacrifice of his son for victory in Snorri's *Óláfs saga Tryggvasonar* (Hollander, *Heimskringla*, p. 185).
[93] Richards, *Poems*, vol. I, p. 64.
[94] Prologue, in Faulkes, *Edda*, p. 4.
[95] Richards, *Poems*, vol. I, p. 102.
[96] Richards, *Poems*, vol. I, p. 104.

The Chorus laments Odin's exile, but he remains triumphant in defeat:

> The warrior, born to liberty, admits
> No charm of soil: wherever he is free,
> There is his native land.[97]

Liberty is here represented not as a national, or political achievement, but as a virtue inherent in members of the Gothic races; it will travel with them wherever they go. Richards's work not only harks back to the time-honoured association of liberty with the Gothic tribes, but also picks up on theories of racial supremacy which were to become ever more influential.

The most thorough-going historicist treatment of Viking themes is Walter Scott's *Harold the Dauntless* (1817). Scott's knowledge of Old Norse literature and Viking age history was very considerable, and the library at his home in Abbotsford was stocked with a remarkable collection of scholarly work on Old Norse themes. And Scott's linguistic skills were impressive, too: the 1847 edition of *Northern Antiquities* included his abstract of the Old Norse *Eyrbyggja saga*.[98]

Walter Scott's historical verse romance could not be more different from George Richards's solemn, pompous, classically influenced *Odin*. He immediately and merrily introduces *Harold* as a piece which "well may serve to while an hour away" if one is very, very bored, and he archly claims not to care about its reception by critics.[99] The action is very precisely and authentically located in time and place: in the time of the generations following the Norse settlement of northern and eastern England, around the "broad lands on the Wear and the Tyne". The poem opens with a rollicking account of the mayhem caused by the old Danish Viking Count Witikind, who had raided and pillaged all over northern Europe until retiring to England. In old age, Witikind (the name is not Norwegian, or Icelandic, but is presumably designed to reflect more authentically its bearer's continental origins) repents of his Viking activities, and converts to Christianity, handing over his estates to the Church. His son, Harold the Dauntless, is appalled that a Viking who had once raided Christian shrines and melted down their silver as "bracelets for Freya and Thor",[100] and had devoted himself to Odin, god of battle, should become a Christian. Harold's curse on his father is that skalds should immortalize his shame.

[97] Richards, *Poems*, vol. I, p. 111.
[98] Percy, *Northern Antiquities*, ed. I. A. Blackwell (London: Henry G. Bohn, 1847), pp. 517–40.
[99] Walter Scott, *Harold the Dauntless: A Poem, in Six Cantos* (Edinburgh: James Ballantyne and Co., 1817), p. 6.
[100] Scott, *Harold*, Canto I, IX, p. 19.

There is a light-heartedness and inventiveness about Scott's allusions to Norse myth which is almost comic. Harold proudly boasts that he was brought up to warfare, "rocked in a buckler and fed from a blade".[101] The motifs of Ragnarök are the common parlance of the Norse characters: Harold's pageboy, Gunnar, complains about the terrible weather— there is thunder and lightning "As if Lok, the destroyer, had burst from his chain!".[102] Harold's devoted servant "Gunnar" is in fact Eivir, the daughter of his old nurse, a girl who has always loved him. Harold has an inkling that Gunnar is not what he seems, since he doubts the "boy's" capacity to "wade ankle-deep through foeman's blood".[103] The ferocity of the Viking has a comic book quality here.

No reader could doubt that the poem will end happily, as indeed it does. But there is a darker sub-plot. Harold's fancy is taken by a local girl, the daughter of an outlaw and a witch, who is already engaged to be married to Lord William, the local squire, and he plans to abduct her. With this comes a curious unleashing of Slavic mythological references, as the girl's mother, with the very unGermanic name of Jutta, prays and sacrifices to the god Zernebock (presumably the eastern European pagan deity Chernobog) who is said to be worshipped by "Estonian, Finn and Lett" on his "Pomeranian throne".[104] It seems that if Norse paganism is the cheerful domestic currency of the Norse characters, darker rituals must be attributed to more alien systems.

Scott is well able to employ the familiar clichés of Norse-inspired English works. Interestingly, such references—runic rhyme, quaffing mead from an enemy skull in Valhalla, and so on—are carefully set in the context of poetic practice within the narrative of *Harold*—as when Harold demands a song from Gunnar, or recalls the skalds of his grandfather's court. And when Gunnar obliges with a song, Scott gives him a version of Percy's translation of the Death Song:

> Hawk and osprey scream'd for joy
> O'er the beetling cliffs of Hoy,
> Crimson foam the beach o'erspread.[105]

But *Harold* also contains some interesting new details which Scott's Norse scholarship could provide. It was well known that court poets— the skalds—might praise the fame of their lords, but Gunnar's eulogy for

---

[101] Scott, *Harold,* Canto I, XI, p. 22.
[102] Scott, *Harold,* Canto I, XV, p. 27.
[103] Scott, *Harold,* Canto I, XVII, p. 31.
[104] Scott, *Harold,* Canto II, XVII, p. 66.
[105] Scott, *Harold,* Canto III, VI, p. 85; for similar stanzas in Percy's 'Dying Ode', see Clunies Ross, *The Old Norse Poetic Translations of Thomas Percy*, pp. 101–2.

Harold's grandfather does not please Harold himself, who points out that skalds also had a role as truth-tellers and even satirists:

> At Odin's board the bard sits high
> Whose harp ne'er stooped to flattery.[106]

However, and again a little comically, Harold does not like Gunnar's mild attempt at criticism either: "it is not thine/To judge the spirit of our line".[107]

Harold demands his father's lands back from the Church, and when the clerics inform him that the estate has been given to local supporters of the Church, Anthony Conyers, and Alberic Vere, Harold only laughs, and:

> A head and a hand on the altar he threw.
> Then shudder'd with terror both Canon and Monk,
> They knew the glazed eye and the countenance shrunk,
> And of Anthony Conyers the half-grizzled hair,
> And the scar on the hand of Sir Alberic Vere.[108]

The clerics behave badly, too; their discreditable response is to plan to poison him. Viking violence seems honest and open by comparison. But now the poem takes a strange turn. The Bishop of Jarrow has a better plan: Harold will be challenged—at a feast, naturally—to spend a night in a haunted castle, as described in the song of a minstrel. Harold cannot resist. But on his way there, like Peacock's Fiolfar and Richards's Odin, he is challenged by a Voice, a dark phantom which Gunnar cannot see, and which urges Harold to repent, as his father did. Harold is shaken, and when he happens across the bridal feast of Lord William and his betrothed, urged by Gunnar to show mercy, he refrains from killing the bridegroom; thus "Fierce Witikind's son made one step towards heaven".[109]

The horrors of the night in the castle, in which Harold sees a vision of Hecla, the mouth of hell, and is welcomed home by the god Zernobock, culminate in Harold's vision of his own father, desperately trying to save him from his fate, and revealing, though still obscurely, the secret of Gunnar's real identity. The climax of these visions is the appearance of Odin,

> His cloak the spoils of Polar bear:
> For plumy crest, a meteor shed
> Its gloomy radiance o'er his head.[110]

[106] Scott, *Harold*, Canto III, VII, p. 88.
[107] Scott, *Harold*, Canto III, VIII, p. 90.
[108] Scott, *Harold*, Canto IV, V, pp. 112–3.
[109] Scott, *Harold*, Canto V, XVI, p. 163.
[110] Scott, *Harold*, Canto VI, XIII, p. 189.

The vision is as massive as "when in stone/O'er Upsal's giant altar shown". This terrifying figure berates Harold for thinking of deserting him:

> Wilt thou then forfeit that high seat,
> Deserved by many a dauntless feat
> Among the heroes of thy line,
> Eric and fiery Thorarine?[111]

But Harold's last act of Viking violence is to attack Odin, and the phantom, revealed as a spirit sent by "a higher will"—the devil, one supposes—vanishes. Harold converts, and marries Eiver, so that, as Scott wittily concludes, "on the same morn he was christn'd and wed".[112]

Harold the Dauntless is an entertaining and readable poem, which in spite of its foray into the Gothic horror of a haunted castle offers in verse the equivalent of a historical novel, in which setting, characters, and central theme—the conversion to Christianity of Scandinavian settlers in immediately post-Viking-age England—are both entertainingly fictional and at the same time historically plausible. The plausibility, such as it is, arises from Scott's extensive Norse learning. But he ends *Harold* by mocking precisely the research his predecessors boasted of:

> Be cheer'd 'tis ended—and I will not borrow,
> To try thy patience more, one anecdote
> From Bartholine, or Perinskiold, or Snorro.
> Then pardon thou thy minstrel, who hath wrote
> A Tale six cantos long, yet scorn'd to add a note.[113]

A very much more solemn piece is the Rev. James Prowett's version of 'The Voluspa, or Speech of the Prophetess; Extracted from the remains of the Runic Mythology, as preserved by Olaus Wormius, Bartholinus and others' (1816).[114] As might be expected, there are gloomy caverns and a raven banner; and much of the traditional paraphernalia of the Gothic—a "horror brood" of monsters, a "pathless cheerless wild", and "hollow ey'd demons"—is used to conjure up Ragnarök. There are also a number of echoes of Gray. But Prowett's *Völuspá* takes a high moral tone which readily complements Christian dogma: of the Norse pantheon only Odin is named, and though he is footnoted as a "Supreme deity of the Goths and Celts"—an old confusion—Prowett notes further that *Völuspá* alludes to "a Being superior to Odin, who existed before the world", and ascribes

---

[111] Scott, *Harold*, Canto VI, XIV, p. 191.
[112] Scott, *Harold*, Canto VI, XIX, p. 199.
[113] Scott, *Harold*, p. 200.
[114] James Prowett, *The Voluspa, or Speech of the Prophetess, with other poems* (London: Payne and Foss, 1816).

the Norse apocalypse to "deeds of guilt" and "Crimes of more than mortal birth", explaining that it will come to pass on "the day by Heaven decreed". Prowett's novel depiction of Loki presiding over Hell "in adamantine chain" is clearly Miltonic, thus inviting comparison of Loki and Lucifer. Readers would have no difficulty in seeing Old Norse myth as a precursor of Christianity.

Sir William Drummond's long poem *Odin*—though not as long as it was apparently projected to be, since only the first four parts of eight were ever published, in 1817—follows quite closely the conventions of earlier Odin epics.[115] Although some reviewers were by now sceptical of the "Odin myth",[116] Drummond boldly identifies Odin as the deified son of Mithridates, Pharnaces, who vows to avenge his father's defeat by the detested Romans. He is directed by a "grisly spectre" to a "gloomy grot, exhaling vapours foul" where the Vola, the prophetess, resides.[117] The poem is packed with the standard motifs of what had come to be known as "Gothic" horror: a howling watchdog, ("conscious of disaster"), a croaking raven, and "at the midnight hour/The cock, unnatural, his clarion sounds".[118] Pharnaces, in a Dantean echo, is conducted by the Vola—"a Sibyl to the new Aeneas"—through the Old Norse mythic cosmos. Drummond's presentation is dramatic and inventive, with a wonderful Jötunheim all made of ice, a magnificent World Serpent, and the "hot whirlwinds" and "seas of molten ore" in Surtur's realm of fire. Pharnaces accepts a Faustian pact: the promise of victory over Rome, and deification, if he will worship Loki and his monstrous progeny. Back in the "real"—that is, pseudo-historical—world, war thus comes to Scandinavia, and Odin's troops again "quaff the blood of foes from brimming skulls" just as their eighteenth-century literary forebears did.[119] But as William Taylor notes in his review, Pharnaces is not a character with whom one can sympathize; in spite of its Miltonic grandeur and epic drama, *Odin* only intermittently engages the reader, and there are a number of implausible etymologies (for instance, the claim that the term "Vola", itself after all an anglicization of the Norse word *völva*, literally means "the frantic woman" as may be seen in the French word for one such: *la folle*). These etymological connections are rendered all the more unlikely by the persistent garbling of proper names,

[115] Sir William Drummond, *Odin: A Poem, in Eight Books and Two Parts* (London: Law and Co., 1817).
[116] See for instance William Taylor's review of Drummond's work in the *Monthly Review* (January 1819), 38–44; Taylor much preferred Sayers' 'Descent of Frea'.
[117] Drummond, *Odin*, p. 47.
[118] Drummond, *Odin*, p. 58.
[119] Drummond, *Odin*, p. 122.

most notably "Mignard" for the World Serpent. Drummond claims in his preface that Norse mythology is "now nearly forgotten".[120]

This chapter began with the translation work which was inspired by the publication of the Copenhagen edition of the *Edda* in 1787. Walter Scott was himself one of the reviewers who noted that the translator William Herbert's knowledge of Old Norse marked out his *Select Icelandic Poetry* as a completely new departure from publications whose authors did not know the originals in their original language. In his review, Scott is modest, even self-deprecating about his own skills, but clear about Herbert's expertise, and shrewd about its significance: "We do not pretend any great knowledge of the Norse; but we have so far 'traced the Runic rhyme,' as to be sensible how much more easy it is to give a just translation of that poetry into English than into Latin; and, consequently, how much is lost by the unnecessary intermediate transfusion".[121]

But Herbert did not confine himself to the purely scholarly, and in the preface to his 1815 poem 'Helga' he very carefully analyzes the difference between translation and free adaptation; describing his own experience, he writes:

> I was...forcibly struck with the poetical images which the manners and religion of the northern nations appeared to present; and, feeling that I was prevented from giving them full effect by the fidelity which I deemed necessary in the translation of writings which derived their principal interest from their antiquity and peculiarities, it occurred to me that, by undertaking an original poem of which the scene might be laid amongst the ancient Scandinavians, I should be able to illustrate their manners and religion, and superstitions, in a form that would be more pleasing to the reader, and to avail myself of a wide field for poetical composition, which had as yet been untouched by any writer except in a few short and unconnected translations.[122]

There are some surprising assumptions here. It seems that what struck Herbert about eddic poetry was not the poetic quality of the poems themselves, but their "poetical images"—that is, the mythology itself. And he regarded the translation of these poems as something to be done as faithfully as possible, because of their significance as historical survivals, yet his aim in undertaking "an original poem" seems to have been not to imitate the form and diction of Old Norse poetry originals—which is perhaps what might have been expected, given his direct, and probably unprecedented, engagement with the originals—but to use the poem as a means of producing what Herbert goes on to call "a faithful picture of the manners and superstitions of the period". Indeed, he continues, he has attempted to give the work

[120] Drummond, *Odin*, p. i.
[121] Scott, Review of Herbert, *Miscellaneous Poetry, The Edinburgh Review*, vol. IX (October 1806-January 1807), Article XV, pp. 211–23 (212).
[122] William Herbert, *Works* (London: H. G. Bohn, 1842), vol. I, p. 26.

"the colouring of poetry"—in order, presumably, to enhance its readability, although he explicitly draws the line at imitating "the rude wildness of Scaldic diction".[123]

But in spite of the superior standard of Herbert's Norse learning, the resulting poem, 'Helga', is unexpectedly retrograde, especially in its style and diction. Herbert confines himself to familiar clichés. The subject matter is based on events in the part of *Hervarar saga* adjacent to the verses in the saga which gave rise to the endlessly translated and re-translated versions of an old favourite, 'The Waking of Angantyr'. But Herbert tells his part of the story from the perspective of Hjalmar, Angantýr's opponent in the original Old Norse. The heroine of the poem, Helga, is the daughter of King Yngvi, and Hialmar is his champion, challenged by Angantyr who means to carry her off. Yngvi's hall is like the Valhalla English readers would be used to— Helga pours out the drink, like a valkyrie, and warriors duly "quaffed the mantling bowl", and "pour'd the wild notes of Runic rhyme".[124] Helga, like Odin, originally, or in Gray's 'Descent', or Sayers's Carril, travels to the gate of Hel to consult Vala, the sibyl of *Völuspá*, wanting to know what the outcome of a duel between Hialmar and Angantyr will be. Her journey explicitly references Gray's 'Descent of Odin'—in fact, in his notes to the poem, Herbert writes that he recognized that it was "rather dangerous" to describe "the dog of the infernal regions" after Gray had done it so well in what Herbert terms his "beautiful translation".[125] When Hialmar, doomed to die in spite of Helga's efforts, imagines the "Valkyriur" (note the borrowing of Gray's form of the plural in his notes to 'The Fatal Sisters') coming for him, their solemn form is clearly derived from their depiction in the poem *Hákonarmál*, which Percy translated as 'The Funeral Song of Hacon'.

On the other hand, the extent of less usual allusions to Norse myth in 'Helga' is very marked. For example, Helga prays to the goddess Freyja by the gems in her necklace—an allusion to the notorious Brísingamen—and when actually dying, Hialmar has a vision of Odin himself, and his two iconic birds Huginn and Muninn:

> Near him two ravens black as night,
> Memory and Observation hight.
> On never-tiring pinion borne
> The wonderous pair go forth at morn;
> Through boundless space each day they sail,
> At eve return to tell their tale,
> And whisper soft in Odin's ear
> The secrets of each rolling sphere.[126]

---

[123] The last word is printed as "fiction"—a typographical error, I think.
[124] 'Helga', Canto I, 35 and 38, in Herbert, *Works*, vol. I, pp. 27–142 (28).
[125] Herbert, *Works*, vol. I, pp. 128–9.
[126] Herbert, *Works*, vol. I, pp. 109–10, Canto VI, 2574–81.

Hialmar's dying vision is the occasion for a detailed description of the whole Norse pantheon which is not limited to the usual three or four deities. Along with Odin, Tyr, Thor, and Heimdallr, Hialmar sees, and Herbert includes and imaginatively elaborates, Iduna, "Queen of Youth", with her "fragrant fruit of loveliest hue" which "tasted makes the wrinkled brow/Again like polish'd ivory glow"—an allusion to the goddess Íðunn with her apples of immortal youth. Her spouse, according to Herbert, is Braga, god of poetry itself; Freyr and Freyia are both accurately enough spelt and properly identified as brother and sister; even Njörðr and the giantess Skaði—"his mountain bride"—whose union was doomed because he hated living in the mountains, and she could not abide the coast—feature amongst a number of gods only very barely alluded to in Norse sources. And Baldr is mentioned, but is not present; his death and translation to Hel must be understood to have taken place earlier in mythological time. This roll-call of the gods ends, unsurprisingly, with a brief account of Ragnarök, heralded by the sound of Heimdallr's horn, and presaged by "three long continuous winters". After this, "gods shall fall... But Might and Majesty shall stand... And when old Odin's glories fail,/Silence and Strength alone prevail"—as Herbert's notes explain, a reference to—and in fact, a literal translation of—stanza 51 of *Vafþrúðnismál*.[127]

On occasion, Herbert's allusions to Norse myth are so recondite that without his notes, the relevant lines in the poem would not be comprehensible. Thus Hialmar sees

> he, at heaven's extremest verge,
> Who broods o'er Ocean's swelling surge,
> With giant form, and frequent flings
> The tempest from his eagle wings.[128]

As Herbert's note explains, this is the giant Hræsvelgr ("corpse-swallower") who, as described in *Vafþrúðnismál*, lives at the edge of the known world in the form of a giant; the world's winds are whipped up by the flapping of his wings. Similarly, there exists

> that mighty Power,
> Who, in the hot meridian hour,
> Spreads his broad shield thro' ample space
> Before the Sun's refulgent face[129]

—this is Svalin ("Coolness") who appears only in stanza 38 of *Grímnismál*.[130]

---

[127] Herbert, *Works*, vol. I, pp. 109–13, Canto VI, 2572–2691; see Larrington, *The Poetic Edda*, p. 48.

[128] Herbert, *Works*, vol. I, p. 112, Canto VI, 2647–50.

[129] Herbert, *Works*, vol. I, p. 112, Canto VI, 2651–4.

[130] Dronke, *The Poetic Edda*, vol. III, p. 121.

Taken together, Herbert's notes to 'Helga' comprise an informative and accurate essay on Old Norse myth. His allusions to Norse myth are carefully documented, and their prose and poetic sources cited. When Vala is introduced in the text, the relevant note not only claims the form of the name "Vala" to be the nominative form of the genitive "völu", as in the title of the poem, but also refers the reader to *Völuspá*, and offers the first of many quotations in Old Norse.[131] He is scrupulous about the extent of his own learning: of the valkyries, he notes "thirteen are enumerated in Grímnismál... I have never seen their exact number stated", but cites the relevant lines from *Völuspá* in which six valkyries are named, in support of his description of the "six maids in complete armour dight... With pensive brow and look sedate" which Hialmar sees on his way to fight Angantyr.[132] One of the rivals for Helga's hand is named as Orvarod, a version of the legendary character Örvar-Oddr ("Arrow-Odd"), but Herbert admits "I have never been able to procure a copy of Orvarodds saga, and am only acquainted with its contents... through a free translation, or at least a tale founded upon it, in the works of Professor Suhm".[133]

Herbert was also ready to speculate on the historical origins of certain aspects of Old Norse myth: the giants, for instance, he supposes may have been "men of larger stature" whom Odin's smaller Asiatic followers encountered when they settled in Scandinavia, or that "Niorder" (Njörðr) was "one of the nation of the Vanir, a Grecian colony".[134] Rindr, the mother of Vali, a son magically begotten by Odin, the sole purpose of whose existence was to avenge the death of Baldr, is called the daughter of the sun in the quasi-eddic poem *Hrafnagaldr Óðins*,[135] and Herbert picks this up and deduces that Rindr, or her historical counterpart, came from Russia (east of Scandinavia, where the sun rises). He also considers in his notes the possible historicity of the whole story of Hialmar and King Yngvi, but sensibly draws back from affirming more than a very general basis in Danish history, concluding that in any case "the exact date is of very little importance".[136]

For Herbert, then, mythic allusion is a fundamental aspect of depicting the "manners and superstitions of the northern nations" in a roughly defined early period of their history. Visions of the Norse gods, and intimations of Ragnarök, are part of his characters' world view. And the narrative

[131] Herbert, *Works*, vol. I, pp. 127–8.
[132] Herbert, *Works*, vol. I, pp. 97–8, Canto VI, 2182–2219, and note on pp. 134–5.
[133] Herbert, *Works*, vol. I, p. 141.
[134] Herbert, *Works*, vol. I, pp. 133, 137.
[135] Annette Lassen (ed.), *Hrafnagaldur Óðins (Forspjallsljóð)* (London: Viking Society for Northern Research, 2011), st. 23.
[136] Herbert, *Works*, vol. I, pp. 141–2.

itself, though sensational in its incident, is not actually fantastic. The reality of Helga's journey to the sibyl, for instance, is carefully undermined on her return: having apparently been rescued from the jaws of Hel by the goddess Freyja, to whom she has prayed for assistance, she awakes "as from a feverish dream" in her bower the next morning.[137] Herbert's final stamp on the broad historicity of 'Helga' comes in the conclusion to the poem: Herbert, having described the building of a huge funerary mound over Hialmar (who has died of grief, and been burnt and buried along with her dead lover—like Brynhildr, indeed, in the *Edda*) reflects on what has become of all this heroism and grandeur, concluding that "The great, the fair, whate'er their lot/Sleep undistinguished and forgot".[138] Nothing remains of them but "strange tales"—the *Edda* and its related sagas?—and the mound itself. But of course this paradoxically attests to an actuality behind the narrative—there are monumental mounds in northern landscapes, and Norse literature has survived.

In his poem 'Hedin' (dated 1820), Herbert executes an even more intriguing historicist strategy on his Old Norse sources. 'Hedin' is the story of what is known in Norse mythology as the *Hjaðningavíg*—the never-ending battle of the Hjaðningar, the people of Heðinn, Herbert's Hedin. This story is hard to categorize as either heroic or mythic. In its most remarkable form, it is one of the four mythic, or legendary, subjects depicted in the earliest Old Norse skaldic poem to have survived, *Ragnarsdrápa*.[139] This poem purports to describe four scenes painted on a shield, a lavish gift for which the poem is a grateful and impressive acknowledgement. The *Hjaðningavíg* scene, described in a highly cryptic skaldic fragment, tells of the woman Hildr (a valkyrie name, and also the common noun for battle itself) who, as "the desiring goddess of the excessive drying up of veins", is depicted as both utterly merciful—playing the female role of staunching warriors' wounds after a conflict—and at the same time, paradoxically, insatiably bloodthirsty, for she heals their wounds in order that the battle may resume every day, in a curious parallel to the Valhalla myth. Putting together the allusions in this difficult poem with the story as extrapolated by Snorri,[140] we learn that Hildr, the daughter of Högni, has been abducted by Heðinn. Like so many female characters in Germanic story, she is thus caught between husband and father, a victim to be fought over. But Hildr is far from passive, and to her

[137] Herbert, *Works*, vol. I, p. 52, Canto II, 803.
[138] Herbert, *Works*, vol. I, pp. 121–3, Canto VII, 2945–92.
[139] Finnur Jónsson, *Skjaldedigtning* B I, pp. 1–4.
[140] Faulkes, *Edda*, pp. 122–3.

is credited the never-ending battle which can have no victory, and thus no defeat.

Herbert, whose knowledge of Old Norse poetry went beyond the *Edda,* and beyond those skaldic or semi-skaldic poems which Percy had translated, knew *Ragnarsdrápa* as well as the prose versions of the story, such as Saxo's account, and refers his reader to a Danish scholar's reconstruction of the narrative. He speculates in a long note about the relationship of the story to any historical events or characters, but concludes "it is absurd to regard it as genuine history".[141] However, he takes pains in 'Hedin' to create a psychologically naturalistic backstory: Hedin and Hagen (Högni) are said to have fought together in Orkney, but Hedin has betrayed his fellow warrior by seducing Hilda. Hilda offers her own life as a sacrifice, rather than that the two should fight, but there is a duel, and both are killed.

Hilda's grief for her lover is so overwhelming that she goes to Hedin's tomb at night—"but not to mourn". Like Hervör, in the story of Angantýr, she casts spells to wake Hedin from the dead, and succeeds. He is a shockingly corporeal revenant: not "the airy shape of human kind", writes Herbert, but "bodily" and "palpable".[142] As "by her burning mouth his icy lips are pressed" the inevitable ensues: Högni too rises from his grave, and the duel recommences. From this single narrative occasion, a legend arises:

> There still each eve, as northern stories tell,
> By that lone mound her spirit wakes the spell;
> Whereat those warriors, charmed by the lay,
> Renew, as if in sport, the deadly fray.[143]

And at dawn, the "spectre pageant" vanishes. The mysterious *Hjaðningavíg* has been turned into a Gothic ghost story.

Herbert's 'Song of Vala' appears in the 1842 edition of *Works* as a free-standing mythic poem, a version of the Old Norse *Völuspá,* which was not included in the 1804 translations since the editors of the Copenhagen *Edda* had not included it in the first volume of 1787.[144] Herbert explains in his notes that this song "was written with an idea of inserting it into the second canto of *Helga*"—one assumes, as part of the dialogue of one of the characters, perhaps Helga herself, as part of her expedition to visit the sibyl. It is a direct representation of a mythological poem—unlike 'Helga' and 'Hedin', which, as we have seen, transpose myth into legendary or romantic narrative. In fact, surprisingly for a writer like Herbert whose

[141] Herbert, *Works*, vol. I, p. 25.
[142] 'Hedin', in Herbert, *Works*, vol. I, pp. 3–25 (19–20).
[143] Herbert, *Works*, vol. I, p. 22.
[144] Herbert, *Works*, vol. I, pp. 143–8.

reputation rests on the generally accepted excellence of his translations, 'Vala' is not a success. Its four-line stanzas, rhyming abab, rattle along at a pace oddly inappropriate to the solemnity of the wisdom being presented. The stanzas are full of busy exclamation marks and questions, and the omission of articles also increases the pace, to something approaching telegraphese: as, for instance, "I was rock'd in giant's cradle" (5), or "Strand was none or rocky shore" (12). The giant Imir (Ymir) is perfunctorily brought to life as he presides over chaos—"Imir sat with lonely sadness/ Watching o'er the fruitless globe" (21–2), but there is little sense of the sibyl herself delving deep into her memory, or unwillingly revealing her unique store of wisdom; she speaks with rapid fluency as if commenting on action taking place before her. All in all, the metre is not right for the eschatological visions of an ancient sibyl, but towards the end of the poem, when she envisages a new order, the diction and style evoke the quality of a Christian hymn:

> He shall come in might eternal,
> He whom eye hath never seen!
> Earth, and heaven, and Powers infernal,
> Mark his port and awful mien.[145]

Thus the climax of 'Vala' is the stanza—regarded by many modern scholars as a Christian interpolation—describing the "one from above" who will descend in judgement. This is surely not accidental: one might even see it as another way of dealing with the paganism of Norse myth. As one might expect, then, Ragnarök is passed over cursorily, although as in the other poems, some of the allusions are so arcane as to be incomprehensible without referring to Herbert's notes.[146] In the notes, Herbert firmly contextualizes the poem as "the creed of the old Scandinavian nations", and wonders at the way it "holds out the expectation of a time when some greater unknown power would come in majesty to judge the world"[147]— pagan Scandinavians were, in other words, Christians *avant la lettre*.

In his poem 'Brynhilda', Herbert takes the tragic love story of Brynhildr and Sigurðr as his subject. Since the material comes from the heroic poems of the *Edda*, it is not strictly mythological, though Herbert included a good deal of mythic reference to contextualize his characters. But very significant is the emphasis on female psychology in Herbert's work. His tragic heroines—Hilda, Helga, Brynhilda—are not passive figures, mere

---

[145] 'The Song of Vala', 89–92, in Herbert, *Works*, vol. I.
[146] For example, the line "Hark! Another bird of morning" refers to the "soot-red cock in Hel" as mentioned in *Vǫluspá*; the question "Who are those in pride advancing?" is unanswered in the poem, to be revealed as Odin, Vili, and Ve in the notes (p. 144).
[147] Herbert, *Works*, vol. I, p. 148.

ciphers like Peacock's Nitalpha, whose abduction drives the narrative but who barely appears in it. Further, the heroines are portrayed in a strongly sexualized way. Hilda physically desires her dead lover Hedin, and has been seduced by him, and not merely chastely carried off, like Nitalpha. Brynhildr is already emotionally attached to Sigurðr when she is married to Gunnarr, though most versions of the story include the placing of a sword between them when they first sleep together—as Herbert does. Herbert's Brynhilda is described both sentimentally—"lovely she moved, like the silvery beam/Of the moonlight that kisses the slow-gliding stream"—and erotically: an ex-valkyrie, she has been imprisoned in sleep on a hill top by Odin, and Herbert describes her womanly form in considerable detail, with "Those soft-rounded arms now defenceless and bare", and "that snowy bosom, thus lovely reveal'd [which]/Has been oft by the breastplate's tough iron conceal'd".[148] The sexual attractiveness of Hilda and Helga is similarly and repeatedly emphasized.

Sexual love, with its attendant jealousies and rivalries, is a theme more evident in the heroic poems of the *Edda* than in the mythological ones. Here we can look forward to William Morris, whose much later poetry based on the Sigurðr story explores more fully the tragedy of the female characters. In Morris's work, especially 'The Lovers of Gudrun', the women take centre stage. Even Herbert's most immediate successor, Walter Savage Landor, who gratefully acknowledged his debt to Herbert—"I owe my *Gunlaug* to his stories from the Icelandic"[149]—went for the tragic love story rather than a mythological subject. In this case, the source was the prose saga of Gunnlaugr nicknamed "Serpent-tongue" who, in common with the other poets in the Icelandic tradition, fails to marry his beloved— a narrative element Icelandic saga authors had themselves found in heroic poetry.[150] Landor seems to have been completely uninterested in Old Norse myth. His characters make no reference, for instance, to "their" gods. In one extraordinary footnote, having mentioned a giant—a "Jotun"—in his text, Landor explains that the existence of jotuns was "not fabulous. In the north at all times have existed men of enormous stature. We ourselves have seen them from Ireland".[151] The giant is no longer a mythic personage, but the human product of genetic mutation.

---

[148] 'Brynhilda', 172–3 and 11–22, in Herbert, *Works*, vol. I, pp. 149–56.

[149] See Farley, *Scandinavian Influences*, p. 170. *Gunlaug* was first published in 1806.

[150] *Gunnlaugs saga ormstungu*, in Sigurður Nordal and Guðni Jónsson (eds.), *Borgfirðinga sögur*, Íslenzk fornrit III (Reykjavík: Hið Íslenzka Fornritafélag, 1938), pp. 51–107; for a translation see Jones, *Eirik the Red and Other Icelandic Sagas*, pp. 171–217.

[151] 'Gunlaug', in Walter Savage Landor, *Gebir, Count Julian, and Other Poems* (London: Edward Moxon, 1831), pp. 263–83 (279).

What thrilled Landor about the literature of the North was not myth, but the heroism of "Regnor Lodbrog", about whom he had read in Mallet, and the spirit of Viking adventure. Nevertheless, the world of his characters is cosily domestic: the "sandy-dog rose" grows in the hedgerows, Helga wears sandals, and she has a pet rabbit and a pet dormouse; her lover Gunlaug feeds the rabbit with "crispest parsley" and crumbs of "breakfast bread".[152] We are coming close to a replay of Orchard's sanitizing, humanizing, Christianizing impulse of the Anglo-Saxon author[s] of *Beowulf*.[153] Another product of such transformation—with the addition of "classicizing"—is Arnold's 'Balder Dead', which I will discuss in Chapter 4. And an extension of the "humanization" of Old Norse myth is the continued interest in the old "Odin myth" with Odin repeatedly identified as an historical personage deified by early Scandinavians.

However, as we shall see in Chapter 4, the most significant change in the reception of Old Norse myth in the nineteenth century was its scholarly treatment as evidence of "old Thought", as Thomas Carlyle put it, of the broader history of the development of the human race (or, more sinisterly, of one of its supposed races), as an allegorical code which needed informed interpretation, of interest not only in itself, but as the religion or wisdom of the Indo-European race to which English (and German)-speaking peoples believed they belonged. Here we see the dark side of the attractions of Old Norse myth—a fascination with, or even revivification of, the philosophies of "our forefathers", and the belief in a racial supremacy inherited from them. With this later development in mind, a passage in Herbert's 'Helga' looks oddly proleptic. The sibyl has advised Helga that in order to defeat Angantyr, Hialmar must procure for himself a sword which is in the keeping of "the pigmy race"—the dwarves who live underground. Herbert describes them as "A loathsome, wan and meagre race/With shaggy chin, and sallow face".[154] We might be reminded here of Wagner's characterization of the Nibelungs, the people of Alberich the Dwarf Smith.

The Scottish poet William Motherwell (remembered today for his sentimental ballad 'Jeanie Morrison') declares in the preface to his *Poems Narrative and Lyrical* (1832) that notes would spoil the appearance of his slim volume, but that he will have to make an exception for the first three poems: 'The Battle-Flag of Sigurd', a lively but old-fashioned account of a Viking battle, with verbal echoes of Gray's 'Norse Odes' (lowering clouds, red slaughter, and dusky standards), the customary raven banner, and a maiden called

---

[152]   Landor, *Gebir, Count Julian, and Other Poems*, pp. 264–6.
[153]   See Prologue to this work, n. 4.
[154]   Herbert, *Works*, vol. I, p. 70, Canto IV, 1349–50.

Brynhilda, a "pale watcher by the sea";[155] 'The Wooing Song of Jarl Egill Skallagrim'—"entirely a creation...nothing of it...historical";[156] and 'The Sword Chant of Thorstein Raudi', about a Viking who owes everything (naturally) to his sword, which he apostrophizes in a series of stanzas as Land Giver, Might Giver, Joy Giver, Fame Giver, Death Giver, Heart Gladdener, and Song Giver; each stanza ends "I kiss thee". As Motherwell cheerfully notes, Thorstein probably "never said so much in all his life about his sword or himself, as I have taken the fancy of putting into his mouth".[157] We can see here the imaginative, if naïve, engagement with the supposed spirit of the Vikings which took hold so dramatically in Victorian England, and which Andrew Wawn has documented so well.[158] But a nation thrilled by its Viking past does not amount to poets engaging with Old Norse myth.

Three more poems may serve to show how tired and clichéd English poetry on Norse themes had become. Dilnot Sladden's *The Northmen* (1834) is set in the Viking age, and opens with a raid on Anglo-Saxon England by Eric, with his raven banner. On the advice of a sibyl, Bertha, he has "quaffed" ceremonial ale to Odin and heads off to attack the kingdom of King Ella, like Ivar and Ubba avenging the death of their father Ragnar Lothbrok at Ella's hands. Eric is killed in the ensuing battle, but his long dying speech drops a bombshell: Eric is no Norseman, but an Anglo-Saxon who was forced to flee to Norway when Ella objected to his marriage to the lovely Thora (who did not escape: "Poison obscured young Thora's bloom/She drooped, and sought an early tomb").[159] Bertha the Sibyl prophesies the glorious future of "Albion"—that is, of course, nineteenth-century England—and although the Vikings conquer this land, harmony breaks out:

> And the rough warriors gave the hand
> Of friendship to the Saxon band,
> And vowed, by Odin, they would be
> Their comrades through eternity.[160]

Thus, concludes Sladden, apostrophizing England, although

> A thousand years have changed thee, yet the hand
> Of a true sea-king o'er the isles does reign.[161]

---

[155] William Motherwell, *Poems Narrative and Lyrical* (Glasgow: David Robertson, 1832), pp. 9–20 (15).
[156] Motherwell, *Poems*, p. 2; 'The Wooing Song of Jarl Egill Skallagrim', pp. 21–9.
[157] Motherwell, *Poems*, p. 3; 'The Sword Chant of Thorstein Raudi', pp. 30–5.
[158] Andrew Wawn, *The Vikings and the Victorians: Inventing the Old North in Nineteenth-Century Britain* (Cambridge: D. S. Brewer, 2000).
[159] Dilnot Sladden, *The Northmen* (Canterbury, 1834), p. 92.
[160] Sladden, *The Northmen*, pp. 122–3.
[161] Sladden, *The Northmen*, p. 126.

For Sladden, as for many later writers, this Viking blood explains the past and present military successes—and, indeed, technological progress—of his native land. Wawn quotes the scholar and translator George Webbe Dasent comparing the spirit of the Vikings with that of nineteenth-century industrialists.[162] More fancifully still, the historian J. A. Froude argued that the god Heimdallr might be regarded as "the precursor and patron of the Macadams and Stephensons of English road-engineering".[163]

Finally, Wawn has drawn our attention to the prize for poetry at Oxford in 1850, when the prescribed topic was "The Hall of Odin".[164] T. F. Rawlins, who won first prize, combines the staple motifs of the old Gothic horror—"beetling rocks", and "funeral cypress"—with familiar clichés: "grisly heroes" ("their bowls, the reeking skulls of enemies") "quaff potent draughts of luscious hydromel" in Valhalla.[165] There follows a sensationalist description of the "mangled dead" sacrificed to Odin at Uppsala, and a triumphant allusion to the Christian temple built in its place. W. C. Valentine's second prize poem also "shuffles motifs from Percy's *Five Pieces*", as Wawn tartly notes, including the mead drunk from skulls. Valentine even falls into a paraphrase of the Death Song—"We fought with swords," and so on—and borrows from Robert Southey's early Odin poems. But he is anxious to dispel the notion that Valhalla is all male warriors fighting, claiming:

> They err who dare deny, that Love doth dwell
> Among those happy spirits,[166]

citing the presence of valkyries ("fair damsels") and Frigg ("sweet lady").

Women poets also took Norse themes for their poetry, and did not necessarily feminize them. Anna Seward, for instance, whose work, as we have seen, was edited by Walter Scott in 1810, produced an extremely successful version of Percy's 'The Incantation of Hervor' which she described as a "bold paraphrase": she called the poem 'Herva at the Tomb of Argantyr' (sic). In a letter dated 1796, she records that a male acquaintance asserted that it "excels Gray's descent of Odin in sublimity".[167] But perhaps the most popular female poet of the nineteenth century to have taken up Norse themes was Mrs Felicia Hemans. Although she is celebrated now only for

[162] Andrew Wawn, 'The Cult of "Stalwart Frith-thjof" in Victorian Britain', in Wawn (ed.), *Northern Antiquity*, pp. 211–54 (218).
[163] J. A. Froude, 'The Odin-Religion', *The Westminster Review* (October 1854), pp. 165–83 (176).
[164] Wawn, *The Vikings and The Victorians*, pp. 206–7.
[165] T. F. S. Rawlins and W. C. Valentine, *The Hall of Odin* (Oxford, 1850), pp. 2–5 (3).
[166] Rawlins and Valentine, *The Hall of Odin*, pp. 6–13(8).
[167] Farley, *Scandinavian Influences*, p. 56.

the much repeated first line of her patriotic poem 'Casabianca'—"The boy stood on the burning deck"—she has been described as "the most widely read woman poet of the nineteenth century", and was the highest paid contributor to *Blackwood's Magazine*, "rated above Scott, Godwin and de Quincey".[168] Hemans has been characterized as a poet with peculiarly feminine concerns: "home, nation, femininity and religion" with "a particular investment in religion".[169] And amongst her large and varied output she published in 1825 two Norse-themed poems, 'Valkyriur Song' and 'The Sword of the Tomb'.[170]

In 'Valkyriur Song' (Hemans has used the Icelandic plural of the word for valkyrie, as Thomas Gray did, and follows Gray in labelling the valkyries "choosers of the slain"), a sea king Regner awakes on the morning of a battle to see mysterious female figures:

> there seem'd, through the arch of a tide-worn cave,
> A gleam, as of snow, to pour;
> And forth, in watery light,
> Moved phantoms, dimly white,
> Which the garb of woman bore.[171]

He at once recognizes them as valkyries, and hears them calling himself, his "fair-haired bride", his brother, and his "raven-steed" to Odin's Hall. Hemans refers her reader to Mallet for confirmation of these details, and there is also a reference to Herbert's 'Helga'. The poem ends with the fulfilment of doomed Regner's vision: that evening, he "Lay cold on a pile of dead!"

'The Sword of the Tomb' refers the reader to the legend of the Norse hero Starkaðr, dramatized by Adam Œhlenschläger, the Danish Romantic poet. In the poem, the hero Sigurd hopes to vanquish his foes by reclaiming his father's sword from his tomb. He is warned that he must on no account disturb the urn containing his father's ashes, but fumbles the sword, smashes the urn, and the shade of his father is driven out of Volhalla (sic). Hemans's verse is crammed with Gothic details: hollow chants, sepulchral hills, Northern pines, and sinister light. And the Voice which guides him to the sword speaks a "Runic rhyme". In both of these poems, the content is nugatory; atmosphere is everything. Hemans does not engage with myth

---

[168] Emma Mason, *Women Poets of the Nineteenth Century* (Tavistock: Northcote House, 2006), pp. 17, 25–6.
[169] See Mason, *Women Poets*, pp. 19–20.
[170] Mrs Hemans, *The Forest Sanctuary, and Other Poems* (London: John Murray, 1825), 'The Sword of the Tomb: A Northern Legend', pp. 112–19, and 'Valkyriur Song', pp. 120–3.
[171] Hemans, *The Forest Sanctuary, and Other Poems*, p. 121.

itself, beyond figuring Odin's Valhalla as a mysterious destination for her heroes.

While the canonical Romantic poets of the British Isles turned to Mediterranean themes for their inspiration, and away from the indigenous (or more or less indigenous) literary cultures of the North, Romantic movements across Europe, but especially in Scandinavia and Germany, did the opposite and turned to Old Norse literature—and myth in particular—as the ancient bedrock of their various cultures. This European romanticism struck a strong chord in North America. What Erik Ingvar Thurin has described as a brief but intense engagement between American poets and novelists and Old Norse literature reflects their direct contact with continental Romantic writers, such as the extended visit to Scandinavia by Henry Wadsworth Longfellow in 1835.[172] In fact, by this time, according to Thurin, the Norse revival there was already "past its prime".[173] But although it ran its course very quickly in America, in a matter of two or three decades, "while it lasted, a majority of writers got involved in one way or another".[174] In fact, rather few became involved with Old Norse myth, and essayists seemed more interested in the idea of the North than poets did. Such interest in Gothic trappings as there was was probably due to the influence of Thomas Gray's poetry. No tradition of learning Old Norse itself, let alone translating its literature, developed in America,[175] and there was practically no interest in the particular literary qualities of skaldic verse, though the term "skald" was often used. Unlike in England, there was also little interest in the *Poetic Edda*; Snorri's *Gylfaginning* was the main source for what mythological material was produced. Of course, one of the major special interests of Old Norse literature for Americans was the story—not mythological at all—of the Norse discovery of America, and it is no coincidence that most of the writers we are concerned with were based in New England.[176]

Longfellow's first engagement was not with mythological literature. In common with many English Victorian poets and their readers, as Andrew Wawn has shown, Longfellow's great passion was the Swedish poem *Frithiofs saga,* based by Bishop Esaias Tegnér on the Old Norse

---

[172] Erik Ingvar Thurin, *The American Discovery of the Norse: An Episode in Nineteenth-Century American Literature* (Lewisburg, 1999), p. 143.

[173] Thurin, *The American Discovery of the Norse*, p. 20.

[174] Thurin, *The American Discovery of the Norse*, p. 143.

[175] Longfellow thought that Old Norse has "a harsh, sharp and disagreeable sound"; see Andrew Hilen, *Longfellow and Scandinavia: A Study of the Poet's Relationship with the Northern Languages and Literature* (New Haven: Yale University Press, 1947), p. 89.

[176] For a full account of these writers and their response to Old Norse, see Thurin, *The American Discovery of the Norse*.

Friðþjófs saga.[177] According to Andrew Hilen, what attracted Longfellow
to Tegnér's poem was the ways in which it departed from some "authentic" flavour: "What [Longfellow] admired most in the Swedish poet was
his ability to draw a curtain on the violence and brutal reality of the
ancient legends of the North at the same time that he brought to full
poetic bloom the wild freedom, the vigor of life, and the emotions of
the heart which were potential in the saga literature".[178] Even so, after
reviewing the poem with tremendous enthusiasm and translating parts
of it, Longfellow, in spite of the urging of Tegnér himself, never actually translated the whole poem. This was not Longfellow's only omission: he planned to write an epic about Jarl Hákon, but never did, and
according to Erik Kielland-Lund, "in his *Journals* he describes a number
of Saga-inspired projects that never came to fruition".[179] But Longfellow
found success with his long poem in several parts, 'The Saga of King Olaf',
one of the *Tales of a Wayside Inn* told by "a blue-eyed Norseman" about
"the dead kings of Norroway".[180] 'The Saga of King Olaf' is a series of
entertaining and often dramatic scenes from Snorri Sturluson's saga of
Óláfr Tryggvason, which Longfellow read in Samuel Laing's recently published English translation.[181] This King Óláfr (not to be confused with the
later St Óláfr Haraldsson of Norway) struggled to Christianize Norway,
and sent the missionary priest Thangbrandr in a failed attempt to convert
the Icelanders. Longfellow's poem begins with a stirring sequence he had
composed earlier, 'The Challenge of Thor', in which the god Thor, "the
War God", "the Thunderer", reigns "amid icebergs" with his mighty hammer and chariot, his red beard "blown by the night wind", and issues a
challenge to King Óláfr and the "Galilean".[182] As Hilen concludes, and
this opening peroration confirms, Longfellow's "conception of the Norse
past lacked authenticity".[183] Similarly, Longfellow's ballad 'The Skeleton in
Armour', declaimed by the ghost of an old Viking, dramatizes the building

[177] See Wawn, 'The Cult of "Stalwart Frith-thjof"', pp. 225–7.
[178] Hilen, *Longfellow and Scandinavia*, p. 61.
[179] Erik Kielland-Lund, '"Twilight of the Heroes": Old Norse Influence in Longfellow's
Poetry', in Inga-Stina Ewbank, Olav Lausund, and Bjørn Tysdahl (eds.), *Anglo-Scandinavian
Cross-Currents* (Norwich: Norvik, 1999), pp. 71–83 (74). See also Hilen, *Longfellow and
Scandinavia*, p. 93, who quotes from Longfellow's 'Book of Suggestions': "'Northern
Mythology'. A book on this subject might be made highly agreeable. Not pedantic, but
lively. Consult Grimm, Pigott".
[180] *The Poetical Works of Henry Wadsworth Longfellow* (London: George Routledge,
1867), pp. 379–98.
[181] Samuel Laing (trans.), *The Heimskringla, or Chronicle of the Kings of Norway*
(London: Longman, Brown, Green, and Longmans, 1844), 3 vols.
[182] Longfellow, *Poetical Works*, p. 380.
[183] Hilen, *Longfellow and Scandinavia*, p. 106.

of the Round Tower at Newport which was once supposed to be a relic of the Norse discovery of America.[184] As Hilen notes, this old Viking is somewhat reminiscent of Frithiof: he is "more worldly than Frithiof, and lacks his semidivine and heroic characteristics, but he leads in many ways a similar life"[185]—another stereotypical and inauthentic Northern hero.

I want to conclude this section on Longfellow and the American engagement with Norse literature with two works by Longfellow which exemplify his failings of incompletion and inauthenticity. Nevertheless, these two works seem to me to be remarkable evidence of clear engagement with the heart of Norse mythology, its particularity, and distinctive voice. The first is Longfellow's unfinished foray into Old Norse creation myth: "Ymer. A poem on the Giants of the Northern Mythology. The subject is very grand. It should be in blank verse".[186]

Longfellow's immediate intuition that the subject demands blank verse—Miltonic metre—shows at once that he recognizes the significance of the subject; these Hrimthursar—frost giants—are not the comic lumberers of fairy-tale tradition, but the terrifying precursors of all living things. Longfellow relies on Snorri's account of creation in *Gylfaginning* for his verse, but fills out the narrative with Homeric similes. Thus, the warmth which in Snorri comes from Muspell to meet the ice of the *ginnunga gap* is described by Longfellow as "a warm wind" which

> Rose, and blew steadily, as the hot Sirocco
> From Afric's coast, or Trade wind in the Tropics,
> Blowing the pennons at the mast abroad
> And swelling the big sails of some armada.[187]

As we shall see with regard to Matthew Arnold's Homeric similes in 'Balder Dead', there is a real attempt here to re-imagine in conventional poetic terms the unimaginable strangeness of the Old Norse source—which, indeed, Snorri himself may not have understood or envisaged clearly enough to make sense of. Snorri's resultant thaw is vividly re-imagined by Longfellow: the snowy mountains let fall a "soundless Avalanche", and "fields of ice/Cracked suddenly across, in broken chasms". Snorri's barely figured (or understood) vivifying principle is squarely identified—"the breath of the All-father"—and the first frost giant, Ymer, is created, "Huge, disproportioned, ponderous and wild". Longfellow actually imagines the creature seeing and hearing the sounds of creation which "God

[184] Longfellow, *Poetical Works*, pp. 62–4.
[185] Hilen, *Longfellow and Scandinavia*, p. 63.
[186] Longfellow's first note on the idea in his 'Book of Suggestions', 18 October 1848, quoted in Hilen, *Longfellow and Scandinavia*, p. 94.
[187] The poem is printed in Hilen, *Longfellow and Scandinavia*, pp. 94–7 (94).

alone" had heard so far: pinnacles of ice, shining in a far-off light; the "gurgling runnels" of the thaw; and the sound of footsteps "Crushing the icicles and frosty snow", a sound "as when on winter nights, is heard afar/ Amid the pauses of the gusty storm,/The awful roar of the implacable sea". This is the great cow Idumbla (Auðumbla in Snorri), Ymer's monstrous wet nurse, who proceeds to lick three more giants out of the ice.

Nothing in the rest of this fragment quite matches the eerie drama of its opening. Longfellow gets entangled in the improbable genealogy of the gods such that the subsequent slaughter of Ymer, and building of the earth from his corpse, is unmotivated and unconvincing. But the fragment ends on a tantalizingly high note: the gods create the first humans from driftwood—or, in a sudden imaginative leap from Longfellow, "perhaps the broken oar/Of Bergelmir", the "Old man of the Mountain", the only frost giant to escape—perhaps, Noah-like, on a boat—the flood caused by the great flow of Ymer's blood. And Ymer's ghost seems to respond to this memory: "Loud moaned the distant sea; as if the blood/Of the slain Ymer cried aloud to heaven"—like the vengeful blood of Abel. And we know that the gods will face, in due course, a final apocalypse.

The author of *Frithjofs saga*, Esaias Tegnér, died in 1846. The following year, Longfellow wrote in his *Journal* that he had finished "a mystic poem on Tegnér's death, in the spirit of the Old Norse poetry".[188] This was 'Tegnér's Drapa'. Longfellow originally entitled the poem 'Tegnér's Death'. The term *drápa* in Old Norse signifies a formal sequence of skaldic stanzas (in general, skaldic verse is preserved as single stanzas or short sequences of stanzas, not as complete long poems). *Drápa* is used to designate not subject matter, but the degree of formality: a *drápa* was a poem fit for a king, who might take offence at being offered a less ambitious production, one which perhaps lacked a formal refrain, or the full force of the semantic density engendered by the complex interweaving of extended kennings and poetic synonyms. Though Thurin is justified in objecting to Longfellow's use of the term *drápa* for his English poem, since it does not reflect to any degree at all the technical aspects of skaldic metre or lexis,[189] nonetheless, Longfellow's elegiac solemnity more than validates his use of the term in his title.

The poem begins with a disembodied voice—sounding like "the mournful cry/of sunward sailing cranes"—announcing the death of Baldr: "Balder the Beautiful/Is dead, is dead!"[190] Nature, as represented by the ethereal migration of the birds, and indeed the whole cosmos, for

[188] Hilen, *Longfellow and Scandinavia*, p. 61.
[189] Thurin, *The American Discovery of the Norse*, p. 99.
[190] Longfellow, *Poetical Works*, pp. 166–7.

Longfellow imagines a mist-shrouded sun as a "pallid corpse" which is "Borne through the Northern sky", echoes the departure and demise of Balder, figured by Longfellow, and by so many of his predecessors, as a Sun God. But his death heralds more than the coming of winter. Baldr may be, for Longfellow, "God of the summer sun", but he is also a spirit of more symbolic enlightenment, for "Light from his forehead beamed", and most tellingly, it is implied that he is the god of poetry: "Runes were upon his tongue". Thurin complains that "Longfellow fails to show with any degree of precision" how the poem as a whole relates to Tegnér,[191] but it seems to me that darkness and silence aptly follow both passings.

Longfellow, having implicitly linked Baldr and Tegnér, moves to recount, with impressive economy, a few telling details of the Baldr myth, which he would almost certainly have found in an English translation (perhaps Dasent's) of Snorri's *Edda*. He recalls the terms of Baldr's inviolability, according to which all living things except the mistletoe agreed never to harm Baldr, and re-imagines the blind god Höðr as being not only blind, but old, "whose feet are shod with silence". The whole Loki conspiracy is nicely encapsulated with the phrase "by fraud", and Baldr's funeral is a dignified digest of Snorri's grotesque gathering. Crucial details are carefully included: Odin "placed/A ring upon his finger/And whispered in his ear". In harmony with the poem's opening, Baldr is accorded a ship burial, not in Snorri, in which his burning pyre, afloat, disappears gradually beneath the waves, like the setting sun itself.

All this has nothing to do with Tegnér, of course, except by implication and extension. But the poem moves to lament the passing of the Norse gods in the historical sense: "So perish the old Gods!". And in an elegant echo of the sibyl's post-apocalypse vision in the mythological poem *Völuspá*, in which she sees, Revelation-style, a new Heaven and a new Earth arising from the conflagration of Ragnarök, Longfellow foresees a new world of literature: "out of the sea of Time/Rises a new world of song/Fairer than the old." Like the Norse gods who will inhabit the regenerated cosmos, Longfellow's imagined new inhabitants will "Feed upon morning dew", but they are not gods, but poets, and their subject—Longfellow's long-held literary ideal—will be not the violence and revenge of the old poetic order, but the moral edification and romantic sweetness he admired in Tegnér. "Thor, the Thunderer" is dead in two senses, for Tegnér has initiated a new sensibility, and "The law of love prevails!" In a somewhat bathetic conclusion, Longfellow amplifies this sentiment: northern poets will no longer celebrate violence and revenge—"the deeds of

---

[191] Thurin, *The American Discovery of the Norse*, p. 99.

blood"—though they will preserve the traditional virtue of the North: freedom.

Such pacifism has been identified as the key, if at first glance paradoxical, characteristic of Longfellow's distinctive take on Old Norse. But back in England, valour continued to be seen as the distinguishing feature of Old Norse culture. In 1840, Thomas Carlyle, for instance, concluded his first lecture 'On Heroes, Hero-Worship, and the Heroic in History: The Hero as Divinity. Odin. Paganism: Scandinavian Mythology' with the claim that "the primary seed-grain of the Norse religion" was valour, and that indeed, Old Norse religion was in essence a "Consecration of Valour".[192] His biographer, J. A. Froude, in an article entitled 'The Odin-Religion', went further: "Somnolent contemplation may be suitable to the languid Hindoo, passive humility and acquiescence to the enslaved Asiatic, but the supreme virtue of the free, vigorous, cheery Teutonic man was *valour*".[193] Although the attraction of Old Norse myth for many eighteenth-century poets had been the novelty, the strangeness, and the sublime wildness of the poetic material, throughout the nineteenth century legendary protagonists, such as Odin the Asiatic chieftain, or fictional creations like Harold the Dauntless or Sladden's Eric, proved more tractable as human characters. They could have affairs of the heart, and be seized by the passions of sexual or familial drama, and might therefore be presented with freer imaginative rein than the more rigid abstractions of even the strikingly human Norse pantheon.

As we shall see in Chapter 4, major developments in the reception of Old Norse mythology served rather to dehumanize the Old Norse pantheon, and return its divinities to the status of allegorical abstractions. Typically, Old Norse myth was systematized and allegorized, treated to scholarly analysis as the remnants of an ancient religion which might offer comparison with Christianity itself. The dominant divinity in the Old Norse pantheon—for so long the quasi-historical warrior leader Odin— now emerges as Baldr, the beautiful young god whose premature death is the greatest sorrow to come upon men and gods, a death which might teach readers about the transience of truth and beauty, and about how the passing of what was believed in its time to be immutable had something to tell a contemporary audience about the nature of faith itself.

---

[192] Thomas Carlyle, *On Heroes, Hero-Worship, and the Heroic in History: Six Lectures* (London: James Fraser, 1841), pp. 53, 65.
[193] Froude, 'The Odin-Religion', p. 169.

4

Paganism and Christianism:
The Victorians and Their Successors

As Andrew Wawn has shown, Old Norse myth excited a "vigorous Victorian debate" amongst scholars in Britain and Europe, primarily Germany and Scandinavia: the issue was not the literary qualities of the material, but what it "really meant"—and thus, what could be learned from it about humanity in general, and European humanity in particular.[1] This debate is fascinating in itself, for as Froude's piece in the Westminster Review demonstrated,[2] many of the ideas which underpin twentieth-century racist ideologies have their beginnings, and are developed or aired, in the course of it. But for our purposes, a brief account of this debate will explain the unique poetic popularity of one subject from Old Norse myth: the death of Baldr.

In 1828, Thomas Keightley had published a review of the work of the Icelandic mythographer Finnur Magnússon. Finnur had won a prize given by the Danish Royal Society of Science on the subject of "A historico-critical solution of the connection between the religion of the Old Northerns, especially the Scandinavians, and that of the Indo-Persian nations".[3] Old Norse myth is placed in the context of a much wider family of mythologies which were held to be related to one another exactly as the comparative philologist Sir William Jones had shown to be the case with Indo-European languages at the end of the previous century.[4] Such comparativism became a staple of Norse scholarship in the nineteenth century, and increasingly inventive and implausible similarities were proposed: Heremod is identified with Hermes, for instance, or even, at a greater philological stretch, Woden with Buddha. Thus, the study of Old Norse myth came to be regarded as a crucial element in the study of universal human cultural development and anthropology. This put Old Norse material on an equal footing with

---

[1] Wawn, *The Vikings and the Victorians*, p. 188.
[2] Froude, 'The Odin-Religion'; see Chapter 3 of this work.
[3] Thomas Keightley, *The Foreign Quarterly Review* vol. II (February-June 1828), Article VII, pp. 210–43 (212).
[4] William Jones, 'Third Anniversary Discourse' (1786), in *The Works of Sir William Jones* (London: John Stockdale and John Walker, 1807), vol. III, pp. 24–46.

its old rival, Greek and Roman mythology. Keightley's triumph is clear: "it surely is gratifying to reflect, that the nobler Gothic race was in physical and moral knowledge at least on an equality with those Romans who so contemptuously styled them Barbarians".[5] And, as is already evident in Keightley's championing of the Goths—"our" ancestors—it excited a pride in either national or Indo-European origins which inevitably morphed into a doctrine of racial supremacism and purity. Froude's celebration of the "Odin-Religion" captures this latter development especially well: Norse religion, claims Froude, was "original and indigenous; it was not imported from a foreign people of different character and conditions, but of home-growth, nursed in native forests, and in the hearts of men of the same blood and race".[6] His concern for the "Heilige Deutsche Reich" and celebration of "*one* soul breathing through the whole—the Language; and *one* common ground of intelligence: the Literature"—a combination which keeps together the otherwise "dispersed, disunited children of the Fatherland"[7]—certainly strikes a sinister note for present-day readers. The family of philosophical, civilized, and progressive cultures repeatedly cited by comparative mythographers (and inherited from their predecessors in comparative linguistics) maps very precisely on to those languages which later came to be labelled Aryan—as opposed to Semitic, for instance, or African, or Chinese.[8]

But Old Norse myth had to be properly glossed to make its contribution to anthropology. Finnur Magnússon propounded an allegorical reading of Old Norse myth, to "raise the symbolic veils", as Keightley put it, under which the scholar might be able to decode and restore "old Thought".[9] Keightley claimed that the apparent strangeness of Old Norse myth paradoxically guaranteed its serious import: "the more absurd a mythos appears, the more certain we may be of its containing an important meaning—the thicker and more grotesquely shaped the shell the sounder the kernel".[10] For example, the story of creating the world from the slain body of the giant Ymir is held to be an allegory of creation from "primitive undigested chaotic matter",[11] or the battle of the gods and giants at Ragnarök an allegory of "conflict between the powers of nature".[12] Keightley is politely

---

[5] Keightley, *FQR* II, p. 242.
[6] Froude, 'The Odin-Religion', p. 169.
[7] Froude, 'The Odin-Religion', p. 167.
[8] See Leon Poliakov, *The Aryan Myth: A History of Racist and Nationalist Ideas in Europe* (London: Sussex University Press, 1974).
[9] Keightley, *FQR* II, p. 210.
[10] Keightley, *FQR* II, p. 216.
[11] Keightley, *FQR* II, p. 218.
[12] Keightley, *FQR* II, p. 242.

sceptical of some of Finnur's ideas, noting that his etymologies are a little fanciful, and that some of the most fundamental elements in Old Norse myth are no doubt echoed in other mythic systems because their common source is not so much Indo-European culture as the human mind. He does not engage at all with Finnur's most extraordinary allegorical excursion: that the twelve gods of the Norse pantheon and their residences correspond to the signs of the zodiac, and are in effect an elaborated calendar.

Mary Busk, writing in *Blackwood's Edinburgh Magazine*, is vehemently opposed to allegorical methods which "turn the Asa gods into showers, winds, or signs of the zodiac, and the touching tale of Ballder's fate into a fanciful description of the summer solstice"; they cause her to "recoil" with "filial abhorrence".[13] But she champions the Danish scholar N. F. S. Grundtvig, who, she explains, "considers all mythology as metaphysical allegory"[14]—that is, that it encodes—reasonably enough—the fears and aspirations of mankind. Thus, for instance, for Grundtvig, Yggdrasill represents "the great struggle between *life* and *death*".[15] Much more fantastical allegorical systems had been propounded to "explain" Old Norse myth. Most notable, perhaps, was Benjamin Thorpe's "physical mode of interpretation" which consisted in "showing the accordance between the myths and the later systems of chymistry", as one (hostile) contemporary reviewer of Thorpe's theory's describes it; this involved seeing Thor's belt of strength as an electrical condenser, and recognizing Thor's exploits in the land of the giants as an allegory of terrestrial magnetism.[16] However, Busk's acceptance of even Grundtvig's relatively moderate degree of allegorization gives way to a completely straight re-telling of "our favourite Asa legend"—the story of the death of Baldr, which she relates in a form "free from the Dane's violence and the German's mysticism", to be enjoyed as entertainment.[17]

In a review of Grundtvig's work, Busk quotes approvingly his highly edifying account of the Baldr story: far from the crude celebration of violence and defiance in the face of impending death which had characterized so much of the hitherto favourite Norse material—the Death Song, or the Odin myth, and indeed, the continuing popularity of broader Viking themes amongst Victorian writers—the story of Baldr's death, says Grundtvig, is "a deep expression, a grand image of the splendour

[13] Mary Busk, 'Scandinavian Mythology, and the Nature of its Allegory', *Blackwood's Edinburgh Magazine* vol. XXXVIII (July 1835), pp. 25–36 (27).
[14] Busk, 'Scandinavian Mythology', p. 29.
[15] Busk, 'Scandinavian Mythology', pp. 32–3.
[16] See William Roscoe's review of Thorpe's work in Roscoe, 'The Eddas', *The Prospective Review* 32 (October 1852), 456–89 (475), and also Wawn, *The Vikings and the Victorians*, pp. 193–4.
[17] Busk, 'Scandinavian Mythology', p. 34.

surrounding life, when viewed with an innocent eye in the light of eternity; but which, as the noblest human lives testify, may, upon occasion of great misfortune, vanish from the earth, for the sons of men, irrecoverably".[18] Grundtvig was a Lutheran pastor; his reading of the myths also stressed their compatibility (when carefully interpreted) with Christian doctrine. It is arguable that we can see here the seeds of the future of Old Norse myth—and especially the story of the death of Baldr—as morally edifying reading suitable for general readers and even children. Thomas Smith, for instance, singled out Old Norse myth as differing from its Indo-European counterparts in the moral purity of its gods, just as Gothic architecture "bears the stamp of elevation, and awe, and holiness"—even if, as we have seen, offending parts of *Lokasenna* had to be disguised in Latin by translators such as Amos Cottle, who primly noted that Loki's worst insults "would not admit with propriety of an English version".[19] These shifts in the reception of Old Norse myth all tended to militate against the taking up of individual poems or themes from Old Norse mythological literature by serious poets. Myths were instead being taken over by scholars and storytellers, their original poetic forms obscured, and their "meaning" given precedence over their aesthetic or literary qualities. A number of poets and scholars produced versions of Old Norse myth in which mythological materials from different sources were knitted together as continuous narrative, producing a coherent "story" of the Norse gods, and effectively disguising the heterogeneity of the original texts. The Danish Romantic poet Adam Œhlenschläger, for instance, whose work was translated into English in 1845 by W. E. Frye as *The Gods of the North*,[20] managed very skilfully—but totally factitiously—to weave his sources into just such a narrative. Frye's translation opens with a merry invitation: "come young and old!/And listen to my varied rhyme".[21] In his summary of Œhlenschläger's narrative, we find that the violent and sinister poem *Skírnismál*, in which Freyr's phallic emissary Skírnir threatens the giantess Gerðr with hideous sexual torments if she refuses to accede to Freyr's demands, has been completely transformed: "Frey's messenger... shows to Gerda the portrait of Frey, and softens her heart. Her father gives his consent".[22] This is much more suitable material for the general reader, especially if young, or female.

---

[18] *Nordens Mythologi*, quoted in Busk, *FQR*, vol. XVI (1836), pp. 437–44 (443).

[19] Thomas Smith, *The Völuspá: read before the Leicestershire Literary Society* (Leicester, 1838), p. 60, and Cottle's *Icelandic Poetry*, p.161.

[20] William Edward Frye, *The Gods of the North: An Epic Poem* (London: William Pickering, 1845).

[21] Frye, *The Gods of the North*, Canto I, p. 1.

[22] Frye, *The Gods of the North*, 'Argument of the Poem', p. lxxx.

In 1878, the American author Julia Clinton Jones published *Valhalla*, a long poem in twelve parts, which she called "a saga". In his book on the American discovery of the Norse, Erik Ingvar Thurin calls this piece "the symbolic end product of the Norse revival in America",[23] and her verse epitome of Old Norse myth, as well as being itself a poetic response to the mythology, illustrates some of the features of the synthetic accounts of Old Norse myth which, following Œhlenschläger's work, became popular amongst general readers. Jones based *Valhalla* on R. B. Andersen's prose account of Norse myth, *Norse Mythology; or, the Religion of our Forefathers* (1875), which had only recently been published; Andersen writes in the preface to his work that "What we claim for this work is, that it is the *first complete and systematic presentation of the Norse mythology in the English language*".[24]

Jones's preface to *Valhalla* is surprisingly old-fashioned in the way it introduces Old Norse myth to readers. She deplores, for instance, the fact that "so slight a knowledge of Scandinavian Mythology prevails, popularly",[25] and like Thomas Smith, praises its "purity", in explicit contrast to classical myth—though again like Cottle, Jones had to take measures with such poems as *Lokasenna*, completely omitting Loki's obscene taunts which are referred to simply as "words of insult vile".[26] Rasmus Andersen, the son of Norwegian immigrants to America, similarly pays tribute to the purity of Old Norse myth, and tellingly identifies himself (and possibly, by implication, his readers) with the Goths: "We Goths are a chaste race, and abhor the loathsome nudity of Greek art".[27] Andersen notes proudly that "there will not be found a single nude myth" in the *Poetic Edda*—though he bowdlerizes the substance of the eddic poem *Þrymskviða*, in which the god Thor dresses up as Freyja and verges on a wedding night with a giant in an attempt to reclaim his stolen hammer, calling it "a very beautiful myth",[28] and claiming that there is "not an impersonation of any kind that can be considered an outrage upon virtue or a violation of the laws of propriety".[29] Jones errs on the side of caution and omits it altogether.

Jones's praise of Old Norse culture recalls Montesquieu's eighteenth-century ideas of the morally bracing effects of a cold climate: the

[23] Thurin, *The American Discovery of the Norse*, p. 120.
[24] R. B. Andersen, *Norse Mythology; or, the Religion of our Forefathers* (Chicago: S. C. Griggs and Company, 1875), p. 9; the italics are Andersen's.
[25] Julia Clinton Jones, *Valhalla: The Myths of Norseland, A Saga, in Twelve Parts* (San Francisco: Edward Bosqui and Co., 1878), p. 7.
[26] Jones, *Valhalla*, p. 110.
[27] Andersen, *Norse Mythology*, p. 113.
[28] Andersen, *Norse Mythology*, p. 328.
[29] Andersen, *Norse Mythology*, p. 113.

"Southerner", she derides, became "effeminate and sensuous" because of the warm weather, while "lost in the contemplation of the ice-bound peaks of his native land...the Norseman's hardy spirit was lifted up...thus did his nature become nobler...and so gave birth to a purer Mythology".[30] She even slips into the old confusion of Celtic and Scandinavian cultures, claiming that "our ancestors sang their runic rhymes in groves of oak around the sacrificial stone".[31] The Goths are celebrated in familiar, traditional terms as bearers of political liberty, whose religion and culture are based on "principles of temperance, freedom, and chastity; bravery and justice were its key-stones".[32] But one detail illustrates her poetic alertness to this tradition: the outpouring of the Goths from Scandinavia, for so long figured in metaphors of hives and swarms and bees, is deftly transformed: Jones's Goths "rushed like an avalanche from their snow-capped fastnesses, to fall upon Rome".[33]

Jones also emphasizes, as one might expect, the specifically North-American angle on Norse mythology: that, as she puts it, "the first European who trod American soil was a Norseman", and that the Vikings were "the revolutionists" of their age.[34] Tied in with this is an implicit allusion to the old euhemeristic story of Odin as an actual chieftain; Jones sees the blood of the Vikings as flowing in American veins, and these Vikings as "descendants of the old Norse-Gods".[35] Old Norse mythology is the racial and cultural inheritance of white Americans.

Reflected in Jones's preface are the ideas of more recent German mythographers such as Grundtvig—mediated through Andersen—and this is especially evident in her light allegorizing of the material: Loki as the demon of fire, the Giants as the powerful and feared personifications of frost and ice.[36] Loki's monstrous offspring, the serpent, the wolf, and the goddess Hela, are identified as Sin, Pain, and Death.[37] And like Carlyle, Jones dwells on the parallels between Norse myth and Christianity. Her valkyries are "bright-winged", explicitly termed "bright angels";[38] three Norse gods Odin, Vili, and Ve are suggestively called the "Aesir-trinity", and Heimdallr, the watchman of the gods, who will warn Asgard about the coming of Ragnarök, is compared to the archangel Gabriel, with Ragnarök itself identified with the Christian day of Judgement. But most striking of all are the parallels Jones explores between Baldr and "Christ slain". For Jones, Baldr was not only, in familiar and uncontroversial mythographical

[30] Jones, *Valhalla*, p. 12.
[31] Jones, *Valhalla*, p. 8.
[32] Jones, *Valhalla*, p. 8.
[33] Jones, *Valhalla*, pp. 8–9.
[34] Jones, *Valhalla*, pp. 10, 11.
[35] Jones, *Valhalla*, p. 7.
[36] Jones, *Valhalla*, p. 13.
[37] Jones, *Valhalla*, p. 17.
[38] Jones, *Valhalla*, pp. 14, 19.

terms, "the personification of the summer sun slain by the long dark winter of the North", but also "Innocence,—the Light of the world".[39] The reference to the Gospel of St John, in which Christ repeatedly uses the phrase of himself, recalls Holman Hunt's celebrated and enormously popular devotional representation of Jesus with a lantern, the Light of the World.

The poem *Valhalla* itself is a perfect example of a unified, simplified and homogenized synthesis of Norse myth and legend. Its twelve parts cover Old Norse myth in a pleasingly ingenious structure. The narrative is dominated by the imminence of Ragnarök, which is alluded to in almost every section, and gives a teleological perspective to everything. Jones alters the myths in various ways, and as Thurin notes, "factual mistakes are not always easy to tell from the free play of the poetic imagination".[40] But a major alteration is Jones's complete omission of an episode which seems to have been extremely popular and prominent in the Middle Ages: Thor's encounter with the World Serpent, Miðgarðsormr. Jones substitutes an account of an encounter between Thor and the Daughters of Ægir—the waves. Thor, half personified as a storm, is a disturbingly aggressive lover to these wave-women who are themselves highly sexualized with "billowy breasts/Heaving high" and "dimpling smiles o'er soft cheeks breaking".[41] Thor is rough with them: "lustful" and "filled with passion" he tries to overcome them, and they resist, "Fiercely the billows strive,/Madly they toss and writhe".[42] Thor relishes the struggle, and eventually, "his wrath appeased" he departs, laughing. Jones's depiction of life in Valhalla is similarly sexualized: valkyries "recline . . . on warm bosoms", and Odin's warriors are plainly treated to sex as well as drink.[43] *Valhalla* would perhaps not have been thought especially suitable for younger readers.

Andersen quotes some stretches of eddic poetry in translation, and there is an extremely brief account of eddic alliteration in *Norse Mythology*,[44] but Jones evidently made no attempt to recreate any of the metrical effects of Old Norse. Her one foray into Old Norse poetic diction is notably misguided: in one of her very few footnotes, she explains the terms "dragon's bed" and "dwarf's dew" as "personifications of gold".[45] Whilst the first is in fact a kenning for gold, the second is not, though it could just about refer to the mead of poetry. It seems unlikely that Julia Clinton Jones

[39] Jones, *Valhalla*, p. 18.
[40] Thurin, *The American Discovery of the Norse*, p. 124.
[41] Jones, *Valhalla*, pp. 82, 84.
[42] Jones, *Valhalla*, pp. 85, 86.
[43] Jones, *Valhalla*, p. 45.
[44] Andersen, *Norse Mythology*, pp. 117–18.
[45] Jones, *Valhalla*, p. 70.

knew any Old Norse and Thurin criticizes her use of an ungrammatical plural—valkyriar—for Old Norse *valkyrjur* ("valkyries"), though it might be noted that he himself seems to take the plural noun Æsir ("the gods") as a singular, and adds an extra plural (Æsirs).[46]

The eighth section of *Valhalla* concerns Odin's visit to the sibyl—the subject of Gray's Norse ode 'The Descent of Odin', and, as we have seen, much re-worked. Jones's version includes the obligatory cliché used by so many other writers of the gods "quaffing" ale in Valhalla, but it is not especially indebted to Gray's work: though Jones's Odin, like Gray's, "up rose" for the journey to Hel, Jones's hound Garmr is not at all threatening, and all in all Jones's version of the material is rather colourless. But she echoes Longfellow's alliterative elegy: "Baldur the Beautiful must die",[47] and her account of Baldr's funeral is staid, dignified, and very short.

Julia Clinton Jones produces a poetic synthesis of Old Norse myth in which, like its prose predecessors, the original materials from which it was drawn are obscured. One striking objection to such homogenization is vehemently expressed in a review by William Roscoe of the work of Benjamin Thorpe, William and Mary Howitt, and the German poet and mythographer Karl Simrock. Roscoe notes that "with the main outlines of northern mythology everyone is familiar; fewer are acquainted with the exact nature of the materials from which those outlines have been constructed".[48] Old Norse poets transformed the mythic kernels into great poems, and "what we have transmitted to us in the *Edda* are *poems,* their best value is as poems, and there can scarcely be a doubt that it was as poems they were enjoyed and valued among the people for whom they were recited or sung".[49] His critique of mythographers is still valid now, especially what he calls "that very tempting but very false practice of dealing as if there had at some time existed a perfect and orderly system of mythology, of which we possessed only imperfect remains, and which it is the investigator's business to reconstruct".[50]

Roscoe's argument is testimony to how far the original mythic texts had been lost sight of in the synthetic systems of scholars. But the story of the death of Baldr proved to be an exception. Of all the elements in Old Norse myth, this was the one which repeatedly escaped incorporation into an over-arching narrative, and continually tempted writers and reviewers to "tell the story" instead of analyzing or assessing it. Grenville Pigott

---

[46] Thurin, *The American Discovery of the Norse*, p. 122.
[47] Jones, *Valhalla*, p. 92.
[48] Roscoe, 'The Eddas', p. 466.
[49] Roscoe, 'The Eddas', p. 475.
[50] Roscoe, 'The Eddas', p. 487.

called the death of Baldr "the principal event in the Mythological drama of the Scandinavians".[51] Adam Œhlenschläger omitted it altogether from his synthetic account of Old Norse myths, and turned the episode into a stand-alone piece, *Balder hin Gode*—provoking his translator Frye to tell the story in the preface to his translation.[52] William and Mary Howitt, in their impressive (though somewhat over-enthusiastic) overview of Old Norse-Icelandic literature (and therefore myth), explain its centrality through allegory: Baldr's death is "a symbol of the life of the year slain by Winter" and further symbolic of "the general destruction of virtue and justice". Moreover, they argue, the story provides clear evidence of a belief in "the true and only God".[53]

Paradoxically, the most accessible account of Baldr's death in Old Norse is related not in poetry, but in Snorri's *Prose Edda* (repeatedly compared unfavourably with the *Poetic Edda* by nineteenth-century commentators). This means that it already had its own narrative cogency and almost novelistic motivation, characters, and sentiment. Even the somewhat carnivalesque detail of the otherwise dignified gods throwing missiles at Baldr because it was diverting to watch them bounce off his inviolable body could be made to seem more natural; Grenville Pigott imagines that after he had ominous dreams, the gods threw things at Baldr as a kindness, to reassure him about his inviolability.[54] Froude, for all his racist celebration of valour and Northern courage, yet praises the tenderness and pity evident in the story of Baldr, as Frigg, and indeed, almost the whole of creation, weeps at his death, and Nanna "breaks her heart and goes with him"[55] (though perhaps Nanna's presence on Baldr's funeral pyre had a more sinister origin). The elements of human drama are all there: Baldr's worries; Frigg's maternal instincts; Loki's deception. And no-one could miss the resonances with Christian mythology (not to mention echoes of the myths of Adonis and the Babylonian deity Tammuz): the young and beautiful god, whose death caused great grief, and whose resurrection is imperative. The death of Baldr was also the first portent of Ragnarök, of the end of the world, and might prompt meditation on apocalypse and a regenerated new order. It was a solemn, even grand, subject, with a

---

[51] Grenville Pigott, *A Manual of Scandinavian Mythology, containing a Popular Account of the Two Eddas and of the Religion of Odin* (London: William Pickering, 1839), p. 22.

[52] Adam Œhlenschläger, *Balder hin Gode* (Copenhagen, 1806), and Frye, *The Gods of the North*, pp. xx–xxiv.

[53] William and Mary Howitt, *The Literature and Romance of Northern Europe* (London: Colburn and Co., 1852), vol. I, p. 52.

[54] Pigott, *A Manual of Scandinavian Mythology*, p. 289.

[55] Froude, 'The Odin-Religion', p. 169.

morally edifying protagonist and not too much "wild" detail. It was ideal matter for a Victorian poet.

Matthew Arnold probably began writing 'Balder Dead' in 1853; he wrote to his sister at the end of 1854 saying that the poem was finished.[56] His main source was Percy's translation of Mallet—*Northern Antiquities*—and although he owned a copy of I. A. Blackwell's revised edition of 1847, to write 'Balder Dead' he relied on one of the two earlier editions: either the original of 1770, or the very similar second edition of 1809.[57] So 'Balder Dead', though ostensibly a product of the mid-nineteenth century, is rather "based on the scholarship of the late eighteenth century... *Balder Dead* is a late-blooming fruit of the antiquarianism of the romantic revival".[58] There are some details in the poem which betray this reliance on old scholarship, perhaps most obviously a reference to the gods drinking wine from "gold-rimmed skulls" (I.14), which Blackwell, following Grenville Pigott, had corrected in the 1847 edition. But more significantly, Mallet's gods had not become the allegorized forces of nature proposed by nineteenth-century scholars, and Arnold's most distinctive transformation of the Old Norse myth is to classicize it, to tell the story of Baldr's death in the style of classical epic, as Homer, or more particularly, Virgil, might have framed it. The poem duly opens with the off-stage action of Baldr's death as a fait accompli: "So on the floor lay Balder dead" (I.1). W. E. Buckler argues that Arnold was attracted to and developed the distinctively Virgilian qualities of the original story: "The Homeric tale of the epic hero—solitary, self-reliant, vulnerable but indomitable even in the face of catastrophic circumstances—has been replaced by the Virgilian tale of the tribe—socialized, circumscribed, dwarfed by prudence and responsibility".[59]

The primary effect of classicizing the original material is what some (but by no means all) critics have recognized as what the poet W. E. Henley called its "simple majesty of conception, sober directness and potency of expression, sustained dignity of thought and sentiment and style".[60] But another striking effect is that the human interest inherent in the story is very fully realized. The gods are oddly domesticated, and so too is their dwelling place in Asgard, which is described in detail with its streets, and

---

[56] See *The Poems of Matthew Arnold*, ed. Kenneth and Miriam Allott (London: Longman, 1979), p. 376.

[57] See Mary W. Schneider, 'The Source of Matthew Arnold's "Balder Dead"', *Notes and Queries* 14:2 (1967), 56–61.

[58] Schneider, 'The Source of Matthew Arnold's "Balder Dead"', 61.

[59] William E. Buckler, *On the Poetry of Matthew Arnold: Essays in Critical Reconstruction* (New York: New York University Press, 1982), p. 155.

[60] W. E. Henley, quoted in Carl Dawson (ed.), *Matthew Arnold, The Poetry: The Critical Heritage* (London: Routledge & Kegan Paul, 1973), p. 289.

harbour, and lighted windows. Hoder (Höðr), condemned to wander in
Hel, regrets the loss of what looks like a distinctly Victorian respectability:

> I too had once a wife, and once a child,
> And substance, and a golden house in Heaven. (III.403–4)

Even Hel is more like a pale version of the real world than the fantastical
realm of horrors earlier poets depict; Balder, for example, occupies his time
acting as a sort of local magistrate there, as "the wan tribes of dead" come to
him to settle "Their ineffectual feuds and feeble hates" (III.464–6). The harsh
northernness of the setting is replaced by a Mediterranean mildness, with
warm evenings scented with honeysuckle. The more extraordinary elements
of the original description of Baldr's funeral—such as the god Thor kicking a
dwarf on to the funeral pyre, or Freyja's chariot pulled by cats—are absent.[61]

Arnold's deployment of Homeric similes is very striking. They stand out
very markedly because they compare the events of the narrative with pastoral scenes more English than Scandinavian or even classical. Thus when
Hoder lightly touches his brother Hermod in the darkness, Arnold likens
the contact to "a spray of honeysuckle flowers" which

> Brushes across a tired traveller's face
> Who shuffles through the deep dew-moistened dust,
> On a May evening, in the darkened lanes,
> And starts him, that he thinks a ghost went by. (I.231–4)

Balder's ghost (Arnold's own invention) fades from sight "as the woodman
sees a little smoke/Hang in the air, afield, and disappear" (I.335–6). These
are light and pleasing additions. A more major intervention is Arnold's
depiction of Hermod's difficulty in crossing the bridge over the River
Gjöll, which marks the boundary between the world of the living and the
world of the dead. In the Old Norse, the bridge is guarded by a female
figure named by Snorri as Móðguðr ("battle-weary"); we know nothing
else about her. Arnold describes Hermod's passage across, blocked by the
bridge guardian, as being like

> when cowherds in October drive
> Their kine across a snowy mountain-pass
> To winter-pasture on the southern side,
> And on the ridge a waggon chokes the way,
> Wedged in the snow; then painfully the hinds
> With goad and shouting urge their cattle past,
> Plunging through deep untrodden banks of snow
> To right and left, and warm steam fills the air. (II.91–8)

---

[61] Arnold's source Percy had omitted these details.

One nineteenth-century critic quite reasonably complained that "the comparison of a damsel to a wagon is not specially poetical; and the minute details of drovers and cattle are vastly ineffective and irrelevant".[62] Even more extraordinarily ill-fitting is the simile Arnold puts in the mouth of the malevolent Lok, who jeers at Hermod's return to Asgard without Balder

> Like as a farmer who has lost his dog,
> Some morn, at market, in a crowded town—
> Through many street the poor beast runs in vain,
> And follows this man after that, for hours;
> And, late at evening, spent and panting, falls
> Before a stranger's threshold, not his home,
> With flanks a-tremble, and his slender tongue
> Hangs quivering out between his dust-smeared jaws,
> And piteously he eyes the passers-by. (III.8–16)

The focus of the comparison has shifted uncomfortably from Hermod being like a farmer to Baldr being like his lost dog. As the poet Ian Hamilton has remarked, when Arnold is "'at home' with his materials" he is "wildly out of tune with his main purpose".[63] But this cannot be inadvertent or unwilled. Every one of Arnold's carefully observed countryside scenes serves to relate the events of the myth to a distinctively real, contemporary world, and provides a strikingly successful backdrop to the central allegory inherent in the original myth: all creation weeping for the death of Baldr as the universal natural phenomenon of the thawing of a frozen landscape. Just as Snorri compares this weeping to a thaw, "when things are brought out of frost and in to heat", so Arnold compares it to what happens

> in winter, when the frosts break up,
> At winter's end, before the spring begins,
> And a warm west-wind blows, and thaw sets in—
> After an hour a dripping sound is heard
> In all the forests, and the soft-strewn snow
> Under the trees is dibbled thick with holes,
> And from the boughs the snowloads shuffle down;
> And, in fields sloping to the south, dark plots
> Of grass peep out amid surrounding snow,
> And widen, and the peasant's heart is glad... (III.307–16)

[62] H. B. Forman, in Dawson, *Matthew Arnold... The Critical Heritage*, p. 198.
[63] Ian Hamilton, *A Gift Imprisoned: The Poetic Life of Matthew Arnold* (London: Bloomsbury, 1998), p. 183.

Norse myth is here re-cast in startlingly familiar terms. Of course, some critics regretted such acculturation. Clare Jerrold found it disappointing as well as surprising that Arnold, "who wrote when Norse literature had become a field of eager research, should so strip an old legend of every natural characteristic as to render it practically unrecognizable".[64] Jerrold goes on to complain that "the whole picture is foreign to the wild forces of nature which the myth is meant to portray".[65] On the other hand, there were those who praised Arnold's transformations. H. G. Hewlett evidently despaired of Old Norse myth as a poetic source: "The delineation of beings so anomalous as the Gods of Scandinavian mythology is attended with difficulties that Art can scarcely hope to overcome",[66] praising Arnold's decision to "disregard as accidental the national peculiarities of the literatures that have furnished his themes".[67] Why, then, did Arnold choose to work with this subject?

As we have seen, he was reading Mallet, but this choice demands explanation in itself. I have indicated above the attractions of the Baldr myth—as opposed to other Old Norse subjects—for a serious poet. Clyde de L. Ryals writes further of the qualities that might have attracted Arnold: "a fatalistic conception of the universe and a brooding, melancholy atmosphere".[68] W. E. Buckler sternly suggests a more didactic purpose: "broadening the base of the reader's literary experience, connecting a mythology largely foreign to him with a stylistic manner [which is] part of the mainstream of the European poetic consciousness".[69] And Froude, reviewing *Poems* (1853), with characteristic chauvinism commended Old Norse myth as a subject for Arnold: "why should not the Teutonic poet sing of the Teutons?"[70] Finally, topoi such as the funeral preparations are shared by both the heroic epic and the Norse myth. But much-documented connexions between Arnold and Thomas Carlyle may both explain why Arnold committed himself to the story of Baldr, and show more clearly what he made of it.

Arnold became an undergraduate in 1841, the year after Carlyle delivered his lecture on Odin. Ruth apRoberts speculates that Arnold's interest in Baldr may have been "piqued" by Carlyle's reference to Baldr as "the White God, the beautiful, the just and benignant (whom the early

---

[64] Clare Jerrold, 'The Balder Myth and Some English Poets', *Saga-Book of the Viking Society* III (1901–3), 94–116 (105).

[65] Jerrold, 'The Balder Myth and Some English Poets', 108.

[66] Dawson, *Matthew Arnold... The Critical Heritage*, p. 242.

[67] Dawson, *Matthew Arnold... The Critical Heritage*, p. 240.

[68] Clyde de L. Ryals, 'Arnold's *Balder Dead*', *Victorian Poetry* 4:2 (1966), 67–81 (68).

[69] Buckler, *On the Poetry of Matthew Arnold*, p. 156.

[70] J. A. Froude, 'Arnold's Poems', *The Westminster Review* (January 1854), 146–59 (159).

Christian Missionaries found to resemble Christ)".[71] Carlyle tells the story
of Baldr's death, and apRoberts concludes that "there is little question that
the Odin lecture was the inspiration for... 'Balder Dead'".[72] As apRoberts points out, "the whole lecture...can be seen as a disguised account
of the nature of Christ and the development of Christianity",[73] although
while Odin is a man who comes to be worshipped as a god, Christ is
a divinity who becomes human.[74] Perhaps, then, what struck Arnold
about Carlyle's work was his bold analogy between Old Norse paganism and Christianity—or "Christianism", as Carlyle pointedly terms it.
For Carlyle, Norse myth as much as Christianity had "a *truth* in [it], an
inward perennial truth and greatness".[75] Carlyle, influenced by his reading
of the German philosopher and theologian Johan Herder, saw in Norse
myth, and especially its account of Ragnarök, of which Baldr's death is the
first portent, a demonstration that belief systems rise and fall, each to be
replaced by something better—a theme which Arnold continually stresses
in 'Balder Dead'. One might argue, then, that Arnold took from Carlyle
the inspiration for using the story of Baldr's death for his own reflections
on the nature and development of Christianity.

Frederick Page reads 'Balder Dead' as an allegory of Christian
faith: "Balder is Christianity as it has fared among men. Lok is the critical spirit, 'the all-corroding, all-dissolving scepticism of the intellect in
religious enquiries'. Hoder (that innocent Judas) is popular opinion".[76]
In fact, since Arnold describes Balder as a poet, and even usurping Odin's
role, as the inventor of poetry, his death might also be taken to represent the demise of creativity. But as Ryals argues, it is not Balder himself,
but the poem's powerfully negative depiction of life in Valhalla which is
so redolent of Arnold's view of the spiritual condition of England in the
mid-nineteenth century. "Life in Valhalla is aimless", Ryals observes, citing the pointless throwing of missiles at Balder. "Compassion and love find
little place [there]", as can be seen in the cruel depiction of blind Hoder
as "ill-fated, child of bale" (I.112). Frea is "a nagging wife who also wants
her prominence recognized", and Odin is "powerless to avert the coming

---

[71] Ruth apRoberts, 'Arnold and Natural Supernaturalism', in Clinton Machann
and Forrest D. Burt (eds.), *Matthew Arnold in His Time and Ours: Centenary Essays*
(Charlottesville: University Press of Virginia, 1988), pp. 17–29 (18).
[72] apRoberts, 'Arnold and Natural Supernaturalism', p. 18.
[73] apRoberts, 'Arnold and Natural Supernaturalism', p. 22.
[74] See Anne Varty, 'Carlyle and Odin', in Ewbank, Lausund and Tysdahl (eds.),
Anglo-Scandinavian Cross Currents, pp. 60–70.
[75] Carlyle, *On Heroes*, p. 42.
[76] Frederick Page, '*Balder Dead* (1855): An Interpretation', *Essays and Studies* 28 (1942),
60–8 (60).

doom".[77] Balder is glad to have left behind its "storm of carnage" and when Hoder offers to go to Hel in place of Balder, Frea tells Hoder—in unmistakably Miltonic terms—that would be no shortage of volunteers,

> For many Gods in Heaven, not thou alone,
> Would freely die to purchase Balder back,
> And wend themselves to Hela's gloomy realm.
> For not so gladsome is that life in Heaven
> Which Gods and heroes lead, in feast and fray,
> Waiting the darkness of the final times. (I.119–24)

There is no future in or for Valhalla.

In 'Balder Dead', we can see Arnold transforming Old Norse myth to produce a poem with a topical reflex and profoundly personal concerns. In doing so, he has deepened the tenor of the myth itself, even as he has turned his back on the stylistic features of his original, and substituted classical features and blatantly ill-fitting Homeric similes of English pastoral life. Stripping Old Norse myth of its dubious incidental particularities has only laid bare its core, an imaginative truth which, as Carlyle would have it, is as valid as the truth of Christian dogma, which itself might survive the rationalist attacks on the supernatural features of Christian faith. And this core of truth may outlast the inevitable passing of Christianity itself, to be itself replaced by another future, almost incoherently predicted by Arnold: "Another Heaven, the boundless—no one yet/Hath reached it" (III.519–20).

'Balder Dead' never became a popular poem. In 1881, a caricature of Matthew Arnold was published with the caption:

> Admit that Homer sometimes nods, that poets *do* write trash,
> Our bard has written "*Balder Dead*" and also, Balder-Dash.[78]

At almost the same time as Arnold was writing 'Balder Dead', Sydney Dobell was beginning a very different Baldr poem. The eponymous hero of *Balder* is not a Norse god, but a Victorian husband and father. However, his child is dead—apparently by Balder's own hand—and his wife, driven insane, presumably by grief, longs for death. For Balder, the temptation to kill her—and add that experience to his store of extreme sensations—proves too great to resist. The poem, presented as a verse drama, largely comprises a series of intense, soul-searching monologues by Balder, interspersed with the pathetic ramblings of his wife Amy, and

[77] Ryals, 'Arnold's *Balder Dead*', 70–3.
[78] Edward Linley Sambourne, 'Punch's Fancy Portraits, No. 59: Mr. Matthew Arnold', *Punch* (26 November 1881), p. 250.

what are apparently readings from Balder's own works. The poem was pilloried and parodied by William Aytoun, who dubbed Dobell and poets who wrote in a similar vein about extreme inner turmoil "the Spasmodic school".[79] According to Mark Weinstein, spasmody was a post-Romantic development, heavily influenced by the work of Shelley and Byron, and Weinstein declares that "Spasmody reaches its extreme limits in Sydney Dobell's *Balder*".[80]

Two points of connexion between Balder and Baldr are already evident. Firstly, Weinstein notes that "the Spasmodic hero is...a Byronic poet" and as we have seen, in Arnold's 'Balder Dead' for instance, the mythological figure of Baldr is sometimes presented as a poet. And secondly, Balder's morbid fascination, not to say obsession, with death, is a strong link with the god whose death is the focal point of the story of the Old Norse gods—a connexion even more clearly evident in Robert Buchanan's long poem *Balder the Beautiful*, which I will come to shortly. Dobell's Balder is much given to pondering immortality: early on in the poem he voices his uncertainties:

> Am I not immortal?
> And if immortal now, immortal then;
> And if immortal then, existent now;
> But where?[81]

Further, Dobell himself called his hero "a nineteenth-century pagan"[82]; Pittock notes "repeated solar imagery" in the poem;[83] and Amy rather histrionically refers to her husband as a god. Otherwise, the Norse references in *Balder* are incidental allusions. Balder has ominous prophetic dreams, like Baldr; not, apparently, about his own demise, but about the possibility that poetic inspiration will be withheld from him, though he also muses on resurrection.[84] Balder dismisses Fame as little more than a brassy trumpet, "Tho' it blow Regnarok (sic) and wake the graves".[85] And at one point, Balder imagines seeing the world from the perspective of a tiny child, such that, "This chequered field shall be my vast

[79] See Mark A. Weinstein, *William Edmondstoune Aytoun and the Spasmodic Controversy* (New Haven: Yale University Press, 1968).

[80] Weinstein, *William Edmondstoune Aytoun*, p. 94. At one point in the poem, words seem to fail to express the depth of Balder's emotional responses, and he utters the wordless interjection "ah" thirteen times; a little later on, Amy manages only eight repetitions.

[81] Sydney Dobell, *Balder* (London: Smith, Elder, and Co., 1854), Scene III, p. 21.

[82] Malcolm Pittock, 'Dobell, *Balder* and Post-Romanticism', *Essays in Criticism* 42:3 (1992), 221–42 (223).

[83] Pittock, 'Dobell, *Balder* and Post-Romanticism', 229.

[84] Dobell, *Balder*, Scene XVIII, p. 71.

[85] Dobell, *Balder*, Scene III, p. 15.

expanse;/Yon tree Igdrasil".[86] Perhaps more significantly, Balder the poet may be writing about Ragnarök: he reads aloud from his own poetry which describes a scene of chaos, in which "Old ocean made invasion/And advanced with all his waves" and "earth/With deadly fear did shiver to her core".[87] Further on in the poem, a great cosmic war is described, "In horrid rank/Sinister, front to hostile front opposed".[88] Finally, when the doctor unsuccessfully treating Amy looks through Balder's writings, he notes in one set of scrolls "Thor—Balder—a Viking—a Runic Skald".[89] Balder is clearly writing about Baldr, creating an extremely odd moment of fictional self-referentiality in the poem.

Balder was mocked by some of Dobell's contemporaries, a hostile critical reception which was perhaps the main factor in Dobell's failure to complete his original plan of writing another two parts.[90] But although, as Weinstein puts it, the spasmodic poets were censured for "their violent language, non-functional imagery, emotional vicissitudes and poetic digressions"—all features very evident in *Balder*—Tennyson admired the spasmodic poets, and Dobell in particular.[91] And Dobell himself thought that *Balder* was his best work. The same dislocation between the author's assessment of his work, and its wider critical reception, is true of Robert Buchanan's long poem, *Balder the Beautiful*.

Robert Buchanan began his literary career translating Scandinavian poetry, especially ballads, into English.[92] In 1877, he wrote *Balder the Beautiful*, with its heavily portentous subtitle, "A Song of Divine Death". Buchanan's Balder is a Christ-figure, and in Buchanan's long poem, the events of his life (and death) are given a remarkable new twist. Buchanan's epigraph to the poem reveals at the outset one radical feature of his representation of Balder: gods, says Buchanan, are "brethren", all "fashion'd of the self-same fire"; Balder, metaphorically at least, is the younger brother of Jesus. Balder's divine Father back in Asgard (never named as Odin by Buchanan, but left in patriarchal anonymity) is a terrifying and hostile figure. Balder's mother Frea (the usual mistake for Frigg) therefore leaves

---

[86] Dobell, *Balder,* Scene XXXIV, p. 237.

[87] Dobell, *Balder,* Scene VII, pp. 39–40.

[88] Dobell, *Balder,* Scene XII, p. 53. A. S. Byatt's novel *Possession* features a fictional Victorian poet, Randolph Ash, who is writing a poem about Ragnarök. The Spasmodic school was held by some to have influenced Tennyson's 'Maud'; Byatt has written about 'Maud', so there is a possibility that Ash was modelled by Byatt on Balder.

[89] Dobell, *Balder,* Scene XXIII, p. 103.

[90] See his preface to the second edition (London, 1854), and Weinstein, *William Edmondstoune Aytoun*, p. 165.

[91] Weinstein, *William Edmondstoune Aytoun,* pp. 173–4.

[92] See Christopher David Murray, *Robert Buchanan (1841–1901): An Assessment of his Career*, D.Phil thesis (University of London, 1974).

Asgard and gives birth to him on earth—"By the pangs of a woman/the goddess was torn".[93] Buchanan implicitly figures this birth in lyrical seasonal terms: springtime comes to the Earth. The reason—beyond the Freudian commonplace—for the Father's grim hostility is the prophecy associated with Balder that he will cause the downfall of the gods:

> Yet the spell had been woven
> Long ages ago,
> That the clouds should be cloven,
> The Father undone.[94]

Moreover,

> In runes it was written,
> With letters forlorn.[95]

And so, leaving him "on a bank of flowers", Frea tells the Father and the other gods back in Asgard that Balder is dead, and the gods "Drank deep, and breathed again".[96]

On earth Balder grows up at one with nature, fed honey by wild bears, in an idealized paradisiacal childhood lyrically described by Buchanan:

> And wheresoe'er he sets his feet
> Fair ferns and flowers spring,
> And honeysuckles scented sweet
> Grow where his fingers cling.
>
> He calls, and wood-doves at the cry
> Come down to be caress'd;
> Curl'd in his arms the lynx will lie,
> Its lips against his breast.[97]

But like his Norse original, he has bad dreams; the threatening presence of the Father continues to haunt him. Further, his closeness to earth has brought him intimations of mortality; in his dreams he has seen "he whom mortal men have christen'd Death".[98] Buchanan develops the seasonal metaphor by figuring Baldr's departure as the coming of winter. Frea, wrongly but sweetly convinced that once the Father sees his son, he will love him for his beauty and radiance, takes Balder back to Asgard (and winter comes to earth). But Balder is not at all welcome to the Father, since he signifies,

---

[93] Robert Buchanan, *Balder the Beautiful: A Song of Divine Death* (London: William Mullan & Son, 1877), p. 8.
[94] Buchanan, *Balder the Beautiful*, p. 13.
[95] Buchanan, *Balder the Beautiful*, p. 13.
[96] Buchanan, *Balder the Beautiful*, p. 17.
[97] Buchanan, *Balder the Beautiful*, p. 19.
[98] Buchanan, *Balder the Beautiful*, p. 41.

in psychological as well as prophetic terms, his father's death, and as Frea is forced, succinctly, to admit to Balder, "Thy Father loves thee not, but casts thee forth".[99] Balder returns to earth (bringing with him the advent of spring). Unlike his father, Balder loves mankind, and still grieves for human mortality. So he sets off to find death (his plea for help unanswered by his father, who sits "Immortal, terrible and desolate" in Asgard).[100]

The goddess Ydun (Old Norse Íðunn) appears to Balder, offering him the apples of immortality, but Balder will only accept them if he can pass them on to his beloved mankind. Ydun therefore offers to take him to see Death, leading him to a sinister altar where a female virgin has been sacrificed to the Father. Death, still unsatisfied, hovers above the altar, singing a grim song. Balder is, naturally, appalled. He prays again to the Father in familiar terms: "Father, Father, who art in heaven", and begs that he may be allowed to die "that men may live".[101] The identification of Balder and Christ is complete.

As Balder falls asleep in Death's arms, snow falls on earth. But through the darkness slowly approaches a silent shape with a red lantern in its hand: this is, unmistakably, the Light of the World, as painted by Holman Hunt; his hands and feet are pierced, and, as Balder had hoped to do, he has died for mankind. Christ explains to Balder that the gods of Asgard are simply not powerful enough to bargain with Death, and Balder must resume divinity and immortality; he must be resurrected from his brief death. But Christ, Balder, and Death head north to Asgard—that is, Death is brought to the pitiless gods. Balder's triumphant greeting—"Behold, I am risen, my father"[102]—signals to the Æsir that the ancient runic prophecy is fulfilled. In a dreadful peroration, the gods give vent to their hatred and contempt for Balder and all earthly things; Balder, by returning, has killed the Father.

C. D. Murray writes that in *Balder the Beautiful*, Buchanan attempted to address "the overwhelming question concerning man's immortality that beset him throughout his life".[103] But equally evident in the poem's philosophy is the explicit expression of the comparability and indeed equality of gods such as Balder and Christ who suffered for the good of mankind, and, implicitly, the equivalence of their hostile or at best indifferent fathers. Plainly, the divine Father of Christian tradition is not flattered by the comparison.

---

[99] Buchanan, *Balder the Beautiful*, p. 98.
[100] Buchanan, *Balder the Beautiful*, p. 134.
[101] Buchanan, *Balder the Beautiful*, pp. 198, 201.
[102] Buchanan, *Balder the Beautiful*, p. 270.
[103] Murray, *Robert Buchanan*, p. 55.

Balder the Beautiful was not a critical success, perhaps because of its theological position. But Buchanan was even prouder of his Baldr poem than Arnold and Dobell were of theirs, in spite of a lack of critical appreciation. In letters to friends, Buchanan expresses what might even be called inordinate pride in his work. To William Canton, accompanying proofs of the poem, Buchanan writes "I think you will admit its originality whatever you think of its beauty. For my own part, I am conceited enough to think it in some respects the finest conception of this generation!!!" (original punctuation).[104] To Roden Noel, he is no less enthusiastic, although anticipating less enthusiasm from the public: it is "a work...pregnant with subtle ideas...I fancy you will admit the conception to be grandiose and striking in the extreme...it is not a poem for the public—it is likely to be caviar to the general".[105]

Close engagement with the Baldr myth evidently summoned up profound responses in some Victorian poets. The application of the myth not only to human emotions—pity, grief, filial affection and lack of it, and so on—but also to philosophical issues such as mortality and transience and the value of beauty—played a part in how engaged they became with their source material. But what is particularly significant is the versatility of the myth of Baldr, the way in which an individual poet might take the original story and turn it into something entirely different. As Buchanan added in his letter to Canton about *Balder the Beautiful*, "In reading it, forget—if you remember—anything about the vulgar myths of the Edda. This Balder is my own—his story mine—although he is the Northern Apollo as well as the Northern Christ".

In 1897, the composer Howard Orsmond Anderton produced yet another very different adaptation of the myth of Baldr: though published as what looks like a verse drama, *Baldur* was evidently planned as the libretto of a tragic operetta, though I cannot find any trace of its ever having been performed. The myth as presented by Anderton is surprisingly suitable for theatrical performance, with its troops of gods, goddesses, heroes, valkyries, skalds, fantastically dancing fire-spirits, and gnomes. The setting is elegantly classicized: the opening scene is set in Baldur's garden, with a palace of white marble, "half-covered with golden lattice", and even a perch of doves.[106] Baldur's wife Nanna is to be dressed in a gown of gold and white, and she greets the dawn, "clad in dewy veil/Of hazy splendour and opal sheen". She lyrically expresses her love for Baldur, who enters also

---

[104] See Harriett Jay, *Robert Buchanan: Some Account of His Life, His Life's Work, and His Literary Friendships* (London: T. Fisher Unwin, 1903), p. 209.

[105] Jay, *Robert Buchanan*, p. 210.

[106] H. Orsmond Anderton, *Baldur: A Lyrical Drama* (London: T. Fisher Unwin, 1893), p. 5.

dressed in gold and white, "his golden hair falling about his shoulders", addressing him as "Lord of Love and Peace".[107] But Baldur has had prophetic dreams, and we see at once that his worries are justified: a sinister character called Thralsyn (not anywhere found in Old Norse) appears, armed with a dagger; he is Loki's creature, sent to kill Baldur. Christ-like, Baldur does not defend himself, and forgives Thralsyn for what he was about to do. In Act II of *Baldur*, Loki tries to force Thralsyn to kill Baldur with mistletoe, but in spite of Loki's vicious threats, Thralsyn refuses to be his accomplice, and is saved by trusting in Baldur's forgiveness. This little narrative of Thralsyn's redemption is Anderton's own invention, increasing Baldur's moral stature, and deepening the pathos of his own death.

Alongside this free invention, Anderton demonstrates his close knowledge of Old Norse by scattering mythic details throughout his work. Baldur says that his premonitions are reliable, for he, like Odin, has "drunk of Mimir's well",[108] but dreads his imminent exile in Hel, where he will have to contend with

> the serpent that lies curled
> Encircling the world,
> Pouring his poison-flood
> Into its heart and blood.[109]

The magic ring "Dröpner" (Draupnir) is invoked and there is a wonderfully theatrical appearance—announced by a mysterious humming—of Norns whose actions plainly owe a good deal to Thomas Gray's fatal sisters:

> As they spin the fibre thin
> And weave the web of Fate,
> Woof and warp of will and deed.[110]

There is even some quaffing of nectar. Anderton's valkyries are sexual beings: in Valhalla, Odin's warriors sink into their arms in slumber. Loki's progeny are termed a "monstrous brood", and named, reasonably accurately, as "Fenris, Jormungand and Hela". Loki reminds the gods of their wrongful deeds –"Who coveted Andvari's gold?/Who cheated the Jötuns of their pay?",[111] referring to the story Snorri tells about the gods sending Loki to steal Andvari's gold to pay the otter's ransom, and to his account of the so-called "master-builder tale", in which the gods—with Loki's help—avoid paying a giant who has been commissioned to repair the walls of Asgard (his agreed reward was marriage to Freyja). And of course Ragnarök is alluded to, as a distant apocalypse which "draws/Ever more near".[112]

---

[107] Anderton, *Baldur*, p. 6.   [108] Anderton, *Baldur*, p. 7.
[109] Anderton, *Baldur*, p. 9.   [110] Anderton, *Baldur*, p. 11.
[111] Anderton, *Baldur*, p. 22.   [112] Anderton, *Baldur*, p. 31.

Anderton reproduces the command to all things animate and inanimate not to harm Baldr, but dramatizes it by having Odin address "Ye
powers of Water, Earth and Air". There is even a false oath: Loki swears
that he shall not raise his hand to Baldur, but Baldur spots the deceit at
once: "Not thine hand,/Tho' thine the will and brain".[113] And so it proves,
just as in the original myth. Loki has found out that the mistletoe has
not been included in the oath Frigg sought from all things not to harm
Baldur (not through a meeting with Frigg, but "hidden lurking nigh" he
overheard), but having failed to coerce Thralsyn into using it, he stirs up
a fight in Valhalla. In the confusion Höder fires the fatal shot. As well as
the fight, Anderton invents some thoughtful details to increase the drama
and reduce the strangeness of this episode. Loki has made fire spirits create a lethal weapon from the mistletoe, so that a plant thought "Too small
a bud,/Too weak and mean" will serve his purpose, and he rejoices that
"Small to great things grow".[114]

After Baldur's death, Anderton follows his Norse sources in having an
emissary sent to Hel's underworld to reclaim Baldur, though here the god
Thor undertakes the journey, mounted on Sleipnir. In another departure from the original, Thor challenges Hel directly, and wrestles with
her; her bringing him to one knee is an allusion to one of Snorri's stories
about the exploits of Thor at the court of the giant Útgarða-Loki, when
Thor is brought down to one knee by the old woman Elli, who is actually a personification of old age; Útgarða-Loki purports to be amazed at
this feat, since all living things are brought to both knees by old age.[115]
Thor's response here—"Foiled by a woman!"—seems a little comic today,
and recalls an earlier moment in *Baldur* when Loki, irritated by the gods'
attempt at self-righteousness, mocks "Bah! Purity's for girls, not men".[116]

In line with the myth, Hela offers to release Baldur if all things will
weep for him. But in another radical departure from the original, "a veiled
figure is dimly seen seated in the darkness beside the bier", and this strange
creature tells a mysterious fable claiming that the gods will never be able
to escape their doom: they have been seduced by an enchanter's magic
drink which has given them knowledge.[117] There is immediate uproar
in Valhalla, the gods divided against each other, some denouncing the
fable, others defending the figure—who will not weep. Thor threatens to
attack, and the figure is revealed to be Loki, to the acclaim of the rebellious
Æsir, who demand the mead of oblivion whatever the cost. The gods are

[113] Anderton, *Baldur*, p. 13.   [114] Anderton, *Baldur*, p. 17.
[115] Faulkes, *Edda*, pp. 43–6.   [116] Anderton, *Baldur*, pp. 30, 24.
[117] Anderton, *Baldur*, pp. 35–7.

doomed, and as darkness falls on the scene, Loki triumphantly cries out that he himself is Fate. There is no need for a Ragnarök, which, as Richard Wagner anticipated, was impossible to dramatize on stage.

But Anderton's libretto does not end here. A vision of Prometheus bound appears, and a voice identifies the bringer of fire to mankind as a Loki-figure, whose crowning triumph was the death of Baldur. But a voice explains that Baldur's purity cannot be extirpated, and the vision of Prometheus gradually changes into the shape of Christ's Cross, and finally, into a vision of Baldur, "in fullest intensity of glory".[118] Anderton has expressed in visual terms the argument we have seen verbally expressed in the other Baldur poems of this period: Old Norse myth is equated, and assimilated, with Christianity, and thus raised from its status as the bizarre and essentially untrue (if diverting) beliefs of a past age.

It only remains to note the spelling of the hero's name: "Baldur" is the modern Icelandic form of the name of the Norse god Baldr. By the end of the nineteenth century we are beginning to see fewer of the misconceptions, inaccuracies, and plain garbling which betrayed the imperfect grasp of the sources characteristic of earlier poets. And as Karl Litzenberg points out, by 1905 "virtually all the Old Norse documents which might be of general interest had been published", marking the end point of what Litzenberg calls "the golden age of Old Norse study in England".[119] He dates the beginning of this "golden age" to the publication of George Webbe Dasent's translation of Snorri's *Edda*, in 1842, and as his word "study" suggests, he is at pains to make a clear distinction between the part previously played by poets in popularizing Old Norse literature, and the work of translators such as Samuel Laing and Dasent himself. But Litzenberg chooses 1905 for his end point because it is the year in which the final volume of the Saga Library—William Morris and Eiríkr Magnússon's set of saga translations—was published. Like his enormously influential predecessor Thomas Gray, Morris combined the skills of both scholar and poet—Litzenberg notes that he "was more closely acquainted with Scandinavian literature, myth and custom than any English *poet* [my italics] before him".[120] So before moving on to the next phase, the influence of Old Norse myth on twentieth-century poets who could draw on a great and fast-increasing reservoir of scholarly studies and translations of Old Norse literature, I want to turn to William Morris and his epic poem *Sigurd the Volsung*, published in 1876.

---

[118] Anderton, *Baldur*, p. 40.
[119] Karl Litzenberg, *The Victorians and the Vikings* (Ann Arbor: University of Michigan Press, 1947), p. 14.
[120] Litzenberg, *The Victorians and the Vikings*, p. 2.

The Old Norse *Völsunga saga* is a prose rendering of the main substance of the heroic poems of the *Poetic Edda*. It centres on the celebrated story of the great hero and dragon-slayer Sigurðr the Völsung, though it begins much further back in heroic time with his Odinic ancestry and ends much later with the terrible death of his daughter Svanhildr at the hands of the Gothic tyrant Jörmunrekkr, and the subsequent revenge taken on him by the sons of Guðrún. Sigurðr's career—slaying first Fafnir, the dragon-keeper of a cursed gold-hoard, and then Fafnir's brother Reginn, having learnt from birdsong of Reginn's treachery towards him—is perhaps the most celebrated in Germanic heroic legend, and the central relationships of the saga—and thus, of *Sigurd the Volsung*—are familiar if only in their Wagnerian versions: Sigurðr's betrothal to the valkyrie princess Brynhildr, his subsequent disastrous marriage to Guðrún and his murder at the hands of Gúðrún's brothers. In a further phase of the narrative, Guðrún's brother Gunnarr is executed in a snake pit by her second husband Atli—Attila the Hun. Morris, having learnt Old Norse with the Icelander Eiríkr Magnússon, translated the saga with him in 1870, and appended translations of the poems on which the main events of the saga are based. Not long after, apparently inspired by the texts he and Eiríkr had translated, Morris began writing *Sigurd the Volsung*.

Völsunga saga and the poems it is based on are thus strictly speaking heroic, rather than mythic texts; their characters are legendary heroes, not gods—although Odin, as the legendary progenitor of the Völsung line, does intervene in human affairs. In fact, as David Ashurst has pointed out, Morris developed the naturalistic, human dimensions of the story a stage further than the saga had done with its heroic lay sources; he gave the story "an essentially novelistic treatment... filling out the thoughts and emotions of the characters and floating the narrative on a stream of incidental details".[121] Elsewhere in his poetry, Morris alludes to Norse myth in depicting his heroic characters. In the early poem *Aslaug*, for example, as J. N. Swannell notes, there are "careful touches of local colour... references to Baldur and Freyja", though Swannell rather tartly describes the limitations of this effect: "We could change the names of the characters

---

[121] David Ashurst, 'William Morris and the Volsungs', in David Clark and Carl Phelpstead (eds.), *Old Norse Made New* (London: Viking Society for Northern Research, 2007), pp. 43–61 (53). Ashurst further suggests that Morris may have been especially drawn to and compelled by the "love triangle" theme in *Völsunga saga* because of its resonances with his own personal life (p. 47). For specific details of what Morris did to *Völsunga saga*, see George Tremaine McDowell, 'The Treatment of the *Volsunga Saga* by William Morris', *Scandinavian Studies and Notes* 7 (1922–3), 151–68.

from Old Norse to Celtic or Old French without any sense of incongruity".[122] Similarly, in *The Lovers of Gudrun*, which Morris based on *Laxdoela saga*, although the substance of the poem is not mythic, Morris alludes to mythological scenes on the panelling in the grand hall of an Icelandic chieftain, as indeed the saga itself does.[123] And in *Sigurd*, the characters frequently make reference to the gods: King Siggeir, for instance, warns against the dangers of sea voyages with a reference to the rapacious sea goddess Ran, always lurking beneath the waves;[124] and Signy, hatching a plan to sleep with her brother Sigmund in order to conceive a true Völsung child, ponders the incestuous origins of the Æsir and the Vanir.[125] But in *Sigurd*, mythological content goes far beyond this. Firstly, the gods are depicted as ever present, watching events unfold, and responding to the emotions of the human characters they look down upon, functioning "as an audience within the narrative itself".[126] Secondly, and even more insistently, the mythic concept of Ragnarök dominates not only the whole action of the poem, but also Morris's depiction of history and time as expressed in it. It is Morris's use in *Sigurd* of Ragnarök—the "God's dusk" of *Aslaug*—I now turn to.

Morris's echoes of Ragnarök as it is described in the poem *Völuspá* introduce a grim note of proleptic irony. The inhabitants of Lymdale, King Heimir and his sister-in-law Brynhild, have forgotten what civil war—here described in terms borrowed from *Völuspá's* account of Ragnarök—is like:

> the axe-age and the sword-age seem dead a while ago,
> And the age of the cleaving of shields, and of brother by brother slain,
> And the bitter days of the whoredom...[127]

But as Andrew Wawn points out, "no Victorian reader...would need reminding that *Völuspá* refers not to a past that will never return...but rather to a future from which none may escape".[128] These horrors are about to engulf Lymdale; its own Ragnarök looms. Morris, echoing the long stretch of *Völsunga saga* from the time of the far-off progenitors of the Volsung line, recalls a distant Golden Age of dwarves and gods; the implication is that just as that time has passed, so will the present time of the

[122] J. N. Swannell, *William Morris & Old Norse Literature* (London: William Morris Society, 1961), pp. 6–7.
[123] Einar Ól. Sveinsson (ed.), *Laxdoela saga*, Íslenzk fornrit V (Reykjavík: Hið Íslenzka Fornritafélag, 1934), ch. 29, p. 80.
[124] William Morris, *Sigurd the Volsung*, ed. Jane Ennis (Bristol: Thoemmes Press, 1994), p. 9.
[125] Morris, *Sigurd*, p. 27.
[126] Ashurst, 'William Morris and the Volsungs', p. 55.
[127] Morris, *Sigurd*, pp. 143–4.
[128] Wawn, *The Vikings and the Victorians*, p. 274.

poem (and perhaps, even, our own era) pass, giving way to a new creation. But further, as Charlotte Oberg shows, this extended timescale enables Morris to build up an implicit but highly intricate series of parallels in mythic and heroic time. Thus, the "Grey and Ancient" serpent who kills Gunnar in the snake-pit at the end of *Sigurd* is "the same one who gnaws at the root of Yggdrasil... its success in killing the tree is to cause the final destruction of the universe supported by Yggdrasil. And so the victory of the 'Grey and Ancient' over Gunnar is an intimation of the end, when Thor will die by the venom of the Midgard Serpent".[129] Fafnir, the dragon killed by Sigurd himself, is, tellingly, "ash-grey".[130] Similarly, Signy's burning of her family is a type of Gudrun's burning of Atli, and Brynhild's suicide on Sigurd's funeral pyre; all three foreshadow the conflagration of Ragnarök. In this way, Morris uses Ragnarök as a unifying absent (but imminent as well as immanent) signifier. By contrast, the author of *Völsunga saga* never alludes to Ragnarök, either from the characters' point of view, or as authorial comment.

It has been argued that the poem reflects not only Norse myth itself, but also contemporary Victorian debates between mythologists and archaeologists. Amanda Hodgson describes the former group as operating with "a degenerative model of time", by which the world is in decline from a former Golden Age, which must be returned to; while the latter, embracing new ideas of evolutionary progress, and linking historical scholarship to stratified archaeological finds, such as those at Troy, see time as linear and progressive rather than cyclic. Hodgson suggests that the opposition between Sigurd and Regin "almost exactly duplicates the terms of this debate",[131] culminating with the birds urging the human hero Sigurd to take action against Regin, "lest the world run backward" while the gods "sit deedless, dreaming"[132]—recalling Orsmond Anderton's Æsir, drunk on the mead of oblivion.

Hodgson's conclusion is that, given that Sigurd himself embodies many of the attributes of a solar deity and might therefore be felt to represent cyclic time, so with *Sigurd the Volsung* Morris has "produced... a text deeply involved with contemporary preoccupations and contradictions";[133] as she puts it, "One way of reading the poem... is to see it as

[129] Charlotte Oberg, *A Pagan Prophet: William Morris* (Charlottesville: University Press of Virginia, 1978), p. 87.

[130] Morris, *Sigurd*, p. 113.

[131] Amanda Hodgson, 'The Troy Connection: Myth and History in *Sigurd the Volsung*', in Peter Faulkner and Peter Preston (eds.), *William Morris: Centenary Essays* (Exeter: University of Exeter Press, 1999), pp. 71–9 (77).

[132] Morris, *Sigurd*, p. 116.

[133] Hodgson, 'The Troy Connection', p. 79.

encoding the triumph of linear, progressive time: a victory, if you like, of history over myth".[134] Partly in contrast to this, Simon Dentith has seen Morris's composition of *Sigurd the Volsung* in the form of heroic epic as a complete departure from any contemporary context, literary or philosophical: as illustrating a Hegelian notion of history and culture moving ineluctably on, leaving behind forever "those partly misshapen and barbaric ideas" which constitute Norse myth.[135] Dentith argues that "despite the claim made for racial and linguistic continuity...what the extraordinary diction of the poem emphasizes is precisely the massive historical and social distance which divides readers in the nineteenth century from the world that produced the story".[136] This view of the poem decisively distinguishes it from the work of poets such as Arnold who, following Carlyle, stressed the compatibility of Norse myth and Christianity, and therefore the relevance of the myth for present-day audiences. However, at least one near-contemporary of Morris felt what seems to have been a disturbingly visceral connexion with *Sigurd*, perhaps because of rather than in spite of its oddly alien formal properties:

> The long overlapping lines, the unending sea of song, swelling and dying and surging again like the wind in some mighty primæval pine-wood, touching us with sudden suggestions or wakening ancestral memories of billowing green and singing-birds and keen Northern scents, joyously shattered here and there by the golden echo of huntsmen's horns or the clash of battle, or barbarously torn by the savage jungle-cries of the elemental passions, these qualities of the music of the poem irresistibly remind us of some of Wagner's greatest work.[137]

Wagnerian echoes and ancestral stirrings: there was to be no politically acceptable future for such responses to Old Norse myth.

As Karl Litzenberg has shown, the concept of Ragnarök was to become of central importance in Morris's political philosophy.[138] For Morris, inevitable revolution would be like Ragnarök, violence and destruction necessarily preceding a new world order of harmony and social justice. Here we see the influence of Old Norse myth on the political thought of a poet.

---

[134] Hodgson, 'The Troy Connection', p. 77.

[135] Simon Dentith, '*Sigurd the Volsung*: Heroic poetry in an Unheroic Age', in Faulkner and Preston, *Centenary Essays*, pp. 60–70 (61).

[136] Dentith, '*Sigurd the Volsung*', p. 64.

[137] Alfred Noyes, *William Morris* (London: Macmillan, 1908), pp. 118–19.

[138] Karl Litzenberg, 'The Social Philosophy of William Morris and the Doom of the Gods', *Essays and Studies in English and Comparative Literature X* (Ann Arbor: University of Michigan Press, 1933), pp. 183–203.

It might seem to be a huge leap from William Morris's medievalism to the poetry of the literary movement termed "modernism". For example, many would agree with John Gross that at the very least, modernism "came to signify a drastic break with the past".[139] Thus it might seem perverse to include in a chapter on nineteenth-century poets who engage with Old Norse myth two poets now usually identified as modernists, though oddly, rarely included in surveys or anthologies of modernism: David Jones and Hugh MacDiarmid. But I shall argue nevertheless that the characteristics of these two poets which have led to them being termed "modernists"—primarily, their recourse to an alternative, quasi-mythical history of national culture and origins—have been inspired and shaped by the engagement with Old Norse myth.

In his intellectual autobiography *Lucky Poet* ("A Self-Study in Literature and Political Ideas") Hugh MacDiarmid claims that in his early teens he already had an impressive knowledge of Old Norse.[140] Particularly significant is his mention of "William Herbert and his Scandinavian poetry"— the first translation of Norse poetry by an English poet who worked from the Icelandic originals. An examination of MacDiarmid's sustained and fundamental use of the three central symbols in Old Norse mythology— the serpent, the tree, and the mead of poetry—reveals his close knowledge of Old Norse myth.

The World Serpent—the Miðgarðsormr—looms threateningly over the whole course of Old Norse mythic time. Snorri tells the story of the god Thor's expedition to fish for the World Serpent as a thrilling, half-comic, cartoonish adventure.[141] Thor, having been humiliated by a giant into thinking he was picking up a cat with its back arched and extended, when he was actually pulling, fruitlessly, on one of the mighty loops of the World Serpent itself, determines to get his revenge by hooking the World Serpent on a fishing line. He recruits a giant, the cowardly Hymir, to row him way out to sea, and baits his line with an ox head. The World Serpent takes the bait, and the god struggles mightily to land his enormous prize, his feet crashing through the floor of the boat so that he ends up bracing himself against the sea bed itself. The World Serpent's head finally breaks the surface of the waves, and for a few brief moments of heart-stopping tension, Thor and the Miðgarðsormr glare ferociously at each other, until the giant

---

[139] John Gross (ed.), *The Modern Movement: A TLS Companion* (Chicago: University of Chicago Press, 1992), p. xi.

[140] Hugh MacDiarmid, *Lucky Poet: A Self-Study in Literature and Political Ideas* (London: Methuen, 1943), p. 328. For a fuller account of MacDiarmid's engagement with Old Norse myth, see Heather O'Donoghue, 'Miðgarðsormr' in *Archipelago* (Number three, Spring 2009), pp. 20–31.

[141] *Gylfaginning*, ch. 48, in Faulkes, *Edda*, pp. 46–7.

Hymir cuts the line, and ends the stand-off. In fury, Thor lashes out at Hymir, and he topples overboard, "showing the soles of his feet", as Snorri playfully adds. This is a story of the one that got away. Two much older Old Norse poems—*Ragnarsdrápa*, perhaps from as early as the beginning of the ninth century AD, and *Húsdrápa*, reliably dated to 978 AD—purport to describe a dramatic depiction of the scene, the first as part of a shield decoration, the second, a section of the panelling on the walls of a rich Icelandic farmer's hall.[142] And there are a number of Viking-age stone carvings of the encounter, from Sweden, Denmark, and the British Isles; the encounter powerfully engaged the imaginations of those who knew it.[143] Unsurprisingly, the most successful representation is the one in which the World Serpent itself is not pictured: on the Danish Hørðum stone, Thor's boat is held at a terrifyingly steep angle by the unseen weight at the end of a long slender line which runs right off the edge of the stone.

Thor's encounter with the World Serpent had far greater import than Snorri's exciting but essentially light-hearted narrative might suggest. The many poetic names for the World Serpent are indicative of the creature's significance. Even its commonest name, Miðgarðsormr, translates literally as "Middle-Garth's Snake", with the word "garth" denoting an enclosed space, here the earth itself, of which the serpent is the encloser. This interpretation is confirmed by some of the other poetic terms for the World Serpent: the *jarðar reistr* (twist of the earth); the *endiseiðr allra landa* (edge-rope—or edge-fish, a pun here—of all lands); very elaborately, the *borðróins barða brautar þvengr enn ljóti* (the ugly thong of the path of the gunwhale-rowed boat); or the *stirðþinull storðar* (the stiff boundary rope of the world).[144] The World Serpent is the living manifestation of the circular horizon itself; like a vast belt, it holds the earth together. With that one appalling exception which so mesmerized poets and artists, it is always just out of reach, just out of view. When Thor hooked it on his line, and dragged it up from the deep, the whole created world hung by a thread. And the snake will not surface again until Ragnarök.

In MacDiarmid's early poem 'Sea-Serpent', the monster "fits the universe man can ken/As a man's soul fits his body"[145]—a clear reflection of the

---

[142]   For the two poems see Finnur Jónsson, *Skjaldedigtning*, B I, pp. 1–4 and 128–30.

[143]   For a discussion of the scene and its depictions in visual art, see Preben Meulengracht Sørensen, 'Thor's Fishing Expedition', in Gro Steinsland (ed.), *Words and Objects: Towards a Dialogue between Archaeology and History of Religion* (Oslo: Norwegian University Press, 1986), pp. 257–78.

[144]   *Ragnarsdrápa*, st. 14, 15, 17 and *Húsdrápa*, st. 5; see also *Skáldskaparmál*, ch. 4, in Faulkes, *Edda*, pp. 72–4.

[145]   *The Complete Poems of Hugh MacDiarmid*, ed. Michael Grieve and W. R. Aitken (Harmondsworth: Penguin, 1985), vol. I, pp. 48–51 (48).

cosmic scale of the Old Norse creature. Its strange status in MacDiarmid's poetic imagination as half abstraction, the unifying principle of God's first creation, and half boisterous living creature—it "walloped in rings", "blithe as a loon in the swings"—is also just like the Miðgarðsormr.[146] But its elusive imperceptibility, in spite of its almost unimaginable size and the wild grandeur of its movements, is especially similar to the Norse serpent. The sea-serpent's "fer-aff coils" are only indicated by "keethin's"— according to MacDiarmid's favourite lexicographical source, Jamieson's *Dictionary of the Scottish Language*,[147] movements on the surface of water which betray the presence of a salmon swimming beneath. More mysteriously, the serpent is simply too immense to be seen—like a wood which proverbially cannot be seen for the trees, or "tint as the mid-day sun is tint/ In the glory of its rays".[148]

MacDiarmid constantly re-worked his protean image of the cosmic serpent—most obviously in *A Drunk Man Looks at the Thistle* and *To Circumjack Cencrastus*.[149] Of course, a great serpent is prominent in many mythologies, and MacDiarmid himself linked his various serpent forms with the biblical Leviathan, Melville's great white whale, and Indian world serpents. But there are many indications that the Norse World Serpent was at the forefront of MacDiarmid's mind. The challenging title of *To Circumjack Cencrastus* is significant here. The verb "to circumjack" is ultimately based on the Latin *circum jacere*, to lie around, and the Miðgarðsormr is precisely the ultimate circumjacker of the world—a physical and metaphysical impossibility. Like the Miðgarðsormr, Cencrastus, always out of reach and barely apprehended at best, is also the one that got away. As Julian Meldon D'Arcy points out, throughout the poem MacDiarmid imagines the poet as fisherman; like Thor, the poet "may always struggle desperately with the monster, but he must never actually land it, for to do so would signify the poet's doom as well as the serpent's".[150] At Ragnarök, Thor will finally kill the Miðgarðsormr, but will die himself in the attempt. In *A Drunk Man Looks at the Thistle* MacDiarmid had already acknowledged the hubris inherent in trying to capture this great thought-serpent. Early on in the poem, he cannily observes that "Content to glimpse its loops I dinna ettle/To land the sea serpent's sel' wi' ony gaff"[151]—a clear

[146] MacDiarmid, *Complete Poems*, vol. I, p. 49.
[147] John Jamieson, *An Etymological Dictionary of the Scottish Language* (Edinburgh: University Press, 1808), vol. I, under "keething sight".
[148] MacDiarmid, *Complete Poems*, vol. I, p. 49.
[149] MacDiarmid, *Complete Poems*, vol. I, pp. 81–167 and 181–292.
[150] Julian Meldon D'Arcy, *Scottish Skalds and Sagamen: Old Norse Influence on Modern Scottish Literature* (East Linton: Tuckwell Press, 1996), p. 96.
[151] MacDiarmid, *Complete Poems*, vol. I, p. 87.

allusion to the god Thor's overweening, and almost catastrophic, revenge attack on the Miðgarðsormr.

One can also recognize the story of Thor and the World Serpent behind an anecdote MacDiarmid tells in *Lucky Poet* about his childhood.[152] In 1927, a longer version of this incident had been published by MacDiarmid in the *Glasgow Herald* as a short story about his brother "Andy", and its relation to the Norse is very evident. Andy hooks the trout—"By jings, it's a whopper"—and the concentration on his face as he tries to land the fish is "like a thunderclood—as if there was naethin' in the warld but him and this wallopin' troot and the need to land it". The scale has suddenly turned cosmic. Andy "rung in till his rod was like a hauf-hoop and his line as ticht as the gut o' a fiddle—and there was its heid! It was a whopper and nae mistak'!...snap! the line broke...Andy dived into the pool heid first."[153] W. N. Herbert describes this anecdote as being "linked to personal experience";[154] but all it lacks to match the myth is a reference to the soles of Andrew Grieve's feet.

The other great looming symbol in Old Norse myth is the World Tree, Yggdrasill. Snorri describes the ash tree Yggdrasill with a respect which is close to awe; it is "of all trees the biggest and best. Its branches spread out over all the world and extend across the sky."[155] The well beneath one of its great roots is the sacred meeting place of the Norse gods, where they make their judgements every day. The well beneath another is the source of all wisdom and the god Odin pledged one of his eyes for a single drink from it. As the immensely memorious prophetess declaims in *Völuspá*, it is "a tall tree...It stands forever green".[156] But it is not immune to the passage of time; in fact, it suffers continuous attrition: a mischievous squirrel runs up and down its trunk, four stags nibble its foliage, a malevolent serpent gnaws its roots, and its sides are gradually rotting. And when Ragnarök is at hand, the great ash will shudder and creak, harbinger of the second appearance of the Miðgarðsormr, and the end of the world.

MacDiarmid embarks on his sustained and calculated play on the identification of the Drunk Man's thistle and Yggdrasill with playful, almost teasing delicacy. As early as the second stanza, the Drunk Man ruefully concedes that his throat is not as supple as it once was: "nae langer up

---

[152] MacDiarmid, *Lucky Poet*, p. 225.

[153] 'Andy', in Hugh MacDiarmid, *Annals of the Five Senses and Other Stories, Sketches and Plays*, ed. Roderick Watson and Alan Riach (Manchester: Carcanet, 1999), pp. 170–4 (173).

[154] W. N. Herbert, *To Circumjack MacDiarmid: The Poetry and Prose of Hugh MacDiarmid* (Oxford: Clarendon Press, 1992), p. 50.

[155] Faulkes, *Edda*, p. 17.

[156] *Völuspá*, st. 19, in Dronke, *The Poetic Edda*, vol. II, p. 12.

and doun/Gleg as a squirrel speils the Adam's apple".[157] Most critics have drawn attention to Adam and the apple as allusions to the biblical Tree of Knowledge, and Kenneth Buthlay has noted an allusion to a Gaelic proverb "cho grad ri feòraig-Chéitein"—as quick as a summer squirrel—but in this densely packed simile there is a clear reference to the squirrel in Yggdrasill.[158] Later on in the poem, MacDiarmid compares humankind to a mere and shambolic "stick-nest" in a World Tree which he names "Ygdrasil", even though his vision of the tree at this point seems to be rather of the Tree of Knowledge, which constitutes "the facts in ilka airt/ That breenge into infinity,/Criss-crossed wi' coontless ither facts/Nae man can follow...".[159] But as if to pull the image back into the Norse ambit, MacDiarmid, in a manoeuvre constantly repeated in *A Drunk Man*, associates the tree with the familiar sea monster story: a man's brain whirls, he says, like a fishing reel from which "A whale has rived the line awa'".[160] We are back with Thor and the Miðgarðsormr, with a tree whose branches are "sibness to snakes".[161] And the voice of the thistle itself unmistakably and longingly alludes to Yggdrasill towards the end of the poem:

> O for a root in some untroubled soil,
> Some cauld soil 'yont this fevered warld,
> That 'ud draw darkness frae a virgin source,
> And send it slow and easfu' through my veins... [162]

Throughout *A Drunk Man*, MacDiarmid stresses the ironic disparity between the thistle, "this sorry weed", and the cosmic magnificence of the World Tree. In part, the disparity is due to the physical circumstances of the Drunk Man lying on a hillside, looking up at the thistle. From his perspective it "fills the universe". It is a growth which "yet'll unite/Man and the Infinite".[163] Most memorably, it is a tree "wi' centuries for rings,/Comets for fruit, November shoo'ers/For leafs that in its Autumns fa'/—And Man at maist o' sic a twig/Ane o' the countless atoms is!"[164] But MacDiarmid's thistle is not only presented in its (ironic) majesty and glory. Like Yggdrasill, it too shudders (though in a classic MacDiarmidian shift of register, the movement is compared to "A horse's skin aneth a cleg"[165]) and shrivels.

[157] MacDiarmid, *Complete Poems*, vol. I, p. 83.
[158] MacDiarmid, *A Drunk Man Looks at the Thistle: An Annotated Edition*, ed. Kenneth Buthlay (Edinburgh: Scottish Academic Press, 1987), p. 5.
[159] MacDiarmid, *Complete Poems*, vol. I, p. 129.
[160] MacDiarmid, *Complete Poems*, vol. I, p. 129.
[161] MacDiarmid, *Complete Poems*, vol. I, p. 156.
[162] MacDiarmid, *Complete Poems*, vol. I, p. 150.
[163] MacDiarmid, *Complete Poems*, vol. I, p. 98.
[164] MacDiarmid, *Complete Poems*, vol. I, p. 130.
[165] MacDiarmid, *Complete Poems*, vol. I, p. 128.

Only a drunk man—or a poet—could make this visionary transformation from thistle to World Tree. In Old Norse myth, poetic inspiration is
represented as the mead of poetry—as in *A Drunk Man*, with its whisky
which "aince moved [Burns's] lyre",[166] inebriation and inspiration go hand
in hand. The Norse account of how the gods came to secure the mead of
poetry—a heady brew of blood, spittle, and honey—tells how the god
Odin stole it from a giant (who had himself taken it from the dwarves)
by drinking it, and then flying back to Asgard in the shape of an eagle.[167]
The giant pursues him, and though Odin manages to vomit up most of it
into containers which the other gods provide, in his panic he defecates a
little before he reaches Asgard; this is the comparatively meagre and grossly
degraded drink which human poets have for their inspiration—an even
fouler liquid than the Drunk Man's inferior whisky.

The link between poetry and inebriation in *A Drunk Man* and Norse
myth is not merely coincidental or inevitable; MacDiarmid plainly knew
firsthand the story of Odin's mead. Snorri names one of its containers
Óðrærir, and in his 'Cornish Heroic Song for Valda Trevlyn' which begins
"Come, let us drink", MacDiarmid proposes to toast his beloved (in
Gaelic) with "*Odhaerir*".[168] This strange form is evidently a typographical error (going back to the poem's first publication in 'The Criterion' in
1939) for *Odhraerir* (MacDiarmid always used "dh" for the Old Norse
letter "ð"). Only in the eddic poem *Hávamál* is the mead of poetry itself
called *Óðrærir*; the name may be derived from the noun *óðr* (poetry, or
soul) and the verb *hræra* (to stir up).[169]

It is clear that MacDiarmid appreciated the deepest and darkest corner
of Old Norse myth: that Yggdrasill was the tree on which Odin hanged
himself, a god sacrificed to himself, and wounded with a spear in his
side, like Christ. Though it may seem to fill the universe, in *A Drunk
Man* Yggdrasill also "like a reistit herrin' crines" (shrivels like a dried her-
ring).[170] MacDiarmid has buried an Odinic allusion here, for Jamieson
in his *Dictionary* cites the Scots poet Dunbar as a source for "reistit" and
"crynd"—both words applied by Dunbar to a "hangit man on a hill".[171]
Odin's sacrifice was an attempt to gain the wisdom of the other world—
specifically, knowledge of runes and by extension, poetry. As Julian Meldon

---

[166] MacDiarmid, *Complete Poems*, vol. I, p. 85.
[167] See *Skáldskaparmál*, ch. 58, in Faulkes, *Edda*, pp. 62–4.
[168] MacDiarmid, *Complete Poems*, vol. I, pp. 704–12.
[169] *Hávamál*, st. 140, in Dronke, *The Poetic Edda*, vol. III, p. 31.
[170] MacDiarmid, *Complete Poems*, vol. I, p. 126.
[171] 'The Flyting of Dunbar and Kennedy', in *William Dunbar: The Complete Works*,
ed. John Conlee (Kalamazoo: Medieval Institute Publications, 2004), pp. 181–98 (l. 187).

D'Arcy notes, "MacDiarmid's use of this aspect of the Yggdrasill myth has very apt and powerful references to his own self-sacrificing struggle to establish the Scots language as a medium for the Scottish Renaissance".[172] In *A Drunk Man*, MacDiarmid clinches this implicit identification:

> A Scottish poet maun assume
> The burden o' his people's doom,
> And dee to brak' their livin' tomb.
>
> Mony ha'e tried, but a' ha'e failed.
> Their sacrifice has nocht availed.
> Upon the thistle they're impaled.[173]

Like Odin and Christ, they are nailed to their "ain crucifix".

Throughout his work, we can see MacDiarmid not merely alluding to Old Norse myth, but using its iconic elements as dynamic and even protean symbols in his own work.

MacDiarmid was insistently concerned with the mix of Celtic and Norse ethnicity in Scotland, and adopted the figure of the Hiberno-Norse matriarch Auðr the Deep-Minded—a character from the Old Icelandic *Laxdoela saga*—as his muse. The tradition of recovering or re-creating a united past for the British Isles stretches back, as we have seen, to poets like Thomas Gray, whose great unfinished magnum opus was an anthology of poetry encompassing Anglo-Saxon, Norse, and Celtic verse, or William Blake, who used Old Norse myth and literature extensively in his elaborate creation of a mythic prehistory of Albion.

David Jones also explores the mixed origins of British people and culture, but uses Norse myth for very different ends in his two major works, *In Parenthesis* (1937) and *The Anathemata* (1952). Although Jones himself speaks of his companions at the Front as embodying "the genuine tradition of the Island of Britain",[174] and might therefore be expected to include an Old Norse element, in fact he only alludes explicitly to Old Norse myth in *In Parenthesis* on two occasions. Both allusions are nevertheless extremely significant. The first occurs before the terrible battle which forms the central climax of the work. Jones steadily builds up the tension and dread of the soldiers who are marching in ignorance and appalling physical conditions to some unknown (to them) fate and goal, following their progress from England to France, and then across country. Private John Ball, acting as sentry, sees a wood through the "breakfast-fire smoke" of early

---

[172] D'Arcy, *Scottish Skalds and Sagamen*, p. 95.

[173] MacDiarmid, *Complete Poems*, vol. I, p. 165.

[174] David Jones, 'Preface', *In Parenthesis* (London: Faber and Faber, 1937, repr. 2010), p. x.

morning, and is deeply affected by the sight. Jones explains the effect on
Ball as a response to an age-old connexion between men and woods: "To
groves always men come both to their joys and their undoing".[175] We are
reminded of Tacitus's *Germania* here, for he writes of groves as the sacred
places of the Germanic tribes.[176] The Anglo-Saxons were of course once
part of that Germanic people; indeed Jones saw the First World War as a
fratricidal conflict. When Ball "sees and loses, thinks he sees again, grey
movement..." he may be catching a significant first glimpse of the hitherto unknown and unseen German enemy, in their grey field uniforms.
But woods are also the haunt of wolves, and like their ancient counterparts
in Old English and Old Norse verse, they too are a "grey war-band".[177]
Jones seals this identification with an endnote reference to Christopher
Dawson's book *The Making of Europe:* Dawson quotes from the Old Norse
poem *Eiríksmál* "it is not surely known when the grey wolf shall come
down upon the seat of the Gods".[178] As it happens, Private Ball, unlike
the mythic watchman of the gods, Heimdallr, does not sound the alert;
"indeterminate of what should be his necessary action" he lets the enemy
bide. But he cannot take his eyes off the ruined wood,

> to where great strippings-off hanged from tenuous fibres swaying,
>   whitened to decay—as swung
> immolations
> for the northern Cybele.
> The hanged, the offerant:
>   himself to himself
>   on the tree.[179]

Jones's reference to Cybele, the Phrygian earth goddess, returns us back to
Tacitus, who identifies a deity worshipped by a large number of Germanic
tribes as Terra Mater, the earth mother. But more striking is the explicit
allusion to the sacrifice of the god Odin, hanging from the tree Yggdrasill,
a god who sacrificed himself to himself in pursuit of knowledge. Jones's
note refers to Frazer's *The Golden Bough*, in which the crucial lines from
Hávamál, "dedicated to Odin/myself to myself", are quoted.[180] In fact,
Jones misattributes the lines (his note reads "Quoted from the Icelandic
poem, the *Volospa*") but the relevance of self-sacrifice in this context is very
powerful. Jones ends this section with a reference to the Anglo-Saxon missionary Boniface—the "apostle to the Germans"—who is said to have cut

175   Jones, *In Parenthesis*, p. 66.
176   Tacitus, *Germania*, ch. 9, p. 109.
177   Jones, *In Parenthesis*, p. 67.
178   Jones, *In Parenthesis*, pp. 204–5.
179   Jones, *In Parenthesis*, p. 67.
180   Jones, *In Parenthesis*, p. 204.

down a tree which was held sacred by the pagan Saxons; sacrifice is averted on this occasion too, for Ball identifies the enemy as neither bestial, nor apocalyptic, but as his fellow soldiers: "they were at breakfast and were as cold as he".[181]

Jones does not allude to Norse myth again until the final section of *In Parenthesis*. Here, the god Balder is used as a figure for young men of both sides being killed: "Fair Balder falleth everywhere",[182] the archaic language suggesting the long history of lethal warfare. A little further on in the work, we see Balder used in the same way: the Queen of the Woods is handing out "bright boughs of various flowering" to the dead. They are a tellingly and carefully representative group: Emil, and Fatty, Balder, and Ulrich, and "that swine [Major] Lillywhite".[183]

Following on from Jones's first reference to Baldr, the effects of shrapnel in battle are associated with the god Thor in another allusion to *The Golden Bough*. Jones describes how "thunder-besom breakings/bright the wood";[184] Frazer explains a thunder besom as "a shaggy, bushy excrescence on branches of trees... popularly believed to be produced by a flash of lightning"—in other words, a thunderbolt, or shrapnel.[185] The key effect of shrapnel is that it pierces the body; Jones's note to this passage makes it clear that this action links the death of Baldr with the crucifixion of Christ—"how any chosen thing suffers a kind of piercing and destruction".[186] It is striking that David Jones does not use images of the collapse of the World Tree, or of the destruction at the Norse apocalypse, Ragnarök, in his account of the fighting. His focus is on those aspects of Old Norse myth which relate to human suffering—the death of Odin's young and beautiful son—and Christian sacrifice: death by hanging and piercing. These are the aspects which are repeatedly foregrounded in *The Anathemata*, in which Jones sees the Cross on which Christ was crucified as a sign parallel to Yggdrasill, since, as Neil Corcoran puts it, "Christ is viewed as the fulfilment of all the poem's mythic heroes".[187]

Throughout most of *The Anathemata*, Jones's allusions to Old Norse myth are sporadic, fleeting, and to some extent even predictable. In the poem's first section, 'Rite and Fore-Time', for instance, there is a reference to the so-called Venus of Willendorf, a celebrated prehistoric figurine of

---

[181] Jones, *In Parenthesis*, p. 67.
[182] Jones, *In Parenthesis*, p. 177.
[183] Jones, *In Parenthesis*, p. 185.
[184] Jones, *In Parenthesis*, p. 177.
[185] James George Frazer, *The Golden Bough: A Study in Magic and Religion*, abridged edition (London: Macmillan, 1963), p. 867.
[186] Jones, *In Parenthesis*, p. 223.
[187] Neil Corcoran, *The Song of Deeds: A Study of The Anathemata of David Jones* (Cardiff: University of Wales Press, 1982), p. 71.

a woman, usually interpreted as a fertility symbol. Jones ponders what ancient artist, mimicking divine creativity, might have modelled, or "god-handled" her, and suggests that she is a precursor of the Norse Venus, the goddess Freyja, whom he calls Vanabride.[188] In Old Norse, Freyja is one of the Vanir, the gods associated with sex and fertility; indeed, she is the only female member of the Vanir to be named. Similarly, the second section, 'Middle-Sea and Lear-Sea', in which Jones explores and celebrates the Mediterranean roots of British culture, and imagines the sea-borne transmission of that culture to the British Isles, is dominated by nautical references, and Jones duly makes reference to "nine white grinders/riding the daughters of the quern of islands"—in a note accurately identifying the Norse god of the sea as Ægir, whose nine daughters were the waves.[189] But towards the end of this section Jones reveals how his vision of Eucharistic unity effected by the coming of Christianity to Britain calls to his mind the parallel pagan sacrifice of Odin; in a note he explains that "what is pleaded in the Mass is precisely the argosy or voyage of the Redeemer…It is this that is offered to the Trinity (Cf. 'Myself to myself' as in the *Havamal*…)".[190]

This analogy remains dormant (but should perhaps be present in the reader's mind) through the succeeding sections of *The Anathemata*, in which Norse allusions are largely confined to historical events or characters, and are associated with sea-faring, as one might expect from Viking culture. In 'Redriff', for instance, set by the Thames in Rotherhithe, we hear of "Galley Wall", a local name which according to Jones's note derives from a story about the beaching of the Danish King Canute's ships there.[191] Similarly, in 'The Lady of the Pool'—"an attempt to celebrate the sign that is 'London'"[192]—there are references to Norse texts such as *Ragnars saga loðbrókar* and Snorri's historical compendium *Heimskringla* which mention Viking activity in London, and repeated use of the Norse version of place names such as Ongulsey (Anglesey) or "Thor's own haven" (Thorshavn, in the Faroes), as actual, not mythic, destinations. In colloquial speech, the Norse inheritance is still evident: lightning is "the Hammerer's summer-flashers" and thunder "the full rant/of the Roarer"[193] in such obvious reference to the Norse god Thor that Jones does not even provide a footnote. But at the close of the section, there is a sudden

[188] David Jones, *The Anathemata* (London: Faber and Faber, 1952, repr. 2010), p. 59.
[189] Jones, *The Anathemata*, p. 99.
[190] Jones, *The Anathemata*, p. 106.
[191] Jones, *The Anathemata*, p. 120.
[192] Corcoran, *The Song of Deeds*, p. 60.
[193] Jones, *The Anathemata*, p. 141.

startling reference in the midst of what Jones calls "our collective London myth" to the World Serpent: Elen Monica threatens the sea captain with the most fearsome of sea monsters: "May the Loathly Worm have you".[194]

'Keel, Ram, Stauros' plays on the interconnected central significances of timber; as planks for ship-building; as items of warfare; and as the wood of the Cross. But the phrase "the trembling tree"[195] is markedly inappropriate to denote the mast of a ship; it refers rather to Yggdrasill, the great World Tree of Norse myth, which shudders in expectation of Ragnarök. Indeed the ship in 'Keel, Ram, Stauros' is built in "the Æsir's yard",[196] as if the Norse gods, the great builders of Asgard, were the proprietors of a river-side shipyard. And there is one more faint allusion to the analogy between Yggdrasill as the site of Odin's sacrifice, and the Cross on which Christ was crucified: towards the end of the section, the climax of a series of questions is "Agios Stauros/*stans*?" ("Holy Cross standing?").[197] In *Völuspá*, Yggdrasill is *askr standandi* (the ash which stands), even as it trembles, about to fall.[198] But it is not until the final section that this allusion is expanded. In 'Mabinog's Liturgy' we are halfway there: references to Nordic sea voyages continue, and Yggdrasill is named when the "cruising old *wicing*...stepped the Yggdrasil for mast".[199] The allusion here may either be to the idea of Odin, in shamanistic role, climbing the tree in pursuit of knowledge, or to early voyagers using the axis of the great tree like the North Star, as a pointer to due north. The religious climax of 'Sherthursdaye and Venus day' completes the complex allusion, however: David Jones quotes the crucial lines from *Hávamál* ("nine nights on the windy tree?/Himself to himself?"), a sacrifice, like Christ, "wounded with *our* spears",[200] and creates a remark-able Nordic version of the crucifixion:

> On rune-height by the garbaged rill
>   the scree-fall answers the cawed madrigals
> and there are great birds flying about.
> And (to sustain his kind)
>   the mated corbie
> with his neb
>   forcipate, incarnadined—
> prods at the dreaming *arbor*... [201]

[194] Jones, *The Anathemata*, p. 168.
[195] Jones, *The Anathemata*, p. 173.
[196] Jones, *The Anathemata*, p. 177.
[197] Jones, *The Anathemata*, p. 180.
[198] *Völuspá*, st. 45, in Dronke, *The Poetic Edda*, vol. II, p. 19.
[199] Jones, *The Anathemata*, pp. 199–200.
[200] Jones, *The Anathemata*, p. 225.
[201] Jones, *The Anathemata*, p. 240.

"[T]he hydromel/that moists the mortised arbour" is glossed by René Hague as the blood of Christ, but evident too is the nurturing dew which according to *Völuspá* drops from Yggdrasill.[202] The climax of *The Anathemata* finally locks tight the analogy of the Cross and Yggdrasill. The sacrificed god rides "the Axile tree" as Odin "rides" his gallows, Yggdrasill, and the Axile tree is the fixed point around which the world turns: either in Christian tradition ("stat crux dum volvitur orbis") or in Norse myth, in which Yggdrasill is the fixed axis which links heaven and earth.

Apart from Elen Monica's threat of an encounter with the Loathly Worm—the Miðgarðsormr—David Jones's use of Old Norse myth takes two distinct forms. Firstly, there is the establishment of the Norse, or Viking element, in British culture—less prominent, in fact, than Jones's celebration of the Celtic, or Welsh element, or the Roman, but nevertheless inescapably part of "the genuine tradition of the Island of Britain", and evident in the staples of Anglophone culture such as the days of the week, which Jones so often reproduces in etymologized form as Frigg's day or Thor's day. Secondly, there is Jones's constant awareness of the sacrifice of Odin as an analogue to the sacrifice of Christ on the Cross. Far from sensationalizing Odinic sacrifice, or using it as convenient local colour to identify Norse pagans, Jones actually performs an act of recuperation by insistently relating it to Christian theology and liturgy. No doubt he was influenced by mythographers such as Frazer who explored the basic similarities between different human belief systems, but Jones's creative use of this central, mystical facet of Norse mythology restores to new life one of the central elements of Old Norse myth.

Insofar as he is recognized as a poet, rather than as a novelist, critic, and Christian polemicist, C. S. Lewis has also been termed a modernist, and he too used Old Norse myth in relation to Christian theology. However, the poetry written before his reversion to Christianity does not so much recuperate the mythic theology as use it to voice opposition to a Christianity which Lewis both doubted and opposed. In his autobiography, *Surprised by Joy,* Lewis describes his first encounter with Norse-derived material: the sight of a journal advertising a book called *Siegfried and the Twilight of the Gods* (in fact, a translation of Wagner's libretto) with illustrations by Arthur Rackham.[203] This sight recalled an earlier memory of having read *Tegner's Drapa,* Longfellow's Norse-influenced elegy, with its evocative

---

[202] Rene Hague, *A Commentary on The Anathemata of David Jones* (Wellingborough: Skelton, 1977), p. 243; *Völuspá,* st. 19, in Dronke, *The Poetic Edda,* vol. II, p. 12.
[203] C. S. Lewis, *Surprised by Joy: The Shape of My Early Life* (London: Geoffrey Bles, 1955), p. 74.

mention of "sunward-sailing cranes".[204] Lewis vividly recounts the emotional force—the joy—of this memory: "Pure 'Northernness' engulfed me... I was returning at last from exile". Having next read a synopsis of the *Ring* story, Lewis embarked on turning it into a Miltonic poem in rhyming couplets which he never finished; he got no further than the opening of *Das Rheingold*.[205]

A year or so later, when Lewis was still barely sixteen, he began work on his own libretto, for an opera which he called *Loki Bound*; only a few fragments of this have survived.[206] Since, and presumably as a result of, being engulfed by what he terms Northernness, Lewis had read a great deal more Norse material, including Mallet's *Northern Antiquities*, and even the huge scholarly edition of Old Norse poetry, Vigfússon and Powell's *Corpus Poeticum Boreale*; he describes how he "tried, vainly but happily, to hammer out the originals from the translation at the bottom of the page".[207] But the most significant aspect of Lewis's Norse reading was its impact on not his literary, but his spiritual life. As his doubts about Christianity grew, "Northernness" seemed, he writes, "a bigger thing than my religion... because my attitude towards it contained elements which my religion ought to have contained and did not".[208] He concludes "I can almost think that I was sent back to the false gods there to acquire some capacity for worship against the day when the true God should recall me to Himself".[209]

From what survives of *Loki Bound*, we can see clear evidence of Lewis's further reading. The piece opens with a grand description of Asgard spoken by Loki himself:

> This is the awful city of the gods,
> Founded on high to overlook the world

and passes to Odin's throne, "whence once the impious Frey/With ill-starred passion eyed the demon maid".[210] This is an allusion to the eddic poem *Skírnismál*, in which the god Freyr falls in love with a giant's

---

[204] See Chapter 3, p. 145.
[205] Unpublished, but reproduced in Appendix 1 of Don King, *C. S. Lewis, Poet* (Kent, Ohio: The Kent State University Press, 2001), pp. 245–65. In fact, the opening of *Das Rheingold* is the part of Wagner's work which is least dependent on Old Norse sources; see Árni Björnsson, *Wagner and the Volsungs* (London: Viking Society for Northern Research, 2003), pp. 130–54.
[206] See King, *C. S. Lewis, Poet*, Appendix 1, pp. 265–9.
[207] Lewis, *Surprised by Joy*, p. 112.
[208] Lewis, *Surprised by Joy*, pp. 77–8.
[209] Lewis, *Surprised by Joy*, p. 78.
[210] King, *C. S. Lewis, Poet*, p. 266.

daughter whom he has glimpsed from Odin's all-seeing seat *Hliðskjálf.*
There are references too to the giant Ymir, from whose murdered corpse
the earth was created, and to Loki's "monster children". In another fragment, a giant with the Wagnerian name Fasolt tells how he has built a
defensive wall for the gods—but this action accurately represents Norse
myth, rather than its Wagnerian version, in which a pair of giants builds
Valhalla itself. And Lewis's brother Warren, alluding to a missing passage
of *Loki Bound,* mentions a "maddened horse".[211] According to Snorri's
Norse version of the story, the giant intended to use a stallion to help him
complete his gargantuan task. Loki cunningly distracts it from the work
with a mare, the sight of which maddened the stallion. This mare—which
we can infer was Loki himself—had sex with the stallion, and gave birth to
a foal, Odin's celebrated eight-legged horse Sleipnir.[212] One wonders how
much of this story Lewis the teenager retold, and indeed why the relevant
passages were destroyed.

Lewis also makes major changes to his sources. His Loki—motivelessly
malevolent in Norse myth—is a rational and even sympathetic figure used
to voice Lewis's own antagonism towards God. Loki views Odin's creation of Man and earth as "awful error and injustice dread". He challenges
Odin: "Who art thou/To bring forth men to suffer in the world/Without
their own desire?".[213] Lewis himself describes how *Loki Bound* reflects the
angry contradictions in his attitude towards divinity, summed up by Don
King as "God does not exist but how dare He create a world".[214] And
as King points out, Lewis's first published collection of poems, *Spirits in
Bondage* (1919), also reflects this contradiction.

The prevalence of binding imagery in these titles and in their content
is striking. In Norse poetry, Ragnarök will be a time of chaos when what
had been bound hitherto—Loki, the wolf Fenrir, the giants' ship Naglfari,
and even the cosmos itself, with heavenly bodies in fixed positions—will
come loose; a time when, in W. B. Yeats's terms, "Things fall apart; the
centre cannot hold". Freedom from bondage is also a central theme in
Lewis's early long poem, *Dymer,* published in 1926, but begun a decade
earlier, the very title of which recalls Lewis's spelling of the primordial
giant: "Ymer". Lewis, when he began the poem years before, had called it
The Redemption of Ask, recalling the name given to the piece of driftwood

---

[211] King, *C. S. Lewis, Poet,* p. 268.
[212] *Gylfaginning,* ch. 42, in Faulkes, *Edda,* pp. 35–6.
[213] King, *C. S. Lewis, Poet,* p. 267.
[214] King, *C. S. Lewis, Poet,* p. 42.

which the gods transform into the first human: Askr.[215] The poem was badly received by critics and readers, and is hard to follow.[216] It opens in an unspecific future time, with its hero Dymer escaping from the constraints of "The Perfect City", an imaginary totalitarian settlement in which everything and everyone is strictly regimented. Dymer has a series of strange, visionary adventures, including a sexual encounter with a beautiful young woman who, at the very end of the poem, he finds to have borne him a son—a bizarre monster which, in Old Norse fashion, he must take on; like the Norse gods and their monstrous opponents, both Dymer and his foe are killed in the battle which ensues.

There are also a number of other possible traces of Old Norse myth in this poem. For instance, a hideous old crone, described by Lewis with disturbing ferocity and distaste, who blocks his way when he searches for the woman he has slept with, is perhaps reminiscent of the old woman who humiliates the god Thor when he wrestles against her in the court of the giant Útgarða-Loki; she is Old Age personified, against whom no-one can prevail. But *Dymer* both begins and ends with explicit references to Old Norse myth. In the first edition, the title page has a quotation from the Old Norse poem *Hávamál* (the words of the High One—Odin himself). It is perhaps significant that the quotation—"Nine nights I hung upon the Tree, wounded with the spear as an offering to Odin, myself sacrificed to myself"—takes the form of prose, not verse; Lewis was more concerned with its content than with its poetic form. Odin here describes his self-sacrifice, followed in the poem by his revival. In a letter to Arthur Greeves, Lewis writes that he was very much attracted to this complex of ideas, and was "mysteriously moved by it"—though at that time only in the context of pagan myth, and not in its Christian context.[217] But there are clear parallels with Christ's crucifixion in the relevant passage of *Hávamál*.

At the end of the poem, when Dymer fights his monstrous son, a strange double transformation takes place. The monster is replaced by a "wing'd and sworded shape"[218] like the clearly protective (but also distinctly Nordic) angel depicted on the title page of *Dymer*, and, as George

[215] Lewis points this out in a letter he wrote to Arthur Greeves in 1918, quoted in Walter Hooper's introduction to Lewis, *Narrative Poems* (London: Bles, 1969), p. ix.
[216] For a very useful outline of it, see George Sayer, 'C. S. Lewis's *Dymer*', *SEVEN* 1 (1980), 94–116.
[217] C. S. Lewis and Arthur Greeves, *They Stand Together: The Letters of C. S. Lewis to Arthur Greeves, 1914–1963*, ed. Walter Hooper (London: Collins, 1979), p. 427, letter dated 18 October 1931.
[218] *Dymer*, in Lewis, *Narrative Poems*, pp. 1–91 (91), Canto IX, st. 34.

Sayer puts it, Dymer's death "seems to have set into motion a process of cosmic rebirth".[219] As a sign of his redemption, there is heard

> A noise of great good coming into earth
> And such a music as the dumb would sing
> If Balder had led back the blameless spring
> With victory...[220]

As we have seen throughout this chapter, Baldr was widely recognized as a Christ figure by later interpreters of Old Norse myth, as the young and radiant god, perhaps even sacrificed by his father. By beginning and ending *Dymer* with the two great divine deaths in Old Norse myth, Lewis definitively situates his own hero Dymer in this mythic tradition, though he writes that the exact form of the myth on which the poem is based "arrived, complete" in his imagination when he was seventeen.[221] Lewis's description of his first attempt at this poem makes clear that the idea of regeneration and succession was a crucial part of this myth: the son both replicates and supersedes the father, in what the young Lewis called "a future and higher generation". In *Loki Bound,* Odin was a powerful and heartless creator against whom Lewis could rehearse his own confused and angry feelings about Christianity. But in *Dymer,* Lewis implies his demise, re-formulating the myth of the dying and reviving god to develop an ideology of succession and progress.

After his reversion to Christianity in 1929, Lewis continued to reflect Old Norse material in his poetry, but with significant differences. In his prose piece *The Pilgrim's Regress* (1933), Lewis's hero faces up to a "Northern" dragon, but now Northernness has come to mean "tension, hardness, possessiveness, coldness, anaemia", and the dragon, which, like the Norse dragon Fafnir, speaks (or, as Lewis specifies, "sings"), is a pure personification of greed, or cupidity, and addresses God in distinctly Christian style (though with distinctly un-Christian sentiments):

> Lord that made the dragon, grant me thy peace,
> But say not that I should give up the gold.[222]

This dragon is a grotesque and even grimly comic creature who only regrets having eaten his wife because it means that he no longer has a helpmate with whom to share the guardianship of the gold hoard. A second dragon poem is a long cry of victory from a dragon-slayer, but there is no allusion

[219] Sayer, 'C. S. Lewis's *Dymer*', 112.
[220] Lewis, *Dymer*, Canto IX, st. 35.
[221] See Sayer, 'C. S. Lewis's *Dymer*', 95.
[222] 'The Dragon Speaks' and 'Dragon-Slayer' in Lewis, *Poems*, ed. Walter Hooper (London: Bles, 1964), pp. 92–5 (93).

to Sigurðr or anything Norse apart from the dragon-slaying itself, and in fact the warrior celebrates his triumph in Latin and Greek.

Finally, in 'A Cliché came out of its Cage', a poem first published in 1950, Lewis mocks the modish literary revival of classical mythology, and compares it unfavourably with "another kind of heathenry"—Norse myth. Freedom from bondage is still an anxiety: "The Wolf, admittedly, is bound;/But the bond will break, the Beast run free".[223] However, the focus has moved from the gods as overbearing creators and rulers of the seasons; these are "weary gods,/Scarred with old wounds" who will "limp to their stations for the last defence". They are mortal, like the human characters from Icelandic sagas whom Lewis holds up as examples of how to face death bravely. In place of a personal and spiritual engagement with pagan myth, Lewis turns to the familiar brave Viking who scorns death. Indeed, for Lewis, "Northernness" is now so much situated in the actual, human sphere that with his reference to men of "decent blood" and "tall women with yellow plaits" Lewis evokes Nordic racial stereotypes.

Like C. S. Lewis's *Dymer*, David Jones's vision in *The Anathemata* might well of course be termed mythic in itself; as Jones writes in the preface, it is not "a history of any sort" but is set in a mental space, "in the time of the Mass".[224] The events and figures of myth do not exist in any real historical time or geographical space. Nevertheless a distinctive intersection of the two—Bakhtin's chronotope[225]—comes in the twentieth century to dominate a British tradition of difficult, allusive poetry centring on national histories and origins. But unlike the times and places of myth, this poetry is set in real northern locations, and in medieval times. For instance, Basil Bunting, in *Briggflatts* (1966), a poem very clearly in the modernist tradition, anchors his poetry in his native Northumberland, the location of both the opening and the close of the poem. *Briggflatts* is dominated by the symmetrical poles of Eric Bloodaxe and St Cuthbert: both medieval Northumbrian figures—one Norse, one English—who achieved almost legendary status after their deaths.[226]

In *Mercian Hymns* (1971), Geoffrey Hill's chronotope is articulated in the voice of another semi-legendary medieval figure, King Offa of Mercia, who ruled 757–96 AD, a century after Cuthbert, and a couple before Bloodaxe. Hill playfully juxtaposes modern and medieval references—most

---

[223] 'A Cliché came out of its Cage', in *Poems*, pp. 3–4 (4).
[224] Jones, *The Anathemata*, p. 31.
[225] See 'Forms of time and of the chronotope in the novel', in M. M. Bakhtin, *The Dialogic Imagination: Four Essays*, trans. Caryl Emerson and Michael Holquist (Austin: University of Texas Press, 1981), pp. 84–258.
[226] Basil Bunting, *Briggflatts* (London: Fulcrum, 1966).

celebratedly, perhaps, in his description of Offa's funeral, hilariously attended by "Merovingian car-dealers" and "a shuffle of house-carls", fusing past and present.[227] Ted Hughes and Seamus Heaney have also both established a past in their work which can be brought into close relation with the present, though each very differently. Hughes repeatedly reinvented a mythic and oddly timeless past inspired by a present landscape and its animal inhabitants, and based very largely on Celtic models, though he also incorporated some Old Norse and Near Eastern material. But when he turns to history, rather than speculating on or creating its originary myth, the Norse element proves problematic. As Paul Giles has said, in the poem 'The Warriors of the North', in *Wodwo*, Hughes describes how "acquisitive and ruthless Norse invaders trampled underfoot the Anglo-Saxon heritage", as well as looting what Hughes calls the "elaborate, patient gold of the Gaels".[228] In *Remains of Elmet*, the Vikings who "got this far" into Elmet are compared with much later mindless young vandals who wreaked destruction; both then "trailed away homeward aimlessly".[229] But Elmet was historically a British—that is, ethnically Celtic—principality sandwiched between the Anglo-Saxon kingdoms of Northumbria and Mercia, ruthlessly conquered by Northumbria at the beginning of the seventh century. Pre-Christian Celtic—not Germanic—myth is thus necessarily Hughes's inspiration and model; neither the Anglo-Saxons nor the Norse are easily acculturated into this imagined West Riding past.

Seamus Heaney's most celebrated—and controversial—conjunction of the medieval and the present is worked out primarily in *North*, in which the violence of Vikings in the ninth and tenth centuries is seen as analogous to the Troubles in Northern Ireland in the twentieth. But again, the focus is Viking history, and not Old Norse myth. One poem in particular engages directly with the old view of Norsemen—until recently, standard in Ireland especially—who raided and then left. (There's even a significant trace of this in Basil Bunting's historical picture of Northumbria, with "the Viking inheritance all spent save the faint smell of it".[230]) In 'Belderg' Heaney shows the poem's speaker being forced by an archaeologist to

---

[227]   Geoffrey Hill, *Mercian Hymns* (London: Deutsch, 1971), XXVII.

[228]   Paul Giles, 'From Myth into History: The Later Poetry of Thom Gunn and Ted Hughes', in James Acheson and Romana Huk (eds.), *Contemporary British Poetry: Essays in Theory and Criticism* (Albany: State University of New York Press, 1996), pp. 143–73 (156), and Ted Hughes, 'The Warriors of the North', from *Wodwo*, in *Collected Poems*, ed. Paul Keegan (London: Faber and Faber, 2003), pp. 145–83 (167).

[229]   Hughes, 'For Billy Holt' and 'Mill Ruins', from *Remains of Elmet*, in *Collected Poems*, pp. 483–4, 464.

[230]   Letter to Louis Zukovsky, September 1964; see Victoria Forde, *The Poetry of Basil Bunting* (Newcastle upon Tyne: Bloodaxe, 1991), p. 207.

accept the historical and material fact that these "fabulous raiders" became part of the genetic fabric of Irish people, their "congruence" figured in the image of a tree-ring.[231] The poem's speaker—we may assume Heaney himself—is rocked back for a moment, but quickly sees the force of this correction: the name of his home place, Mossbawn, is a compound derived from the Scandinavian word for "bog", *mos*, and a word for "an English fort", a "planter's walled–in mound", which by philological chance recalls the Irish word "bán", (white) and thus the image of ceannabhán bán—white bog cotton, which grows everywhere on Irish bogland. Here, philology— the language itself—testifies to a mixed ethnic and political heritage.[232]

These poets are not concerned so much with the persistence and transcendence of the cultural symbol—the sign, as David Jones would term it—throughout historical time, as with the actual historical congruence of successive generations of humans, and the continuance of their basic preoccupations. To put it crudely, for them, Old Norse myth is one aspect of Viking culture, and the Vikings are part of "our" history, and were perhaps our ancestors. For Jones, as well as providing evidence of "the Norse ring on our tree"—the Norse, or Germanic, element in British history and culture—Old Norse myth provides meaningful and indeed usable signs of direct, if mystical, relevance to our own spirituality.

W. H. Auden's life-long engagement with things Icelandic—and especially its medieval literature and myth—is well known.[233] In *Letters from Iceland,* Auden writes that having listened to his father reading Icelandic folk tales to him, he now "know[s] more about Northern mythology than Greek".[234] And towards the end of his life, in 1969, he and Paul Taylor published *The Elder Edda*, an English translation of a selection of Old Norse verse which very largely comprises the mythological poems of the *Edda*.[235]

Auden completed his verse play *Paid on Both Sides* in 1928, the year he finished his undergraduate degree in Oxford.[236] The title is taken from the

---

[231] Seamus Heaney, 'Belderg', in *North* (London: Faber and Faber, 1975), pp. 13–14.

[232] See Heather O'Donoghue, 'Heaney, *Beowulf* and the Medieval Literature of the North', in Bernard O'Donoghue (ed.), *The Cambridge Companion to Seamus Heaney* (Cambridge: Cambridge University Press, 2009), pp. 192–205.

[233] See Sveinn Haraldsson, '"The North begins inside": Auden, Ancestry and Iceland', in Wawn, *Northern Antiquity*, pp. 255–84.

[234] W. H. Auden and Louis MacNeice, *Letters from Iceland* (London: Faber and Faber, 1937), p. 210.

[235] Paul B. Taylor and W. H. Auden, *The Elder Edda* (London: Faber, 1969). After Auden's death, a fuller selection including heroic pieces was published as *Norse Poems* (London: Athlone Press, 1981).

[236] See *The English Auden: Poems, Essays and Dramatic Writings 1927–1939*, ed. Edward Mendelson (London: Faber, 1977), p. xiii. All quotations from *Paid on Both Sides* are from this edition.

Old English poem *Beowulf*,[237] and the poem's debt to both Old English poetry and Old Norse saga prose is evident.[238] But there are also a number of allusions to Old Norse myth.

Auden associates the death of John Nower in the play's grim and point-less feud with the central tragedy of the Old Norse pantheon—the death of the young god Baldr, radiant, Christ-like, and, as Odin's son, bearing the future hopes of the whole divine dynasty. When Baldr falls to the earth, fatally wounded, the gods are paralyzed with horror, and speech fails them; so too does the power to lift up Baldr in their arms. All they can do is weep.[239] Anne Shaw-Nower's reaction to her husband's death surely alludes to this myth: "The hands that were to help will not be lifted,/And bad followed by worse leaves to us tears".[240]

Odin's response, we learn from *Völuspá*, is to beget another son who magically reaches maturity in one night, his whole being "dedicated to vengeance"; as Dronke puts it: "A brother of Baldr/was born quickly:/he started—Odin's son—/slaying at one night old".[241] In the opening scene of *Paid on Both Sides*, we see Joan Nower with her new-born baby, and the corpse of her dead husband. That baby reaches maturity almost immedi-ately—seconds, in fact, in stage time, after his birth, and vengeance for the death of the father duly follows.[242] And there is one last faint reverberation of Odinic myth: a reference to "one drawn apart" who learns "a secret will/ Restore the dead; but comes thence to a wall"[243] reminds us of Odin who is able to "call to life dead men out of the ground", and to know a magic spell which enables him to speak with hanged corpses.[244] But of course Odin did not succeed in resurrecting Baldr, or in averting Ragnarök. He came up against a brick wall here, in spite of his sorcery.

In *Völuspá*, the mysterious seeress who prophesies the end of the gods and the created world—Ragnarök—foresees yet further, to the

---

[237] See Edward Mendelson, *Early Auden* (London: Faber, 1981), p. 42, and *Beowulf*, 1304–5: "That was not a good exchange, that they on both sides had to pay with the lives of friends".

[238] See Heather O'Donoghue, 'Owed to Both Sides: W. H. Auden's double debt to the literature of the North', in David Clark and Nicholas Perkins (eds.), *Anglo-Saxon Culture and the Modern Imagination* (Cambridge: D. S. Brewer, 2010), pp. 51–69.

[239] See Faulkes, *Edda*, p. 49.

[240] Auden, *The English Auden*, p. 17.

[241] *Völuspá*, st. 32, in Dronke, *The Poetic Edda*, vol. II, p. 15.

[242] This apparently miraculous maturation is considerably helped by Auden's forget-ful omission of a stage direction to explain the passage of time; see Mendelson, *Early Auden*, p. 48.

[243] Auden, *The English Auden*, p. 7.

[244] Hollander, *Heimskringla*, p. 11, and *Hávamál*, st. 157, in Dronke, *The Poetic Edda*, vol. III, p. 34.

establishment of a new world order, a new heaven and a new earth. In her
lyrical vision of rebirth, she speaks of the earth rising, green again, out of
the sea. Cornfields will grow, though unsown. And above these verdant
hills flies an eagle, hunting fish.[245] *Paid on Both Sides* ends on the same
note of hope, expressed in remarkably similar terms: feuding has created a
wasteland, "... though later there be/Big fruit, eagles above the stream".[246]

Auden continued to allude to Old Norse sources, and Old Norse myth,
throughout his life's work, as Paul Taylor has shown,[247] and his long poem
The Age of Anxiety, which he began writing in 1944, is peppered with
allusions to Old Norse. In fact, *The Age of Anxiety* is fundamentally struc-
tured around the Old Norse myth of Ragnarök, the Norse apocalypse. In
Völuspá, the time leading up to Ragnarök is dramatically, even hectically,
figured by the seeress as "an axe age, a sword age... a wind age, a wolf
age".[248] Auden presents us with a modern version of this headlong descent
into apocalypse which is yet bathetically less violent and more cerebral; it
is an anxious age.

The action of *The Age of Anxiety* takes place on All Souls night, as four
figures in a Manhattan bar in the 1940s at first soliloquize, in turn, and
then fall into a stylized conversation before setting off for an after-hours
drink together. The epigraph to the poem consists of three lines from
the thirteenth-century Latin hymn *Dies Iræ*—Day of Wrath—heralding
the Last Judgement, with its terrifying blend of retribution and apocalypse, when heaven and earth will be reduced to ashes. For Auden's four
characters, Rosetta, Quant, Malin, and Emble, a destructive apocalypse
is apparently imminent. But it is clear that there are distinctively Norse
elements to it.

The beginning of the whole Ragnarök story is that the god Baldr has
ominous dreams.[249] Auden echoes this when Malin envisages a human
infant, perhaps himself as a baby:

> helpless in cradle and
> Righteous still, yet already there is
> Dread in his dreams...[250]

[245] *Völuspá*, st. 56, in Dronke, *The Poetic Edda*, vol. II, p. 23.
[246] Auden, *The English Auden*, p. 17.
[247] Paul Taylor, 'Auden's Icelandic Myth of Exile', *Journal of Modern Literature* 24:2 (2000–1), 213–34.
[248] *Völuspá*, st. 44, in Dronke, *The Poetic Edda*, vol. II, p. 19.
[249] Faulkes, *Edda*, p. 48.
[250] *The Age of Anxiety*, in *W. H. Auden, Collected Poems*, ed. Edward Mendelson (London: Faber and Faber, 1976, revised edition 2007), pp. 445–533 (463).

Similarly, Quant sees himself in the bar-room mirror, marked with "the brand of a winter/No priest can explain"[251]—perhaps a reference to the first event of the coming Ragnarök, a winter called *fimbulvetr*, as long as three winters run together, with no summers in between, an obvious terror for the pagan north.[252] On their mysterious dream journey later on in the poem, Rosetta's disquiet also seems to reference Ragnarök: she fears "These hills may be hollow; I've a horror of dwarfs".[253] In *Völuspá*, the dwarves are said, in the cryptic language of the poem, to groan in their stone doorways; these creatures who are accustomed to being imprisoned in caves in rocks and mountains now gather ominously on their thresholds.[254] Thus three of Auden's four speakers in *The Age of Anxiety* are associated with the first signs of Ragnarök. Emble, the youngest of the four, is also associated with a sort of beginning: his name is a close echo of the name Embla, which the poet of *Völuspá* gives to one of the pairs of first humans, transformed from inanimate driftwood by the gods who endow Ash and Elm—Askr and Embla in Old Norse—with breath, spirit, and flesh.[255] According to *Völuspá*, this driftwood lacked destiny before the gods' intervention; it was not merely physically inanimate, but stood outside the world of gods and men as a non-participant in that world's events and outcomes. Auden's Emble is preoccupied by his status as a young man who has yet to find his place in life; in an unexpectedly touching expression of this, Emble reflects that:

> To be young means
> To be all on edge, to be held waiting in
> A packed lounge for a Personal Call
> From Long Distance, for the low voice that
> Defines one's future.[256]

Quant, too, is associated with beginnings. When, at the end of his soliloquy, he concludes sardonically that "One-Eye's mistake/Is sorry He spoke", then it is natural to assume that this is a reference back to Polyphemus.[257] But the Norse god Odin was one-eyed, too, and is known in Old Norse as "All-father", which is comparable with Auden's labelling of One-Eye as "Ur-Papa". And Auden's bored Ur-Papa creates the universe with a "Primal

---

[251] Auden, *Collected Poems*, p. 449.
[252] Faulkes, *Edda*, pp. 52–3.
[253] Auden, *Collected Poems*, p. 486.
[254] *Völuspá*, st. 49, in Dronke, *The Poetic Edda*, vol. II, pp. 20–1.
[255] *Völuspá*, st. 17, in Dronke, *The Poetic Edda*, vol. II, p. 11.
[256] Auden, *Collected Poems*, p. 472.
[257] Auden, *Collected Poems*, p. 475; see John Fuller, *W. H. Auden: A Commentary* (London and Princeton: Faber and Faber, 1998), p. 377.

Yawn", a phrase which instantly recalls the primordial void of Norse myth, the *ginnunga gap*.[258] Quant's own cautious maxim—"The safest place/Is the more or less middling: the mean average/Is not noticed"[259]—is clearly derived, in its tripartite form as well as its substance, from three verses in the Old Norse mythological poem *Hávamál* which all begin "Middling wise/must every man be,/he should not be overwise ever" followed by one of three perceived advantages to mediocrity.[260] As Fuller reminds us, Quant (like Auden) is an authority on mythology; "he had spent many hours one winter in the Public Library reading... books on Mythology".[261]

Ragnarök is repeatedly figured as a time when all fetters and bonds will be broken and torn apart.[262] Auden's version of this fantastic chaos is more cerebral, but equally and wittily destabilizing; as Malin puts it,

> The primary colors
> Are all mixed up; the whole numbers
> Have broken down,[263]

and a few lines later, "Our ideas have got drunk and drop their H's".[264] Malin has made specific reference to the end of the world:

> we cannot be deaf to the question:
> "Do I love this world so well
> That I have to know how it ends?"[265]

and Rosetta wonders at the last moment if their dreams—like Baldr's—really do herald apocalypse:

> Does it exist,
> That last landscape
> Of gloom and glaciers and great storms
> Where, cold into chasms, cataracts
> Topple, and torrents
> Through rocky ruptures rage forever
> In a winter twilight watched by ravens,
> Birds on basalt,
> And shadows of ships long-shattered lie,
> Preserved disasters, in the solid ice
> Of frowning fjords?[266]

---

[258] *Völuspá*, st. 3, in Dronke, *The Poetic Edda*, vol. II, p. 7.
[259] Auden, *Collected Poems*, p. 498.
[260] *Hávamál*, st. 54–6, in Dronke, *The Poetic Edda*, vol. III, p. 13.
[261] Auden, *Collected Poems*, p. 448.
[262] Faulkes, *Edda*, p. 53.
[263] Auden, *Collected Poems*, p. 511.
[264] Auden, *Collected Poems*, p. 512.
[265] Auden, *Collected Poems*, p. 508.
[266] Auden, *Collected Poems*, p. 509.

This vivid depiction of winter is plainly situated in a Viking north. In swift succession, the four characters comment on cosmic horrors: "thunderheads threaten the sun"; "the clouds explode"; "the scene dissolves, is succeeded by/A grinning gap"; "Violent winds/tear us apart"; "The sullen South has been set on fire".[267] We can compare this with the events of Ragnarök: "The wolf will swallow the sun", and "Surtr will come from the south with fire".[268] The grinning gap is a sinister distortion (found also in Joyce's *Finnegans Wake*) of the primal void of Old Norse myth, the *ginnunga gap*, or yawning gape.

But for Auden's Manhattan quartet, Ragnarök is just a dream. They awake, and with wonderfully theatrical bathos, it is revealed that the cosmic darkness with which their dream came to an end is the bartender turning off the lights. Even this moment of apparently modernistic iconoclasm is paralleled in Old Norse, for Snorri ends his lengthy narrative of Norse mythology, climaxing in Ragnarök, with the same manoeuvre: the mysterious authorities in Asgard, who act as Snorri's mouthpiece for delivering the myths to an insistent questioner, suddenly disappear before his eyes, together with their great hall, in Snorri's equivalent of a puff of smoke. Only the stories remain.[269]

The dream of Ragnarök leaves Auden's characters with an ill-defined sense of disquiet, and a powerful sense of loss. They lament the absence of "some semi-divine stranger with superhuman powers"[270] and grieve for a world without belief or meaning, without structures imposed upon it. Ironically, it is here that Auden presents his clearest reference to Ragnarök, as

> In the high heavens
> The ageless places,
> The gods are wringing their great worn hands
> For their watchman is away, their world-engine
> Creaking and cracking.[271]

In Norse myth, the watchman of the gods is Heimdallr, who will blow his horn when he sees the first signs of impending Ragnarök. While the gods, ageless beings paradoxically nearing the end of their lives, gather to hold urgent counsel about their response, the cosmic World Tree, Yggdrasill, begins to show its own great age: like a real tree, it bends and creaks.[272] In

---

[267] Auden, *Collected Poems*, p. 510.
[268] See Faulkes, *Edda*, pp. 53–4.
[269] Faulkes, *Edda*, p. 57.
[270] Auden, *Collected Poems*, p. 513.
[271] Auden, *Collected Poems*, p. 514.
[272] *Völuspá*, st. 45, in Dronke, *The Poetic Edda*, vol. II, p. 19.

Auden's world, with Heimdallr away, Ragnarök would catch the gods unawares; that is why Auden's old gods are wringing their hands. Like Lewis's weary, battle-scarred gods, they are objects of pity now; no longer leaders, and indeed leaderless themselves. And Yggdrasill, the unifying symbol of their cosmos, is still splitting apart.

Amongst others, Paul Muldoon has continued this tradition of learned, allusive textual playfulness; it is perhaps significant that two poems of Muldoon's which relate to Old Norse myth, 'Yggdrasill' and 'Rune', both play on the obscurity and arcane nature of past mythologies, and their capacity to make meaning unstable, or even non-existent: the empty message at the top of Yggdrasill, and the unexplained runic stave.[273]

Old Norse myth has always been used by poets as a cultural marker for a group of people who formed part of the history and culture of the British Isles and Ireland, and thus features in an account of that history, whether actual or imagined. But in the twentieth century, we can see the central figures of Old Norse myth itself redeployed as new symbols in modernist poetry such as MacDiarmid's. In the work of David Jones, the wars against Germany are figured as a fratricidal tragedy, with Old Norse myth, and the clear connexions between the Germanic languages as evidence of that relationship. More especially in *The Anathemata*, the religious symbolism of Old Norse myth is revived by association with Christian theology. This same connexion is rather differently made by C. S. Lewis in his early poetry. By contrast, Old Norse myth, as encountered by poets such as Auden or Muldoon, can be used in a playful, academic way, for witty or ingenious effect. I shall argue in an epilogue, which is the final section of this book, that contemporary poets who use Old Norse myth manifestly continue these distinct traditions.

---

[273] Paul Muldoon, *Poems 1968–1998* (London: Faber and Faber, 2001), pp. 118 and 450.

Epilogue
New Images: Contemporary Poetry
and Old Norse Myth

It seems right to begin this brief survey of contemporary poetry draw-ing on Old Norse myth with the poetry of Pauline Stainer, because of all the poets considered here, her mythic allusions are the most sustained, and her debt to the work of David Jones is evident throughout, not only in the dense allusiveness of her work (more than one reviewer has com-plained that "one could ask for more clues",[1] and the poet David Morley has explicitly compared her to Jones and Geoffrey Hill in precisely this respect[2]) but also in the insistently religious themes and lexis she uses. The title of a poem from her first collection, *The Honeycomb* (1989), for instance, 'Flora in Calix–light', references the name of a watercolour by David Jones, with the religious symbol of the chalice—the flowery "calix" of the title—as its central focus. In the poem itself, Stainer sees the chalice as radiant with both light and religious significance, and she makes a char-acteristic link with archaeology: after all, she asks,

> did not the Saxon king
> in the ship-burial
> suffer ten silver bowls
> chased with crosses
> at his shoulder?[3]

The religious symbol is universal, transcending any one particular faith: the unnamed Saxon king in the Sutton Hoo ship burial (the subject of a sequence of poems, 'Little Egypt', in *Parable Island*, a later collection by Stainer) may well have been a pagan ruler who yet recognized the power of Christianity.

Although in *The Honeycomb* Stainer explores the related themes of the presence of the past in the landscape and in ritual, her ultimately mythic world is more a timeless spatial *imaginaire* than an actual chronotope.

---

[1] Kevan Johnson, 'Four ounces of raven', *Times Literary Supplement* (23 June 1995), p. 30.

[2] David Morley, 'A spring in her heels', *The Guardian* (22 November 2003).

[3] Pauline Stainer, *The Honeycomb* (Newcastle upon Tyne: Bloodaxe Books, 1989), p. 44.

John Greening has said of *The Lady and the Hare*, Stainer's 2003 collection of new and selected poems, that "we never really leave the mind and imagination of Pauline Stainer".[4] However, the title sequence from *The Ice-Pilot Speaks* (1994), a collection generously represented in *The Lady and the Hare*, opens with deceptively specific indications of time and place: "It is Ascension Week" (but the religious calendar is cyclic rather than chronologically linear) in *"ultima thule"*—the very far North, somewhere beyond the actuality of the map.[5] It is the physical expanse and various cultures of the frozen far North which dominate this sequence; Stainer's graphic realization of an icy world counters the vagueness of mythic time. The Ice-Pilot himself, whose voice is not always distinguishable from Stainer's own, cannot quite be pinned down to any distinct point in historical time; several allusions in the poem come from Sir William Parry's 1821 *Journal of a Voyage for the Discovery of a North-West Passage*, but the sequence is a tissue of allusions to various journals of Arctic and indeed Antarctic discovery, such as the reference to Amundsen's dogs, driven to death—"the only dark memory of my stay in the South", as Amundsen wrote in his account *The South Pole*.[6] In fact, the overriding theme of 'The Ice-Pilot Speaks' is the ultimate human constant—death—tempered to some extent by what is arguably the other: sex. The first section of the sequence opens with the claim that there is

> No such thing
> As a routine death—
> In *ultima thule*...[7]

and continues thick with allusions to its various manifestations: the dead walrus whose skin provides the shaman with his drum; the black crepe veils—usually mourning gear—worn by the crew to combat snowblindness; the birds shot for food, one snowy owl itself "thawing its prey/against its breast";[8] and Amundsen's dogs. Textuality—like maps—is useless: volumes of saga literature, Old Icelandic chronicles of life in Iceland in the early Middle Ages, serve only to stoke the ship's furnace. Some sections of the poem are framed as memories of the warmth of human sexual contact, but these memories seem infinitely distant, even hallucinatory. More urgent is the repeated questioning in the poem, apparently an attempt to

---

[4] John Greening, 'An irreproachable eye', *Times Literary Supplement* (30 April 2004), p. 32.
[5] Pauline Stainer, *The Ice-Pilot Speaks* (Newcastle upon Tyne: Bloodaxe Books, 1994), p. 9.
[6] Roald Amundsen, *The South Pole* (London: John Murray, 1912), vol. I, p. 237.
[7] Stainer, *The Ice-Pilot Speaks*, p. 9.
[8] Stainer, *The Ice-Pilot Speaks*, p. 9.

express the bleakness and purity of the sights and sounds of this strange
half-imaginary landscape. Stainer invokes the haunting music of Satie and
Varese, and the dreadful and unimaginable noise of the Piper Alpha oil rig
fire in the North Sea. She asks too about sounds which can only be potential, and perhaps never heard:

> What is song
> when the shroud
> is left unlaced at the mouth
> and the arctic tern
> has a radio transmitter
> lashed with fuse-wire
> to its leg?[9]

Inexpressibility inevitably leads Stainer to the idiom of religious myth. In
a section about the plague ("Who says plague is monotonous?" the poem
asks, echoing the poem's opening claim about the variety of death) comes
a startling allusion to Christian and Norse myth:

> Christ turns
> on Yggdrasill
> under the strobe lights... [10]

Yggdrasill, the great World Tree, is the supporting link between heaven
and earth, and the central symbol of a world which is mighty but also
organic, and therefore subject to old age and decay. Yggdrasill was the tree
on which the god Odin, the High One, hanged himself for nine nights
in pursuit of wisdom—specifically, the knowledge of runes. In the Old
Norse poem *Hávamál*, the power of runes is magical, but one might see
this as ultimately referencing mastery of written language.[11] Stainer also
alludes to Odin and the runes in *Parable Island*: in 'Sourin' (a place on the
island of Rousay, where Stainer was living at the time) the pitiful sight of
a swan hanging from power-lines evokes Odin hanging from Yggdrasill;[12]
Stainer's connection is perhaps the folk belief in the swansong—the mystical singing of the dying bird—as if death brought it, like Odin, new means
of articulation.

That Christ should "turn" on Yggdrasill echoes David Jones's repeated
conflations of Christian symbol and Norse myth; for both divinities, sacrifice involved hanging and resurrection. The most obvious link, perhaps,

[9] Stainer, *The Ice-Pilot Speaks*, p. 12.
[10] Stainer, *The Ice-Pilot Speaks*, p. 14.
[11] *Hávamál*, st. 138–44, in Dronke, *The Poetic Edda*, vol. III, pp. 30–1.
[12] Pauline Stainer, 'Sourin', from *Parable Island*, in *The Lady and the Hare* (Tarset: Bloodaxe
Books, 2003), p. 139.

is with the climax of *The Anathemata*, where Christ's crucifixion is figured as his "riding" (the word always used of Odin's sacrifice in Old Norse sources) of "the Axile Tree"—the tree which forms the axis between heaven and earth; that is, again, Yggdrasill, in Norse cosmology, or the Rood, in Christian sources.[13] Some modern mythographers have suggested that Yggdrasill as a symbol originated as an ancient Lappish conception of a great central axis culminating in the Pole Star, around which the heavens seem to turn, and Stainer's constant concern with the quality of light— evident in all her work—finds here its most evocative site: the Northern Lights whose eerie flickering illuminates a distinctively northern crucifix- ion, the reference to strobe lighting bringing what is distant into sudden contact with the here and now.

From this point in the sequence, explicit allusions to Old Norse myth begin to build up. A ship, sunk with its heavy cargo of southern sugar, rises to the surface as the sugar dissolves, like ice melting; this physical evanescence is compared to the yet more ephemeral imprint of the hooves of Odin's eight-legged horse, Sleipnir, on a glacier.[14] The weapon which killed Odin's son, Baldr, was an apparently harmless missile, a mistletoe stem which was mysteriously transformed (perhaps by Odin himself?) into a rigid javelin.[15] Stainer evokes this scene, describing the mistletoe, perhaps, in ancient myth, a symbol of resurrection, as well as the instru- ment of Baldr's death, as "shafting" Baldr[16]—a graphic rendering of the parasitic plant's transformation, but also playing on the word as a term for a beam of light, which so very often in Stainer's verse is described in terms of a weapon, especially a blade, physically perilous. In a classic "bog body" poem, 'Lindow Man', we see another veiled reference to the death of Baldr: archaeologists "found mistletoe in [his] gut" and he suffered "a triple death"—a ritual execution like Baldr. But Lindow Man is not given voice: again, the topos of inexpressibility dominates the poem. Even the significance of his death is labelled "unspeakable".[17]

In 'The Ice-Pilot Speaks', the death of Baldr leads Stainer to think of the Argentinian author Jorge Luis Borges, a devotee of Old Norse myth and literature, who was blind, like Höðr, and how his touch of a pillar in a Reykjavík hotel room brought back to his mind the geometrical diagrams—reminiscent, perhaps, of lines on a geographical chart—of

---

[13] Jones, *The Anathemata*, p. 243.
[14] Stainer, *The Ice-Pilot Speaks*, p. 15.
[15] See Faulkes, *Edda*, p. 49.
[16] Stainer, *The Ice-Pilot Speaks*, p. 15.
[17] Pauline Stainer, *The Wound-dresser's Dream* (Newcastle upon Tyne: Bloodaxe Books, 1996), p. 48.

his youth, which he can no longer see. The lyrical description of a pool beneath a waterfall—"an unspilled moon"—is also a site of transformation: Stainer imagines a painter drawing five strings across it, which would transform it as visual image into a musical instrument with its dark bowl from which the sound issues. All of these transformations culminate in the ultimate creative transformation,

> as on the evening
> of the first day
> a man's hair
> comes out of the ice[18]

—a reference to the creation narrative in Old Norse myth, as described by Snorri in *Gylfaginning*: the mythic cow Auðumbla licks blocks of ice, and on the first day, a man's hair appears: Auðumbla licks him into shape.[19] Here, significantly for Stainer's purposes, man is created not from earth, or dust, but from ice.

Stainer next links the graphic bloodiness of a whaling station with the savagery of Viking funeral practices:

> The whalers could be
> gods, butchering
> Balder's horse against
> the midnight sun.[20]

In fact, in his account of Baldr's funeral, Snorri rather fastidiously restricts himself to noting that Baldr's horse was led to the funeral pyre,[21] but we know from many Scandinavian Viking graves that the butchering of horses was a not uncommon accompaniment to the inhumation of a high-status human. In a more fantastic episode in Old Norse myth, the half-god Loki, the perpetrator of Baldr's death, is fettered by the gods: Snorri tells us that the fetters were made of the guts of Loki's own son, torn to pieces by a brother whom the gods had transformed into a ravening wolf.[22] Stainer, whether by accident or design, compresses this bizarre story and presents Loki as "bound/with his own entrails".[23] Both this and the previous allusion focus on the physical horror of violent death—the blood and the guts—whether actual or mythic.

---

[18] Stainer, *The Ice-Pilot Speaks*, p. 16.
[19] Faulkes, *Edda*, p. 11.
[20] Stainer, *The Ice-Pilot Speaks*, p. 16.
[21] Faulkes, *Edda*, p. 50.
[22] Faulkes, *Edda*, p. 52.
[23] Stainer, *The Ice-Pilot Speaks*, p. 16.

The next section turns to the sequence's second theme—human love—and again alludes to Norse myth, this time the love story of the hero Sigurðr and the valkyrie Sigrdrífa, whom he encounters, sleeping on a mountain-top, having been instructed by the speech of birds.[24] Stainer picks up the element of blood in this story, for Sigurðr came to understand the speech of birds through accidentally tasting the blood from the dragon Fafnir's heart, which he was roasting on a spit; Stainer dramatically shifts this epiphany into the human sphere as the poem's speaker tastes with a finger a lover's menstrual blood.[25] Sigrdrífa's mailcoat was so tight, according to a prose link in the *Edda*, that "it was as if it had grown into her flesh"[26]—again, Stainer compresses the simile and has the lover "slit the mailshirt/grown into her flesh/as Sigrdrifa slept", implying bloody penetration. But this action demonstrates not so much blood-letting as plenitude, for "not a drop runs over/but there is no room for another".[27] This is in contrast to the excessive gore of the whalers (and, by extension, the Viking mourners), who cause the animal's blood to "boil from the heart", unlike the fleeting touch of Sigurðr's finger on the dragon's heart, or the lover's dipping into the menstrual blood.

The final allusion to Old Norse myth in 'The Ice-Pilot Speaks' is, fittingly, to neither sex nor death, nor even apocalypse, but to the elegiac and oddly archaeological element of the chess board of the gods. In *Völuspá*, the golden age of innocence enjoyed by the gods in Asgard is characterized by their carefree game of chess in the meadow, but this idyll is disrupted by the arrival of three mysterious giantesses, and all manner of violent and faithless events ensue, culminating in Ragnarök.[28] But as in Christian tradition, there is life after apocalypse, and after cataclysm and conflagration a new earth will arise, and "There will once more/the miraculous/golden chequers/be found, in the grass,/those that in the old days/they had owned".[29] The chess pieces are like archaeological finds, material evidence of an antediluvian world which is otherwise no more than the memory of stories. In Stainer's lines, the playing of chess is almost an illicit activity, for the gods are "discovered" at it, and quite at odds with the sign of renewal and recovery in the Old Norse poem, Stainer sees their play as "the game

[24] It is clear that there has been some merging of the legend of Brynhildr the valkyrie with this story; Sigrdrífa herself only appears in the *Poetic Edda* and not in Snorri's account, where Sigurðr's beloved is Brynhildr (Faulkes, *Edda*, pp. 102–3, and see *Sigrdrífumál*, 'The Lay of Sigrdrifa', in Larrington, *The Poetic Edda*, pp. 166–73).

[25] Stainer, *The Ice-Pilot Speaks*, p. 16.

[26] Larrington, *The Poetic Edda*, p. 166.

[27] Stainer, *The Ice-Pilot Speaks*, p. 17.

[28] *Völuspá*, st. 8, in Dronke, *The Poetic Edda*, vol. II, p. 9.

[29] *Völuspá*, st. 58, in Dronke, *The Poetic Edda*, vol. II, p. 23.

that must be lost".[30] Although *Völuspá* represents the chess set as itself a
material recovery from a past age, these old gods and their world have now
gone, and their only recovery is through poetry.

In a later collection, *A Litany of High Waters* (2002), Stainer quotes
actual Old Norse mythological poetry (in translation) to give voice to
medieval speakers in the poem 'Falcon on a blue field'. The speakers are
thirteenth-century falconers sent to Iceland by King Hakon of Norway
to fetch back gyrfalcons. They endure the harsh conditions which are the
constant hallmark of Stainer's northern landscapes, and to keep up their
spirits, they declare:

> we sang
> from the sagas
> '*We are snowed on with snow*
> And smitten by rain
> *And drenched with dew.*
> *We have long been dead.*[31]

Stainer's note acknowledges Ursula Dronke's edition of the *Poetic Edda* for
these lines, but as Stainer would have known from this edition, eddic poems
are not sagas. Further, the original lines are framed in the first person singular, and are spoken by the mysterious sibyl whom the god Odin summons
from the underworld to answer his questions about the death of Baldr;
the taxing journey is from the world of the dead to speak to Odin.[32] Here
Stainer uses "sagas" as a convenient, uncomplicated sign for Old Norse
literary sources. But she also suggests an implicit parallel between travelling
through Iceland—the classic Northern landscape—and the journey from
Hel—and perhaps too the strange power of Norse mythological verse, for
as the falconers chant their lines, "the falcons/fall out of the middle air".[33]

Elsewhere in *A Litany of High Waters* Stainer alludes to Old Norse myth
in a medieval context. A young fisher-wife in medieval King's Lynn dreams
of marrying an Icelandic merchant; whether in recognition that this is
an impossible dream, or that her wedding night will be a revelation, she
alludes to Ragnarök, enjoining "Brother Wolf, swallow the moon"—a reference to one of the cosmic calamities presaged for the end of the world.[34]
In 'The Last Sorcerer', a shape-shifting shaman hears increasingly mystical
and sinister sounds, culminating with "Thor pulling on his iron gloves".[35]

[30] Stainer, *The Ice-Pilot Speaks*, p. 17.
[31] Stainer, *The Lady and the Hare*, p. 184.
[32] *Baldrs draumar*, st. 5, in Dronke, *The Poetic Edda*, vol. II, p. 155.
[33] Stainer, *The Lady and the Hare*, p. 184.
[34] 'The Ballad of Ruby Tuesday', in Stainer, *The Lady and the Hare*, p. 187.
[35] 'The Last Sorcerer', in Stainer, *The Lady and the Hare*, p. 187.

Stainer's volume *Crossing the Snowline* contains poems written after a long fallow period following the death of her daughter. The title is of course ambiguous: is Stainer coming back out of the cold—like Le Carré's spy George Smiley—or is she at last returning to a familiar spatial *imaginaire*, that polar wasteland which proved so productive? The poet Frances Leviston has described Pauline Stainer as "guarding the power of our occult and mythological heritage".[36] This concern, in tandem with her fascination for Northernness, means that Old Norse myth is an inescapable focus in her poetry. Myth is not only a means of giving local colour and period detail to the world of the past, but also an instrument for expressing the continuity of sign and symbol—as David Jones did—and the transformative power of art in general, and poetry in particular.

The Scottish poet Kathleen Jamie, though also concerned with the mythic, or the numinous, presents a marked contrast to Pauline Stainer. Jamie has been called "a strikingly unbookish poet"[37] and much of her work consists in the immaculate depiction of directly observed scenes or images, most often from the landscape. It is perhaps in keeping with this that Jamie's use of myth is not confined to explicit allusion or quotation. Instead, she transforms mythic motifs and patterns into wholly new narratives. In 'One of us', the plural speaking voice announces "We are come in a stone boat,/a miracle ship".[38] 'The Witch in the Stone Boat' is the title of an Icelandic folk tale collected by Andrew Lang in his *Yellow Fairy Book*, though it occurs too as an element in folk tales of other traditions.[39] The travellers in the stone boat are also associated with Celtic motifs: they wear "sealskin cloaks" and "penannular brooches" and their slippers are made from "feathery/gugas' necks"—*guga* being the Gaelic word for a young gannet. Perhaps what we see here is the intermingling of Celtic and Norse elements which is—as Hugh MacDiarmid insisted—characteristic of Scotland. The medieval ethos is suddenly shattered as the mysterious travellers pick their way past "rusty tractors" and see "No-one,/nothing, but a distant/Telecom van". They are clearly time travellers, arrived from an unknown past into a desolate present; like the Telecom van, they are involved with messages across big distances.

Jamie presents their arrival into this world—a classic collision of past and present—as richly comic: they describe their solemn sacred symbols ("the/golden horn of righteousness,/the justice harp") as "our tat"—"what

---

[36] Frances Leviston, 'Shiver of satisfaction', *The Guardian* (20 December 2008), p. 15.
[37] Gerald Mangan, 'Romantic risks', *Times Literary Supplement* (16 August 2002), p. 22.
[38] Kathleen Jamie, *The Queen of Sheba* (Newcastle upon Tyne: Bloodaxe Books, 1994), p. 43.
[39] Andrew Lang, *The Yellow Fairy Book* (London: Longmans, Green and Co., 1894).

208 *Epilogue*

folks expect" of them—and their shape-shifting abilities as "silly magic". But they can still cause a stir: transformed into swans, they literally stop the traffic: "a dormobile/slewed into a passing place; cameras flashed".

So who are these enigmatic visitants? As swan-maidens, their arrival recalls the Old Norse mythic poem *Völundarkviða*, in which three swan maidens take three brothers as lovers, but seven years later depart as mysteriously as they arrived, impelled by a force as ineluctable as that which drives the migration of actual birds.[40] But the end of Jamie's poem moves beyond the recollection of old myths. The visitants seem to be carrying out an undercover assignment. They make use of safe houses; they "hold/ minor government jobs, lay plans, and bide [their] time". They have infiltrated our society. This project taps into a series of related contemporary myths. Are they fifth columnists, "the enemy within", as Thatcherite rhetoric would have it? Or, more sensationally, aliens from Outer Space? Or simply the bearers of a yet-to-flourish ideology, whose day will come? The sinister power of this modern myth needs no specificity to do its work; the poem's title, 'One of us', with its negative implication "*not* one of us", exploits the anxiety we all feel about the difficulty of locating a threat to our security. Jamie has transformed an old myth into a new one.

In 'The horse-drawn sun' Jamie invests another ancient mythic idea with modern relevance. At first, the poem's speaker seems to be the ubiquitous bog body: "We may lie forsaken in the earth's black gut". But the speaker who experiences a thrilling exhumation—a "struggle to surface/after thousands of years", and then "the plough-share/tearing the earth overhead" is "a horse of the light"—a beast of burden drawing the sun behind it.[41] The figure of the sun being moved across the sky by a horse-drawn chariot is familiar from a number of mythologies, including Old Norse, and, insofar as it has survived, perhaps Anglo-Saxon too. It is sometimes regarded as a rather naïve way of understanding the movement of heavenly bodies, even a reductive one. But Jamie's horses—rather like the mythic horses in Edwin Muir's 'The Horses'—are not only sentient, but also wiser than the human world, and comprehend the inadequacies of a decayed modern age. As revenants from a long-gone past, their curiosity about contemporary humanity is terrifyingly condescending: "Let's see what they've lost. What they've become".

In both *Nominies* (1998) and *The Lammas Hireling* (2003), Ian Duhig's attitude towards the past splits between a bloke-ish jokiness and a serious exploration of the place of poetry in the relationship between the two. As

[40] *Völundarkviða*, in Dronke, *The Poetic Edda*, vol. II, pp. 243–54.
[41] Jamie, *The Queen of Sheba*, p. 52.

Stephen Burt has observed, "Duhig wants above all to reveal a continu-ity between archaic (religious, folkloric) and contemporary (quotidian, urban) experience".[42] But this aim is often expressed through a satirical mode, a debunking of the past; David Kennedy maintains that "we roman-ticize history into something grand to counteract the absurdities of the human predicament. Duhig wants us to know that history just isn't worth it".[43] *Nominies* presents ample evidence of this latter approach. 'Shanty', for instance, reduces Vikings to the butt of a (fictitious) children's rhyme:

> Seven fly:
>> salmon feast.
> Seven salmon:
>> seal feast.
> Seven seal:
>> shark feast.
> Seven shark:
>> whale feast.
> Seven whale:
>> Norse feast.
> Seven Norse:
>> fly feast.[44]

The poem 'A Line from Snorri Sturluson' purports to quote from *Skáldskaparmál*, in which many synonyms are listed: "*I would say the names of the Sea*".[45] But Duhig, while acknowledging that as a poet this is his job too, goes on to describe a squalid contemporary seascape, with used con-doms, discarded ice-cream cornets and piles of dogshit. In burlesque spirit, Duhig calls his own dog "Fenris, wolf to Loki!", alluding to the malevolent half-god Loki, who sired monsters, including the apocalyptic wolf Fenrir (not "Fenris").[46] Duhig's dog, in its unattractive snuffling around, knows "more depths than Thor's lip", probably a reference to Snorri's account of Thor's humiliations at the court of the giant Útgarða-Loki, in which he fails to drain a drinking horn whose furthest end dips into the ocean itself.[47]

---

[42] Stephen Burt, 'To wake the fiddlers underneath', *Times Literary Supplement* (26 September 2003), p. 25.
[43] David Kennedy, 'Historical vulgarities', *Times Literary Supplement* (18 October 1991), p. 23.
[44] Ian Duhig, *Nominies* (Newcastle upon Tyne: Bloodaxe Books, 1998), p. 17.
[45] Duhig, *Nominies*, p. 20; for Snorri's list of names for the sea, see *Skáldskaparmál*, ch. 75, in Faulkes, *Edda*, pp. 160–1.
[46] Faulkes, *Edda*, pp. 26–7.
[47] Faulkes, *Edda*, pp. 42–6.

Duhig is gaily playing fast and loose with the tradition he invokes. In similar fashion, in *The Lammas Hireling*, Duhig debunks the celebrated story of the great Icelandic saga hero Njáll, whose peaceable instincts and legal skills are not enough to avert tragedy, or halt the course of a violent feud; he and his wife and grandson are burnt to death in their house.[48] Duhig, in 'Wise, Brave Old Njal', attributes to Njáll a series of tedious, invented aphorisms and then provocatively claims that if he'd been there, he'd have "lent a match".[49]

On the other hand, the object of Duhig's satire can be the crude trans-formation of Norse myth in contemporary culture. In 'Ken's Videos, Seahouses'—Seahouses being a small fishing village on the ever-resonant Northumbrian coast—Duhig represents himself as pondering whether to rent a Hollywood film, *The Vikings*. Ken presses the attractions of "a recent *Beowulf*" ("the hero an exiled Arab poet played by Antonio Banderas") and Duhig wittily picks up on the most familiar cliché of Viking tradition to represent his indecision: "On the horns of a helmet, I hesitate, lost".[50]

Duhig's references to history and myth are of course primarily book-ish—they play with textual traditions, rather than being inspired by actual landscapes or artefacts. Even the quartet 'Four More Sides to the Franks Casket', a poem ostensibly inspired by the delicate and cryptic eighth-century ivory reliquary of that name, tells us less about the object itself than about Duhig's a-historicist and esoteric medieval learning.[51] When Duhig won a Northern Arts fellowship, commissioned to produce "something commending the literature and landscape of the region", the resulting poems in *The Lammas Hireling* were still overwhelmingly "book-ish", several of them adopting the familiar technique of ventriloquizing voices from the past, though not for comic effect.[52] Not all of them found favour with critics, but the title poem won universal acclaim, though many readers found it mysterious. 'The Lammas Hireling' returns to a familiar chronotope, the northern past, though the title and the first line suggest a Northern Irish setting. However, the mythic quality of the poem's narra-tive transcends time and place, and there are no proper names. The poem's speaker has hired a farmhand, and like the sacral kings of old tradition, the new help, though silent and unsociable, seems to have caused the farm to prosper: the cattle "only dropped heifers, fat as cream".[53] But apparently

---

[48] Cook, *Njals saga*, pp. 216–32.
[49] Ian Duhig, *The Lammas Hireling* (London: Picador, 2003), p. 36.
[50] Duhig, *The Lammas Hireling*, p. 30.
[51] Duhig, *The Lammas Hireling*, pp. 34–5.
[52] See Alan Brownjohn, 'Warriors, Warlocks and Video Shops', *The Independent* (23 January 2004), p. 18.
[53] Duhig, *The Lammas Hireling*, pp. 4–5.

haunted by the voice of his dead wife, the farmer kills the hireling, whose corpse undergoes a strange transformation into the shape of a hare—a sinister animal in many folk traditions. The farmer's cattle no longer prosper (they are "elf-shot", a term from Anglo-Saxon charms) and he is wracked by irrational guilt.

I do not know of any Germanic myth or narrative which matches these events, although as we have seen there is no reason to expect that Duhig will slavishly reproduce his sources or influences. And yet aspects of this elliptical tale are strongly reminiscent of the Old Icelandic saga of Grettir, with its celebrated analogues to the action of the Old English poem *Beowulf*.[54] In the saga, Grettir, an outlaw, pits himself against a series of humanoid creatures: trolls, the zombie-like ghost of a Swedish farmhand, and berserks. One of his adversaries is the silent and unsociable Glámr, who is first killed by some unknown force and then returns as an *aptrganga* —one of the walking dead. Just as Grettir is about to kill this creature, in support of the farmer who has hired him, the moon comes out from behind the clouds—as, indeed, "the moon came out" in Duhig's poem as the farmer kills the hireling. The killing has a permanent effect on Grettir, as it does on Duhig's farmer, although in the saga we are told that Grettir was ever afterwards afraid of the dark—a disastrous weakness in an outlaw. The weird hired hand, the farming context, the murder, the moon, and the continued psychological reverberation of the killing, combined with a similar atmosphere of menace and the uncanny, all suggest some influence from the saga on Duhig's poem. But he has transformed the narrative into something more powerful and sinister—we would not expect in a family saga an event so blatantly magical as the shape-shifting to the form of a hare—just as Kathleen Jamie created her new myth about the enemy within in 'One of us'.

Deliberately arcane references characterize 'Behoof', in which Duhig muses on the many manifestations, definitions, and identities of the horse in Western (and indeed Eastern) culture, apparently as a comic riposte to Dickens's reductive Gradgrind. Early definitions are medieval: "Siege engine. Saxon land art./Ritual bride for Celtic kings".[55] But as the poem progresses, references are piled up in an a-historical jumble, and include two specific allusions to horses of Old Norse myth, Skinfaxi ("Shining mane"—according to Snorri, the horse which pulls Day's chariot, thus lighting up the world)—and Hrimfaxi ("Soot", or "Frost-mane", pulling Night's chariot, its bit-spittle spraying the earth with dew).[56] It is not clear,

---

[54] See Guðni Jónsson (ed.), *Grettis saga Ásmundarsonar*, Íslenzk fornrit VII (Reykjavík: Hið Íslenzka Fornritafélag, 1936), and Byock, *Grettir's Saga*, ch. 32–5, pp. 91–103.

[55] Duhig, *The Speed of Dark*, p. 18.

[56] See Faulkes, *Edda*, p. 14.

however, whether these names contribute to the overall theme, or meaning of the poem, or whether they are simply arcane additions, useful to carry a bit of light-hearted morphological word-play:

> Hack for taxi, tack for Faxi,
> Brass facts. That's that.[57]

Don Paterson is another distinctively "bookish" poet who has been compared with Paul Muldoon in this respect. His tricksy collection *God's Gift to Women* (1997)—with what Robert Potts has called an "overarching denial of any theme"[58]—contains many allusions to many myths. Several of the poems are named after the stations on an old Scottish railway line, including, as if this were a timetable, the time of day—a wonderfully textual chronotope. In '00:00 Law Tunnel' a walled-up railway tunnel is a depository for cultural and historical odds and ends.[59] The casual reference to "Fenrir, Pol Pot,/Captain Oates" suggests that Paterson is simply heaping up larger-than-life figures from the past—there is no apparent link between these names. Here, then, Old Norse myth is simply part of a wide-ranging "myth-kitty" on which poets can draw without particular purpose; neither Northernness nor a specific point in the past is at issue here.

Paterson has described himself as "not really a poet of place"[60] and in 'The Alexandrian Library' in *Nil Nil* (1993), history is purely and literally a textual construct—it is represented by a nightmarish journey through a post-industrial wasteland to a shop selling a vast and various array of unwanted and outdated books. This post-modernist depiction of the past naturally contains a medieval component (interpolated with a quick joke about amnesia):

> . ... a grimoire in horrible waxpaper,
> a lost Eddic cycle of febrile monotony,
> *Leechdom and Wortcunning; Living with Alzheimer's*
> and Tatwine's gigantic *Aenigmae Perarduae*.[61]

In *Rain* (2009) there is, with one extraordinary exception, no explicit reference to a northern medieval. We have seen Jamie and Duhig arguably transforming mythic material into new narratives; the obvious problem with identifying this is that the deeper the poet's engagement, and

[57] Duhig, *The Speed of Dark*, p. 19.
[58] Robert Potts, 'Reflected glare', *Times Literary Supplement* (12 September 1997), p. 21.
[59] Don Paterson, *God's Gift to Women* (London: Faber, 1997), pp. 6–7.
[60] Interview with Marco Fazzini, http://www.donpaterson.com/files/interview1.htm (accessed 5 March 2014).
[61] Don Paterson, *Nil Nil* (London: Faber, 1993), p. 30.

the greater the transformation, the more uncertain identification of the possible source becomes. Thus, for instance, writing of one of his twin sons, in 'Correctives', Paterson, apparently working from direct observation, describes how the child stills a slight shudder in his left hand "with one touch from his right". Paterson represents this as a sort of small but hugely significant epiphany, a demonstration of "the one hand's kindness to the other" not granted to everyone to have either experienced or seen.[62] Anyone familiar with Old Norse poetry will be struck by the parallel with the eddic poem *Hamðismál*, in which two brothers, setting out on a doomed revenge mission, are offered help by their half-brother, who promises to support them "as one foot another". His offer, which implies that he is as integral a part of their brotherhood as two feet are part of one body, is not understood by the two full brothers, who mock his metaphor in terms which only serve to make its meaning clearer: "How can a foot/help a foot,/or a hand grown from the body's flesh/help a hand?"[63] Paterson's short poem seems to explore precisely this idea: his son "understands/that the whole man must be his own brother". If this is indeed inspired by the Old Norse legend of Hamðir and his brother Sörli, it is very far from the casually explicit incorporation of proper names from a myth-kitty.

Rain is dominated by the long sequence 'Phantom', in memory of the poet Michael Donaghy. In section V, Paterson imagines a cosmic otherworld and inverts long-held conceptions of the relationship between life and death:

> We come from nothing and return to it.
> It lends us out to time, and when we lie
> in silent contemplation of the void
> they say we feel it contemplating us.
> This is wrong...[64]

Paterson's contention is that earth itself is the void, only brought to life and meaning by the paradoxical (and oddly Platonic) play of "bright shadows" on it from a "something vast and distant and enthroned". But what happens when "the dark light stills", and this vast mind rests? It is at this point that Paterson reaches for the great image of the Old Norse World Tree to express a sort of cosmic regression from enlightenment:

[62] Don Paterson, *Rain* (London: Faber, 2009), p. 16.
[63] *Hamðismál*, st. 13, in Dronke, *The Poetic Edda*, vol. I, p. 164.
[64] Paterson, *Rain*, p. 55.

> the tree will rise untethered to its station
> between earth and heaven, the open book
> turn runic and unreadable again.

This too is very far from the casual name-dropping of Old Norse mythic references; it is a precisely measured and considered deployment of mythic allusion appropriate to the lofty solemnity of Paterson's elegy. Old Norse mythology is not funny, or arcane, or symbolic of a shared past which poets in English can recover: it is testimony to an unwelcome, unwanted, and essentially unlit prehistory.

I made it clear in the introduction to this book that it cannot be exhaustive in its survey of the influence of Old Norse myth on poetry in English. I expect—indeed, I hope—that other readers and critics will have found, and will continue to find, allusions to Old Norse myth, and will write about them. Moreover, if a myth—in its broadest definition—denotes a story of such significance to its hearers or readers that it bears, even demands, continual repetition and re-telling,[65] then a history of the use of Old Norse myth by poets in English can necessarily have no conclusion. I am aware that even as I write this, poets are in the process of producing ever more work which draws on Old Norse myth. And as time goes on, more and different reasons for turning to Old Norse myth will surely emerge.

[65] See Heather O'Donoghue, *From Asgard to Valhalla* (London: I. B. Tauris, 2007), pp. 1–4.

Bibliography

Anon., Review of Jerningham, *The Rise and Progress of the Scandinavian Poetry,* *Literary Review* (1784), Article LII, pp. 237–9.

Anon., Review of Sterling, *Poems, The English Review* vol. 10 (October 1787), Article 13, pp. 281–4.

Anon., Review of Sterling, *Poems, The English Review* vol. 15 (March 1790), Article 22, p. 229.

Adam of Bremen, *History of the Archbishops of Hamburg-Bremen*, trans. F. J. Tschan (New York: Columbia, 1959).

Alyal, Amina, '"In what Scythian sorte soeuer": Tudor Debate on Rhyme', in Z. Almási and M. Pincombe (eds.), *Writing the Other: Humanism versus Barbarism in Tudor England* (Newcastle: Cambridge Scholars, 2008), pp. 159–76.

Amundsen, Roald, *The South Pole: An Account of the Norwegian Arctic Expedition in the 'Fram', 1910–1912*, trans. A. G. Chater (London: John Murray, 1912), 2 vols.

Andersen, R. B., *Norse Mythology; or, the Religion of our Forefathers* (Chicago: S. C. Griggs and Company, 1875).

Anderton, H. Orsmond, *Baldur: A Lyrical Drama* (London: T. Fisher Unwin, 1893).

Armstrong, John, *Taste: An Epistle to a Young Critic* (London: R. Griffiths, 1753).

Arnamagnæan Commission, *Edda Sæmundar hinns Fróda. Edda Rhythmica seu Antiquior, vulgo Sæmundina dicta* (Hafniæ: Sumtibus Legati Magnæani et Gyldendalii, 1787, 1818, 1828), 3 vols.

Arngrímr Jónsson, *Brevis Commentarius de Islandia* (Hafniæ: Iohannes Stockelmannus, 1593).

Arngrímr Jónsson, *Crymogaea, sive Rerum Islandicarum libri tres* (Hamburg, 1609).

Árni Björnsson, *Wagner and the Volsungs* (London: Viking Society for Northern Research, 2003).

Arnold, Matthew, *The Poems of Matthew Arnold*, ed. Kenneth and Miriam Allott, 2nd edition (London: Longman, 1979).

Ashfield, Andrew, and de Bolla, Peter (eds.), *The Sublime: A Reader in British Eighteenth-Century Aesthetic Theory* (Cambridge: Cambridge University Press, 1996).

Ashurst, David, 'William Morris and the Volsungs', in David Clark and Carl Phelpstead (eds.), *Old Norse Made New* (London: Viking Society for Northern Research, 2007), pp. 43–61.

Auden, W. H., *The English Auden: Poems, Essays and Dramatic Writings 1927–1939*, ed. Edward Mendelson (London: Faber, 1977).

Auden, W. H., *Collected Poems*, ed. Edward Mendelson (London: Faber and Faber, 1976, revised edition 2007).

216		*Bibliography*

Auden, W. H., and MacNeice, Louis, *Letters from Iceland* (London: Faber and Faber, 1937).

Auden, W. H., and Taylor, Paul B., *Norse Poems* (London: Athlone Press, 1981).

Bailey, Richard N., *Viking Age Sculpture in Northern England* (London: Collins, 1980).

Bakhtin, M. M., *The Dialogic Imagination: Four Essays*, trans. Caryl Emerson and Michael Holquist (Austin: University of Texas Press, 1981).

Barakat, R. A., 'Odin: Old Man of the Pardoner's Tale', *Southern Folklore Quarterly* 28 (1964), 210–15.

Bartholin, Thomas, *Antiquitatum Danicarum de Causis Contemptae a Danis adhuc Gentilibus Mortis* (Hafniæ: Joh. Phil. Bockenhoffer, 1689).

Bethurum, Dorothy (ed.), *The Homilies of Wulfstan* (Oxford: Clarendon Press, 1957).

Bindman, David, *Blake as an Artist* (Oxford: Phaidon, 1977).

Birkett, T. E., *Ráð Rétt Rúnar: Reading the Runes in Old English and Old Norse Poetry*, D.Phil thesis (University of Oxford, 2011).

Bjarni Aðalbjarnarson (ed.), *Heimskringla*, Íslenzk fornrit XXVI–XXVIII (Reykjavík: Hið Íslenzka Fornritafélag, 1941–51), 3 vols.

Blackmore, Richard, *Prince Arthur: An Heroick Poem in Ten Books* (London: Printed for Awnsham and John Churchil, 1695).

Blake, William, *The Complete Poems*, ed. Alicia Ostriker (London: Penguin, 2004).

Blake, William, *The Complete Poems*, ed. W. H. Stevenson, 3rd edition (Harlow: Pearson, Longman, 2007).

Blake, William, *The Complete Poetry and Prose of William Blake*, ed. David V. Erdman, revised edition (Berkeley: University of California Press, 2008).

Bloom, Harold, 'William Blake', in Frank Kermode and John Hollander (eds.), *The Oxford Anthology of English Literature* (New York and London: Oxford University Press, 1973), 2 vols, vol. II, pp. 10–14.

Boorde, Andrew, *The Fyrst Boke of the Introduction of Knowledge*, ed. F. J. Furnivall, Early English Text Society extra series 10 (London: N. Trübner, 1870).

Boswell, James, *Life of Johnson*, ed. R. W. Chapman (Oxford: Oxford University Press, 2008).

Bowles, W. L., *Sonnets, and Other Poems* (London: T. Cadell, 1801), 2 vols.

Boyse, Samuel, 'The Triumphs of Nature', *The Gentleman's Magazine* XII (June–August 1742), pp. 324, 380–2, 435–6.

Boyse, Samuel, 'The Vision of Patience', in *Bell's Classical Arrangement of Fugitive Poetry, vol.XI: Poems imitative of Spenser and in the Manner of Milton* (London: John Bell, 1790), pp. 49–60.

Bremmer, Rolf H., 'The Anglo-Saxon Pantheon according to Richard Verstegen (1605)', in Timothy Graham (ed.), *The Recovery of Old English: Anglo-Saxon Studies in the Sixteenth and Seventeenth Centuries* (Kalamazoo, Mich.: Medieval Institute Publications, 2000), pp. 141–72.

Brodeur, Arthur G., *The Art of Beowulf* (Berkeley: University of California Press, 1959).

Browne, William, *Britannia's Pastorals* (London, 1613–1616), 2 vols.

Brownjohn, Alan, 'Warriors, Warlocks and Video Shops', *The Independent* (23 January 2004), p. 18.

Bruce, Michael, *Poems on Several Occasions* (Edinburgh: J. Robertson, 1770).

Buchanan, Robert, *Balder the Beautiful: A Song of Divine Death* (London: William Mullan & Son, 1877).

Buckler, William E., *On the Poetry of Matthew Arnold: Essays in Critical Reconstruction* (New York: New York University Press, 1982).

Bunting, Basil, *Briggflatts* (London: Fulcrum, 1966).

Burt, Stephen, 'To wake the fiddlers underneath', *Times Literary Supplement* (26 September 2003), p. 25.

Busk, Mary, 'Scandinavian Mythology, and the Nature of its Allegory', *Blackwood's Edinburgh Magazine* vol. XXXVIII (July 1835), pp. 25–36.

Busk, Mary, Review of Grundtvig, *Norden's Mythologi*, *The Foreign Quarterly Review* vol. XVI (1836), Article VIII, pp. 437–44.

Butlin, Martin, *William Blake* (London: Tate Gallery, 1978).

Byock, Jesse (trans.), Snorri Sturluson, *The Prose Edda: Norse Mythology* (London: Penguin, 2005).

Byock, Jesse (trans.), *Grettir's Saga* (Oxford: Oxford University Press, 2009).

Camden, William, *Britannia* (London, 1586), trans. Philemon Holland, *Britain, or A Chorographicall Description of the most flourishing Kingdomes, England, Scotland and Ireland, and the Ilands adioyning, out of the depth of Antiquitie* (London, 1610).

Campbell, John, *The Polite Correspondence: Or, Rational Amusement; Being a Series of Letters, Philosophical, Poetical, Historical, Critical, Amorous, Moral and Satyrical* (London: John Atkinson, 1750).

Carlsen, C., 'Old Norse Visions of the Afterlife', D.Phil thesis (University of Oxford, 2012).

Carlyle, Thomas, *On Heroes, Hero-Worship, and the Heroic in History: Six Lectures* (London: James Fraser, 1841).

Casaubon, Meric (ed.), *A True and Faithful Relation of what passed for many Yeers Between Dr. John Dee... and Some Spirits* (London: D. Maxwell, 1659).

Chadwick, Nora, 'The Story of Macbeth: A Study in Gaelic and Norse Tradition', *Scottish Gaelic Studies* 6:2 (September 1949), 189–211.

Clunies Ross, Margaret, *The Norse Muse in Britain 1750–1820*, with appendix by Amanda J. Collins (Trieste: Edizioni Parnaso, 1998).

Clunies Ross, Margaret (ed.), *The Old Norse Poetic Translations of Thomas Percy: A New Edition and Commentary*, Making the Middle Ages 4 (Turnhout: Brepols, 2001).

Clunies Ross, Margaret (ed.), *Poetry on Christian Subjects, Part 1: The Twelfth and Thirteenth Centuries*, Skaldic Poetry of the Scandinavian Middle Ages VII (Turnhout: Brepols, 2007), 2 vols.

Coburn, Kathleen (ed.), *The Notebooks of Samuel Taylor Coleridge* (New York: Pantheon Books, 1957–2002), 5 vols.

Cook, Robert (trans.), *Njals saga* (London: Penguin, 2001).

Corcoran, Neil, *The Song of Deeds: A Study of The Anathemata of David Jones* (Cardiff: University of Wales Press, 1982).

Cottle, A. S., *Icelandic Poetry, or The Edda of Saemund Translated into English Verse* (Bristol: N. Biggs, 1797).

Cottle, Joseph, *Early Recollections, chiefly relating to the late Samuel Taylor Coleridge* (London: Longman, Rees and Co., 1837), 2 vols.

Damico, Helen, '*Sörlaþáttr* and the Hama episode in *Beowulf*', *Scandinavian Studies* 55 (1983), 222–35.

Damon, S. Foster, *A Blake Dictionary: The Ideas and Symbols of William Blake* (London: Thames and Hudson, 1973).

D'Arcy, Julian Meldon, *Scottish Skalds and Sagamen: Old Norse Influence on Modern Scottish Literature* (East Linton: Tuckwell Press, 1996).

Davis, Craig, *Beowulf and the Demise of Germanic Legend in England* (New York and London: Garland, 1996).

Dawson, Carl (ed.), *Matthew Arnold, The Poetry: The Critical Heritage* (London: Routledge & Kegan Paul, 1973).

Deacon, A. N., *The Use of Norse Mythology and Literature by some 18th and 19th Century Writers, with special reference to the work of Bishop Thomas Percy, Thomas Gray, Matthew Arnold and William Morris*, B.Litt thesis (University of Oxford, 1964).

De Luca, Vincent Arthur, *Words of Eternity: Blake and the Poetics of the Sublime* (Princeton: Princeton University Press, 1991).

Denham, John, *Coopers Hill* (London: Humphrey Moseley, 1655).

Dentith, Simon, '*Sigurd the Volsung*: Heroic poetry in an Unheroic Age', in Peter Faulkner and Peter Preston (eds.), *William Morris: Centenary Essays* (Exeter: University of Exeter Press, 1999), pp. 60–70.

Dobell, Sydney, *Balder*, 2nd edition (London: Smith, Elder, and Co., 1854).

Donne, John, *The Elegies and The Song and Sonnets*, ed. Helen Gardner (Oxford: Clarendon Press, 1965).

Downman, Hugh, *The Death-Song of Ragnar Lodbrach, or Lodbrog, King of Denmark, translated from the Latin of Olaus Wormius* (London: Fielding and Walker, 1781).

Dronke, Ursula, '*Beowulf* and Ragnarök', *Saga-Book of the Viking Society* 17 (1966–9), 302–25.

Dronke, Ursula (ed.), *The Poetic Edda* (Oxford: Clarendon Press, 1969–2011), 3 vols.

Drummond, William, *Odin: A Poem, in Eight Books and Two Parts* (London: Law and Co., 1817).

Dryden, John, *The Works of John Dryden: Poems 1681–1684*, ed. H. T. Swedenburg, The Works of John Dryden vol. II (Berkeley: University of California Press, 1972).

Dryden, John, *The Works of John Dryden: Plays*, ed. V. A. Dearing, The Works of John Dryden vol. XVI (Berkeley: University of California Press, 1996).

Duhig, Ian, *Nominies* (Newcastle upon Tyne: Bloodaxe Books, 1998).

Duhig, Ian, *The Lammas Hireling* (London: Picador, 2003).

Duhig, Ian, *The Speed of Dark* (London: Picador, 2007).

Dunbar, William, *The Complete Works*, ed. John Conlee (Kalamazoo, Mich.: Medieval Institute Publications, 2004).

Einar Ól. Sveinsson (ed.), *Laxdœla saga*, Íslenzk fornrit V (Reykjavík: Hið Íslenzka Fornritafélag, 1934).

Einar Ól. Sveinsson (ed.), *Brennu-Njáls saga*, Íslenzk fornrit XII (Reykjavík: Hið Íslenzka Fornritafélag, 1954).

Einar Ól. Sveinsson and Matthías Þórðarson (eds.), *Eyrbyggja saga*, Íslenzk fornrit VI (Reykjavík: Hið Íslenzka Fornritafélag, 1935).

Farley, Frank Edgar, *Scandinavian Influences in the English Romantic Movement*, Studies and Notes in Philology and Literature IX (Boston: Ginn, 1903).

Faulkes, Anthony (ed.), *Two Versions of Snorra Edda from the 17th Century* (Reykjavík: Stofnun Árna Magnússonar, 1977), 2 vols.

Faulkes, Anthony (trans.) Snorri Sturluson, *Edda* (London: Dent, 2003).

Faulkner, Mark, 'Archaism, Belatedness and Modernisation: "Old" English in the Twelfth Century', *Review of English Studies* 63 (2011), 179–203.

Fell, Christine (trans.), *Egils saga* (London: Dent, 1975).

Fell, Christine, 'The first publication of Old Norse literature in England and its relation to its sources', in Else Roesdahl and Preben Meulengracht Sørenson (eds.), *The Waking of Angantyr: The Scandinavian Past in European Culture* (Aarhus: Aarhus University Press, 1996), pp. 27–57.

Finch, R. G. (ed.), *Völsunga saga: the Saga of the Volsungs* (London: Nelson, 1965).

Finnur Jónsson (ed.), *Den norsk-islandske skjaldedigtning* (Copenhagen: Gyldendal, 1912–1915), 4 vols.

Fjalldal, Magnús, *The Long Arm of Coincidence: The Frustrated Connection between Beowulf and Grettis saga* (Toronto: University of Toronto Press, 1998).

Forde, Victoria, *The Poetry of Basil Bunting* (Newcastle upon Tyne: Bloodaxe, 1991).

Frank, Roberta, 'Skaldic Verse and the Dating of *Beowulf*' in Colin Chase (ed.), *The Dating of Beowulf* (Toronto: University of Toronto Press, 1981), pp. 123–39.

Frazer, James George, *The Golden Bough: A Study in Magic and Religion*, abridged edition (London: Macmillan, 1963).

Froude, J. A., 'Arnold's Poems', *The Westminster Review* (January 1854), pp. 146–59.

Froude, J. A., 'The Odin-Religion', *The Westminster Review* (October 1854), pp. 165–83.

Frye, Northrop, *Fearful Symmetry* (Princeton: Princeton University Press, 1947; 4th printing 1974).

Frye, William Edward (trans.), *The Gods of the North: An Epic Poem, by Adam Œhlenschläger* (London: William Pickering, 1845).

Fuller, John, *W. H. Auden: A Commentary* (London: Faber and Faber, 1998).

Gade, Kari Ellen (ed.), *Poetry from the Kings' Sagas 2: from c.1035 to c.1300*, Skaldic Poetry of the Scandinavian Middle Ages II (Turnhout: Brepols, 2009), 2 vols.

Garmonsway, G. N. (trans.), *The Anglo-Saxon Chronicle* (London: Dent, 1972).

Garmonsway, G. N., and Simpson, Jacqueline (eds.), *Beowulf and its Analogues* (London: Dent, 1968).

Giles, Paul, 'From Myth into History: The Later Poetry of Thom Gunn and Ted Hughes', in James Acheson and Romana Huk (eds.), *Contemporary British Poetry: Essays in Theory and Criticism* (Albany: State University of New York Press, 1996), pp. 143–73.

Gordon, E. V., An Introduction to Old Norse (Oxford: Clarendon Press, 1927).

Greening, John, 'An irreproachable eye', *Times Literary Supplement* (30 April 2004), p. 32.

Griffith, Mark, 'Some difficulties in Beowulf, lines 874–902: Sigemund reconsidered', *Anglo-Saxon England* 24 (1995), 11–41.

Gross, John (ed.), *The Modern Movement: A TLS Companion* (Chicago: University of Chicago Press, 1992).

Guðni Jónsson (ed.), *Grettis saga Ásmundarsonar*, Íslenzk fornrit VII (Reykjavík: Hið Íslenzka Fornritafélag, 1936).

Guðni Jónsson (ed.), *Fornaldar sögur Norðurlanda* (Reykjavík: Íslendingasagnaútgáfan, 1950), 4 vols.

Hague, Rene, *A Commentary on The Anathemata of David Jones* (Wellingborough: Skelton, 1977).

Hakluyt, Richard, *The Principal Navigations, Voyages, Traffiques and Discoveries of the English Nation* (London, 1599–1600, 3 vols, repr. Glasgow: J. Maclehose and Sons, 1903–5, 12 vols).

Halverson, John, 'The World of *Beowulf*', *English Literary History* 36:4 (1969), 593–608.

Hamilton, Ian, *A Gift Imprisoned: The Poetic Life of Matthew Arnold* (London: Bloomsbury, 1998).

Haraldsson, Sveinn, '"The North begins inside": Auden, Ancestry and Iceland', in Andrew Wawn (ed.), *Northern Antiquity: The Post-Medieval Reception of Edda and Saga* (Enfield Lock: Hisarlik Press, 1994), pp. 255–84.

Hart, Edward, 'Portrait of a Grub: Samuel Boyse', *Studies in English Literature 1500–1900* 7 (1967), 415–25.

Heaney, Seamus, *North* (London: Faber and Faber, 1975).

Heaney, Seamus, *Beowulf* (London: Faber and Faber, 1999).

Hemans, Felicia, *The Forest Sanctuary, and Other Poems* (London: John Murray, 1825).

Herbert, W. N., *To Circumjack MacDiarmid: The Poetry and Prose of Hugh MacDiarmid* (Oxford: Clarendon Press, 1992).

Herbert, William, *Select Icelandic Poetry, Translated from the Originals, with Notes* (London: T. Reynolds, 1804).

Herbert, William, *Works, Excepting Those on Botany and Natural History, with Additions and Corrections by the Author* (London: H. G. Bohn, 1842), 3 vols.

Herford, C. H., *Norse Myth in English Poetry* (Manchester, 1919), reprinted from *The Bulletin of the John Rylands Library* 5:1–2 (August 1918–March 1919).

Heywood, Thomas, *Gunaikeion, or Nine Books of Various History concerning Women* (London: Adam Islip, 1624), republished as *The Generall History of Women* (London: W. H., 1657).

Hickes, George, *Institutiones Grammaticæ Anglo-Saxonicæ et Meso-Gothicæ* (Oxford: E Theatro Sheldoniano, 1689).

Hickes, George, *Linguarum Vett. Septentrionalium Thesaurus Grammatico-Criticus et Archæologicus* (Oxford: E Theatro Sheldoniano, 1705) 2 vols.

Hilen, Andrew, *Longfellow and Scandinavia: A Study of the Poet's Relationship with the Northern Languages and Literature* (New Haven: Yale University Press, 1947).

Hill, Geoffrey, *Mercian Hymns* (London: Deutsch, 1971).

Hodgson, Amanda, 'The Troy Connection: Myth and History in *Sigurd the Volsung*', in Peter Faulkner and Peter Preston (eds.), *William Morris: Centenary Essays* (Exeter: University of Exeter Press, 1999), pp. 71–9.

Hole, Richard, *Arthur, or The Northern Enchantment: A Poetical Romance, in Seven Books* (Dublin: Zachariah Jackson, 1790).

Hollander, Lee M. (trans.), *Heimskringla: History of the Kings of Norway* (Austin: University of Texas Press, 1964).

Howitt, William and Mary, *The Literature and Romance of Northern Europe* (London: Colburn and Co., 1852), 2 vols.

Hughes, Ted, *Collected Poems*, ed. Paul Keegan (London: Faber and Faber, 2003).

Jack, George (ed.), *Beowulf: A Student Edition* (Oxford: Clarendon Press, 1994).

Jamie, Kathleen, *The Queen of Sheba* (Newcastle upon Tyne: Bloodaxe Books, 1994).

Jamieson, John, *An Etymological Dictionary of the Scottish Language* (Edinburgh: University Press, 1808), 2 vols.

Jay, Harriett, *Robert Buchanan: Some Account of His Life, His Life's Work, and His Literary Friendships* (London: T. Fisher Unwin, 1903).

Jerningham, Edward, *The Rise and Progress of the Scandinavian Poetry: A Poem, in Two Parts* (London: James Robson, 1784).

Jerrold, Clare, 'The Balder Myth and Some English Poets', *Saga-Book of the Viking Society* 3 (1901–3), 94–116.

Jesch, Judith, 'Skaldic Verse in Scandinavian England', in James Graham-Campbell et al. (eds.), *Vikings and the Danelaw: selected papers from the proceedings of the Thirteenth Viking Congress, Nottingham and York, 21–30 August 1997* (Oxford: Oxbow, 2001), pp. 313–25.

Johnson, D. F., 'Euhemerisation versus Demonisation: The Pagan Gods and Ælfric's De Falsis Diis' in T. Hofstra, L. A. J. R. Houwen, and A. A. MacDonald (eds.), *Pagans and Christians* (Groningen: E. Forsten, 1995), pp. 35–69.

Johnson, Kevan, 'Four ounces of raven', *Times Literary Supplement* (23 June 1995), p. 30.

Johnson, Samuel, *The Lives of the Poets*, ed. John H. Middendorf, The Yale Edition of the Works of Samuel Johnson vols. 21–23 (New Haven and London: Yale University Press, 2010).

Johnston, Arthur, 'Poetry and Criticism after 1740', in Roger Lonsdale (ed.), *Dryden to Johnson*, History of Literature in the English Language IV (London: Sphere, 1971), pp. 357–95.

Jones, David, *In Parenthesis* (London: Faber and Faber, 1937, repr. 2010).

Jones, David, *The Anathemata* (London: Faber and Faber, 1952, repr. 2010).

Jones, Gwyn (trans.), *Eirik the Red and Other Icelandic Sagas* (Oxford: Oxford University Press, 1988).

Jones, Julia Clinton, *Valhalla: The Myths of Norseland, A Saga, in Twelve Parts* (San Francisco: Edward Bosqui and Co., 1878).

Jones, W. Powell, 'The Contemporary Reception of Gray's *Odes*', *Modern Philology* 28:1 (1930), 61–82.

Jones, William, *The Works of Sir William Jones* (London: John Stockdale and John Walker, 1807), 13 vols.

Keightley, Thomas, *The Foreign Quarterly Review* vol. II (February–June 1828), Article VII, pp. 210–43.

Kennedy, David, 'Historical vulgarities', *Times Literary Supplement* (18 October 1991), p. 23.

Kielland-Lund, Erik, '"Twilight of the Heroes": Old Norse Influence in Longfellow's Poetry', in Inga-Stina Ewbank, Olav Lausund and Bjørn Tysdahl (eds.), *Anglo-Scandinavian Cross-Currents* (Norwich: Norvik, 1999), pp. 71–83.

Kiernan, Kevin S., *Beowulf and the Beowulf Manuscript* (Ann Arbor: University of Michigan Press, 1996).

King, Don, *C. S. Lewis, Poet: The Legacy of His Poetic Impulse* (Kent, Ohio: The Kent State University Press, 2001).

Kliger, Samuel, *The Goths in England: A Study in Seventeenth and Eighteenth Century Thought* (Cambridge, Mass.: Harvard University Press, 1952).

Kopár, Lilla, *Gods and Settlers: The Iconography of Norse Mythology in Anglo-Scandinavian Sculpture* (Turnhout: Brepols, 2012).

Laing, Samuel (trans.), *The Heimskringla, or Chronicle of the Kings of Norway* (London: Longman, Brown, Green, and Longmans, 1844), 3 vols.

Landor, Walter Savage, *Gebir, Count Julian, and Other Poems* (London: Edward Moxon, 1831).

Lang, Andrew, *The Yellow Fairy Book* (London: Longmans, Green and Co., 1894).

Larrington, Carolyne (trans.), *The Poetic Edda* (Oxford: Oxford University Press, 1996).

Lassen, Annette (ed.), *Hrafnagaldur Óðins (Forspjallsljóð)* (London: Viking Society for Northern Research, 2011).

Lestley, C., 'The Haunting of Havardur', *The Gentleman's Magazine* (May 1793).

Leviston, Frances, 'Shiver of satisfaction', *The Guardian* (20 December 2008), p. 15.

Lewis, C. S., *Surprised by Joy: The Shape of My Early Life* (London: Geoffrey Bles, 1955).

Lewis, C. S., *Poems*, ed. Walter Hooper (London: Bles, 1964).

Lewis, C. S., *Narrative Poems*, ed. Walter Hooper (London: Bles, 1969).

Lewis, C. S., and Greeves, Arthur, *They Stand Together: The Letters of C. S. Lewis to Arthur Greeves, 1914–1963*, ed. Walter Hooper (London: Collins, 1979).

Lewis, W. S., and Brown, Ralph S. (eds.), *Horace Walpole's Correspondence with George Montagu*, The Yale Edition of Horace Walpole's Correspondence vols. 9–10 (New Haven: Yale University Press, 1941).

Litzenberg, Karl, 'The Social Philosophy of William Morris and the Doom of the Gods', *Essays and Studies in English and Comparative Literature X* (Ann Arbor: University of Michigan Press, 1933), pp. 183–203.

Litzenberg, Karl, *The Victorians and the Vikings: A Bibliographical Essay on Anglo-Norse Literary Relations* (Ann Arbor: University of Michigan Press, 1947).

Longfellow, H. W., *The Poetical Works of Henry Wadsworth Longfellow* (London: George Routledge, 1867).

Lonsdale, Roger (ed.), *The Poems of Thomas Gray, William Collins, and Oliver Goldsmith* (London: Longmans, 1969).

Lonsdale, Roger, 'Gray and "Allusion": The Poet as Debtor', in R. F. Brissenden and J. C. Eade (eds.), *Studies in the Eighteenth Century IV: Papers presented at the fourth David Nichol Smith Memorial Seminar, Canberra, 1976* (Canberra: Australian National University Press, 1979), pp. 31–55.

Lukman, Niels, 'The Raven Banner and the Changing Ravens: A Viking Miracle from Carolingian Court Poetry to Saga and Arthurian Romance', *Classica et Medievalia* 19 (1958), 133–51.

MacDiarmid, Hugh, *The Complete Poems of Hugh MacDiarmid*, ed. Michael Grieve and W. R. Aitken (Harmondsworth: Penguin, 1985), 2 vols.

MacDiarmid, Hugh, *Lucky Poet: A Self-Study in Literature and Political Ideas* (London: Methuen, 1943).

MacDiarmid, Hugh, *A Drunk Man Looks at the Thistle: An Annotated Edition*, ed. Kenneth Buthlay (Edinburgh: Scottish Academic Press, 1987).

MacDiarmid, Hugh, *Annals of the Five Senses and Other Stories, Sketches and Plays*, ed. Roderick Watson and Alan Riach (Manchester: Carcanet, 1999).

Mack, Robert L., *Thomas Gray: A Life* (New Haven and London: Yale University Press, 2000).

Magnus, Johannes, *Historia...de omnibus Gothorum Sueonumque Regibus* (Romæ: J. M. de Viottis, 1554).

Magnus, Olaus, *Historia de Gentibus Septentrionalibus: Description of the Northern Peoples*, ed. Peter Foote (London: Hakluyt Society, 1996–1998), 3 vols.

Mallet, Paul-Henri, *Introduction à l'histoire de Dannemarc, ou l'on traite de la Religion, des Loix, des Mœurs & des Usages des anciens Danois* (Geneva, 1763), 6 vols.

Mangan, Gerald, 'Romantic risks', *Times Literary Supplement* (16 August 2002), p. 22.

Margoliouth, H. M., *William Blake's Vala* (Oxford: Clarendon Press, 1956).

Mason, Emma, *Women Poets of the Nineteenth Century* (Tavistock: Northcote House, 2006).

Mason, William, *The Works of William Mason, M. A.* (London: T. Cadell and W. Davies, 1811), 4 vols.

Mathias, Thomas James, *Runic Odes imitated from the Norse Tongue, in the manner of Mr. Gray* (London: T. Payne, T. Becket, J. Sewell, and T. and J. Merrill, 1781).

McDowell, George Tremaine, 'The Treatment of the *Volsunga Saga* by William Morris', *Scandinavian Studies and Notes* 7 (1922–3), 151–68.

McKillop, A. D., *The Background of Thomson's Liberty* (Houston: Rice Institute, 1951).

McKillop, A. D., 'A Critic of 1741 on Early Poetry', *Studies in Philology* 30:3 (1933), 504–21.

McTurk, Rory, *Studies in Ragnars saga Loðbrókar and its Major Scandinavian Analogues*, Medium Ævum Monographs New Series XV (Oxford: The Society for the Study of Mediæval Languages and Literature, 1991).

Mendelson, Edward, *Early Auden* (London: Faber, 1981).

Meulengracht Sørensen, Preben, 'Thor's Fishing Expedition', in Gro Steinsland (ed.), *Words and Objects: Towards a Dialogue between Archaeology and History of Religion* (Oslo: Norwegian University Press, 1986), pp. 257–78.

Mickle, William Julius, *Almada Hill: An Epistle from Lisbon* (Oxford: W. Jackson, 1781).

Mierow, Charles Christopher (trans.), *The Gothic History of Jordanes* (Princeton: Princeton University Press, 1915).

Miner, Paul, 'Two Notes on Sources', *The Bulletin of the New York Public Library* LXII (1958), 203–7.

Moorman, Charles, 'The Essential Paganism of *Beowulf*', *Modern Language Quarterly* 28 (1967), 3–18.

Morley, David, 'A spring in her heels', *The Guardian* (22 November 2003).

Morris, William, *Sigurd the Volsung*, ed. Jane Ennis (Bristol: Thoemmes Press, 1994).

Motherwell, William, *Poems Narrative and Lyrical* (Glasgow: David Robertson, 1832).

Muir, Bernard J. (ed.), *The Exeter Anthology of Old English Poetry: An Edition of Exeter Dean and Chapter MS. 3501* (Exeter: University of Exeter Press, 1994), 2 vols.

Muldoon, Paul, *Poems 1968–1998* (London: Faber and Faber, 2001).

Murray, Christopher David, *Robert Buchanan (1841–1901): An Assessment of his Career*, D.Phil thesis (University of London, 1974).

Neckel, Gustav, and Kuhn, Hans (eds.), *Edda: Die Lieder des Codex Regius nebst verwandten Denkmälern* (Heidelberg: C. Winter, 1962–1968), 2 vols.

Nordal, Sigurður (ed.), *Egils saga Skalla-Grímssonar*, Íslenzk fornrit II (Reykjavík: Hið Íslenzka Fornritafélag, 1933).

Nordal, Sigurður, and Guðni Jónsson (eds.), *Borgfirðinga sögur*, Íslenzk fornrit III (Reykjavík: Hið Íslenzka Fornritafélag, 1938).

North, Richard, *Heathen Gods in Old English Literature* (Cambridge: Cambridge University Press, 1997).

Noyes, Alfred, *William Morris* (London: Macmillan, 1908).

Oberg, Charlotte, *A Pagan Prophet: William Morris* (Charlottesville: University Press of Virginia, 1978).

O'Donoghue, Heather, 'What has Baldr to do with Lamech? The Lethal Shot of a Blind Man in Old Norse Myth and Jewish Exegetical Traditions', *Medium Ævum* LXXII (2003), 82–107.

O'Donoghue, Heather, *Old Norse–Icelandic Literature: A Short Introduction* (Oxford: Blackwell, 2004).

O'Donoghue, Heather, *Skaldic Verse and the Poetics of Saga Narrative* (Oxford: Oxford University Press, 2005).

O'Donoghue, Heather, *From Asgard to Valhalla* (London: I. B. Tauris, 2007).

O'Donoghue, Heather, 'Heaney, *Beowulf* and the Medieval Literature of the North', in Bernard O'Donoghue (ed.), *The Cambridge Companion to Seamus Heaney* (Cambridge: Cambridge University Press, 2009), pp. 192–205.

O'Donoghue, Heather, 'Owed to Both Sides: W.H. Auden's double debt to the literature of the North', in David Clark and Nicholas Perkins (eds.), *Anglo-Saxon Culture and the Modern Imagination* (Cambridge: D. S. Brewer, 2010), pp. 51–69.

Œhlenschläger, Adam, *Balder hin Gode* (Copenhagen, 1806).

Omberg, Margaret, *Scandinavian Themes in English Poetry, 1760–1800*, Acta Universitatis Upsaliensis; Studia Anglistica Upsaliensia 29 (Uppsala, 1976).

Orchard, Andy, *A Critical Companion to Beowulf* (Cambridge: D. S. Brewer, 2003).

Orchard, Andy (trans.), *The Elder Edda: A Book of Viking Lore* (London: Penguin, 2011).

Owen, A. L., *The Famous Druids: A Survey of Three Centuries of English Literature on the Druids* (Oxford: Clarendon Press, 1962).

Page, Frederick, '*Balder Dead* (1855): An Interpretation', *Essays and Studies* 28 (1942), 60–8.

Page, R. I., 'How long did the Scandinavian language survive in England? The epigraphical evidence', in Peter Clemoes and Kathleen Hughes (eds.), *England Before the Conquest: Studies in Primary Sources Presented to Dorothy Whitelock* (Cambridge: Cambridge University Press, 1971), pp. 165–81.

Paley, Morton, 'The Figure of the Garment in *The Four Zoas, Milton,* and *Jerusalem*', in Stuart Curran and Joseph Wittreich (eds.), *Blake's Sublime Allegory: Essays on The Four Zoas, Milton, & Jerusalem* (Madison, WI, and London: University of Wisconsin Press, 1973), pp. 119–39.

Parker, E. C., *Anglo-Scandinavian Literature and the Post-Conquest Period*, D.Phil thesis (University of Oxford, 2013).

Parsons, D. N., 'How long did the Scandinavian language survive in England? Again', in James Graham-Campbell et al. (eds.), *Vikings and the Danelaw: selected papers from the proceedings of the Thirteenth Viking Congress, Nottingham and York, 21–30 August 1997* (Oxford: Oxbow, 2001), pp. 299–312.

Paterson, Don, *Nil Nil* (London: Faber, 1993).

Paterson, Don, *God's Gift to Women* (London: Faber, 1997).

Paterson, Don, *Rain* (London: Faber, 2009).

Paterson, Don, Official Website, <http://www.donpaterson.com/files/interview1.htm> (accessed 5 March 2014).

Peacock, Thomas Love, *Palmyra, and other poems* (London: T. Bensley, 1806).

Penrose, Thomas, *Flights of Fancy* (London: J. Walter, 1775).

Percy, Thomas, *Five Pieces of Runic Poetry Translated from the Islandic Language* (London: R. and J. Dodsley, 1763).

Percy, Thomas, *Northern Antiquities: or, A Description of the Manners, Customs, Religion and Laws of the Ancient Danes, and other Northern Nations, including those of our own Saxon Ancestors* (London: T. Carnan and Co., 1770), 2 vols; revised edition, edited by I. A. Blackwell (London: Henry G. Bohn, 1847, 1859).

Phelps, William Lyon, *The Beginnings of the English Romantic Movement: A Study in Eighteenth Century Literature* (Boston: Ginn and Company, 1893).

Phelps, William Lyon (ed.), *Selections from the Poetry and Prose of Thomas Gray* (Boston: Ginn and Company, 1894).

Philips, John, *The Poems of John Philips*, ed. M. G. Lloyd Thomas (Oxford: Blackwell, 1927).

Pigott, Grenville, *A Manual of Scandinavian Mythology, containing a Popular Account of the Two Eddas and of the Religion of Odin* (London: William Pickering, 1839).

Pittock, Malcolm, 'Dobell, *Balder* and Post-Romanticism', *Essays in Criticism* 42:3 (1992), 221–42.

Pocock, J. G. A., *The Ancient Constitution and the Feudal Law: A Study of English Historical Thought in the Seventeenth Century* (Cambridge: Cambridge University Press, 1987).

Poliakov, Leon, *The Aryan Myth: A History of Racist and Nationalist Ideas in Europe* (London: Sussex University Press, 1974).

Polwhele, Richard (ed.), *Poems, Chiefly by Gentlemen of Devonshire and Cornwall* (Bath: R. Cruttwell, 1792), 2 vols.

Poole, R. G., *Viking Poems on War and Peace: A Study in Skaldic Narrative* (Toronto: University of Toronto Press, 1991).

Pope, Alexander, *Poetical Works*, ed. Herbert Davis (Oxford: Oxford University Press, 1978).

Pope, John C. (ed.), *Homilies of Ælfric: A Supplementary Collection*, Early English Text Society nos. 259–260 (Oxford: Oxford University Press, 1967–1968), 2 vols.

Potts, Robert, 'Reflected glare', *Times Literary Supplement* (12 September 1997), p. 21.

Prowett, James, *The Voluspa, or Speech of the Prophetess, with other poems* (London: Payne and Foss, 1816).

Purchas, Samuel, *Hakluytus Posthumus, or Purchas His Pilgrimes* (London, 1625, 4 vols., repr. Glasgow: J. Maclehose and Sons, 1905–7, 20 vols.).

Quinn, Judy, and Clunies Ross, Margaret, 'The Image of Norse Poetry and Myth in Seventeenth-Century England', in Andrew Wawn (ed.), *Northern Antiquity: The Post-Medieval Reception of Edda and Saga* (Enfield Lock: Hisarlik Press, 1994), pp. 189–210.

Raglan, Lord, *The Hero: A Study in Tradition, Myth, and Drama* (London: Methuen, 1936).

Rawlins, T. F. S., and Valentine, W. C., *The Hall of Odin: First and Second Prizes* (Oxford, 1850).

Resen, Peder Hansen, *Edda Islandorum* (Havniæ: Henrici Gödiani, 1665).

Richards, George, *Poems* (Oxford: Oxford University Press, 1804), 2 vols.

apRoberts, Ruth, 'Arnold and Natural Supernaturalism', in Clinton Machann and Forrest D. Burt (eds.), *Matthew Arnold in His Time and Ours: Centenary Essays* (Charlottesville: University Press of Virginia, 1988), pp. 17–29.

Roscoe, William, 'The Eddas', *The Prospective Review* 32 (October 1852), pp. 456–89.

Roscommon, Wentworth Dillon, Earl of, *An Essay on Translated Verse* (London: Jacob Tonson, 1684).

Ryals, Clyde de L., 'Arnold's *Balder Dead*', *Victorian Poetry* 4:2 (1966), 67–81.

Sambourne, Edward Linley, 'Punch's Fancy Portraits, No. 59: Mr. Matthew Arnold', *Punch* (26 November 1881), p. 250.

Sammes, Aylett, *Britannia Antiqua Illustrata: or The Antiquities of Ancient Britain* (London: Tho. Roycroft, 1676).

Saxo Grammaticus, *History of the Danes*, trans. Peter Fisher and ed. Hilda Ellis Davidson (Woodbridge: D. S. Brewer, 1979–1980), 2 vols.

Sayer, George, 'C. S. Lewis's *Dymer*', *SEVEN* 1 (1980), 94–116.

Sayers, F., *Dramatic Sketches of the Ancient Northern Mythology* (London: J. Johnson, 1790).

Sayers, F., *Poems* (London: J. Johnson, 1792).

Schneider, Mary W., 'The Source of Matthew Arnold's "Balder Dead"', *Notes and Queries* 14:2 (1967), 56–61.

Scot, Reginald, *Discovery of Witchcraft*, 3rd edition (London: Andrew Clark, 1665).

Scott, Forrest S., 'Earl Waltheof of Northumbria', *Archaeologia Aeliana* 30 (1952), 149–215.

Scott, Forrest S., 'Valþjófr jarl: an English earl in Icelandic sources', *Saga-Book of the Viking Society* 14 (1953–7), 78–94.

Scott, Walter, Review of Herbert, *Miscellaneous Poetry*, *The Edinburgh Review, or Critical Journal*, vol. IX (October 1806–January 1807), Article XV, pp. 211–23.

Scott, Walter, *Harold the Dauntless: A Poem, in Six Cantos* (Edinburgh: James Ballantyne and Co., 1817).

Seaton, Ethel, *Literary Relations of England and Scandinavia in the Seventeenth Century* (Oxford: Clarendon Press, 1935).

de Selincourt, Ernest, and Shaver, Chester L. (eds.), *The Letters of William and Dorothy Wordsworth*, 2nd edition (Oxford: Clarendon Press, 1967–1993), 8 vols.

Seward, Anna, *Llangollen Vale, with Other Poems* (London: G. Sael, 1796).

Seward, Anna, *The Poetical Works of Anna Seward*, ed. Walter Scott (Edinburgh: James Ballantyne and Co., 1810), 3 vols.

Sheringham, Robert, *De Anglorum Gentis Origine Disceptatio* (Cambridge: Joann. Hayes, 1670).

Shirley, James, *The Triumph of Peace* (London: John Norton, for William Cooke, 1633).

Shirley, James, *James Shirley*, with an introduction by Edmund Gosse, The Mermaid Series: The Best Plays of the Old Dramatists (London: Vizetelly, 1888).

Sisam, Kenneth, 'Anglo-Saxon Royal Genealogies', *Proceedings of the British Academy* 39 (1953), 287–346.

Sladden, Dilnot, *The Northmen* (Canterbury, 1834).

Smith, G. Gregory (ed.), *Elizabethan Critical Essays* (Oxford: Clarendon Press, 1904), 2 vols.

Smith, Thomas, *The Völuspá: read before the Leicestershire Literary Society* (Leicester: Combe and Crossley, 1838).

Smollett, Tobias, *Ode to Independence* (Glasgow: Robert and Andrew Foulis, 1773).

Southey, Robert, and Lovell, Robert, *Poems: Containing the Retrospect, Odes, Elegies, Sonnets, etc.* (Bath: R. Cruttwell, 1795).

Spelman, Henry, *Glossarium Archaiologicum* (London: Alice Warren, 1664).

Spence, Joseph, 'On the Royal Nuptials', in *The Annual Register, or A View of the History, Politicks, and Literature of the Year 1761* (London: R. and J. Dodsley, 1762), pp. 225–6.

Stainer, Pauline, *The Honeycomb* (Newcastle upon Tyne: Bloodaxe Books, 1989).

Stainer, Pauline, *The Ice-Pilot Speaks* (Newcastle upon Tyne: Bloodaxe Books, 1994).

Stainer, Pauline, *The Wound-dresser's Dream* (Newcastle upon Tyne: Bloodaxe Books, 1996).

Stainer, Pauline, *The Lady and the Hare* (Tarset: Bloodaxe Books, 2003).

Starr, H. W., and Hendrickson, J. R. (eds.), *The Complete Poems of Thomas Gray: English, Latin and Greek* (Oxford: Clarendon Press, 1966).

Stephanius, S. J. (ed.), *Saxonis Grammatici, Historiæ Danicæ libri xvi* (Soræ: Joachimi Moltkenii, 1644).

Sterling, Joseph, *Poems* (Dublin: Joseph Hill, 1782; 2nd edition London: G. G. J. and J. Robinson, 1789).

Stevens, William Bagshaw, *Poems, Consisting of Indian Odes and Miscellaneous Pieces* (Oxford: J. and J. Fletcher and S. Parker, 1775).

Swan, Mary, and Treharne, Elaine (eds.), *Rewriting Old English in the Twelfth Century* (Cambridge: Cambridge University Press, 2000).

Swannell, J. N., *William Morris & Old Norse Literature* (London: William Morris Society, 1961).

Swanton, Michael (ed.), *The Dream of the Rood* (Manchester: Manchester University Press, 1970).

Tacitus, *The Agricola and The Germania*, trans. H. Mattingly and S. A. Handford (Harmondsworth: Penguin, 1970).

Tacitus, *Agricola and Germany*, trans. Anthony R. Birley (Oxford: Oxford University Press, 1999).

Tayler, Irene, *Blake's Illustrations to the Poems of Gray* (Princeton: Princeton University Press, 1971).

Taylor, Paul, 'Auden's Icelandic Myth of Exile', *Journal of Modern Literature* 24:2 (2000–2001), 213–34.

Taylor, Paul Beekman, and Auden, W. H., *The Elder Edda: A Selection* (London: Faber, 1969).

Taylor, Paul Beekman, *Sharing Story: Medieval Norse-English Literary Relationships* (New York: AMS Press, 1998).

Taylor, William, 'Original Poetry', Review of Cottle, *Icelandic Poetry, The Monthly Magazine* (July–December 1798), vol. VI, pp. 451–5.

Taylor, William, Review of Drummond, *Odin: a Poem, The Monthly Review* (January, 1819), Article IV, pp. 38–44.

Temple, William, *An Introduction to the History of England* (London: Richard Simpson and Ralph Simpson, 1695).

Temple, William, *Miscellanea: The Second Part*, 2nd edition (London: J. R. for Richard and Ralph Simpson, 1690).

Temple, William, *Five Miscellaneous Essays*, ed. Samuel H. Monk (Ann Arbor: University of Michigan Press, 1963).

Thomson, James, *Liberty, The Castle of Indolence, and Other Poems*, ed. James Sambrook (Oxford: Clarendon Press, 1986).

Thomson, James, *The Plays of James Thomson*, ed. Percy G. Adams (New York and London: Garland, 1979).

Thurin, Erik Ingvar, *The American Discovery of the Norse: An Episode in Nineteenth-Century American Literature* (Lewisburg: Bucknell University Press, 1999).

Tickell, Thomas, *A Poem, to his Excellency the Lord Privy-Seal, On The Prospect of Peace* (London: J. Tonson, 1713).

Tolley, Clive, '*Beowulf's* Scyld Scefing Episode: Some Norse and Finnish Analogues', *Arv* 52 (1996), 7–48.

Tolkien, Christopher (ed.), *The Saga of King Heiðrek the Wise* (London: Nelson, 1960).

Tolkien, J. R. R., '*Beowulf:* The Monsters and the Critics', *Proceedings of the British Academy* 22 (1936), 245–95.

Tolkien, J. R. R., and Gordon, E. V. (eds.), *Sir Gawain and the Green Knight*, rev. Norman Davis (Oxford: Clarendon Press, 1967).

Toynbee, Paget Jackson, and Whibley, Leonard (eds.), *Correspondence of Thomas Gray* (Oxford: Clarendon Press, 1935), 3 vols.

Tucker, Susie, 'Scandinavica for the Eighteenth-Century Common Reader', *Saga-Book of the Viking Society* 26 (1962–5), 233–47.

Varty, Anne, 'Carlyle and Odin', in Inga-Stina Ewbank, Olav Lausund, and Bjørn Tysdahl (eds.), *Anglo-Scandinavian Cross-Currents* (Norwich: Norvik, 1999), pp. 60–70.

Verelius, Olaus (ed.), *Hervarar Saga* (Uppsala: Henricus Curio, 1672).

Verstegan, Richard, *A Restitution of Decayed Intelligence in Antiquities, concerning the most noble and renowned English Nation* (Antwerp, 1605).

Warton, Thomas, Sr, *Poems on Several Occasions* (London: R. Manby and H. S. Cox, 1748).

Warton, Thomas, Jr, *The History of English Poetry, from the Close of the Eleventh to the Commencement of the Eighteenth Century* (London: J. Dodsley, 1774), 4 vols.

Watkins, Carl, 'The Cult of Earl Waltheof at Crowland', *Hagiographica* 3 (1996), 95–111.

Wawn, Andrew, 'The Cult of "Stalwart Frith-thjof" in Victorian Britain', in Andrew Wawn (ed.), *Northern Antiquity: The Post-Medieval Reception of Edda and Saga* (Enfield Lock: Hisarlik Press, 1994), pp. 211–54.

Wawn, Andrew, *The Vikings and the Victorians: Inventing the Old North in Nineteenth-Century Britain* (Cambridge: D. S. Brewer, 2000).

Weinstein, Mark A., *William Edmondstoune Aytoun and the Spasmodic Controversy* (New Haven: Yale University Press, 1968).

West, Gilbert, *Stowe, the Gardens of the Right Honourable Richard Lord Viscount Cobham* (London: L. Gilliver, 1732).

Whittaker, Jason, *William Blake and the Myths of Britain* (Basingstoke: Macmillan, 1999).

William of Malmesbury, *Gesta Regum Anglorum*, ed. and trans. R. A. B. Mynors, R. M. Thomson, and M. Winterbottom, Oxford Medieval Texts (Oxford: Clarendon Press, 1998), 2 vols.

Williams, Harold (ed.), *The Correspondence of Jonathan Swift* (Oxford: Clarendon Press, 1963–1965), 5 vols.

Wilson, David, *Vikings and Gods in European Art* (Højbjerg: Moesgård Museum, 1997).

Worm, Ole, *Runer, seu Danica Literatura Antiquissima* (Amsterdam: Apud Joannem Jansonium, 1636).

Wright, Herbert G., 'Southey's Relations with Finland and Scandinavia', *Modern Language Review* 27:2 (1932), 149–67.

Index